Physical Education

Physical Education

Teaching and Curriculum Strategies for Grades 5–12

Daryl Siedentop
Charles Mand
Andrew Taggart

Ohio State University

MAYFIELD PUBLISHING COMPANY

Library of Congress Catalog Card Number: 85-062623
International Standard Book Number: 0-87484-592-0

Manufactured in the United States of America
10 9 8 7

Mayfield Publishing Company
1240 Villa Street
Mountain View, CA 94041

Sponsoring editor: James Bull
Developmental editor: Janet M. Beatty
Manuscript editor: Marie Enders
Managing editor: Pat Herbst
Production editor: Jan deProsse
Art director: Cynthia Bassett
Cover and text designer: Richard Kharibian
Production manager: Cathy Willkie
Compositor: G&S Typesetters
Printer and binder: Malloy Lithographing

Contents

Preface

The idea for this text originated from our dissatisfaction both with what we saw in physical education in middle and secondary schools and with the textbooks that were then available to prepare students to understand and deal with the problems of teaching physical education to adolescent students.

We honestly feel that this text will help to prepare physical educators to develop better programs of physical education for students in both middle and secondary schools. Better teaching is clearly the main ingredient in the improvement of school physical education programs. And better teacher preparation is of course directly related to better teaching.

While doing research for this text we discovered many exciting programs being implemented in physical education on a worldwide basis. Most of the curricular strategies in this text have come directly from existing school programs: We know of no program suggestion in this text that is not currently being implemented by an innovative, effective physical educator. It can be done!

One main strength of this text is that it attends to both teaching and curriculum strategies—and it attends to those strategies for both middle schools and secondary schools. Effective teaching is very important because at that level programs are transmitted to students on a day-to-day basis through the activities of physical education. But curriculum is important too, perhaps more so than previously, because of the diversity of needs and interests among current adolescent student populations. When an innovative, well-designed curriculum is taught effectively to students on an ongoing basis, significant changes take place: Skills are acquired. Attitudes are changed. Commitments that can last a lifetime are forged. Physical education then occupies a central role in the education of adolescent students—which is, of course, exactly the role it ought to play.

It should be obvious that we are deeply committed to the notion that physical education for youth should be a central rather than a peripheral part of their education. A list of the qualities that characterize the best of education for youth should include perseverance, skill, cooperation, independent action, the ability to defer gratification, and responsibility. We believe that our subject matter has as much potential for positively affecting these characteristics as any discipline in the school. But to have that impact, physical education must be taught well. That is perhaps the main message of this text.

Part One of the text covers the background material necessary to understand what physical education can and should mean to the education of adolescent students. Part One focuses on important trends in our culture and how these will continue to affect physical education. It includes a chapter on the authors' beliefs about physical education—a chapter we feel is important not because we think our beliefs are the final word but because they can serve to help readers clarify their own beliefs about physical education. Part One also contains information about the contexts in which physical education is taught, the nature of the developmental stage we call adolescence, and the characteristics of students with special needs. Also included is a frank discussion of some of the real problems associated with being both a teacher and a coach in today's schools.

Part Two of this text focuses on the physical education curriculum. In this section we present six distinct curriculum models. It is conceivable that some schools might profit from adopting one of the models for their curriculum, but schools would more likely choose from among several models to develop a comprehensive program within their school. The first chapter of Part Two shows how programs should be put together and the kinds of goals to which they should be devoted. The following six chapters then describe and provide examples of different approaches to a physical education curriculum for adolescent students. Some of these models will be familiar (the multiactivity program or the fitness model, for example) and others will be new to most readers. Part Two is intended to stimulate thought and discussion about what constitutes an adequate physical education curriculum for young people—adapted, of course, to local needs and constraints. This part of the text culminates with a brief chapter on schools in which physical education has achieved a central, unifying role.

Part Three focuses on implementation of the curriculum. This part of the text contains chapters on management issues, planning, discipline, effective teaching, current issues, and gaining support for the program. These represent topics that are important to any program regardless of its curricular focus. Most of the ideas and suggestions presented in this part of the text originated from research on effective teaching methods and effective schooling. We feel that teacher preparation programs in physical education can no longer afford to ignore the growing body of evidence about effective teaching and effective schooling; we have attempted to include that evidence in these chapters and to do so in a way that translates easily into practice.

We have many people to thank for their contributions to the conceptualization and completion of this text. The physical educators who provided us with information about their programs in a thorough and professional manner were gracious to do so. Their input was so important that we have chosen to recognize them separately in a list following this preface.

We especially want to thank Don Hellison for his work on the social development model. Thanks also to Hal Lawson and Judy Placek for their full development of the conceptually based program. The chapters describing these models were borrowed directly from their previous works. We are also indebted to Neal Earls for his research on distinctive teachers, which we have used in Chapter 6. Our colleague, Paul Jansma, made invaluable contributions to Chapter 7.

Our typists, Carol Norris and Carole Shockley, worked hard and well, often under fairly strict deadlines. We also had a lot of support from family, friends, and students—and from each other—as we completed this project.

DS
CM
AT

Special Acknowledgments

We would like to express our sincere gratitude to the following teachers and schools for their creative efforts to improve physical education and their willingness to share their programs with us.

Linda Adamski and Doug Adams, Westside High School, Lincoln, Nebraska

Lloyd Atwell, Lake Forest High School, Lake Forest, Illinois

Duane Buturusis, Anita Krieger, Lucas Palermo, and Dawn Heller, Riverside-Brookfield High School, Riverside, Illinois

Jack Didalis and Brenda Boivin, Woodward Park Middle School, Columbus, Ohio

Sandy Dunaway, Columbus Alternative School, Columbus, Ohio

Barb Headlee and Chris Bell, Dublin Local Schools, Dublin, Ohio

Jo Mancuso, Lyons Township High School, La Grange, Illinois

Gayle McDonald, Jefferson High School, Portland, Oregon

Gary Moore, Worthington Hills Elementary School, Worthington, Ohio

The physical education faculty of Cincinnati Academy of Physical Education, Cincinnati, Ohio

The physical education faculty of Wirreanda High School, Adelaide, South Australia

Dick Sandstrom, Seattle Preparatory School, Seattle, Washington

Arthur Signore, Northland High School, Columbus, Ohio

Pete Teppler and Bob Blanchette, St. Mary's School, Calgary, Alberta, Canada

Charlene Thomas, All Saints' Episcopal School, Vicksburg, Mississippi

Jeff Walsh, Gregory Heights Middle School, Portland, Oregon

Part One

The Context of
Physical Education

1

Physical Education in Contemporary Culture

The purpose of this chapter is to describe briefly the cultural context within which school physical education exists. This context includes the nature of schools, families, and students, as well as the ways in which sport and fitness are pursued within the general population. We sketch the cultural context for physical education by examining a series of trends and examining the implications of these trends for physical education. The major topics covered in the chapter are as follows:

The general cultural context dealing with families, poverty-affluence, and affirmative action

The current state of adolescence

The status of sport, recreation, and fitness in the private sector

Current reform movements in education

Problems for students and teachers in middle, junior, and senior high school physical education

Schools have traditionally been responsive to trends and influences in the general culture. So too has physical education. In the early part of this century, a high rate of draft rejects for World War I influenced a move toward an emphasis on fitness in school physical education programs. When veterans from World War II came home and began to create new leisure patterns in America, school physical education programs responded by beginning to emphasize lifetime sports such as golf, tennis, and bowling. When American children were shown in the 1960s to be inferior to European children on certain tests of basic fitness, the nation responded with the President's Council on Youth Fitness and physical education responded with another renewal of emphasis on fitness programs in the high schools.

In the 1960s and early 1970s, when the "youth generation" changed so many life-style patterns, physical education responded by including within the curriculum new activities such as the martial arts and cooperative games. In today's society, education is more in the spotlight than at any other time in this century. Surely physical education will need to respond in some way to the current forces operating in the culture at large and in education specifically. How physical education does respond to these forces will shape the future of programs in schools. The purpose of this chapter is to examine those forces.

What will become of the first generation to have spent much of their adolescent years in front of video games in arcades? How will we deal with the emerging evidence that indicates not only an alarmingly high incidence of childhood obesity but the difficulty in remediating a problem begun during childhood?

What does the tremendous increase in youth sports opportunities mean for school physical education? Can a 14-year-old who has been through youth soccer with its blend of skilled performance, parental involvement, snappy uniforms, and meaningful competitions ever be enthusiastic about school physical education?

What will the back-to-basics movement in education mean for physical education? If we have a longer school day and even a longer school year, when will students exercise and play? If the computer assumes a more dominant role in education, will it produce generations of students who move less and think more?

When will substance abuse among adolescent students be challenged and defeated? Does it matter that the nature of substance abuse shifts from marijuana to amphetamines to alcohol and back again? How can teachers be expected to teach well when so many students are rude and disruptive and there is so little support from the home?

Will we be able to realize the promise of equal opportunity in education in general and in physical education and sport in particular? Can we really afford to guarantee equal opportunity to females, to minorities, and to the handicapped? Can we, in a democracy traditionally devoted to equal opportunity, afford not to?

These are important questions, and the answers to them will be recorded in the coming years. Physical education will be affected dramatically by many of these cultural influences. But exactly how and in what directions physical education will move is difficult to predict. What should physical education of the future look like? What goals should it serve? What strategies should it utilize? There are many possible answers to these questions—some no doubt better than others. However, we cannot answer them reasonably without first coming to grips with some larger issues.

To understand fully what is happening to physical education today and what may happen to it in the foreseeable future, it is necessary to focus briefly on the culture in which physical education operates. Although it is risky to attempt to summarize important trends in any culture, it seems worth the risk simply because an understanding of such trends can aid us greatly in interpreting what is going on in physical education and help us to think clearly about what directions physical education may take in the future.

Important trends

We recognize that seemingly clear directions in culture have a way of turning around quickly. For example, the "flower power" and idealism of the 1960s and early 1970s seemed to herald a fairly distinct trend in America. Nevertheless, little more than a decade later the political and social climate of the country had become much more conservative; students today are more interested in jobs and their own personal futures than they are in demonstrations and protests.

In taking a brief look at the culture within which physical education continues to develop, we have made no effort to gloss over clearly difficult problems, but we have tried to avoid a pessimistic point of view. The fact is that most cultural issues are double-edged. Both their positive and negative sides need to be recognized.

Although many forces will affect physical education in the coming years, we have had to be selective. We have tried to identify those forces that seem to be both enduring in their effects and of great importance to schools and to physical education. No doubt you will disagree with some of our choices and perhaps with some of our conclusions. The major purpose here is to stimulate your thinking so that your own philosophy of physical education can be tested in terms of its ability to speak to the important issues of our time.

Continuing changes in the nature and meaning of families and family life

Do not be surprised if nearly half the students in your classes are members of one-parent families. Similarly, do not be surprised that many students from two-parent homes have mothers and fathers who are in second or third marriages. In recent years families have also become more mobile. There has been a well-publicized population shift toward the Sun Belt in the United States, and experts already are predicting a return to the Northeast early in the twenty-first century. What that portends is continued mobility. Mobility tends to make neighborhoods and neighborhood life more transient. It becomes difficult for children to have continued friendships. It makes school populations very changeable. Without question, it creates psychological difficulties for young people growing up. Many of these problems manifest themselves in schools—and teachers are forced to deal with them.

A widening affluence-poverty continuum

There have always been rich and poor in our society. In recent years, however, it has become clear that the differences between rich and poor have widened rather than narrowed. Because of our tradition of local taxation to support schools, schools in very wealthy areas are likely to be well-equipped and well-staffed, while schools in poor areas are likely to be the opposite. Wealthy districts typically have elementary school physical education specialists; poor districts do not. Space and equipment for play and games is abundant in wealthy districts and often absent in poor districts.

Research indicates that children from wealthy districts tend to have many sports education opportunities in the private sector—at tennis clubs, at golf clubs, in gymnastics schools, and in widespread and well-funded community programs. Children who live in poorer districts have little access to opportunities in the private sector and their community programs are not as well funded.

This is a good example of the double-edged nature of trends. The opportunity for sports education in the private sector is wonderful in many ways, but it does create some difficulties for the physical education teacher. First, students come to class with tremendously differing backgrounds in their sports experience. Second, few school programs can match the time and money that make the community programs so exciting. Thus many students are bored with physical education and are often quite willing to show that boredom in ways that are disruptive.

An even more complicated situation exists when children from rich and poor districts are placed together in one school as part of a desegregation program. This makes the teaching situation even more difficult for the physical educator, yet it also presents the opportunity for an important educational experience.

One particularly grim scenario relative to this trend must be mentioned. As the private sector continues to expand in sports education and as the migration to private schools continues, there may be less and less support for physical education in public schools. In wealthy districts, the opportunities in the private sector may become so varied and so available that physical education in school seems redundant (especially when combined with the pressure for more academic time). In poor districts, where tax levies are difficult to pass, schools may not be able to afford physical education. Clearly, this presents a threat to the future of school-based physical education. While there are very different reasons for this in rich and poor districts, physical education as a school subject is threatened with extinction in each of those places.

A continuing national commitment to affirmative action

Probably nothing has characterized the past quarter of a century in the United States more than the changes wrought by affirmative action legislation and court decisions. The civil rights movement, the women's movement, Title IX, desegregation, the ERA, and Public Law 94-142 have all had their days in the headlines. Many of these changes toward a more open and equitable society have come slowly and painfully. But they have come. Schools have been more affected by these movements than most segments of our society. Indeed, as is so often the case, schools have been asked to bear the major burden of social reform for the country as a whole.

These movements ebb and flow from year to year, but it seems clear that we have committed ourselves as a nation to a more open society in which access to education in general and to sport and physical education specifically is more open and more equitable. Physical education and interscholastic sport in the middle, junior, and senior high schools have been affected in fundamental ways. Coeducation instruction is now the law of the land. Handicapped students are to be mainstreamed whenever and wherever this provides for them the most sensible educational experience. Girls are to have access to athletic opportunities to the same extent as and with the same support given to boys.

Here, too, one can clearly see the double-edged nature of progress. Coed instruction is not always as easy as same-sex instruction. Having a handicapped child in one's class can cause difficulties. School budgets that are already strained become even more strained with the pressure for better support for girls' athletic programs. Are the gains worth the pain? We certainly think they are. A society in which more people have more equitable access to physical education and sport is, from our point of view, a better society.

A continuing psychologically difficult climate for growth in childhood and adolescence

Teenage suicides have increased markedly in recent years. Teenage drug abuse and alcoholism are continuing problems in many American homes and schools. Changing family patterns, referred to earlier, create tensions and anxieties that often manifest themselves in disruptive behavior and poor performance in schools. Young people have more choices than ever before, yet that fact, too, tends to create its own anxieties.

For a number of years, expert analysts of the changes in Western culture have cited the growing state of anxiety created by all of these forces. Increasingly, this has been complicated even further by the growing awareness of the horror of nuclear war (see "Let Your Children Live," p. 8). Although nuclear war is not a typical day-to-day item in our conversations, much evidence suggests that it has a severe and pervasive effect on the youth of our society.

All these factors create a climate for growth that is troubled and difficult, and this climate tends to create problems for teachers. Much of the attention of educators in the recent past has been devoted to solving these very real and human problems. There appears to be no likelihood of significant change in these areas in the near future.

LET YOUR CHILDREN LIVE

In September of 1983, a United States Senate Select Committee heard testimony from research experts on the impact of the threat of nuclear destruction on the lives of children as they mature. Yale psychiatrist Robert Jay Lifton told the panel, "There is increasing evidence that young people doubt that they will be able to live out their full lives." Various experts testified that teenagers often believe they are preparing for "nothingness" because they will not live to adulthood. A study of teens in the Los Angeles area showed that they worried about parents dying, bad grades, and nuclear war, in that order.

This pervasive psychological threat is not often spoken about, but it appears to be a powerful force in the lives of students at middle, junior, and senior school ages. It no doubt is yet another factor that makes working with students in these age groups both tremendously difficult and tremendously important.

A 12-year-old boy from Brooklyn, New York told the panel: "We are frightened that a lot of countries have the bomb. We are frightened that we might be hit. You are parents. Let your children live."

SOURCE: Based on *USA Today*, September 21, 1983, pp. 1A, 8A.

Growing sports, recreation, and fitness opportunities in the private sector

Opportunities for sports participation and training in the private sector have traditionally been associated with the very wealthy and restricted to certain sports such as tennis, golf, and yachting. While men's athletic clubs in large cities have always provided for fitness activities, they were used sparingly and accessible to the few rather than the many. During the past several decades, the picture has changed dramatically. This change probably began during the post–World War II period when golf courses and bowling alleys provided sports opportunities that were within the economic reach of a growing middle class. More recently, the phenomenon has expanded considerably. How many tennis clubs, gymnastics academies, fitness centers, health spas, strength training centers, and racquetball facilities have emerged in your geographical area? Boating, skiing, swimming, and wilderness activities are now big business in America, and both instructional and participatory opportunities are offered in the private sector. The sons and daughters of the middle and upper economic classes have increasingly availed themselves of these opportunities.

During the same period, the amount of money spent for instruction and participation in the public sector has decreased proportionately. School physical education used to be the place where most boys and girls learned many of their first lessons about sport and fitness. Today, it is not unusual for students to have many opportunities outside the school. In lower-economic areas the outcome of this long-term historical trend has simply been to reduce the opportunities for children as they grow up. For many such children, their main lessons about sports are learned in streets or alleys, or perhaps at a typically overcrowded city recreation facility. Thus, there is a growing disparity between sports instruction opportunities for children of the poor and children of the affluent.

This is a tremendously difficult problem for physical education to respond to as a profession. Certainly it is to our advantage to be part of training people for work in private-sector sports and fitness industries. When adults go to a health spa, it is certainly better for them to be instructed and advised by a trained physical educator. When children learn soccer or tennis at a private club or in a community program, it is certainly better for them to be taught and coached by a certified professional teacher. On the other hand, this growing disparity in opportunities is a sad departure from our traditional approach to education in general and physical education in particular. Although economic equality is not easily achieved, it should be hoped that children and youth from all socioeconomic levels would have equal access to good fitness and sports programs. At present they do not! And that trend does not seem to be changing.

The growing importance of fitness among adults

There is little evidence to suggest that today's children and youth are more fit than previous generations, but it is clear that for a certain portion of the adult population fitness has become very "in." One does not see the fitness boom among blue-collar workers or in lower socioeconomic groups, but in the middle and upper classes and particularly in the suburbs that ring major cities, fitness activities are apparent everywhere. Joggers and cyclists line the streets. Fitness trails (called *vita parcours*) can be found in city parks and even at corporate centers. Many newly built or recently remodeled business and industry headquarters include large and well-equipped exercise centers. Health spas are common in shopping centers. Strength training centers can be found in many suburbs. The amount of money spent on staying fit seems to grow each year.

There is no sign that this fitness boom is abating, and it has begun to make some inroads into middle, junior, and secondary school programs. Aerobics classes are now common. Many young people are very interested in "cosmetic fitness," that is, in fitness that makes them look better (see Chapter 10 for complete coverage of the many kinds of fitness programs available to schools).

It is difficult to predict how the fitness boom will affect programs in the future. Many of those who support the back-to-basics movement in education are also strong advocates of fitness programs as an antidote to the pressures of academic programs. However, these people typically advocate fitness because of its supposed relationship to academic success rather than as a positive goal in its own right. Nonetheless, physical educators need to think carefully and plan thoughtfully for the fitness aspects of their programs. The public is becoming fairly well educated about the basic parameters of physical fitness in

Fitness courses have become common in communities and schools.

terms of both health and motor performance. A physical educator can no longer suggest that five minutes of exercises prior to the daily lesson contributes to a fitness objective for the students. Too many parents know enough about fitness to understand that it cannot be achieved in any measurable way through that amount of activity. It is also becoming increasingly clear that fitness habits developed in youth can be long-term—the corollary being that obesity and lack of fitness in youth can also be long-term.

Back to basics: Another period of educational renewal

Few college students today remember when, in 1957, Russia launched *Sputnik*, which seemed to signal a technological superiority for the Soviet Union. The United States reacted predictably. Call after call came for educational reform—more mathematics, more science, higher standards. The result was a flurry of activity in those academic areas and an enormous infusion of federal money to support mathematics and science programs in schools. During the early to mid-1960s, the *Sputnik* phenomenon produced not only the math-science emphasis but also ushered in a backlash movement devoted to humanistic education.

It appears that the mid-1980s is the time for another national examination of schools. (See Figure 1.1, p. 12.) Poor test scores by students, rampant vandalism in schools, high rates of disruptive behavior, widespread substance abuse, and a declining American economic position in international markets

Co-ed instruction and participation have become more prevalent.

have combined to create conditions within which a reevaluation seems necessary. In 1983 the National Commission on Excellence in Education produced a report that seemed to shake the foundations of our faith in education and schools. The report indicated in very straightforward language (see "A Nation at Risk," p. 13) that the state of American education would be taken as an act of war had it been arranged by a foreign power. But said the report, the most tragic aspect of the situation is that we committed the transgressions ourselves; we let education get to the sorry state that the commission viewed it to be. The report created enormous controversy, and many people were quick to point out that economic efficiency and a better ability to compete in world economic markets were not the only purposes of education, not even the most important purposes. Still, the controversy over education is certain to have its effect on schools, and physical education will no doubt be included. Curiously, the commission's report barely mentioned physical education except in the negative sense that it was included among all those "frill" subjects that take time away from the academic curriculum. There is absolutely no doubt that physical educators will continue to be under the gun to defend their programs and to resist efforts to discontinue them.

Dwindling state requirements for physical education

During the early to middle part of this century, physical educators worked very hard to achieve the passage of state laws that required physical education

EDUCATIONAL REFORM — AREAS OF AGREEMENT

Nine reform documents published in the past several years have focused on upgrading the nation's schools. Although the documents differ in some respects, they have been in agreement on most important issues. Below are listed these reports and the improvements that most agree are needed:

National Commission on Excellence: A Nation At Risk

Education Commission of the States: Action for Excellence

Twentieth Century Fund: Making the Grade

Ernest Boyer: High School

John Goodlad: A Place Called School

National Science Foundation: Educating Americans for the
21st Century

Theodore Seiser: A Study of High Schools

Business-Higher Education Forum: America's Competitive

The Padeia Group: The Padeia Proposal

1. Career ladders that permit teachers to be promoted to higher levels of responsibility and income.

2. Incentive pay for teachers based on merit.

3. More rigorous teacher training.

4. Incentives to lure bright high school students into teaching.

5. More classroom discipline.

6. Assessment of student progress based on achievement rather than age.

7. More flexibility for teachers and fewer non-teaching duties.

8. The same curricular track for all students.

Figure 1.1 Areas of agreement among current reform documents focusing on education, schools, and teaching.

SOURCE: *USA Today*, February 14, 1984, p. 1.

A NATION AT RISK

In April 1983 the National Commission on Excellence in Education delivered an open report to the American people entitled *A Nation at Risk: The Imperative for Educational Reform*. The following paragraph is from the opening page of that letter.

> If an unfriendly foreign power had attempted to impose on America the mediocre educational performance that exists today, we might well have viewed it as an act of war. As it stands, we have allowed this to happen to ourselves. We have even squandered the gains in student achievement made in the wake of the Sputnik challenge. Moreover, we have dismantled essential support systems which helped make those gains possible. We have, in effect, been committing an act of unthinking, unilateral educational disarmament. (p. 5)

The recommendations of the commission were many and controversial—more emphasis on science and math, higher standards, computer education, reemphasis of foreign languages, reemphasis of literary skills, longer school days, and longer school years. Physical education was not considered to be a "basic" subject in this report. Indeed, our subject matter is mentioned only once, on page 19, where it is listed with remedial English, personal development courses, and marriage courses as evidence of the large proportion of curricular time devoted to "appetizers and desserts" rather than to "main courses."

Clearly, it is up to the physical education and health professions to convince the public and other professionals that fitness and leisure skills are also basic to a meaningful life and a strong nation. At the moment, there is little evidence that we are winning that battle.

SOURCE: *A Nation at Risk: The Imperative for Educational Reform*. A Report to the Nation and the Secretary of Education by the National Commission on Excellence in Education, David Pierpont Gardner, Chairman, April 1983.

for all students. Most states now have laws that provide for a certain number of hours per week or a certain number of academic credits in physical education for graduation. However, the trend over the past two decades has been to dilute these laws—to require less physical education than before. For the most part, the changes in state law have come about as a result of a desire to save money. In some states physical educators have been able to gain sufficient support to defeat such efforts. In a number of other states the efforts have succeeded. It appears that the trend toward reducing or eliminating physical education requirements in the middle, junior, and senior high schools will continue.

What does this mean for physical education? In some schools the loss of state support for required physical education has led to the development of attractive elective programs. In such cases the reduction in state requirements seems to have motivated physical educators to make their programs more attractive to students with the result of better student support. In other situations, however, the result has been lost jobs, badly reduced teaching staffs, program reductions, and a general devaluing of physical education in the schools. Physical educators need to take this trend very seriously. More professionals in our field have to become advocates for our subject matter. More teachers have to plan and implement their programs more carefully so that students, other teachers, administrators, and parents understand the value of physical education and will be willing to support it when it is called into question.

Varied student backgrounds in sports

Two recent developments seem to account for the current diversity in the skills and expectations that students bring to physical education in middle, junior, and senior high school. First, elementary physical education has developed substantially in the past several decades. Students who come to the upper grades with a good background in elementary physical education will be very different from students who come from a school where there is no elementary physical education specialist. Imagine what the differences must be for two students, one of whom had physical education taught by a specialist three days a week for six years, while the other had little more than supervised play at recess!

The second factor in the diversity now apparent is students' previous experiences in youth sports. Years ago most students had no experience in Little League baseball or Pee Wee football, but today youth competition is provided in a wide range of sports. Not only does this affect the students' skill levels but also their expectations. For example, if they have been on the community youth soccer team and played a full schedule, worn a nice uniform, and had parents and fans at the games, they may feel that a three-week soccer unit in the eighth grade is a bit anticlimactic. It is no secret that many students during the adolescent years feel that physical education is "Mickey Mouse." Unfortunately, part of that perspective is based on the fact that some physical education programs are less than they should be. Regardless of the reasons, the varied entry abilities and expectations of students need to be taken into account when planning a physical education program. To ignore these factors is to risk irrelevancy for a certain portion of your students.

The continuing effect of the dual role of the teacher and coach on the quality of teaching in physical education

Many physical education teachers, especially those who have entered the profession in the past decade, come to school early in the morning, teach a full schedule of classes, and then coach an interscholastic team in the after-school program. The coaching often involves road trips, scouting, and post-season competitions. The 12-hour day becomes commonplace during a sports season. Many physical educators coach for two of the three sports seasons in the school year.

The scenario just described is responsible for what has been detailed in our literature as teacher/coach role conflict (for a more thorough treatment of

A high-ropes course in a wooded setting shows a different approach to physical education.

this topic, see Chapter 6). The typical result of the conflict is that one devotes more time to coaching and less time to teaching. When the moment arrives, as it does fairly quickly, that one must decide where to place one's limited energies, the choice is almost inevitably made for the sports setting rather than for the physical education setting. The result is that energy devoted to teaching is less and the teaching is done less well. In certain unfortunate cases the old stereotype of the coach/physical educator throwing out the ball during gym period and retiring to his or her office to work on "plays" actually does occur. As a result, students not only get an inferior physical education, but the profession suffers a setback in its image.

There appears to be no change in our nation's commitment to a full and strong interscholastic sports program. Title IX has opened these opportunities to girls. More sports are now contested than ever before. The end result of all this activity is that more coaches are needed. Thus, the potential for role conflict seems to be more prevalent. This is a difficult situation that our profession needs to deal with honestly and quickly.

The continuing growth of sports cultures

Americans have always been a sporting people, as have the British, Canadians, Australians, and a host of other nationalities. In developed countries everywhere, sport seems to occupy a central role in culture. During this century, as developed nations grew more prosperous, their involvement with sports and their devotion to sporting pastimes accelerated. There is no evidence that this trend will end. The enormous interest generated by Olympic competition, international tennis tournaments, and other such events is evidence at one level. Youth sports opportunities also continue to expand. School sports continue to grow in both the number of sports offered and the number of participants. College and university sports have sparked tremendous interest recently. And professional sports grow with more sports, more franchises, and more media coverage.

To be sure, there are problems—from youth sports abuses to drug scandals in professional sports, from inept coaching to extraordinarily high salaries. But the problems do not negate the fact that sport is alive and well in our culture. The question is What will be the relationship between school physical education and this larger sports movement? Will physical education embrace sport and attempt to contribute positively to its growth? Or will physical education keep sport at arm's length and move in a different direction? (See page 191 for a further discussion of the relationship between sport and physical education.)

Many physical education professionals feel strongly that we must become leaders in establishing sound sports programs, in promoting safe and sane sports practices, and in extending the benefits and joys of sport to more and more students. This group wants to be on the front line of sports reform, building educationally valuable sports programs in schools and influencing positively the sports programs that are conducted outside of schools.

Others within the profession want to put sport at arms length. This group sees sport as corrupt and elitist. They favor a more recreational or intellectual approach to school physical education. They want to deemphasize competition rather than create better competition. The future of physical education will be determined partially by which of these groups prevails.

Skill in competition continues to be an important question for adolescents.

Problems and prospects

We have tried to highlight some issues in society, in education, and in physical education in order to provide a sense of both the problems and the prospects for physical education in the years ahead. It is not an easy time to be a teacher. Yet the possibilities for contributing positively to the development of youth have never been greater.

Some of the problems we have addressed exist at the societal level, and how they are resolved will certainly affect physical education. However, there is little that physical educators can do to influence the direction of some of these developments. On the other hand, a number of issues (youth sport, role conflict, fitness problems, equal access to sports instruction, etc.) can be directly influenced by the individual and collective actions of physical educators and their professional organizations. The question remains: What will be the effects of our future actions?

There is no doubt that we will affect certain issues. We will either be part of the continuing problem, or we will become part of the cure! By *not acting* we probably risk becoming part of the problem. By acting unwisely we certainly risk becoming part of the problem. But by thinking carefully and acting decisively and courageously, physical educators can indeed help to shape the future of their profession and through their actions to influence the lives of youth. This will not happen unless the problems are identified and debated, taken seriously, and challenged by individuals and by organizations. A first step in taking hold of our own future is to develop an honest and coherent set of beliefs about schools and physical education and to forge those beliefs into a philosophy that can serve as a guide for action. We turn to that task in Chapter 2.

Summary

Physical education reflects the culture within which it is practiced and, to a lesser extent, influences that culture. Some cultural trends seem likely to influence the day-to-day practice of physical education. Families are less stable. School populations shift frequently. Teachers often have more responsibilities and also more problems as a result.

Widened differences between rich and poor are also reflected in schools. In addition, the growth of a private sports instruction industry caters primarily to the middle and upper classes, making access to sports and fitness opportunities for youngsters from poor families even less likely.

Our nation's commitment to affirmative action will no doubt have its ups and downs, but it seems that the course we have charted for ourselves is to provide opportunities for all and to continue to break down barriers that are built strictly on race, sex, or handicapping conditions.

Adolescence continues to be a difficult development period. Teenagers often bear the brunt of societal problems as they face an uncertain future. This

makes teaching and coaching adolescent students a difficult task, one requiring sensitivity and patience.

Fitness continues to become more and more important in the healthy life-
style. Adult fitness has become big business. Adolescents have not yet jumped
on the fitness bandwagon, but they are certainly becoming more educated
about fitness. The back-to-basics movement in schools could prohibit a greater
emphasis on fitness, but it need not do so.

State laws requiring physical education for students have been diluted
consistently over the past several decades. While physical educators in some
states have worked together to defeat efforts to reduce requirements, others
have not been so fortunate. The trend toward reduced or eliminated requirements makes good programming and teaching more important than ever.

Students come to the middle, junior, and senior high schools with vastly
different backgrounds in elementary physical education and youth sport. Some
are very skilled. Others are very unskilled. This makes teaching more difficult
and has to be taken into account when planning programs. Role conflict exists
when the dual roles of teacher and coach create task demands that cannot be
met. Typically, the response is to teach less well and devote more energy to
coaching, a phenomenon that is said to account for much of the less-than-
energetic teaching one sometimes sees in high school physical education.

The sports culture in the United States and most of the developed world
continues to grow and prosper. Though not without problems, sport captures
the imagination of millions each year and has become a vital element in contemporary culture. Physical education has an uncertain relationship to sport
that needs to be clarified in the near future.

Suggested activities

1. Read a synopsis of *A Nation at Risk*. Discuss each of the recommendations relative to your experiences in high school.

2. Visit a private-sector sports/fitness center. Report on who goes there,
how much it costs, what kind of place it is, and what people do when
they are there.

3. Develop a list of common school problems. Discuss them from the
point of view of a former student and from the point of view of a new
teacher.

4. Debate the following topic: Physical education should assume primary
responsibility for the future health and vitality of the sports culture.
Have three class members argue the affirmative and three argue the
negative.

5. Develop a list of "difficulties in being an adolescent." In class, discuss
the list in terms of how physical education can respond to each item.

2

This We Believe: A Philosophy of Physical Education

The purpose of this chapter is to stimulate discussion and thought about what physical education means and how it ought to be taught in schools. To accomplish this we present our own philosophy of physical education, its role in schools, and its potential impact on society. Belief statements are generated for each of these areas as a means to provoke thought and discussion. The major topics covered in the chapter are as follows:

Belief statements concerning the nature of physical education

Belief statements relative to the values to be gained from well-conceived and implemented physical education programs

Belief statements relative to activities within physical education and the necessity of achieving tangible outcomes

Belief statements relative to the conduct of physical education in a democratic society

Belief statements about the process of physical education

Belief statements about physical education teachers and their preparation

It is Monday night and the local board of education is meeting. The chairwoman of the high school physical education department is speaking to the board. There has been discussion about reducing the number of physical education teachers at the high school, and she is here to present a case for retaining and even adding to the present teaching staff. To make her case, she has to convince the board of the importance of physical education in the lives of secondary school students. She has decided to begin her presentation with a short statement about what she believes to be the major values of physical education. The viability of her ideas and her ability to present them may well determine the future of physical education at the school.

It is Thursday afternoon in a middle school. The physical education teachers are meeting with teachers from art and music to talk about a unified arts curriculum for the school. Only a limited amount of curriculum time is devoted to these three subject areas, and today's meeting will initiate the process through which that time will be distributed among the three areas. The art and music teachers seem to know a lot about each other's areas, but they are not too sure about what the physical educators are trying to accomplish. Because of this, the first several meetings will be devoted to letting the two physical education teachers describe what they believe to be important about physical education, what they are trying to accomplish, and how this may or may not fit in with what the music and art teachers want to do. Again, the physical education teachers' ability to express their ideas, and the quality of those ideas, will probably affect the amount of physical education that the students at this middle school will receive.

It is July and summer vacation for most teachers. However, the physical education teachers at the three junior high schools in the district are being paid a summer stipend to develop a new physical education curriculum. The six teachers—one man and one woman from each of the three schools—are meeting to begin their task. They decide that the first step in creating a revised curriculum is to develop a philosophy of physical education and then to arrange a curriculum that reflects that philosophy. They decide further that at their first several meetings each of the six will present his or her own set of beliefs about physical education as a way of getting started. These meetings will involve an exchange of ideas. How good the ideas are and how articulately and forcefully they are presented will determine the nature of the new curriculum.

Do you think these vignettes are contrived? Do you feel that clear statements of belief and the ability to articulate a sound philosophy are unimportant in determining what happens to young people when they come to physical education? The scenarios just described happen every school year. Sometimes the outcomes are crucial, as in the case at the school board. In other situations, the results are probably deferred, as in the last situation. Nonetheless, they impact eventually on what happens in the gymnasium and on the playing fields. Professional educators often find themselves in situations where what they say about their subject matter produces consequences. Sometimes this occurs in a formal situation in a meeting or in front of a parents' group, while at other times it occurs in informal situations in a teachers' lounge at school. *What we say and how well we say it does matter!* You will be judged by your fellow teachers, administrators, students, and parents concerning your ability to articulate your beliefs and the soundness and coherence of those beliefs. Eventually, people will make some connection between what you say about physical education and how you teach. People will slowly begin to put together evidence concerning the degree to which what you *say* corresponds to what you *do*, and you will be judged accordingly.

The purpose of this chapter is to get you to think about what you believe and how your beliefs come together in a philosophy of physical education. Your philosophy should be able to respond to the issues raised in Chapter 1. If it does not, then it is not a philosophy that is relevant to the times.

The vehicle we have chosen to get you to think about your own beliefs is to state ours. We think it is only fair that you understand clearly what we believe.

We do not ask that you believe as we do. Indeed, we encourage you to argue and debate our beliefs because in so doing you will sharpen your own ideas. We ask only that you take our beliefs seriously and that you make an honest attempt to form your own set of beliefs and articulate them carefully.

Belief statements

We now present a set of 14 belief statements and a brief rationale for each statement. Together they represent our philosophy of physical education for today's schools.

Physical education derives from play, is best understood in reference to play and best defined as playful motor activity, and in its mature form is institutionalized in culture as sport and dance

People everywhere and in all times *play*. Play is a fundamental form of human behavior. Childhood play is characterized by spontaneity, gaiety, and quickly changing rules and roles. The play forms of childhood are simple, limited in difficulty, and flexible. As people mature, so too does their play. Adult play is characterized by practice, subordination to rules, ritual, tradition, a growing appreciation for difficulty, an emphasis on skill and strategy, deferred gratification, and effort (Caillois 1961).

We believe that physical education is best understood in reference to its expression as playful behavior. As cultures develop, their play forms become more standard; that is, they are *institutionalized* (rules, standards, organizations, etc.) so that people may play them at different times in different places. Children's games are flexible. Youth sport is more institutionalized. High school sport is even more so.

Other kinds of early childhood play become institutionalized in the form of music, drama, art, and dance. Like sport, these adult play forms derive from less structured childhood play. And like sport, they all require education for children to learn the skills and appreciations necessary to take part in the adult forms. We believe that sport and dance are the institutionalized forms of play that come together in physical education. Thus, physical education is a companion subject to art education, music education, and drama education (Siedentop 1980). Each derives from play, and together they can be referred to as the *ludic arts*.

To develop good *players*, in the fullest meaning of that term, is our primary objective. To become good players, students need to acquire the skills and strategies of the activity, and they need to be educated in the rituals, traditions, and appreciations that provide meaning to players. To play well is to play competently, to play within the rules, to play hard, and to respect both the activity and the people with whom one is playing, whether teammates or opponents.

Health-related fitness is of major importance to the well-being of our society and a necessary element in physical education programs

The costs to our society in lost productivity and medical expenses for people who suffer from fitness-related health problems is overwhelming. Beyond that, fitness is a fundamental prerequisite to a healthy life-style and is often related dramatically to one's quality of life. Fitness needs to be viewed as a lifelong endeavor, a way of life. The skills, habits, and attitudes necessary to ensure a healthy life-style have to be inculcated and constantly reinforced during adolescence. Students need to be helped to achieve fitness. They also have to acquire the knowledge to maintain appropriate fitness throughout life. Perhaps most importantly they have to learn to make a commitment to regular exercise as part of the way they live.

WHAT IS THE PRIMARY GOAL OF EDUCATION?

There appears to be no widespread agreement among experts as to which goal or goals are most important in education. But when Research & Forecasts, Inc., asked parents of school-age boys and girls what they felt about various goals, the answer was revealing. Ninety-six percent of the parents polled reported that improving the quality of life should be the primary goal of education. Seventy-five percent agreed that achieving economic success should also be a major educational goal.

Clearly, if quality of life is seen by many to be a major educational goal, then physical education can and should be an important way to achieve that goal.

SOURCE: Based on *USA Today*, September 22, 1983, p. 1A.

Fitness needs to be attended to seriously and regularly or its benefits are lost. This is not to suggest that keeping fit can't also be fun! Swimming, cycling, and running are done by millions of people who not only derive substantial health benefits from them but also enjoy them thoroughly. We believe that physical educators must develop fitness programs that entail regular exercise of an intensity and duration to ensure cardiovascular fitness and that such programs must be conducted in ways that are acceptable and enjoyable to students.

Physical education is valuable in its own right and does not need to be justified by reference to academics

Learning to be a good volleyball player, an expert rock climber, or a competent downhill skiier is a valuable outcome. These activities are not only important in terms of their immediate joys and benefits, but they provide an important long-term contribution to a quality life-style. The culture of sport and dance that we have developed is an important aspect of our collective existence as a society. It sustains many, many people. We do not subscribe to the notion that physical education should be justified as a school subject because it somehow contributes to better performance in the academic area. In fact, to justify physical education by reference to academics is to trivialize it, to make it less than it can and should be.

We believe that fitness is also a worthy goal in and of itself. Becoming more fit is a good thing regardless of whether it makes you perform better in algebra or keeps you more alert in literature class. Those who explain what we do by citing the beneficial effects of an exercise period only in terms of better academic work completely miss the degree to which our subject matter is related to the individual's quality of life and to the future well-being of society.

> **The major values to be gained through participation in physical education are skill, the joy of physical exertion, the realization of clear-cut objectives, appropriate relationships to authority, the acceptance of responsibility, cooperative relationships, security in the rituals of the rules and customs that define sport, the adventure of risk, the ability to defer goals, and measuring oneself against clearly defined and widely accepted measures of quality**

In fact, there appear to be few other endeavors in which youth can better learn some complex and important lessons about cooperation and competition, authority and responsibility, the importance of commonly accepted standards of performance, and the satisfactions derivable from the pursuit of competence.

However, these important outcomes do not accrue automatically just by participating in activities. Programs have to be carefully conceptualized, properly planned, and competently implemented for participants to gain those values. We all understand that some bad values can also be learned in participation, especially in poorly run programs. Participants can learn to cheat, to get by with less than a good effort, to be selfish. It takes professional people running good programs to ensure that positive values are more likely to accrue than negative ones.

> **The values to be derived from participation in physical education are appropriate to females and males, to rich and poor, to normal and exceptional students**

We want to make it clear that our view is egalitarian. We support legislation and rules that guarantee equal access to our subject matter. We believe that cultures can best grow and prosper by guaranteeing equal opportunity in schools and that equal opportunity in schools includes equal access to quality physical education programs for females, blacks, Hispanics, the handicapped, and the gifted.

We are not so naive as to believe that equal opportunity can be achieved without cost. Recent experiences with Title IX (the government act that mandates equal opportunity in sport and physical education to girls and women) show that some difficult adjustments are necessary to rectify a history of inequality. But that price needs to be paid. Our belief in the importance of equal opportunity to learn and enjoy our subject matter causes us to be supportive of women's programs, of taxation schemes that spread available resources more equitably among school districts, of extra support for school and community recreation programs in lower socioeconomic areas, and of a number of other social and political issues with which you may or may not agree. The point is that we believe that a commitment to equal opportunity requires companion commitments to programs that make equal opportunity more likely to occur. It is one thing to support equal opportunity in one's professional rhetoric and quite another to support programs that can actually help to bring it about.

The issue of equal opportunity is particularly important in light of the emergence of the sports instruction industry in the private sector that we described in Chapter 1 (see page 8). As the private sector takes over more of the sports instruction for youth, the public sector tends to support it less (for example, state laws requiring physical education may be eliminated or weakened). This means that the sons and daughters of the well-to-do have more and better opportunities, while the sons and daughters of the poor have fewer and poorer opportunities. In our view this inequality in opportunity to learn our subject matter can only be reduced by reemphasizing the role of physical education and sport in *public* schools.

The values available through participation in sound physical education programs are particularly relevant to the major developmental tasks of adolescence and to ignore this aspect of development is to deny what has been known for centuries

Adolescence has been a special topic in education since 1904 when G. Stanley Hall published his famous book *Adolescence*. Indeed, the junior high school is a unique American innovation that was created specifically to contribute better to the stage of development called adolescence. It has long been recognized that students in their adolescent years are involved in predictable developmental tasks. For example, they are intrigued and concerned over their changing bodies. They are strongly devoted to their peers and crave both the competition and cooperation involved in peer groups. They are acquiring a value system. They need to have experiences in responsibility as they begin to establish identities that are separate from their families' identities. They like to test themselves and to take risks. They are beginning to be able to participate in the adult culture of art, music, drama, and sport. They need experiences in which gratification is deferred and goals can be sought over time.

Ideally, adolescents should be learning dedication, perseverance, loyalty, the relationship of effort to outcome, how to cooperate and compete, and how to lead and follow. The activities of physical education have great potential for meeting these developmental tasks.

The many activities that comprise physical education have no particular hierarchical value in terms of their importance to the participant even though they may have more or less value relative to specific goals for the educator

We understand that soccer is a vastly superior activity to golf if one is concerned with cardiovascular fitness. (Golf, it has been said, is a good way to ruin what otherwise might have been a nice, healthful walk.) But people don't play soccer and golf primarily because they may be healthy activities. To the soccer player and the golfer, the relative contribution to cardiovascular fitness is not a major issue. We know of no *personal* criteria by which one can judge tennis to be better than volleyball, swimming to be better than climbing, or orienteering to be better than hockey. To the participant, the joy and meaning of an activity is not measurable by standard educational criteria.

This belief has importance when it comes to deciding what kinds of activities to include or exclude from a program. We recognize and support both the right and the obligation of professional physical educators to choose activities on the basis of educational criteria. That is, we support the choice of one activity over another because of its fitness implications or of activity X over activity Y because of its risk dimensions. However, we do believe that these choices have little to do with the meaning of the activity to the participant, and we urge caution in activity decisions that can be made to sound educationally appropriate for youth when, in fact, they have little to do with youth. For example, many professionals urge the exclusion of team-oriented activities from the high school curriculum and replacement of them with individual activities that have a "lifetime sport" orientation. There are two potential problems with this kind of reasoning. First, what constitutes a "lifetime sport" is changing dramatically. Long-distance road racing is becoming a lifetime activity for many men and women. We are moving away from the notion that a nice, gentle game of tennis or golf is the only legitimate means of involvement for older people. Second, in promoting lifetime sports over team games, one risks what a physical educator once described as "pedigeriatrics," that is, making young people old before their time. There is absolutely nothing wrong with teaching tennis or golf to youth; let's just be careful about *why* we do it. The young tennis enthusiast could care less that what he or she is learning and participating in is a "lifetime" activity.

If physical education is to survive and thrive as a school subject, it must demonstrate tangible outcomes and students must show recognizable achievement gains

Although there are many legitimate ways to conceptualize physical education in the life of youth, to be successful it must accomplish something. School is the place students go to learn. If physical education wants to continue to be a part of the school curriculum, students must also learn when they go to the gym, the pool, the fields, or the courts. We believe that a major problem began to develop in physical education when teachers provided less accountability for achievement and performance and began to focus their accountability systems on attendance, proper dress, and "participation." The discussion on pages 401–404 shows very clearly the degree to which achievement and performance have been put aside as major elements in accountability systems. This issue must be raised and debated. Either physical education is going to be a school subject in which there is an honest attempt to improve performance and recognize achievement, or it will become a supervised recreation experience for which students need only participate.

What is equally clear regarding this issue is that many different kinds of physical education programs—from fitness programs to sports programs, from wilderness programs to conceptually based programs—have achieved success in recent years. We believe the successful programs have something in common. They all focus on specific goals and achieve them! That is, they accomplish something that is concrete and recognizable. Students know and can do things at the end of the programs that they did not know and could not do at the beginning of the programs.

Equal educational opportunity is fundamental to the maintenance of our democratic society, and physical education should be in all school curricula and equally accessible to all students

Physical educators in the early part of this century worked diligently to bring physical education into the school curriculum as a regular subject. As noted earlier, in recent times these gains have eroded, and presently many question whether physical education should even be in the curriculum. We believe that it should be a centrally important part of the school curriculum. And we believe that all students should have equal opportunity to learn our subject matter.

It seems to us counterproductive to a democratic society that students in wealthier school districts have better facilities, more teachers, and greater opportunity to learn physical education than do students who happen to live in districts where the tax base is less. If physical education is a legitimate part of the school curriculum, then ways must be found for all students to have an equal opportunity to enjoy and benefit from it.

Physical education can be central to the education of youth if it is characterized by commitment, intimacy, and achievement

In our sixth belief statement (see page 24), we made it clear that physical education is a subject that meets the developmental needs of adolescents extremely well. For this reason, physical education has the opportunity to be a subject that is central to the education of youth, to stand at the very heart of

PHYSICAL EDUCATION IN PRIVATE SCHOOLS

Isn't it interesting that in schools where there are ample resources and where parents care a great deal about the education their sons and daughters receive, fitness and physical education typically are strongly emphasized. This advertisement lists 10 major objectives for the school. Two refer directly to our subject matter. It is a fact that throughout history in places where education has been taken very seriously physical education has played a major role.

Wellington
Wellington
Wellington
Wellington
Wellington
Wellington
Wellington

**Wellington
Wellington
Wellington
Wellington
Wellington
Wellington
Wellington
Wellington
Wellington
Wellington
Wellington
Wellington**

Wellington Students:

Become self-educating, self-motivating individuals to as great an extent as their age and ability allow.

Learn to read with fluency, ease and comprehension.

Learn to communicate effectively orally and in writing.

Become knowledgeable in many facets of mathematical learning and be able not only to handle numbers arithmetically, but also to use numbers to solve problems.

Develop an awareness of the world around them--their community, state, nation, and world--and how that world functions and how it came to be what it is today.

Appreciate the importance of health and fitness and understand appropriate measures to achieve such a state.

Learn entry skills in many appropriate sports and gain experience in playing team and individual sports.

Experience inquiry into the scientific world and gain an appreciation and understanding of many formal sciences.

Work creatively in graphic arts, music, dance, and drama and develop an appreciation for others who do so.

Experience working and playing in a community of students and scholars where application, honesty, hard work, achievement, and appropriate behavior are recognized and encouraged.

For more information:

Wellington School
1822 Fishinger Road
Columbus, Ohio 43221
(614) 457-7883

Wellington is an independent, coeducational college preparatory school that admits children of any race, religion, ethnic or national background.

SOURCE: *Columbus Monthly*, October 1983.

the curriculum of the middle, junior, and senior high schools. In fact, however, physical education is too often a peripheral subject, one that does not excite youth or speak to their developmental needs. We believe that this is the case because physical education is too seldom characterized by commitment, intimacy, and achievement. We will continue to emphasize our belief that in order to be considered valuable and exciting by young people, physical education must be dedicated to achievement. Furthermore, this kind of dedication to achievement cannot be fulfilled without developing programs that are of sufficient duration and intensity to breed intimacy between the teachers and students and among the students.

There is no easy way to achieve the kind of central status for physical education that we describe here. It requires effort, sensitivity to the students, the development of standards, careful planning, competent teaching, and perseverance. These, of course, are the very stuff of *commitment*.

To be fully successful, physical education needs to extend beyond the school and the school day

The physical education program conducted within the school grounds between the hours of 8:00 A.M. and 3:00 P.M. is, of course, important. In fact, good programs can be developed strictly within those time and space constraints. However, in order to be as fully successful as they can be and to have the full effect on youth that they can have, physical education programs need to move beyond the school space and the school day.

The community is typically a rich resource for sports and fitness instruction and participation. There are golf courses, bowling alleys, racquetball courts, rivers, and a host of other settings where good physical education can take place in ways that often cannot be reproduced on the typical school grounds. (See Chapter 4 for a complete treatment of this issue.) Beyond the immediate community there are settings for physical education that offer the potential for exciting and important experiences and growth. This is particularly true for activities that fall under the rubric of wilderness sport.

We are a mobile society. People have grown accustomed to going places, and youth seem particularly fond of going places. Travel tends to breed intimacy because people spend a lot of time together, share meals, and have the opportunity to interact in both formal and informal ways. We recognize that this also creates problems; there is a liability problem, and there are administrative problems. As noted earlier, however, there are no easy ways to accomplish important goals. If special outcomes are desired, then special efforts need to be made. We believe that the problems can be overcome and that the potential outcomes outweigh the efforts that must be expended.

The role of the teacher is critical to the success of the physical education program

Do teachers make a difference? In our judgment the evidence is overwhelming in support of a positive answer to that question. Yet it seems equally clear to us that there is no one perfect teaching method or style. We have no desire to make all teachers look alike or behave in identical ways. We do believe that there are teaching skills and strategies that are fundamental to success, but learning and improving these skills and strategies does not necessarily make people alike.

We believe that teachers need to facilitate opportunity, to help students to be task oriented, to provide firm but supportive learning environments, to develop standards, to hold students accountable to those standards, to manage classes and experiences efficiently, and to provide tasks for students that are challenging yet achievable. (Chapter 20 more fully covers these issues.) These teaching strategies are important for a volleyball unit in a school gymnasium, and they are equally important for an orienteering experience in a nearby state forest. In this sense they are *generic* teaching strategies.

In the final analysis, physical education will probably rise or fall on the effectiveness of those who teach it. If they teach well, plan good programs, develop the commitment and intimacy described above, and stress achievement, then physical education is likely to flourish and grow more important as a school subject. Students will learn from it and enjoy it. Their achievement and excitement will become known to administrators, other teachers, and parents. This knowledge will build support among those groups, and this support will further enhance the ability of physical educators to develop and extend their programs. In short, success will breed further success. On the other hand, poor teaching and planning lead to apathy among students. Apathy among students is noticed by teachers, administrators, and parents. Less support is available. People begin to question the role of physical education.

Therefore, have no doubt about who we believe to be the central figure in the drama that will be played out in schools in regard to physical education: It is the teacher of physical education in the schools who will write the future of our subject matter.

Teacher education programs in physical education can equip students with skills and attitudes to design, implement, and maintain vital physical education programs in today's schools

Teacher education programs can help to develop competent, dedicated teachers only if that is their main goal. The skills of teaching need to be the main focus of the programs. Experiences need to be provided for people to practice these skills in schools. Teacher education programs are unlikely to achieve this important goal if they are not aiming for it! That may sound nonsensical, but the statement deserves serious consideration. Dedicated, competent teaching does not happen automatically. Good intentions are not sufficient to produce it. Above all, it will not happen merely as a side effect of a program devoted to other goals, for example, to producing young scholars in the discipline of physical education.

Developing competent, dedicated teachers takes time and effort, just as developing good programs in schools does. The effort must translate into undergraduate curriculum time that is devoted to topics directly related to the teacher's role in schools. The role of good teacher education programs in the future of school-based physical education is vital.

The physical educator needs to be an advocate for our subject matter within the context of the school and to provide a model of involvement and a healthy life-style

Physical education needs people who are willing and able to be advocates for our subject matter. We need people who are able to articulate views that clearly identify the values intrinsic to physical education and to resist efforts to justify it by reference to its influence on academic performance. We need physical educators who refuse to take a backseat to the so-called basic subjects, who recognize that physical education can be *basic* to the growth and development of the student and who are willing and able to argue that point of view with other teachers, administrators, school boards, and parents. If we do not stand up for our subject matter, then who will?

We also believe that physical educators should be models for our subject matter, that they should be active people who participate regularly and joyfully and who are fit. Physical educators do not need to parade their activity and fitness in front of others; neither do they need to use those qualities as hammers to beat down others. They simply need to *be* active, fit people.

The bottom line

The contemporary influences outlined in Chapter 1 represent a set of interrelated problems that will certainly affect the future of physical education. Yet physical education is not a passive phenomenon that will merely react to and be affected by these influences. Physical education has the opportunity to shape its own future. It cannot do so without coming to some clear formulation of basic beliefs.

In this chapter we have tried to inform you of our basic beliefs. We have attempted to be as direct and as honest as possible. There is no value in being either fuzzy or half-hearted when it comes to stating beliefs! We have not stated our beliefs because we expect you to adopt them but because we hope to provoke you to think about your own beliefs, to discuss them with others, to clarify them, and to sort out the degree to which you really believe in certain things. Examining your own beliefs is not always an easy or pleasant task. But it is a necessary task if you are to move forward in your ability to be a professional physical educator.

When you have your day before the school board, or in front of a parents' organization, or in a meeting with your principal, what will you say? How well will you say it? How well will you respond when questioned about something you have said or done? If there is a major debate in your school district as to whether funds ought to be spent for new textbooks or for a swimming pool,

WHAT DO PARENTS EXPECT FROM THEIR CHILDREN'S TEACHERS?

When parents send their children to school, they expect the school will do well for the children. They do not expect that each child will become a superstar in physical education, but they do expect that the child will discover something of his or her potential. It is important to remember that parents do indeed have expectations about what will happen to their children while they are under your care. Here are a few to think about:

1. Parents expect you to care about their children—to regard them as people with interests, fear, and hopes.

2. Parents expect you to teach their children—they want their children to learn the basics of your subject matter, to be fit or to learn fundamental sports skills and how to play important games. They expect more than supervised recreation.

3. Parents expect that you will behave in ways such that their children are excited about what you are doing.

4. Parents expect you to support and encourage the progress of their children, not only through recognition and reinforcement but through higher expectations, nurturing, and even pushing the children a bit.

5. Parents expect you to discipline their children. They understand the need for self-control and cooperation. They are concerned only that the system be fair and open.

6. Parents expect teachers to make a real effort. They work hard at their jobs, and they expect you to work hard too.

7. Parents expect to be kept informed of their children's programs, progress, and problems. They do not like to be kept in the dark. They cannot help if they are not informed. Furthermore, they genuinely appreciate efforts at communication.

SOURCE: Based on Charles, C. M., *Building Classroom Discipline*. New York: Longman, 1981.

how will you react? You obviously cannot be against new textbooks, but can you convincingly argue in favor of the swimming pool? We hope you will be able to influence positively the people to whom you talk. We hope so because of the young people in that district who would benefit enormously from the addition of a swimming pool, from what it could mean in terms of their growth and development. That is the bottom line—the education of youth.

Summary

What a physical educator believes about his or her profession and how well those beliefs are articulated matter a great deal. In order to stimulate discussion and debate about beliefs, we presented our own in this chapter. In summary, our belief statements suggest the following thoughts about physical education and the context within which it is practiced in schools.

1. Physical education derives from play, is best understood in reference to play and best described as playful motor activity, and in its mature forms is institutionalized in culture as sport and dance.

2. Health-related fitness is of major importance to the well-being of our society and a necessary element in physical education programs.

3. Physical education is valuable in its own right and does not need to be justified by reference to academics.

4. The major values to be gained through participation in physical education are skill, the joy of physical exertion, the realization of clear-cut objectives, appropriate relationships to authority, the acceptance of responsibility, cooperative relationships, security in the rituals of the rules and customs that define sport, the adventure of risk, the ability to defer goals, and measuring oneself against clearly defined and widely accepted measures of quality.

5. The values to be derived from participation in physical education are appropriate to females and males, to rich and poor, to normal and exceptional students.

6. The values available through participation in sound physical education programs are particularly relevant to the major developmental tasks of adolescents and to ignore this aspect of development is to deny what has been known for centuries.

7. The many activities that comprise physical education have no particular hierarchical value in terms of their importance to the participant even though they may have more or less value relative to specific goals for the educator.

8. If physical education is to survive and thrive as a school subject, it must be able to demonstrate tangible outcomes and students must be able to show recognizable achievement gains.

9. Equal educational opportunity is fundamental to the maintenance of our democratic society, and physical education should be in all school curricula and equally accessible to all students.

10. Physical education can be central to the education of youth if it is characterized by commitment, intimacy, and achievement.

11. To be fully successful physical education needs to extend beyond the school and the school day.

12. The role of the teacher is critical to the success of the physical education program.

13. Teacher education programs in physical education can equip students with skills and attitudes to design, implement, and maintain vital physical education programs in today's schools.

14. The physical educator needs to be an advocate for our subject matter within the context of the school and to provide a model of involvement and a healthy life-style.

Suggested activities

1. Develop a list of your five major beliefs about physical education. After the lists of all class members are collated, discuss the beliefs in class.
2. Develop your own list of the major values to be gained through participation in physical education.
3. Debate the following issue: Grades in physical education should be assigned primarily on the basis of student achievement. Have three students argue the affirmative and three argue the negative.
4. Examine syllabi from local schools. Are there belief statements in the syllabi? If so, how are they different from or similar to those presented in this chapter?
5. Write brief critiques of any four belief statements given in the chapter.

3

School Settings for Physical Education

It seems that almost everyone considers himself or herself an expert on schools. Just like the Monday morning quarterbacks who offer suggestions regarding last Friday night's game, the "schoolsperts" are always willing to offer a suggestion for any aspect of education and schooling. After all, nearly everyone in this country has attended school, most have graduated, and millions also have children repeating the process. Certainly these consumers of education must be experts!

Not so—schools are a very involved, complex institution, and most of the so-called experts would probably fail a simple test on finance, curriculum design, certification of staff, and a hundred other matters that impinge upon the development and operation of the enterprise. Unfortunately, many teachers also remain aloof, if not ignorant, about the same matters. This is unfortunate because the teacher's role in directing learning for students and representing his or her subject field and school to the public certainly requires a reasonable knowledge of the legal, philosophical, and social factors related to education.

Physical education teachers have some unique responsibilities regarding knowledge about schools. We are involved with students in off-school settings, raise money for certain activities, work in one area that has an unusual safety risk, and above all, seem to be in the public eye as a result of the interesting and appealing nature of our subject.

This chapter attempts to introduce some of the elements that are important to an understanding of schools. As suggested, the matter is complex and the materials in the chapter are sufficient only to stimulate thinking and discussion. The materials are organized around the following topics to assist your understanding:

The goals of equity and quality in U.S. public schools

Various groups of people who work in schools and exert various kinds of influence

Spheres of authority and responsibility

Local, state, and federal funding

Rural, suburban, and urban districting patterns

Grade configurations and the organization of schools

Physical education facilities: opportunity and demand

Projected educational changes in the future

SCENE   JOE *and* BOB, *two businessmen who are visiting a large metropolitan center for a trade exposition, take a walk to escape for a moment the constant round of lectures and exhibits at the show.*

JOE   What's that old building across the street with the high fence around it—the one with trees in front and boarded windows?

BOB   It's a school, an old school, and it seems to be vacant; look at the broken windows to the left.

JOE   It has a big open yard in the rear, a 20-foot fence around it, almost a city block, and look on top, on the roof. That's fenced over, too. Was that a garden? There's a sign—PS 107—that must be the name, a number at that!

BOB   I know you come from a small town, but that's just a typical large-city elementary school.

JOE   An elementary school? It has five stories and must hold hundreds of kids, maybe a thousand. That's as big or bigger than most high schools!

BOB   It is or was an elementary school, five stories. Mine used to have three gyms, a big lunchroom, and an auditorium. The school yard even had a separate fenced area for a garden. The fenced area on top was a gym, but we didn't use it. I think the teachers didn't like to climb the narrow stairs to the roof. The trees in front were probably planted on Arbor Day—a tree for each Arbor Day.

JOE   By the size of the trees, that building must have been constructed 60 or 70 years ago.

BOB   I went to a school like that in the 1940s, grades K–8. All the kids lived in the neighborhood and walked to school. Most of them were there for the entire eight years. Few people moved around. For a lot of them, that elementary school was the last formal school they attended.

JOE   Believe it or not, I went to a high school that only had eight kids in the graduating class. It wasn't a one-room school, but I guess it was close to it. My kids now go to an elementary suburban school. Their school has no windows. That saves heat, no broken glass, cost efficient. Most of the kids are bused to school, but I'm not sure the play area is as large as the school yard over there.

BOB   Basically, that's a good, sound building. It needs to be refurbished, but it could still be used. Instead, they'll ask for another bond issue, an additional levy, higher taxes to build another school. I'm tired of higher and higher taxes; school people are wasteful.

JOE   Well, I don't like taxes either, but look around; there aren't many kids in this area. They've gone to the suburbs. Do you want to bus kids into the city for school?

BOB   I don't like busing!

JOE   Well, here we are at the exposition center. Are you ready for more lectures?

BOB   Let's go. I'll leave the school problem to Jim, my neighbor; he is on the school board. My kids are out of school now.

Yes, schools do come in different sizes and shapes. People have different memories of their own schooling and a very personal sense of responsibility to the future of schools for their children and the community. These facts are important to teachers of physical education because schools are a focal point for instruction in our subject area.

Purposes of schools

Two threads are woven into the educational experience in the United States, opportunity for all and quality of experience: equity and quality. It is simply not enough to provide a series of experiences for all children regardless of race, creed, or economic status. We must also enable each child to reach his or her full potential. It has never been acceptable to imitate the European model of education and provide intellectually stimulating opportunities only to the very bright and relegate other children to a lesser form of intellectual stimulation.

Egalitarian emphasis

We believe in providing many opportunities for children. It is possible to do poorly in elementary and secondary school yet still go to college. We spend millions of dollars helping late bloomers catch up by means of remedial courses and open-admission policies. This concept of equal and multiple opportunities is unique in organized public education. For the most part, systems in other parts of the world classify young people at a relatively early age according to intellectual ability, track them, and make the process of mobility from one track to another the exception. It is a model of education that can be classified as elitist rather than egalitarian.

Some critics of American education maintain that the attempt to accomplish both objectives, equity and quality, is more expensive and wasteful, and neither goal is accomplished satisfactorily. The American system has vacillated between a critical emphasis on the need for social justice in schools, such as the movement to desegregate public education, and the need for more rigorous scholarly standards to match the military or economic competition of the Soviet Union and more recently Japan. Sometimes eminent educational critics and scholars express one viewpoint during a particular phase of their career and then become equally adamant about a diametrically opposed viewpoint at another stage. What is a teacher with 25 to 30 students in the gymnasium on a daily basis to believe?

Education for development

The matter is further complicated by the uses to which society puts schools. Most take for granted eye examinations, lunch and breakfast programs, vocational training, moral education, good citizenship, physical fitness, leisure skills, and myriad educational experiences related to growth and development, not just intellectual achievement. In fact, the purposes of education must be understood in terms of the total development of the student, not just cognitive achievement. This also represents a different view of education from the historical European model. The European view has been much more classical and relates the purpose of education almost exclusively to intellectual and scholarly pursuits. Schools have not been institutions for social purpose as they are in the United States.

Differing purposes of private schools

There is a parallel system of private education in this country that in many ways is similar to that of Europe or attempts to meet unique religious or cultural goals via schools. This system is maintained basically by private sources, and although its right of organization is fundamental in a democratic society, its purposes and goals may differ from those of the public system. Access may be limited for any of several reasons, including ability, sex, financial means, and religious persuasion. Examples of these private institutions include very old prestigious private preparatory schools, military academies, Christian schools, and the largest private school system in the country, Roman Catholic parochial elementary and secondary schools.

Public schools are different from private schools; generally they accept all and try to establish common bonds while recognizing individual imperatives.

Aims of education

Disputes regarding the ultimate aims of education have been common throughout the ages. Here are just a few that are worth your contemplation (Thompson 1951).

> The true aim of education is the attainment of happiness through perfect virtue.
>
> Aristotle (384–322 B.C.)

> Education is the art of forming men, not specialists.
>
> Michel de Montaigne (1533–1592)

Education is a development of the whole man. The ultimate end of man is happiness with God.

Johann Comenius (1592–1670)

Education means a natural, progressive, and systematic development of all powers.

Johann Pestalozzi (1746–1827)

The attainment of a sound mind in a sound body is the end of education.

John Locke (1632–1704)

Education is the instrument of intellectual in the laws of nature.

T. H. Huxley (1825–1895)

The purpose of education is not to stuff the minds but to breed healthy bodies for the state.

Adolf Hitler (1889–1945)

Since growth is the characteristic of life, education is all one with growing; it has no end beyond itself. The criterion of one value of school education is the extent to which it creates a desire for continued growth and supplies means for making the desire effective in fact.

John Dewey (1859–1952)

These statements attest to the fact that the aims of education are not cast in stone. Indeed, it is somewhat surprising that in the United States there is so much agreement about the purposes of public schools. Ours is a country that is populated by people from a variety of backgrounds with different traditions of education, religion, and culture. Yet the public schools receive substantial financial support and usually are criticized because they don't accomplish enough rather than that they are not vital institutions in society.

Indoor climbing walls and rapelling stations in a modern school gymnasium.

You have a task to clarify the goals you expect from the educational process. Are they skill development, happiness for the learner, aesthetic experience, intellectual achievement, good health practices, social adjustment, a sense of fairness, vocational accomplishment, progress for the present or the future? We have made a bold statement regarding our beliefs in physical education. They relate to achievement, opportunity for all, mastery, the total development of the child, and the significance of the teacher's role in assisting students to realize their goals. These beliefs are commensurate with the mainstream view of public education in this century in this country: a belief in both opportunity and quality achievement.

Who works in schools?

Teachers work in schools but so do many other people, and their presence helps to define the way schools work and the purposes they attempt to achieve (see Figure 3.1).

Direct instructional personnel

The most familiar category of school employment is that of direct service for instructional purposes. Teachers, coaches, the band director, the director

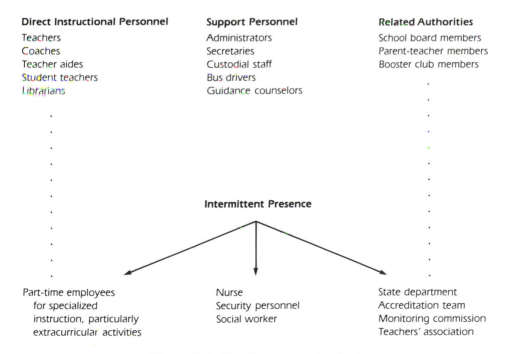

Direct Instructional Personnel

Teachers
Coaches
Teacher aides
Student teachers
Librarians

Support Personnel

Administrators
Secretaries
Custodial staff
Bus drivers
Guidance counselors

Related Authorities

School board members
Parent-teacher members
Booster club members

Intermittent Presence

Part-time employees
   for specialized
   instruction, particularly
   extracurricular activities

Nurse
Security personnel
Social worker

State department
Accreditation team
Monitoring commission
Teachers' association

Figure 3.1 People who work in schools.

of the theater club, and so on are familiar to students, their parents, and the community at large. What is less commonly known is that many of these people serve in school under two contracts. The first is for the traditional certificated teaching assignment in a particular subject. The second or supplemental contract usually employs the individual for a specific task in the extracurricular activities or informal curriculum of the school. This involves an assignment as an athletic coach, club adviser, music or theater director, etc. Some schools still maintain a system whereby teachers upon being hired are obligated to teach and fulfill some extracurricular assignment. Frequently, released teaching time is provided for the teacher during the period of greatest involvement with the additional activity. More and more often, however, the extra assignment is established via a separate contract and specific pay scale. The opportunity for such a supplemental contract has not proven very stimulating to regular teachers. After a few years, many prefer to teach and not accept a supplemental contract. Thus administrators do hire nonteachers with skills in specific fields to fulfill many of the coaching and leadership roles in the informal curriculum. Most of these people only contribute in a particular season of the school year. A typical, large suburban high school may have 80 people on supplemental contract, more than half of whom are not regular teachers.

Support personnel

The major responsibility of the support staff is to facilitate the instructional process. In practice this may mean managing major discipline problems (usually the role of the vice principal), maintaining the physical plant, and protecting teachers or at least acting as an intermediary between the school board, parents, and teachers.

A few support people such as nurses, security personnel, and social workers may not appear in school on a daily basis. In selected schools with unique problems, on the other hand, they may be on hand every day.

Related authorities

Related authorities are those groups who by law or association influence the running of schools. This category includes the school board, the parent-teacher association, and booster clubs that are established for specific purposes. These groups may exert the direct, positive impact of additional resources or the subtle pressure to influence curriculum or the direction of an athletic team.

Another group of organizations may be present, either intermittently or in selected schools. For example, a school district functioning under a court-ordered desegregation plan may have members of a monitoring commission present in classes. A monitoring commission has the task of determining if the plan to remedy desegregation is executed fairly and evenly. Commission members may have to count disciplinary actions, opportunities for use of special equipment, or any of a thousand details in the school day. The report of the monitoring commission is always for the court, not the school authorities.

Every school is accountable to its state department of education. The minimum standards of curriculum are developed at the state level, and schools must abide by those standards. It is possible to exceed the standards, to add more requirements in any subject, but it is not possible to retain school accreditation or state financing without meeting the minimum standards. States often differ in terms of minimum requirements. As noted in Chapter 1, physical education requirements are under attack in some states. However, a majority of states insist that there be a minimum number of minutes of physical education per week for students. In some cases the standard is as little as 45 minutes, and in others it is stated as five times per week for a minimum of 30 minutes per day.

The educational system in the United States is not national but rather controlled by state and local authorities. This is the principal reason why schooling differs dramatically from region to region, from child to child. It is an uneven mix from the very best to the less than tolerable.

Other influence groups such as teachers' unions are also in evidence in schools. The presence of these groups is not necessarily physical but nonetheless influential.

In the broad view, schools involve many people and are more complex than most people realize. Those who work in or are otherwise associated with schools often have different backgrounds and agendas for education. In a sense, we mix professionals, paraprofessionals, lay authorities, parents, state officials, politicians, business leaders, and even religious authorities in 50 different states and tens of thousands of local districts in order to send children to school. Although these disparate groups agree on the importance of schools, they often disagree on the exact means to ensure the best education for each and every child.

Who controls schools?

As suggested in the preceding section, many people work in schools, and each in some manner exerts a measure of influence. However, probably no other profession permits as much authority to a beginner as does the education profession to the beginning teacher.

Authority of the teacher

The teacher is in charge of what goes on in her or his classroom, gymnasium, or wood shop on the first day of work or after 20 years of service. The teacher is the boss, with all the responsibility that accompanies such authority. Major corporations do not permit such opportunity for new employees. Yet the teacher makes vital judgments from the first day on the job. It is a matter of great trust and opportunity.

The teacher's control relates to method, behavior management, course sequence, evaluation, and in some subjects such as physical education even curriculum design. A new physical education teacher can emphasize team games versus individual sports, promote competency teaching, establish standards for fitness, involve the community in the program, develop a leadership corps, construct a contingency management system, and so on. This is heady stuff and may be the single most attractive aspect of teaching as a career.

Think for a moment about a coach and the authority of the position. Is there anything more important to an adolescent than to make the cut, to be on the squad? Then if that is achieved, who plays? Next time you go to a game look down the bench at those not playing, particularly if the score is lopsided. The tension is immense for the players and the coach. All of the authority, however, is with the coach.

Authority of the principal

In a sense, just as the classroom is a function of the teacher's style, the school is a function of the principal's style. Does the principal insist on a tight ship relative to discipline, does the principal support the informal activities of school, does the principal emphasize parental involvement, insist on achievement standards? Being in a position to know what is happening in each classroom and having first access to the community provide the principal with great authority and control mechanisms.

Authority of government

Three governmental bodies have certain control over schools on a legal basis. Generally, the federal government has delegated authority to the states for education since education is not mentioned in the Constitution. Although the amount of authority varies from state to state, most states have passed much power to local school districts. Citizens in the district elect a school board to exercise authority in the schools. The local board generally has authority to raise money, hire personnel, construct facilities, and establish curriculum within state guidelines. The school board is composed of citizens from all walks of life with varying levels of knowledge about education. Most of the members, however, have strong beliefs regarding schools regardless of their background in the area.

The notion of local control of schools derives from this pattern of administration. Obviously, it is not a matter of total local control as is sometimes implied but rather of local authority within state and federal jurisdictions.

The federal government has exercised its authority in two important areas: desegregation and programs for children with special needs.

School boards empowered to construct facilities generally try to place schools in a location that will minimize transportation problems. Thus they build schools, particularly elementary schools, in local neighborhoods. Recall, from the beginning of this chapter, Bob telling Joe about walking to school, a school for over a thousand children. Generally cities have neighborhood schools because the population density is so great that a large enough number of children live within comfortable walking distance to fill each school. Rural areas always bused children, and the neighborhood concept in these areas really refers to a homogeneous population rather than to geography. Rural communities are generally not as diverse as urban residents in terms of race, religion, and family income.

Unfortunately, some school boards deliberately manipulated neighborhood schools to exclude children from their appropriate placement. This was done either by rule or by practice, *de jure* or *de facto* segregation. According to the Constitution, this is a violation of the children's civil rights. Therefore, the federal government's role in education has increased, in part to ensure the civil liberties of its citizens. The courts ordered school boards to develop a plan to correct these violations, to provide a remedy. If the remedy did not redress the liability, then the court developed a plan to do so.

The court solutions generally involved transporting pupils from one area of town to another, thus establishing a conflict with the concept of the neighborhood school. The concern for this concept seems overstated, however, since it was routinely violated for decades in the case of black children.

A second role for federal authorities is to provide direct assistance to children with special needs. Entitlement funds are directed through schools for specific programs. These activities may be instructional or they may relate to health or other such matters.

Large grassy areas are important for good school PE programs.

Only the federal government's insistence on Title IX, an amendment to the ESEA of 1972, has provided girls and women with a chance to use the gymnasium on a shared basis. No other authority, local or state, or professional group had the will or means to accomplish this. Similarly, Public Law 94-142 aids the handicapped in achieving their rights.

Authority of federations and unions

Certain semipublic organizations also exercise influence and control. For example, in most states athletic programs are controlled by a high school federation. Generally a school volunteers to join the federation, which establishes minimum eligibility standards, promotes tournaments, develops statewide rules of play, and monitors the athletic scene. These functions represent a major influence in the conduct of extracurricular activities.

Yet another group that exercises power in the schools is the teachers' union.

> SCENE   *A third-year physical education teacher/coach, who works at a city high school and is pursuing a master's degree, is talking with her former university adviser.*
>
> ADVISER   Are there still repercussions from the teachers' strike last year?
>
> TEACHER/COACH   Some teachers still won't talk to me because I didn't join the strike. In fact, I crossed the picket line to teach. If I hadn't taught, I couldn't have coached after school; the seniors on my team were my main reason for not striking.
>
> ADVISER   I don't see why the team was so important. I can understand your not believing in the strike principle for teachers and in joining a union, but the bit about the time escapes me. Why couldn't you coach after school?
>
> TEACHER/COACH   The school board set the rules on coaching while the strike was on. It's evidently in the labor contract. As far as my volleyball team . . . well, I had two girls in line for college grants. They needed the season to ensure the grants. Also, you know how long it's taken to develop girls' sports. I'm not sure those other teachers even care.
>
> ADVISER   And you say it's still unpleasant?
>
> TEACHER/COACH   For the most part it's fine, but a couple of teachers just won't give up. It's very emotional and tense.
>
> ADVISER   You didn't learn much about that part of teaching while you were in college, did you?
>
> TEACHER/COACH   Not a bit! Why is that? It's the most significant part of my first three years as a teacher.
>
> ADVISER   Frankly, we don't know very much about it. In a sense, you're the expert; you're learning via the school of hard knocks!
>
> TEACHER/COACH   You're right. Maybe I should talk to the undergraduates about the real world. It's a controlling factor.

Two major national federations control teachers' organizations, The National Education Association and the American Federation of Teachers. The teachers in a given school will be members of one or the other of these groups and, in turn, the local teachers' representatives will bargain with the school board on salary and working conditions. Even nonunion members must live and work by the conditions of the bargaining contract.

The union movement in schools, as suggested by the third-year teacher, is a very sensitive and controversial issue among teachers and obviously between teachers and the school board and the public. For many years teachers' associations were organized around curriculum matters with little reference to salary, benefits, or working conditions. Those associations disdained the typical labor-management relationship that existed in most of American industry. There was no thought of establishing an adversarial relationship with the board and using typical tactics of collective bargaining, including sanction, boycott, and strike, to achieve goals. This is *not* the case today.

Frankly, the situation is confusing to teachers, the public, governmental agencies, and school officials including board members. Reasons for the confusion include the following.

1. Patterns of labor-management bargaining developed in the private sector of the economy. Teaching for the most part is in the public sector. The phenomenon of public employees conducting a strike is considered at odds with the police power—that is, the power to protect the health and welfare of the community and its citizens—of the government.

2. In the industrial sector, employees usually bargain over issues of salary and working conditions. Although teachers are raising these matters, too, they are also bargaining over curriculum and program content. This runs contrary to citizen and board control of education.

3. Teachers are generally expected to be satisfied with fewer worldly goods than other people in society. Their rewards are supposedly intrinsic and related to the development of their pupils. The community will care for them, respect them, and ensure their security.

Prospective teachers must learn about and discuss this relatively new force in education. It is important to understand the dynamics of this issue in order to protect oneself against the estrangement and calumny associated with taking a position. And today it is nearly impossible for a teacher to avoid taking a position on collective union or association actions.

How are schools and programs financed?

Public schools are financed primarily by property taxes from local sources and a variety of taxing schemes, including lotteries and state sales and income taxes. The percentage of local versus state money for schools varies according to formula within states and by state (see data in Chapter 1). It is possible to find a school district that receives 100% state funding or 100% local funding. Ordinarily, the school budget is primarily a mix of these two funding sources. As described the federal government supports specific programs based upon unique individual needs. For most schools federal support is a minor part of their budget. In 1983 the national expenditure for elementary and secondary education was $115 billion (*New York Times*, November 13, 1983). Schools and education are America's biggest business.

SCENE   *Two teachers, a veteran and a rookie, meet in the teachers' lounge of a city high school.*

ROOKIE   Well, I finally got some feedback on my job performance from the principal. To put it mildly, he was out of sorts with me.

VETERAN   Don't tell me—the Delaney book—you messed up the Delaney book.

ROOKIE   How did you know? I didn't keep proper attendance records. It didn't have to do with my testing or my choice of materials but with my attendance records!

VETERAN   And the principal's right, of course. We must keep track of the students.

ROOKIE   What do you mean *right*?

VETERAN   Daily attendance is the basis for state aid—less money because of inaccurate records equals less money for salaries. Get on the ball and keep the "book" up to date. Don't ask me, please, who Delaney was! All I know is that Delaney is to attendance what mustard is to a hot dog.

Specialized outdoor facilities can enhance school PE programs.

Daily attendance *is* a major factor in state support for local schools. Obviously, maintaining accurate attendance figures is one of those tasks that doesn't exactly seem vital when one is learning to teach.

SCENE   *Two neighbors,* COREY *and* ADRIANA, *are discussing school funding.*

COREY   School taxes are up again, and another levy for operating monies is on the ballot.

ADRIANA   Yes, but inflation influences schools, and we can't build new schools without money to pay teachers, heat the building, and so on.

COREY   Well, they can save money, be more careful. I don't want to pay for things like sports and music. They're the parents' responsibility.

ADRIANA   But the kids really enjoy them, and the world would be a sad place without music, sports, and art.

COREY   They're frills. They don't help you get a job. I'll spend money on basics.

ADRIANA   Isn't health basic? That's part of physical education—developing a healthy body.

COREY   It's the parents' responsibility, not the general public's.

To a teacher in the area of physical education, Corey's thinking generally necessitates discovering funding sources for athletics and other physical education activities. Although Corey's perception is not universal, it is a significant attitude toward school funding and the purposes of public education. Bob, the businessman whose children are out of school, also represents a group that needs special attention in terms of attitude toward school financial support.

Unfortunately, the preparation of teachers rarely includes training in fund raising any more than in the effects of collective labor practices. The physical education teacher not only steers the ship but tries to get the fuel for it.

Where are schools located?

Why, of course, we build schools where students live! This seems sensible but for the fact that public buildings have a 40-year life expectancy and populations or neighborhoods change more quickly than that. This is exactly the situation that confronts many school boards today. During the 1950s and 1960s a great many schools were constructed in urban and suburban areas to accommodate the baby boom caused by World War II. It was a major task for districts just to build enough classrooms to avoid double sessions. Today the same districts must meet the challenge of what to do with half-empty or vacant schools.

Generally, there are three major school locations in the United States: rural, suburban, and urban areas. Rural schools began to disappear in the 1940s and 1950s as central schools with multiple-program offerings replaced the one-room school. (Note that each time four or five schools were combined into one central school, the result was one basketball team instead of four or five.) The suburban districts expanded tremendously in the 1950s and 1960s and began to depopulate by the middle of the 1970s. The urban schools lost pupils as the move to the suburbs developed, and the nation also lost the multicultural mix that urban education provided. Initially, middle-class white families moved to the suburbs, then more recently middle-class black families followed suit. A disproportionate share of education for economically disadvantaged students, minorities, and recent immigrants has become the responsibility of urban schools. At the same time, the financial base of these districts has also eroded as industry and service occupations have followed the population to the suburbs. A fact of immense importance to the future of public education and to the nation as a whole is that slightly more than a quarter of all students attend elementary or secondary school in the six largest cities. Unless we succeed in the urban schools, there is no success.

One practice still prevalent despite significant changes during the last 40 years involves the typical school calendar. In the day when rural schools were prominent, students worked on farms during the summer months. Schools recognized this need for youth labor and closed in the summer. Today very few students do farm work in the summer. Yet the long summer vacation period, which many believe is too long and counterproductive, is scrupulously maintained.

How are schools organized?

The traditional pattern of schooling kept young people in elementary school, kindergarten through grade 8, until the age of 14. High school or secondary school was established as grades 9 through 12 (ages 15 to 18). Many students left school after elementary school and joined the work force. As increasing numbers of students stayed on to complete high school (few nations have a better record or even seek this as a goal), it became apparent that the traditional K–8 and 9–12 configuration needed review. Students in grades 7, 8, and 9 were quite different from the prepubescent children in the lower grades but not quite able to compete with the later adolescents in high school. Therefore, the junior high school developed, and the common grade configuration became K–6, 7–9, 10–12. This plan was faithful to the knowledge of the growth and development of children, early adolescence, and late adolescence.

More recently the configuration was again modified, this time to K–5, 6–8, 9–12. Grades 6, 7, and 8 comprise middle school, not junior high school, which has become a miniform of high school.

The characteristics of middle school include (1) a flexible environment to accommodate the changing needs of students entering adolescence; (2) a deemphasis of sophisticated activities such as a marching band and interscholastic athletics; (3) exploratory study, including enrichment activities; (4) innovation in team teaching, flexible scheduling, individualized programs, and evaluation of continuous progress; and (5) the dual role of generalist and specialist for the staff.

Let's examine what these characteristics mean. There is recognition that students need a period in which to adapt from the security of one basic teacher to the multiteacher situation in high school. As junior high became more common, it soon evolved into an imitation of high school, not only in regard to academic subjects including college entrance credits but also in the informal curriculum. The sports and music programs became part of a feeder system for high school activities. The middle school's emphasis on exploration rather than achievement of predetermined goals such as admission to college is a reflection of the desire to be patient with young people and let them have some reasonable role in eventual decisions on the basis of alternative experiences.

The major change for teachers, particularly those in areas such as physical education, industrial arts, and music, is the concept of team teaching and flexible scheduling. A typical day in middle school may be divided into three segments: one segment for science and math, another for language and literature, and a third for "unified arts." The last of these includes all nonbasic academic subjects and may be taught as one theme rather than in individual classes. This is a major pedagogical challenge to all concerned.

The popularity and grade configurations of middle schools are illustrated in Figures 3.2 and 3.3, page 50.

At times the conceptual ideas behind grade configuration take a backseat to the need for a place to put students. Too often a school district will maintain a middle school of grades 6, 7, and 8 for several years, then arbitrarily add grade 5 for one year, and then revert to the original scheme. Usually this is in response to population shifts caused by a new housing development.

Critics have voiced a number of other concerns about the concept of the middle school. First, more resources are necessary to promote flexible scheduling, team teaching, and innovative learning modules than in the traditional junior or senior high school. Few middle schools provide the resources along with the model. Second, the elimination of band and varsity sports has not promoted opportunities for extensive intramurals and substitute music experiences. The informal curriculum seems to provide fewer rather than more opportunities for youth. Third, teachers are not prepared for team teaching in the unified arts. Fourth, despite the fact that this is an age of mastery for youngsters in many areas including art, music, and sports, there is little emphasis of this development factor in the middle school exploratory model.

What facilities are available for physical education?

The most significant fact about facilities for physical education and sports is that they are always in short supply and overcrowded during specific periods of the year or the day. This is true for schools with old, run-down facilities as well those with bright, new fields and gymnasiums. In part, it is true because games are seasonal. Basketball is at the height of popularity in the winter, not in the summer. Facilities that are idle in July are overburdened in

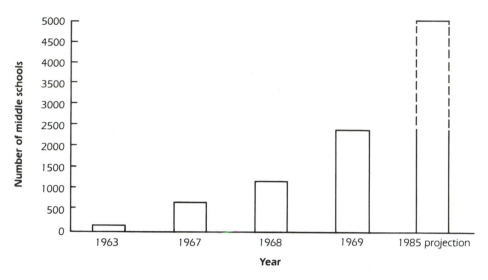

Figure 3.2   Survey of middle schools in the United States.

SOURCE: *Theory into Practice*, Spring 1983, p. 121.

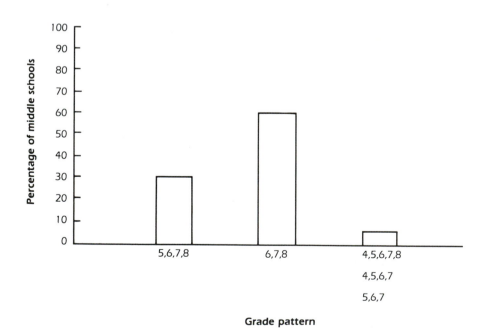

Figure 3.3   Grade configurations of middle schools in the United States.

SOURCE: *Theory into Practice*, Spring 1983, p. 122.

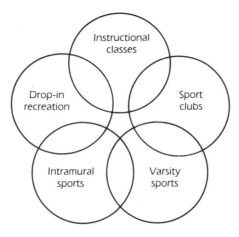

Figure 3.4   Elements of a total physical education program.

January. A second reason for overcrowding and pressure on specific facilities is more subtle but just as important; opportunity spawns demand in physical activity. For example, relatively few high schools have indoor swimming pools. Yet when a school adds such a facility, different groups quickly seek time for instructional classes for elementary as well as high school students, varsity swimming teams for boys and girls, drop-in opportunities, a community tiny tots program, even a water ballet show. In a short time great pressure develops for use of the pool. Before the pool was installed, none of these groups had any opportunity for swimming. Yet given the opportunity, demand ensued. This pattern is common to almost every activity.

Our view of physical education is broad (see Figure 3.4). Elements of a total program may overlap, but each deserves a share of the available facilities.

The need is to establish a facilities council composed of those responsible for various elements of the program to set up priorities for use. The most important consideration is the elimination of proprietary interest. The pool does not belong to the swim coach or the football field to the football coach; rather, these and other facilities serve to meet student needs. Establishing policies and priorities for facilities is a tough task. However, it is essential in every school, and the ability to do so is a mark of professionalism.

Schools in the future

People seem to want more from schools, and their criticisms reflect this point. At times it is difficult for teachers to reconcile the barrage of criticism that seems to plague public education with the notion that teaching is an honored profession. It seems as if someone or some group always wants more, but no one acknowledges the successes and fruitful activities that accrue to millions

By David Seavey, USA TODAY

of young people daily in thousands of schools across the nation. Perhaps teachers are expected to understand that the very nature of the criticism is a testament to the belief that schools make a difference and are worth everyone's attention.

The following changes seem likely to occur in schools in the next decade. If they are realized, the school in which you teach will be quite different from the one you attended as a student.

1. Extension of the services of schools to the very young and to adults on a systematic, routine basis.
2. Development of school facilities that may be converted to private use as demand changes.
3. Providing high school students with the option of interrupted schooling.
4. Creation of summer programs that are enriching and innovative rather than remedial.
5. Development of a number of alternative high schools within metropolitan areas, each with a specific focus such as science, physical education, or the performing arts.

6. Use of more part-time employees with specific skills in the instructional process.

7. Continuation of the interest in and response to affirmative action programs.

8. Negotiation among teachers, administrators, and school boards of curriculum choices as well as salary and working conditions.

9. Response to a school population that will include greater percentages of black and Hispanic children than white children.

10. Improvement of the achievement scores of all students.

11. Attraction of blacks and Hispanics to the teaching field.

12. Development of systematic approaches to influence student behavior related to substance abuse.

13. Expansion of the notion that the school extends to the community and learning occurs beyond the school.

This is a baker's dozen of projected educational changes. Does the list seem sensible or probable to you?

Summary

The idea of universal public education is one of the most cherished in our society. We view an educated citizenry as the most significant factor in maintaining a free and democratic form of government. We can be proud of the progress we have made toward achieving universal education, realizing that many problems related to adequate financing, equal access, and locus of control consistently require our consideration and attention. The support for public schools is generous and has been achieved in a manner that permits and sustains a parallel system of private education.

The purposes of schools vary with the historical period and the form of society. In the United States the major purposes of education include establishing common bonds among people while permitting each individual to realize his or her potential.

Within schools different constellations of people, including administrators, teachers, school board members, parents, and the local community, exert varying degrees of influence. These different groups are important in the system of education as conceived and practiced in the United States, but they also produce controversy and friction. The organization of teachers as a more powerful and militant voice in school affairs represents a major change in education and in the professional life of a teacher.

Principal authority for school resides in the states, with power delegated to local authorities. The federal government has assumed a greater role in school affairs in an effort to protect the civil rights of individuals as guaranteed by the Constitution.

Schools are organized according to prevailing demographic and economic factors. The traditional elementary-secondary form of schooling has changed to include junior high schools and currently middle schools.

Financial practices involving schools follow the pattern of organization. Generally the greater share of money needed to build and operate schools is raised at the local and state levels with a relatively minimal amount coming from the federal government.

Physical education teachers share the same general concerns as other teachers for a living wage and decent working conditions. In addition, the nature of physical education and sports seems to require greater efforts to secure space, facilities, and financial support for programs.

Suggested activities

1. In a short paper, develop and justify your own statement of the aims of education.
2. Attend a school board meeting and record the items of business. Discuss the relevance of the items with classmates who attend other school board meetings.
3. Choose a role as either a teacher representative or a school board member and debate a salary increase as part of a future contract.
4. Outline the curriculum of an "ideal" school of your choosing. Defend your curriculum in class.
5. Debate the following issue: All high schools should organize according to the magnet school concept. Have three class members argue the affirmative and three the negative.

4

The Community and Beyond

He sold trombones, clarinets, bassoons, even tubas, uniforms with bright piping, sheet music, caps, and the conductor's baton. You may not know him or even his music, but your parents did. He was Harold Hill, Professor Harold Hill, salesman deluxe, and his legacy was the songs of Meredith Willson's great show *The Music Man*. For our purposes, Hill left a legacy beyond the music, a line from the score of the overture that is as important to a physical education teacher as to a traveling salesman: "*You gotta know the territory.*"

For a teacher, the territory includes the community in which the school is located. It is complex and diverse, and it involves many people who are interested in and attempt to be involved with programs in the school. In addition, the school itself represents a community of people. Relationships with students, teachers, coaches, and administrators influence daily life and require some balancing and understanding. An effective teacher is able to maintain positive relationships and use the resources of the school and the local community.

This chapter attempts to explore the community of the school and that beyond it. The major topics are as follows:

Arranging for the use of public and private resources for off-campus physical education activities

Ensuring optimal community use of school facilities

The heterogeneous mixture of various groups that may support the school or be self-serving, that can influence the learning process, and that must be recognized by the teacher

Extending the physical education program into the community

The basic purpose of extending professional efforts beyond the school is to increase opportunities for students. The student population has almost infinite interests, but the school has finite resources. If we intend to satisfy the variety of interests for physical activity among students and promote the highest possible levels of skill achievement, then we must find some means to increase personnel, budget, facilities, and time. And we must accomplish this without violating the legal limitations of the school, the traditional schedule, or the nondiscriminatory nature of the operation.

Facilities in the community

Almost every community has additional facilities for physical activity beyond those of the school district. Many times these are private as well as public facilities. At the very least, the community has some open space in the form of parkland that can provide field space or a cross-country course. In addition, many communities also have a swimming pool, golf course, tennis courts, bowling alleys, softball fields, soccer fields, and in some regions ice rinks and ski slopes. Some of the facilities are private, and others are controlled by a public authority such as a recreation department.

Figure 4.1 shows the facilities used by the physical education staff of a suburban high school of 1000 students, located in a municipality of 10,000 people, in a metropolitan area with a population of more than 1 million. The teachers and coaches use both private and public facilities to extend their athletics and also their class programs. The district includes three elementary schools, one middle school, and one high school.

Nontraditional instruction in physical education

Organizing the use of diverse sets of facilities is more complicated than attempting to promote activities solely on the school grounds. Yet the number of schools with sufficient space and funds to provide a great variety of settings for activity is very small and will probably remain so.

At Dublin the teaching staff uses school transportation to reach facilities beyond the school grounds. Weekends, after-school hours, and even vacation periods are used to schedule activities on an elective basis. In other words, the physical education curriculum is a 24-hour, 7-day-a-week operation to take advantage of all possibilities. Also, the teachers who work in this setting do not work a traditional school day of 8:00 A.M. to 3:00 P.M., with extracurricular responsibilities. Rather, these teachers work a variety of schedules at certain periods of the year, depending on the schedule of activities.

We accept these nontraditional practices for school athletic teams without hesitation. Golf teams certainly use community courses to practice and play matches. Many tennis players use private clubs for practice as part of a school-

School	Local Community		Metropolitan Area	
	Private	*Public*	*Private*	*Public*
1 wrestling room	1 Nautilus salon	60 acres of playing fields	1 ski slope	1 adventure center
1 gymnastics room	1 tennis club	24 lighted tennis courts	1 swimming pool	1 high ropes course
1 multipurpose room	2 swimming pools	2 boat launching docks	1 bowling alley	1 ice rink
4 single gymnasiums	3 golf courses	1 jogging course		
1 divided exhibition gym	1 gymnastics club			
1 athletic training room	1 martial arts club			
1 weight training room	1 skeet shooting range			
2 baseball fields	1 scuba center			
2 football fields (lighted)				
1 all-weather 400-meter track				
20 acres of graded fields				

Figure 4.1 Physical education facilities used by the Dublin School District, Dublin, Ohio.

Off-campus neighborhood facilities can be used to expand school programs.

sponsored activity. This chapter emphasizes the use of the same operational schemes for as many regular students as possible. In this way we can help students achieve their level of potential.

Arrangements for using community facilities: Facilities committee

School physical education teachers must sell school administrators and board members on the idea of the use of public and private facilities for off-campus school activities. A practice of some schools is to form a school-community facilities committee that is made up of school and municipal authorities and owners of private facilities, as well as students and residents. Such a committee generally has three functions. The first function is to plan the use of existing facilities by various groups. For example, a municipal pool operation will usually welcome student use of an indoor aquatic center during morning and early afternoon hours on weekdays because a majority of community residents are at work and use the facility in the evening or on weekends.

The second function of such a committee is to plan sensibly for capital additions to facilities. In the case of the Dublin School District, the municipality has 24 lighted tennis courts and the schools none. What happened in this situation was that the municipality assumed responsibility for developing tennis facilities and agreed to stipulated school use on a contractual basis. The schools then assumed responsibility for a different type of facility, in this case an auditorium, and arranged for its use by the community. This arrangement emphasizes cooperation and maximum use of public tax funds.

The third function of the facilities committee is one of influence. School officials and board members respond more favorably to a combination of municipal authorities, private businesses, and residents than to individual teachers or coaches attempting to influence or change the system.

A local golf course can be used on a contract basis for practice and play.

Finances

Although financing off-campus classes and activities is more expensive than staying in school, it is not as expensive as one might think. Frequently facility trade-offs can minimize cash outflows or exchanges. For example, the trade of swim time for gymnasium time between municipality and school is fairly common. The owner of a private tennis club frequently seeks outdoor courts in warm weather and may trade indoor space for them. This negotiation is beyond the responsibility of the teacher, but it is done frequently, requiring only the stimulation of proper personnel to develop the mechanism. After all, everyone appreciates the maximum use of public money, particularly if it appears to be a good bargain.

One item of expense that must be assumed by the school is transportation. This constitutes an operating expense just like paper, pencils, computers, balls, bats, and wrestling mats.

Teaching personnel in the community

Many activities popular with adolescents have developed through the private sector: gymnastics, skiing, tennis, golf, ice skating, even martial arts. These sports have been practiced for many years and attract adults as well as adolescents. As a result, our communities are filled with skilled performers in these activities and many others. Adults represent a rich pool of talent that can assist the physical education teacher. Individuals with diverse backgrounds, rare skills, and an interest in students and schools can be organized to serve as teaching aides or teaching assistants. This is similar to practices of interscholastic coaching in which the roles of assistant coach and even head coach are sometimes assumed by nonregular teachers on supplemental contract.

The country at large is calling for the increased use of talented lay citizens in areas such as science and mathematics to assist in schools. The pool of talented people willing to work with youth in physical education activities is even greater than those in most other classroom subjects. Some of these people expect a modest compensation; many others seek a chance to contribute and to receive recognition. In the concluding chapter of this book we will discuss the means of promoting a program that involves rewarding citizen contributors to the program.

Community use of school facilities

An immediate and pragmatic reason for encouraging adults to use school facilities is to generate support among the voting public for school issues. If the school is immediately valuable to adults as well as an educational vehicle for their children, levels of approval and support will increase. However, there is a philosophical argument that is even more persuasive; learning is a lifetime pursuit, and school is for a broader population than those in the age range of 6 to 18. To educate adults and preschool children, as well as the traditional school-age population, we need a "lighted schoolhouse."

The concept of the lighted schoolhouse or community school is an effort to serve multiple educational needs of the community by employing school facilities many hours of the day and evening throughout the year. The school can be used for vocational training, job retraining, college preparation, adult education, community recreation, and early childhood education. Several different teaching faculties can work in the school to serve different client groups.

School-community continuum

Community use of schools can be better understood by examination of the continuum shown in Figure 4.2. Actually, very few if any schools operate

Point A represents the position that the community is not allowed to use school facilities regardless of the use of the facilities for school functions.

Point B indicates that community groups can use outdoor fields or activity spaces when they are not being used by school groups, according to an established fee schedule.

Point C indicates that community groups may use any school facilities when they are not being used for school functions, according to an established fee schedule.

Point D indicates that the school is a community center acting in partnership with other groups in the community.

Figure 4.2   School-community continuum.

at point A. Some schools act as community centers—point D—and truly attempt a communitywide program, with the school serving as the focus. However, the great majority of schools operate at points B and C. The decision concerning those operations is generally not a cooperative decision but rather the decision of the school board.

Operating principles

Everyone who teaches physical education in school will be involved somewhere on the continuum. Although other teachers are affected, probably none are so involved as those responsible for physical facilities and programs of sports, athletics, and dance. The task is to increase cooperative relationships and minimize adversarial conflicts with the many groups seeking to use school facilities. In this regard, the following actions can be crucial.

1. Establish a formal list for priority use, a fee schedule, and operating arrangements.
2. Develop a districtwide calendar for scheduling facilities.
3. Vest authority in one school representative to oversee the program.
4. Establish a facilities committee of users to allocate space according to priority use and calendar.
5. Publicize procedures, personnel, and community users.

A few of these actions require further amplification. The calendar helps prevent favoritism or certain groups continuing to receive opportunities for facilities on the basis of past practice or tradition of use. For example, in one local community, a boys' youth athletic association had had permission to use certain softball fields in the spring and football fields in the autumn for almost 25 years. The association would not include soccer among the autumn activities or permit girls to participate in the programs at all. Yet it expected to continue to use the facilities because it had traditionally used them for so many years. The establishment of a calendar for request of facilities plus a review of all requests enabled the community and school to break the monopoly with the support of most of the community.

The school representative responsible for overseeing the program should not be the superintendent or principal, whose school administrative demands are too great for them additionally to control day-to-day and seasonal activities of the school-community program.

Sometimes the most ordinary events influence programs. A point of great concern to most physical educators and art teachers whose facilities are used at night by adults is the relative cleanliness of the room, gymnasium, or shop the next day. Frequently, it is not up to standard. It is also the function of the facilities committee to redress such grievances.

The school is a public site. Its use by the community will increase in the next few years as leisure and educational needs of adults grow. There is much in the community to enhance learning for physical education. Creating a

Facility trade-offs can be negotiated between schools and city recreation centers.

straight path to and from the community seems a significant consideration for teachers and other school personnel.

Groups within the school

We suggested in the introduction to this chapter that the school is often a composite of many smaller constellations of people who associate intimately as a result of some common interest, experience, or background.

Subcultures: Loyalty and identity

The individuals within school groups have personal goals but also a loyalty to their particular group. Black students have pride in their racial identity, teams strive for winning seasons, and teachers strive for good working conditions. The task is to somehow meld these many subcultures into a working community, namely, the school. This is not a simple task. In some situations the team, the band, the ethnic group requires such loyalty that the belief in a united school is never realized. The thought that the whole is greater than the sum of the parts is never fully appreciated. Instead of one group's supporting others, it tries to detract from the worth of the others. A prime example of this is the fairly typical rule that prohibits nonfootball teams or classes from using the football field for their activities at any season of the year. This promotes barriers and conflict between groups, not support.

One of the principal means to overcome some of the barriers within schools is to be sensitive to the various groups that have aspirations and common purposes. A description of a few of the subcultures in schools seems appropriate to stimulate further thinking on this matter.

Football boosters

It is 4:30 P.M. on a Friday afternoon in autumn. The football team is filing into the home economics room for a pregame meal before the parents' day home game that is scheduled to start at 8:00 P.M. The menu is traditional for the occasion: steak, spaghetti, garlic bread, salad, soft drinks, and fruit for dessert. The tables are covered with tablecloths, and there are candles and music and favors at each place setting. Even those not able to play this evening—Juan, Randy, Bill, and Leroy, who have leg or arm casts because of earlier injuries—eat with the team. Naturally the coaches, managers, and trainers eat with the team, but in this program the cheerleaders do not. Basically, the coach does not want distractions; this is "real family." Although it is only 4:30 P.M. on a Friday, a working day, the waiters for the occasion are all fathers who are members of the booster club. The meal is prepared by mothers of the players. The parents are also responsible for returning the home economics room to its original state.

Guests for this pregame meal include the parents of the graduating seniors. The parents of the other players will march onto the field before the game. As usual there are a couple of distinguished guests at the dinner. One of them is a former player and alumnus who received a full football scholarship to a Division 1 university, a former all-state performer, a legend in the high school. The second guest is the superintendent of the district. The previous week the local state senator had attended the pregame meal. Usually the guests make a few remarks about the game, the opportunity to play, to contribute, and to defer personal goals for the good of the team and the school.

Tension runs high. The game is the cause of some of it. Also, however, at the conclusion of the affair awards will be made for the previous game: most tackles, the "guts" award, most valuable player award, and so on. Decals for the helmets are passed out as tangible evidence of these achievements. The booster club also has an award or two to complete the affair. Its awards are usually to members of the club for service rather than to the players. A memorable feature of this part of the program is the signing of the cast. Each person present, including guests and parents, signs the cast of Leroy, who went down last week with a fractured arm.

At the conclusion of the meal the coach announces a short movie before the players must dress for the game, curfew for the postgame activities, and the reporting time for tomorrow morning's review of films. Everyone on the varsity squad is also expected to attend the reserve game, which starts at 11:00 A.M. tomorrow.

This is truly a powerful subculture within the school. It includes parents, teachers, coaches, alumni, administrators, community leaders, and of course, the players. Schedules are controlled, rewards seem real, there is a tradition from the past, and there are certainly expectations for the future. In some ways it is remarkable that such a powerful subunit of the school relates at all to other functions of the school. It isn't really a team; it is a program and it captures the loyalties of many who are involved with it. For the players, it is a place to belong, with clear-cut goals, friends, rewards, identity. To some it is almost a shame that such factors as eligibility, study, and other school activities must get in the way of this team and program.

Music boosters

The buses are at the high school, along with a half a dozen cars with adults standing around them. It is a scene of some confusion as personal gear, musical instruments, and other paraphernalia for over 150 high school students are packed for the trip to camp; the marching band is getting ready for another season, not the football season but *its* season. The band plays at halftime at football games, but it also plays in band competitions, in concerts, and for most of the civic affairs in town.

Actually, it is difficult to say if this is the beginning of the band season or the culmination of the year's effort because the band members have raised money during the past school year to support the camp and most of the band operation, including uniforms and some instruments. They do not have gate receipts so it has been a series of fund raisers including weekend car washes, booster drives, concessions, meat sales, laundry soap sales. . . .

The parents contribute money, serve as chaperones or camp counselors, and usually fill many of the seats at the football games to see the band at halftime, not the game. They drive the students around the community for various fund-raising activities and share some sense of resentment at the attention that athletics receives in comparison to music, certainly an activity with greater cultural significance.

Even though the local papers do not devote much space to band activities, the band has a number of award banquets that recognize row leaders, performance, leadership, and other important factors. The band members share bumpy rides to away games, rainy weather, bus drivers who get lost, and uniforms that don't quite fit, as well as many good times.

This, too, is a powerful subunit in many schools. It is made more tightly knit because of some feelings of resentment that other students champion athletics and its masculine image.

Economically impoverished students and parents

The physical education teacher was truly confused. In concert with the guidance counselor and the curriculum coordinator, he had written to and received approval from the state department of education for a summer program grant for middle school students in the district. The school is in the heart of Appalachia; it is a school with limited resources for facilities and equipment, and student scores on reading and math standardized tests are below the median. Also, there are real problems in the health areas of diet, nutrition, and fitness.

The grant provides for the rental of a summer camp that has a lake, athletic fields, craft shops, sleeping cabins, a well-equipped kitchen, and a dining hall. Equipment may also be purchased for gymnastics, other sports, and academic subjects. At the end of the season, the equipment is to revert to the school district. There is money in the budget to hire staff and to pay the cost of each camper's expenses. Camp will not cost the participants anything. The program is fairly traditional: tutoring in academics part of the day, instruction in physical education skills geared to the lake and new equipment for another portion of the day, and time for singing and campfires at night. Students are to attend for three weeks, and money is available for three such sessions. Almost every middle school student can be accommodated.

The teacher sent a message home to parents describing the program and provided a slip for registration. Almost no parents registered their children for the summer camp. They didn't respond with questions or calls; they just ignored the entire matter.

Finally the teacher drove into the hills and began to ask questions of the parents. The answers were very informative.

A principal reason for not registering children for camp was the inability of their parents to provide camp clothing as called for in the registration materials—T-shirts, sneakers, bathing suit, and other such items. "I can't afford it. My child won't have it, and she will be put down, embarrassed because of it. I'm not putting my child in that situation."

A second reason related to the reaction that minority or poor groups of people have toward authority figures and institutions, a fear of foreign people, things, and places. One parent, in as kind a way as possible, told the teacher she really did not trust her child with others, that her family stuck together.

Somehow middle-class authority figures have come to believe that economically poor people are always ready and willing to accept free programs, usually programs that are designed by others for them. Many middle-class people also think that because people are economically poor or come from one-parent families, they don't care about their children. Both thoughts are wrong, absolutely wrong. In fact, the reverse is true. You may as a teacher run into what you consider a perverse obstinacy from the parents of economically poor children based on their need to stick together in the face of a society that takes their feelings and beliefs for granted—or worse—ignores them or attempts to substitute "better values" for them.

Just to finish this story: The teacher changed the budget to buy camp uniforms for the children and included a few of the mothers as members of the camp staff, and the registration changed dramatically. He also learned an important lesson.

Although these parents and their children are not organized as the groups in the situations presented earlier, they too represent a minisociety within the school.

Economically affluent students and parents

Samantha has everything! She is just 16, very bright, popular with the other girls as well as the boys, and seems quite happy. Some other students envy Samantha. She drives a brand new Corvette to school (a gift from her father, who lives across the country), wears beautiful clothes, and has almost complete freedom. She has a boyfriend and plenty of money to spend on clothes, gifts, and whatever else she wants.

Samantha lives with her mother who is a successful real estate broker in the area. Because of the nature of her job, she is usually showing homes to prospective clients on weekends and in the evenings. Her concern is that the school provide enrichment programs to stimulate Samantha's interests.

Vacations and summers are casual for Samantha. Sometimes she visits her father, who has recently remarried, or spends the time at a resort with her mother, or is at home by herself. She once told a friend that she hadn't had a family dinner or sat down to eat at a regular time with her mother since elementary school. She really likes junk food.

Samantha is not on a team or in a club at school. Although she stays after school and seems to be with a group, chatting or talking with other friends who are on teams or in activities, she really isn't. She seems busy going to or coming from someplace. Samantha does not take drugs and has never had a sexual relationship. She is quite ethical and moral by any standard, a very decent person.

Who is Samantha? Is she part of a subculture in the school? We believe she is—a product of affluence and mobility, a young person without roots, goals, or direction. She is passing through, a butterfly flitting from activity to activity, person to person, without any commitment. She does not cause trouble so basically we ignore her and countless other students with too much time, money, and ability but too little direction and commitment from adults. If adolescence represents a period in which to develop mastery, then Samantha and others like her are wasting their adolescence, and the school must be concerned.

Lessons for the teacher

Certainly the school is characterized by complex social relationships. It is equally true that groups related to the school have specific goals of their own. At times a booster club can be overbearing and try to dominate a coach, a sport, or an athletics program. Any specific group may seek to satisfy its own needs without considering that what it seeks may not be beneficial to other groups or to the general mission of the school.

On the other hand, a sense of vitality and excitement surrounds special-interest groups. They generally strive to help students and further their education. The great majority of these groups assist rather than detract from the purposes of education and schools.

It is impossible for a teacher to ignore such groups. Samanthas exist in every school. Parents will always organize to help a reading program, the arts, or the football team. The teacher's task is to be as sensitive to the existence of groups and their imperatives as to the existence of separate individuals in class. As teachers recognize an individual student within the framework of a class, so must they recognize various groups within the fabric of the entire school.

Summary

The mobilization and use of facilities and personnel in the community beyond the school will improve the physical education program. The principal reason that off-school activities are not more common in physical education is a matter of tradition and lack of imagination. Using off-school facilities requires scheduling, transportation, and teaching considerations.

On the other hand, the community has a right to use school facilities because they are supported by the public. Establishing the concept and purposes for the community use of schools can help develop goodwill for schools and encourage lifelong learning. Essential factors such as financing and priority of use must be developed carefully in order to extract the maximum benefit from a community-school program.

The school represents a heterogeneous mixture of various groups. The groups usually develop around program areas or social characteristics. Generally, the groups support student causes and thereby the school. A few groups support little or nothing.

The complexities of the social environment in a school greatly influence the learning process. A teacher must recognize the nature of such groups in the school and their different perspectives just as he or she attempts to recognize individual differences.

Suggested activities

1. Outline and discuss a plan for the community use of the physical education facilities in a school of your choice. Include in your plan factors such as purposes, priorities of use, fees, leadership, and liability.

2. Attend a high school football game and prepare a list of groups who assist in the conduct of the game or who utilize the social occasion of the contest. Write a short paper about the contributions of one group to the school.

3. Think about your high school experience in terms of the groups to which you belonged. Discuss the implications of that association to you, your teachers or coaches, your friends, and the school.

4. Make an inventory of sport facilities within a 10-mile radius of a secondary school of your choice. Compare your list with other lists in a class discussion.

5

The Adolescent Student

Adolescence can be characterized as a period of rapid change, enormous physical and mental growth, and distinct social and emotional development. However, it is probably most important that the teacher understand this period from the perspective of changing roles and behaviors. Adolescence is a time to seek independence, to see if it is possible to make it on one's own. The testing involves establishing relationships, achieving academic mastery and physical competence, earning money, and above all belonging, being accepted. Each of these challenges is really a step to identity, an answer to the question, Who am I? Adolescents do not always listen to or follow the rules of adults. Adults are necessary but as backstops rather than omnipotent, all-knowing sources of wisdom and direction. Obviously these changes produce friction as well as excitement and discovery.

The following major topics are discussed in this chapter:

Adolescence as a developmental stage of life

Four developmental theories of adolescence

Physical and social characteristics of adolescence

Adolescent behaviors that influence a teacher's professional style and work

How economic status can affect adolescence

Failures at adolescence

CHARACTERS

JENNY *a teacher with 20 years of experience*

ARCHIE *a teacher with 5 years of experience*

KAY *a new teacher*

SCENE *The first day of school at a large suburban high school. There is a sense of excitement and anticipation among the students as they search for friends, shout greetings, and gradually proceed to their homerooms. It is a scene of some confusion, a lot of noise, but above all immense energy.* JENNY, ARCHIE, *and* KAY *are standing together, out of the flow of traffic, observing the students.*

JENNY There's George—he repaired my car last month while he was working at a service station. He did a fine job, really competent. They'll miss him while he's in school. Hi, George; good to see you.

ARCHIE Oh, I see that Amy and Joe are still going together. That's been on since they came to high school.

JENNY I've seen 20 opening days, and it's still impressive—the drive, the different styles.

ARCHIE It *is* still exciting, but they all expect so much from us.

KAY It's almost overwhelming; some of the boys are huge, and the girls are so sophisticated. Who's that girl, or is she a teacher? High heels, black dress, pearl necklace. . . .

JENNY That's Terri, a really nice kid. She's been modeling for a couple of years and probably makes more money than any of us. She's quite good at it, I hear. School's a bit of a drag for her at this point.

KAY What do you mean, "they all expect so much from us"?

ARCHIE They expect each of us to wear many hats. We have to be very competent in our subject matter and never get excited or blow up at them. We're supposed to understand that at certain times they have priorities—such as a boyfriend or girlfriend or making the team or earning money or acting in the school play—that are more important than academics. They definitely want us to treat them as individuals, and we're never to embarrass them regardless of their behavior. Above all, it seems that they want us to be adults—not part of the gang. I think they want to test their view of being an adult against real adults.

KAY That really does sound complicated.

JENNY It is, but so are they. For every sophisticated Terri, there are five others who are quite young and naive. For every strong, mature young man such as Robert over there by the locker, there are ninth graders just entering adolescence. In a sense, they're very different from one another; they're at different stages of adolescent development and have different reactions to this period of their lives. On the other hand, there's a sameness or similarity about their energy, mobility, experimentation. We have to react to all of that.

ARCHIE Time for homeroom. Let's talk again in six weeks about differences and sameness. I'm sure we'll have some new observations. Good luck, and smile a lot!

These teachers are reacting to the uncertainty and incongruities that exist among adolescents. Most people agree that adolescence is a dynamic developmental stage filled with the potential for growth, success, and happiness. However, for some youth it seems to be a period that produces unhappiness, fearfulness, rash behavior, and even isolation and withdrawal. Many adults seem confused and preoccupied about adolescence. Our lawmakers demonstrate their inconsistency by passing curfew legislation that makes it illegal for anyone under 18 to be in a public place after 10:00 P.M. whereas other laws permit 16-year-olds to drive automobiles and 18-year-olds to vote. That is certainly a bag of mixed messages.

The nature of adolescence

Adolescence is one of several developmental periods in the life of an individual. Other generally accepted developmental periods are infancy, childhood, early adulthood, middle age, and old age. A developmental period is characterized by certain physical assets, social roles, family responsibilities, and work expectations. The issues of personal identity, body image, relationship to peers, sex, family, childrearing, work, country, and society, which must be resolved by an individual, appear in one form or another in each stage of development. Adolescence represents one step in the developmental journey from birth to death. It is not more significant than other developmental periods—just louder and more obvious.

We will treat adolescence as one period of development since developmental tasks are similar throughout the period. We will, however, advocate different activities, classroom management techniques, and student opportunities for self-direction according to the stages (early to late) of this developmental period. Middle school and junior high school reflect these differences. The changes from early to late adolescence represent a difference in degree, not in kind.

Adults and adolescence

One of the principal reasons for uncertainty about adolescence is that it is a relatively new stage of development. Until the late nineteenth century, children proceeded to adulthood via work or childrearing as a normal course of events. Long periods of preparation for adult life were not necessary in simpler, agricultural societies. In fact, life expectancy was so short and the toil of survival so immense that a period of preparation such as adolescence was unthinkable. All hands and bodies were needed as quickly as possible for the success of family and society.

Industrialization changed this traditional pattern of living. One result was the recognition and acceptance of an intermediate step between childhood and adult life—namely, adolescence. Mere biological change was no longer sufficient to propel individuals into an adult life-style. Additional training and skills became necessary for success in the complex industrial and social society of the twentieth century.

Adolescence as a developmental stage was formally introduced in the first decade of the twentieth century and characterized as a period of "turbulence, ambivalence, danger, and possibilities" (Hall 1904). Unfortunately, the focus on turbulence and danger rather than possibilities created skepticism among authority figures about this period. Adults are often bewildered about adolescence because the rate of change in young people in this period of life is so great. Little girls seem to become young women in the course of a summer vacation. Boys seem to overflow their seats in class. Students who once thought the teacher was always correct now openly question, even defy, the authority. Young people at this stage become taller and stronger, are able to perform at the very highest levels, and demonstrate improved reasoning as well as conceptual powers. They are attracted to the opposite sex and filled with the drive to explore and experiment, and many insist on acting upon their newly found powers. At times, the consequences of these experiments are severe or harmful: drug dependency, an illegitimate child, a tragic accident.

These changes are a radical departure from the stable years of late childhood, and they take place very quickly. They are quite shocking to many parents and make teachers and other authority figures uncomfortable. Parents feel a sense of loss as the dependent child seeks independence and even turns to peers rather than home for advice, support, and intimacy. Teachers in many cases are threatened by the student's size, energy, aggressiveness, and challenge to their authority. At times, teachers feel at a loss, powerless to cope with adolescents.

It is easy to understand why society makes so much of this period in life. Often the focus is negative, on all the things that can go wrong: auto accidents, drinking, violence, sex, defiance. This is unfortunate since adolescence is primarily a time for growth and exultation in newly found powers. The great task of the older generation is to direct the energy of adolescents to the enhancement of self and society. The task cannot be accomplished if adults either routinely forbid experimentation or, at the other extreme, relinquish all sense of order and responsibility.

Developmental theories of adolescence

Those who formulate theories of developmental stages invariably do so from a particular point of view, and theory and reality may differ. Still, theories are useful since they permit us to test reality or behavior against some standard or set of beliefs. No one theory of adolescent development seems to represent all situations or provide all the right answers, but each contributes a bit more to our understanding. Four developmental theories are prominent: learning, cognitive, psychoanalytic, and humanistic.

Learning theory

Basically, learning theorists hold that individuals respond to their environment. A science of human behavior has evolved from this model. Initial efforts at stimulus-response training have generally been replaced by operant conditioning and behavior modification, much more sophisticated methods of influencing behavior. A significant body of research exists to document the effects of this basic model, and teachers and youth workers have adopted techniques developed from it to influence class discipline, improve achievement levels in academic subjects, reduce aggressive acts, improve attendance, and promote punctuality and a host of other behaviors. Behavior modification techniques have been successful with adolescents who seem to have failed in "normal" developmental patterns. For example, adolescents with severe eating disorders or antisocial behavior have demonstrated improvement in response to these techniques.

Of all the theories discussed in this chapter, learning theory provides the most immediate and significant tools for a teacher or youth worker to produce change. Some of the techniques for classroom management and discipline outlined in Chapters 17 and 18 are based on principles of this theory.

Cognitive theory

The names of Jean Piaget and Jerome Bruner are associated most often with cognitive theory. Cognitive theorists generally agree that an individual's intelligence evolves in qualitative steps assisted by interaction with the environment. Adolescence represents a stage in development when young people are able to conceptualize or think beyond appearances. This ability poses challenges for youth since one can conceptualize misfortune or failure as well as happiness and success.

Cognitive theory has also influenced educational practice. If intellectual development proceeds in part from interaction with the environment, then the learning environment must be filled with multiple opportunities for challenge. Sensory objects, teaching aids, audio materials, manipulative devices, and so on are vital to improve stimulation in the classroom. In part, the Montessori system of early education is faithful to this theory.

Cognitive theory emphasizes intellectual development, perceptual ability, and reasoning (Bruner 1971). It does not explore other behaviors or provide much insight into aggression, sexuality, or other potentially motivating factors of adolescence.

Psychoanalytic theory

Perhaps the most pervasive developmental theory in the twentieth century is the psychoanalytical model of Sigmund Freud and his followers. As is typically the case, Freud's followers have changed the original theory in certain ways, and Freud's emphasis on the sexual drive as the fundamental force in development has been replaced by the psychosocial model of Erik Erikson. Erikson's model of development includes eight stages of life (Erikson 1963). See Figure 5.1.

Figure 5.1 Erikson's eight stages of development.

	1	2	3	4	5	6	7	8
VIII Late adulthood								Ego integrity vs. despair
VII Middle adulthood							Generativity vs. stagnation	
VI Young adulthood						Intimacy vs. isolation		
V Puberty and adolescence					Identity vs. role confusion			
IV Latency (years 5½–12)				Industry vs. inferiority				
III Locomotor-genital (years 3–5½)			Initiative vs. guilt					
II Muscular-anal (years 1–3)		Autonomy vs. shame, doubt						
I Oral sensory (infancy)	Basic trust vs. mistrust							

SOURCE: Based on Erikson, E., *Childhood and Society*. 2nd ed. New York: W. W. Norton, 1963.

Adolescence is characterized by identity versus role confusion. Adolescents have the task of resolving what they feel they are with what others believe them to be. According to this model, feeling what and who you are is a product of early experiences and inner drives as well as the effect of what others think. It is a theory based upon the present, the past, and deep instinctual drives. The sense of identity is made difficult by the physiological changes taking place internally and the realization that external expectations differ markedly from those relating to childhood.

Erikson believes that supporting figures in the environment—parents, teachers, coaches, and leaders—have a great impact upon resolution of the conflict between identity and role confusion. Clear-cut demands, reasonable limits to behavior, and appropriate adult role models help adolescents determine just who they are in relation to society.

This theory also responds to the particular difficulties that minority group youth experience in attempting to achieve identity in a culture whose standards are unfamiliar. Imagine the task of students from a foreign culture such as that of Southeast Asia attempting to define a role in the United States. Differences in language or dress are probably less threatening than the different roles of men and women, marriage, family, or job expectation in this country versus their native land.

This model does not provide direct tools for the teacher. Rather, it helps to promote an increased sensitivity to youth at this age. If adolescents have a tendency to view themselves as the center of the universe, teachers have a responsibility to understand the dynamics that underscores the behavior.

Humanistic theory

A current model of development, one affiliated with the existentialist direction of society in the latter half of the twentieth century and associated with Carl Rogers and Abraham Maslow, is the humanistic theory. Maslow (1971) has proposed a hierarchy of needs (see Figure 5.2) that underscores a pattern of development that proceeds from the satisfaction of basic physiological needs to social belonging to the ultimate position of realizing one's full potential, or self-actualization. Basic needs are defined in terms of food, shelter, and security, whereas the expressions of self-actualization are defined in terms of justice, equality, and beauty. For an individual to proceed in a satisfactory developmental pattern, according to this model, he or she must have ample opportunity for self-expression, exploration, and self-directed and creative activities. The end product of this model of development is an individual who acts in a creative manner, has satisfied basic drives, and demonstrates an appreciation for the abstract but qualitative elements of life and society such as truth, justice, and social harmony.

Humanistic theory stresses openness among people, positive relationships, and group support. Therapeutic activities based on this model include encounter sessions and group activities with a great amount of physical contact. At the center of this theory is the right of each individual to satisfy his or her personal needs. Obviously this can create problems in schools, which are

Figure 5.2 Maslow's hierarchy of needs.

SOURCE: Adapted from Maslow 1970.

group structured. Individual freedom and personal choice may create difficulties for a teacher attempting to adhere to these concepts in a school organized about a highly structured, very directive discipline code.

Clearly the four theories of development we have briefly discussed represent a more complex view of adolescence than that put forth by Hall at the turn of the century. Any summary of the changes in the view of adolescence as a result of theoretical considerations must include at least the following points:

1. The growth spurt and physiological changes at pubescence are insufficient to explain the complexities of adolescence.
2. Social experiences that are transitional to adulthood are as significant to adolescence as are physical changes.
3. Adolescence is one of several stages in the development of an individual and not the concluding stage.
4. As adolescents change in their behavior toward adults, so do adults change their behavior toward and expectations for adolescents. Adolescence is a period of reciprocal experience.
5. The behavior of adolescents responds to environmental conditions.

Characteristics of adolescence

Bigger, stronger, faster, brighter—the typical adolescent has greatly increased physical and mental powers in comparison to childhood. These additional capabilities lead to increased social expectations.

Mental characteristics

Upon reaching adolescence, young people are able to think conceptually and most experience an explosion of knowledge. It is a remarkable change from childhood.

Conceptual thinking.   At the age of adolescence a dramatic change in conceptual thinking occurs. For the first time young people are able to project knowledge from one subject to another, to generalize information, to form hypotheses from related subject areas, to develop concepts and assign value from one realm of behavior to another situation. The following examples illustrate the chain of thinking possible at adolescence.

> The explosion of an atom bomb produces radiation that lasts thousands of years. . . . Radiation is a killer, shortens individual lives, destroys plant life, even the soil. . . . Many nations have atom bombs. . . . Nations throughout history have used weapons to settle disputes. What chance is there for me, my friends, my family, my dog? No large nation has been peaceful for as long as fifty years. . . . What sense does it make to prepare for the future, college, a job?

> Some animals reproduce body parts, actually grow another tail or leg if one is destroyed. . . . Scientists are able to manipulate genes to produce new characteristics of life. It will be possible to manipulate DNA and genes to cause nerve cells to reproduce or repair themselves. Spinal cords will be restored; paraplegics will have a chance for full recovery.

Such thinking is representative of a change in style as well as in capacity. The conceptual nature of adolescents' thinking, adding disparate but related information and projecting hypothetical conclusions, is a new-found power of this age level. Note that such ability may lead to depressing conclusions or provide a bright and optimistic hope for the future.

Unfortunately, many adults ignore or refuse to accept the intellectual ability of adolescents. By so doing, they demonstrate a great insensitivity to periods of moodiness caused by the painful nature of such reasoning or appear fatuous and condescending toward the conclusions adolescents reach.

Increased knowledge.   Greater conceptual power and the additional factors of age and time to learn to master information lead to a knowledge explosion during adolescence.

Frequently we read of adolescents who establish world-class records in athletic events and generally now accept the notion that youth are capable of such performances given proper training and opportunity. What we do not realize as readily is that this same age group can perform intellectual feats of comparable worth. A prime example occurs in the computer industry where many major developments are attributed to teenagers rather than established professionals.

It is important to recognize these increased abilities and knowledge and to establish expectations based upon them and thereby foster intellectual development.

Physical characteristics

Four facts appear to be significant when we describe the physical changes of adolescence. The first is that height, weight, strength, and secondary sex characteristics change and develop between the ages of 11 and 18. The second fact is that growth spurts during this stage correspond in rate to those that took place in the first year of life and again in the third to the sixth years. This means growth is very rapid, particularly in the first two or three years of adolescence. The chief reason some authorities believe adolescence should be divided into two stages of development is that the early period is one of rapid change and the later phases are characterized by a relatively slow rate of growth.

The third fact that is significant in the physical changes of adolescence is that girls generally enter adolescence earlier than boys. As a result, for a period of time the physical maturity, as well as the social and emotional maturity, of girls exceeds that of boys. This is probably why junior and senior boys frequently date freshman and sophomore girls. See Figures 5.3 (below) and 5.4 (p. 78). The fourth and last fact to note is that development is an individual matter and some people start earlier than others. For example, just visualize two buddies who shared elementary school, games, and other pastimes on an

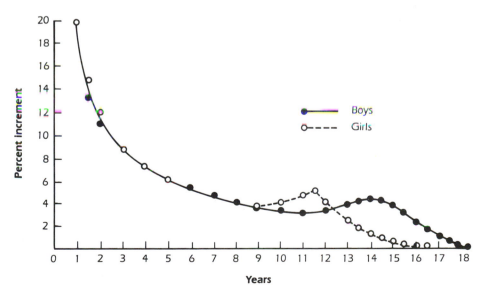

Figure 5.3   Incremental rate of growth—girls and boys.

SOURCE: Tanner 1981, p. 86.

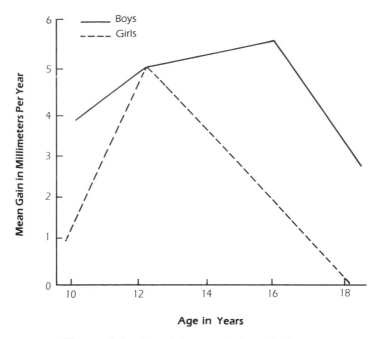

Figure 5.4 Growth in bone and muscle tissue.

SOURCE: Tanner 1981, p. 87.

equal physical footing. Six months after puberty one of them can still pass for a five-foot fifth grader but his pal now towers over him, having grown a foot in the past six months.

Social development

CHARACTERS

FATHER, *old and square according to his daughter*

MOTHER, *old but not so square according to her daughter*

DAUGHTER, *15 years old*

FATHER   What are your weekend plans?

DAUGHTER   Friday night is the football game, and Saturday there's a party at Joe Dalton's house. The party's very casual, just a group of friends. I'm going with Sally and Gretchen.

MOTHER   I want you home by midnight. Who's driving?

FATHER   I thought the three of us might go to the movies on Saturday.

DAUGHTER   Oh, Dad, everyone will be at the party. Gretchen is driving; she's a senior.

FATHER   Things have really changed in this household.

MOTHER   Why don't you realize that?

This is indeed the time when things change, not only for the adolescent but for those close to her or him. Young people want to be with other young people, seeking answers to the question, Who am I?

One tragic result of this emergence from the relative safety of childhood is indicated in Figure 5.5. The data are revealing. Moving into a new social atmosphere, increased opportunity to try new things, and physical capability without corresponding judgment certainly change the consequences for young people.

Adolescents' changing relationship with parents and other authority figures fosters an intimacy among peers within this age group that is quite intense. Boy-girl crushes and other friendships seem to spring up overnight and in many cases fade away just as quickly. However, for many young people serious, intense discussions about significant personal topics happen mostly with peers rather than adults. Yet this discussion is frequently incomplete or needs to be tested with adults, particularly parents or respected authority figures such as teachers. The responsibility of the adult community is to ease young people's task of discussing controversial and sensitive issues as they seek answers to perplexing issues in their world.

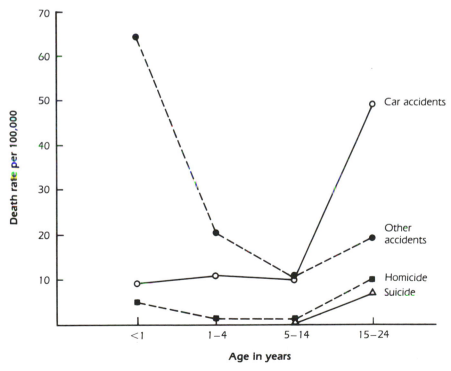

Figure 5.5 Death by accident.

SOURCE: General Mills Family Report, 1978–1979, p. 170.

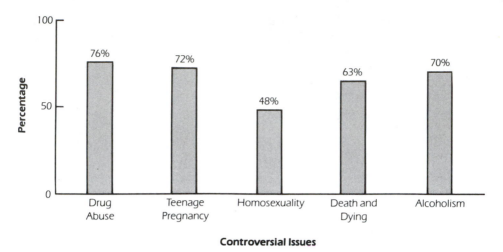

Figure 5.6 Teenage willingness and desire to discuss sensitive health issues.

SOURCE: Adapted and modified from the General Mills Family Report, 1978–1979, p. 170.

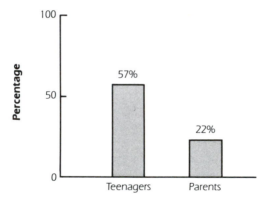

Figure 5.7 Teenage and parental willingness to communicate health problems.

SOURCE: Adapted and modified from the General Mills Family Report, 1978–1979, p. 170.

Figures 5.6 and 5.7 demonstrate young people's interest in such opportunities for discussion; with regard to health issues, a significant number of parents have difficulty in fostering such a family discussion.

Out of the economic mainstream

The range of financial wealth is large in the United States, and students reflect the relative differences in family resources. Adolescents in the same school may come from families of great wealth or be dependent upon governmental assistance for food, clothing, and shelter. Each of these economic groups can pose problems for schools and teachers.

At the very least teachers must recognize the influence of financial resources or the lack thereof on students' lives. Economic factors affect expectations and hopes for the future as well as day-to-day living; they may also influence friendships, values, and the amount of time available for school activities.

Disadvantaged poor

Too few of us really recognize the differences that exist among people, including youth, as a result of economic, racial, or ethnic distinctions.

PRINCIPAL   It's terrific that you opened the gymnasium at South School on Saturday morning to let the youngsters play basketball. I know you did this on your own time because those young people have no other place to go. They have no money for the movies, roller skating, tennis lessons, and all the other activities kids from North High School do on Saturday. Part-time jobs are impossible right now!

TEACHER   They're good kids. Unfortunately, they're so poor that they don't have white-soled sneakers, only street shoes. The wood floor had just been varnished so I had them play in their socks.

PRINCIPAL   Exactly . . . and when they went home each one tried to find a better pair of shoes. My phone is ringing off the hook. There was a clothing allotment just before Easter from the church and settlement house. The boys bought shoes, sharp-looking shoes, some much better than others. You gave them an opportunity to trade up last Saturday.

TEACHER   Do you mean these kids even steal shoes?

PRINCIPAL   Shoes are a status symbol in this community. Furthermore, these people are poor, poor but proud. You'll learn a lot of lessons, but please keep your eyes open, look around, ask questions. There are lots of things different between South High and North High besides the cars in the parking lot.

As the discussion between the teacher and the principal indicates, some young people will steal items such as shoes to "trade up." In addition, welfare agencies or service clubs frequently provide impoverished families a clothing allotment just prior to an important holiday such as Easter or Christmas. Caring teachers usually learn this sort of information by being aware of and sensitive to differences within our society.

Young people from economically poor backgrounds grow up quickly in America. Time for adolescence, the pause to get ready, almost does not exist for them. We are talking here about young people who live in poverty. These are the youth who have been abandoned by at least one parent, brought up in foster homes, lived on welfare or aid for dependent children, taken over the care of their brothers and sisters, and learned the lessons of S.U. (Sidewalk University). The first lesson of the streets is that talk is cheap and the one who receives the first blow also receives the stitches.

This is a different world from the economic mainstream. A certain type of maturity follows responsibility. There is a great desire for some of the material

Adolescent students often care about their strength and are willing to work to improve it.

wealth that flows so easily on television and a drive to escape the crushing burden of poverty and live like others do.

It is a world of loyalty, of togetherness with those who share the hardships, and it is also a world of fierce pride of mothers for children, brothers for sisters, extended family, friends, and neighbors. There are those who belong and there are the outsiders. Most teachers are outsiders. They provide little of value; they do not ease the burdens.

The great challenge in working with such youth, most of whom are in urban school districts, is to recognize that the standard scenario of adolescent development does not apply. Therefore, we must design programs to meet the needs of such young people, programs that take into account the nature of their situation.

Disadvantaged affluent

Poverty promotes one form of variance from normal childrearing practices. Another group of youth are also being raised in unusual economic circumstances. These are the young people from extremely affluent families who typically have a couple of sets of parents, usually on opposite coasts. The parents ply their children with every conceivable material possession. Nevertheless, the children believe that they have been abandoned. Somehow the adults in their lives have forsaken them for something or someone else. Their level of trust for adults is about zero; their desire to "get even" is immense; and their ability to manipulate other people, including teachers, is great. Members of this group lack the sharing of the economically disadvantaged. They are even deprived of working toward a goal of a better material life. The number of young people in this category seems to grow year by year.

As in the case of the economically disadvantaged, programs and teacher response require adjustments to meet the needs of affluent but disadvantaged youngsters.

Behavior at adolescence or what the teacher experiences

SCENE JOE, *a fine young man, a good student, and a superb athlete, is obviously troubled as he talks to his track coach, who helped him win a state championship in the pole vault as a junior. In addition to his success in track,* JOE *has been a starting center in basketball and a member of the football team since his freshman year.*

JOE How can I prepare for the vault if I have to run the high hurdles, high jump, and run a leg in the 1600-meter relay? There's practically no time to practice the vault. When there is time, I'm bushed. It really takes time to prepare for the quarter. . . . I don't want to be embarrassed.

COACH We need points in these other areas for the team score. You can't let the team down. We can win the league meet with your points. We'll work in the vault some way.

JOE You know I have a chance to be really good. You keep telling me that. I'm only a couple of inches from the national high school record, and I'd like to go for it.

COACH You're a lock for the vault at the league meet, and you'll score in everything else. This is important for the team and school.

JOE You know, ever since I was a freshman, I've heard the same story. In basketball, I play center—never handle the ball, always play against giants, guys four or five inches taller than I am. College ball is out for me since I've never handled the ball; my back is always to the basket. Every year I've had a different offensive position in football—wherever the team needed me. Four positions in four years. Same in track. Last year I hardly vaulted in practice until two weeks before the state meet. You know that I don't miss practice. I'm here during spring break, working out while most of the other people are on vacation. When do I get a chance to do it my way—for me?

COACH Let me think about it.

Is Joe selfish or just seeking excellence? Is the coach arbitrary? Has the school exploited Joe's talents without sufficient concern for his needs? Teachers must face these questions.

Competence and a variety of interests

Most people enjoy doing something well. Achievement leads to satisfaction and an increased desire to repeat the experience. Joe not only repeated his successful experiences, he also demonstrated a wide range of interests. That seems to be a key to activity interests for young people. The range of interests in a school population is very great. Any attempt to limit sports activities to the so-called major sports is bound to eliminate many students from participation and a chance to develop competence and a sense of mastery. Apparently, achieving competence is a big step toward a sense of personal worth.

We must note that although sports can be an important source of competency for adolescent girls and boys, so can music, art, computer science, auto mechanics, and stamp collecting. All teachers have a responsibility to develop a curriculum that promotes opportunities for young people to develop their abilities.

Risk and experimentation

Young people take chances. They particularly like to take chances in pursuits that are censored, even illegal. It is not much of a challenge unless the consequences are real. Consequences can be as safe as parent disapproval or as severe as being in trouble with the law.

One of the unfortunate aspects of risk taking at this age is that it is complicated by other factors such as not appearing to be a wimp in front of one's peers or deciding to have sex just because the other person is "the only one who really cares for me." The tyranny of the peer group and the desperate search for belonging lead at times to bad consequences. To compound the problem, these factors are often coupled with high levels of impulsiveness and poor judgment.

It is always amusing and predictable to watch an adult start fooling around with a group of 12- or 13-year-olds at a swimming pool. The adult may initially push one or two of the young people into the water, and eventually everyone pushes someone into the water, including the adult. More often than not, someone gets a cut foot or there is a fight. The lifeguards are angry, and the adult cannot understand how the situation got out of hand. "Why don't those kids have any judgment? Why can't they stop when I do?" The exciting part of being in physical education is that the activities include risk and challenge. It is possible to experiment and still control the consequences.

Authority and independence

Perhaps no other aspect of adolescence provides as much ambivalence as the drive to be independent but also the need for the security of authority. Consider this scenario.

SCENE   *A father is driving 15-year-old daughter (a varsity tennis player who loves sports) to school while on the way to work.*

FATHER   What's happening in school today?

DAUGHTER   We have a homecoming pep rally, and I have a French test.

FATHER   What are you doing in physical education class? I saw some pictures of the new gym in the newspaper.

DAUGHTER   I'm in a volleyball unit with a student teacher.

FATHER   How's the class?

DAUGHTER   Just fair—the student teacher's not very good. In fact, she's nowhere. Yesterday people were making a lot of noise and fooling around and she called us together, had us sit down, and said we had a problem. She wanted us to discuss the problem. She should have told us to shut up and practice; that would've saved time and been more effective. The discussion produced more problems because Jim and Sid really acted like wise guys—just a lot of smart remarks.

FATHER   What's the level of the class?

DAUGHTER   It's a beginning class. Yesterday the student teacher said we could hit the ball on one bounce and ignore the boundary lines. How can you have competition without boundaries? Last year we had teams that stayed together for the entire semester regardless of the unit. We had really good competition—even playoffs.

FATHER   Maybe it'll get better.

DAUGHTER   It's even worse. I'm a beginner, but I have more skills than the teacher does. She can't play!

FATHER   Well, good luck on the French test.

DAUGHTER   See you tonight; thanks for the ride.

The teacher's task is to serve as a conductor, to orchestrate opportunity that permits choices but to establish limits that define boundaries for purposes of security. That is difficult for a parent with one child let alone a teacher with 30 students or a coach with 60 players. The most devastating and perhaps the most common violation of this responsibility is to treat freshmen and seniors according to the same rules, as if there were no difference in their abilities to be independent or their needs for security.

Serving as a model for an age group that is very critical about adult behavior while exceedingly permissive about their own is a difficult task. The teacher who doesn't play volleyball well will truly have a hard time establishing credibility and authority with 15-year-old students, who often see competence as a prerequisite to authority. The situation is made more difficult by class management techniques that the students perceive as ineffective.

Matters of dress and the peer group

Almost everyone in society wears a uniform. For bankers, it usually includes a dark suit and tie. For others it is jeans and T-shirts. For some, the right hair style and the right label are equally important parts of the uniform. Where does all of this lead? Briefly, it leads to belonging, to shared experience, to acceptance by one's peer group.

What adolescents choose to wear is usually a good indication of their values and the importance of the peer group to them. It shows their willingness to abide by the rules and customs of the group. Those who do not participate in the ritual may suffer the tyranny of the peer group and be excluded.

Certain outfits are very precise and seemingly well-defined, such as the uniforms of an athletic team. What does it mean to wear a football uniform? Once encased in pads, helmet, and jersey, the individual truly belongs and represents a particular set of values, usually discipline, dedication, strength, courage, even manhood. It doesn't matter that for a particular person this may not be the case; once in uniform the person is assumed to play the role and is accepted in the group.

When adults take over teenage styles, as in the case of miniskirts several years ago, it forces young people to develop a new style of dress that identifies them exclusively.

Narcissism

Grooming sometimes becomes a way of life among teenagers. Do I look all right? Does my hair lie flat? Am I overdressed? Boys are not exempt from this process and often spend more time styling their hair than girls do. Perhaps the most notable concern of boys, however, is flexing their muscles whenever they pass in front of a mirror.

As noted earlier in the chapter, adolescents are in a stage of introspection, of trying to define their identity. This is particularly important in light of the great physical changes that are occurring at this period of life. Therefore, many actions are self-centered or narcissistic. An important manifestation is appearance. It is better to have clear skin than acne, thick rather than thin hair, for boys muscles rather than no muscles, for girls full breasts rather than flat breasts, and for early adolescents pubic hair rather than no pubic hair. Adolescents are easily embarrassed or humiliated over physical matters that were insignificant five years earlier and will be again ten years hence.

As teachers, we can easily contribute to embarrassment via school physical education programs. Should an obese girl have to wear a bathing suit in front of her peers? Do shy students have to shower and dress in front of their peers? Do students have to shower and dress in a dirty locker room with no opportunity to blow dry their hair or even have time for grooming? Must a frail boy participate in gymnastics when he can't even do a chin-up and his classmates can do five or ten?

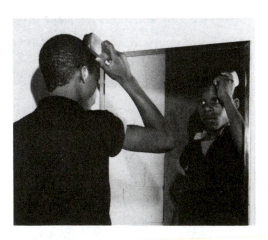

Adolescent students care about grooming and appearance.

Obviously, we must take great care in physical education to protect the right of young people to as much privacy and sensitivity as possible and to defuse narcissistic fears associated with physical matters. If physical education teachers ignore this issue, many young people will despise physical education for years.

Estrangement

SCENE *Two neighbors drive through a suburban housing development on their way to work. Young people from elementary, middle, and high school wait at a series of bus stops for their buses.*

DRIVER *(honking horn and waving)* It's nice to see a response, a wave, a smile. Why do the older kids look so miserable, so sullen?

PASSENGER Yes. The little ones seem so full of vim and pep, so happy to say hello. Then there's Jim over there. He cuts my grass. It seems hard for him to say anything even when I pay him. The older ones really ignore us. And look at her—the girl with the upside-down smile. School days, school days, many happy school days.

DRIVER *(continuing to wave and smile)* What happens to them between fourth and tenth grades?

PASSENGER I don't know, but by eleventh or twelfth grade most of that behavior changes again; they're much more pleasant, willing to say hello to adults. But tell me, why do you wave and smile if you're so unhappy about being ignored?

DRIVER Because they're neat kids. I want them to know I see them and like them and that they count with me. I won't let them ignore me; they're too important. Besides, it hurt my ego to be ignored. I'm important too.

PASSENGER Listen, Ms. Important, it's 7:45; turn on the news and get me to the office on time.

Yes, some young people are sullen, ignore adults, even develop a language that only other adolescents in their group understand. Certainly that is the case with the drug subculture, which has an entire vocabulary that only those on the inside really comprehend.

However, the temporary periods of aloofness from or rejection of adults by youth do not seem to be the most significant aspect of estrangement. Rather, it is apathy, a lack of direction, an unwillingness to try or to believe in deferred goals. Adolescence is a major period in which to develop skills and competency. What does one do with the adolescent who is just standing still and does not seem to care about much of anything? In physical education this may be the nondresser, the person who does not care enough even to try. This person is our greatest challenge, not the student who causes trouble by fighting or acting defiant. At least the latter provides an opportunity for remedial techniques. We understand and can deal with defiance, but we have more difficulty with passivity. One of the greatest responsibilities of a teacher today is to motivate an increasing number of youth to value school and the prospect of learning for the future as well as the present.

Loyalty

Another characteristic behavior of young people is their sense of loyalty. Much of this loyalty is to their peer culture. Friends are very important, and an outsider's criticism of a friend is not easily accepted or readily forgiven. Justice is at stake. At the same time, adolescents seem to look beyond their inner circle and seek to pledge themselves to a larger enterprise. The increased mobility of our society with its accompanying loss of traditional neighborhoods creates a vacuum that needs to be filled. Perhaps this is one reason why various religious groups have attracted such loyalty from adolescents in recent years.

Young people also demonstrate loyalty to their schools and community. The factors of ritual, tradition, standards, and recognition play a large part in this. The informal curriculum of the school, the part that supports theater, art, music, and sports, provides a great opportunity to create a climate that engages the loyalty of youth.

As one teacher suggested to her colleagues, being a teacher is complicated. Young people show competence, take risks, and seek authority but also test it; they behave in self-centered ways but also focus on a group; they develop a strong sense of justice; many want to be part of school yet a few seem empty and without ambition.

Failure at adolescence

The true failures at adolescence are not in schools but rather in hospitals or other treatment centers. Students in regular classes have a history of success that enables them to be in school. Success can be measured by the relative ability to live within the basic rules of a school or community, to retain a relationship with family, to make progress in acquiring the skills of society, and to feel sufficiently satisfied about the self in relation to others. Those who fail do so in more than one of these categories, do not make it to public school, or must be removed for assistance. Consider the following two examples.

A boy at war with himself and others

His name is Paul Oz, but the kids called him Odd Oz the minute he walked into camp. He is a tall, gangly boy with curly hair, a nice smile, and a swaggering air. Part of his right hand is missing; in fact, he has only a thumb and a reconstructed index finger. That finger is the main reason why the kids call him Odd Oz; it is a composite of his three other fingers, which were blown apart as he attempted to light a self-made rocket when he was 14.

It is a remarkable finger. It is longer than a normal index finger by about one-third. When the accident occurred, Paul picked up the pieces he could find and made it to the hospital a half mile away. The surgeons used what was available from among the parts and pieces. The fact that his new index finger has phalanges from the other fingers accounts for its unusual configuration. Paul can actually chin himself with one hand, or rather with his thumb and index finger and demonstrates amazing strength. Paul also uses his hand as a tool. There is no feeling in the very end of the finger, merely an extremely hard callous. He files the callous and uses the finger as a screwdriver.

Paul is considered different not only because of his unusual finger but because of the three major accidents in his life. He once rode his bicycle down a steep hill and somehow crashed through the plate glass window of a department store. A couple of years later he fell from the balcony of a movie theater, fracturing several ribs and puncturing a lung. His third accident was the rocket explosion. The story among the camp staff is that each accident occurred after Paul had engaged in homosexual activity.

Paul is now 16. He is in a treatment center because of troubles with the law. He has been consistently robbing lobster traps and continues to do so after being caught and punished. He maintains that his is no crime since he only steals the "shorts" (less than legal size lobsters that the professional lobstermen return to the sea) and isn't robbing the fishermen. He seems to be at war with himself and others.

A girl headed nowhere

CHARACTERS

SALLY   *an emotionally disturbed 16-year-old*

LEONARD   *camp director at a residential treatment center for emotionally disturbed adolescents*

SALLY   I've come to say goodbye. From the funny farm to the hospital—to the hospital again—never home.

LEONARD   I wish you could stay, but the risks are too great if you continue to cut yourself.

SALLY   I'm not trying to kill myself.

LEONARD   You cut yourself incessantly with a razor blade, up and down the inside of your forearms and on your thighs. Last night instead of just drawing a little blood, you cut too deeply and almost got an artery. We can't seem to keep you from getting razor blades or stop the cutting. You need more help than we can give you, Sally.

SALLY   I hate this place.

Both of these adolescents have failed and are in a different setting from the traditional school. Society does not place young people in residential treatment centers or long-term hospital settings without great consideration. That merely adds one more failure in a life replete with failure. The young person is usually dangerous to himself or herself or to others in society, not making progress at the ordinary tasks of adolescence and without adequate support from parents, teachers, or other authority figures.

Frankly, it is impossible for the typical school to administer properly to those unable to meet certain minimal measures of behavior. Teachers have other responsibilities, the environment is educational, not therapeutic, and few people in public schools are properly trained to respond to the special needs of truly disturbed adolescents.

Teachers' energy must be directed to the positive elements in the personalities of those in their classes. In this way, schools promote the greatest good for the greatest number.

A more normal situation

MOTHER   Hi, honey, how was school today?

DAUGHTER   Just terrific. Mrs. Anthony, the art teacher, hung my charcoal drawings in the main corridor. I got most of my homework done in study hall, and we won in volleyball. We're taking a trip to the high school tomorrow to see what it will be like next year. No more middle school.

MOTHER   Just a lowly freshman.

DAUGHTER   I know, but we have a terrific class. Great athletes, girls and boys, smart kids. We'll make the high school a better place.

MOTHER   It's nice to feel so good about yourself.

Summary

Adolescence is one of many developmental stages in the life cycle. Theories of adolescence emphasize cultural, cognitive, affective or behavioral factors. No one theory seems to explain fully all of the changes and varied behaviors characteristic of this period of life.

Adolescents demonstrate remarkable and rapid changes in physical size, strength, speed, agility, and intellectual capacity. Their personal and social behavior changes from that of childhood to include strong loyalty to the peer group rather than to adults, great expectations for achievement, increased concern about personal appearance, interest in the opposite sex, and a willingness to experiment and take risks. Each of these factors can be a challenge for adults, particularly parents and teachers.

It is obvious that adolescence differs among cultures and in the United States is very much influenced by economic factors. Youth from poor financial circumstances do not have as much time for adolescence and routinely assume greater responsibilities at earlier ages than their mainstream counterparts. At the other end of the economic spectrum are the disadvantaged affluent, adolescents whose parents ply them with material goods but have somehow left them rudderless. These youth see little meaning to their lives, have few goals, and generally distrust adults.

Certain young people fail at adolescence and are remanded to institutional care. Others fail in a more consequential manner in that violent acts and suicide rates escalate during this period of development.

The task for the teacher is to focus on the positive aspects of adolescence and not be derailed by the noise, confusion, and mobility of the age. The teacher must help the student to higher levels of performance; to the attainment of competency, self-direction, and focused loyalty; to be proud of their bodies; to like themselves and to find an answer to the major question of the age: Who am I?

Suggested activities

1. Attend a high school sports event and observe and record student behaviors related to competence, risk taking, reactions to authority, matters of dress, narcissism, estrangement, and loyalty. Then discuss your observations with the class.

2. Draw up a very general outline of a physical education program that might meet the special needs of poverty youth. Discuss it in class.

3. Write a paper justifying or denying the justification of dress codes for high school students during school hours and also for members of school athletic teams.

4. Prepare to discuss in class guidelines for behavior a school might adopt related to boy-girl relationships particularly with respect to public displays of affection.

5. In what ways would you treat a physical education class of seniors differently from a class of freshmen?

6. Prepare a list of techniques that a teacher or coach could use to reward or reinforce the accomplishments of adolescents.

6

The Teacher/Coach

The purpose of this chapter is to introduce you to the complexities of teaching and coaching, the various roles involved, and how those roles may conflict with one another. Both the positive benefits of teaching and coaching and the potentially negative features are discussed. In addition, some characteristics of distinctive physical educators are examined. The major topics covered in the chapter are as follows:

The major tasks a teacher/coach typically fulfills throughout a school year

The concepts and technical language involved in the study of role conflict

What is known about role conflict in teaching and coaching

Teacher stress and coping mechanisms for dealing with it

Teacher burnout and strategies for dealing with it

The characteristics and attitudes of distinctive physical educators

SCENE   *A modest house in one of the city's middle-class neighborhoods. It is 7:00 P.M. and a physical education teacher and reserve team basketball coach at one of the city high schools is just getting home from school, having taught his classes and just having finished his basketball practice.*

JAKE   Hi, Barb, I'm home!

BARB   *(from the kitchen)* Hello, Jake. Dinner's almost ready. I'm in the kitchen.

JAKE   *(entering the kitchen)* That smells good—sorry it's such a rush.

BARB   That's O.K. How was your day?

JAKE   Well, we had a fair practice. The kids seem to be working harder. I wish Brian was a nicer kid. The others really dislike him, and it's showing up on the court. Things don't always go the way they should. I guess it's hard to expect 14- and 15-year-olds to put aside their personality differences, but unless they learn to in this case, we'll never be as good as we can be.

BARB   Is Brian the cause of the trouble?

JAKE   Not really—I mean he really doesn't set out to create problems. He's just a different kind of kid, and his personality really grates on the others. Maybe it'll get better once we get over these early games and into the season. I hope so.

BARB   How were your classes today?

JAKE   O.K.

BARB   What team are you scouting tonight?

JAKE   Eastland High School. They're playing one of the suburban schools. It's our only chance to see them before we play them next week.

BARB   We'd better eat now so you can get going!

The teacher/coach is a busy person. The preceding scene is true of male and female, suburban and urban teacher/coaches. Even this small slice of a teacher/coach's daily life reveals several features that will be highlighted in this chapter. First, it shows the incredible amount of time put in by a teacher/coach during a season, teaching all day, coaching after school, and scouting during the evening. Second, it shows that the job is not all teaching skills and strategies; it also involves working with young people who are in their growth years and often have personal problems and differences. Third, the scene at least implies that this teacher/coach, when asked about his day, responds with detailed information about coaching and only a simple O.K. about teaching, suggesting an imbalance in concern and interest between the two roles.

Many people persist in believing that teaching in today's schools is an easy job. It is a difficult job! It is also not a very well-paid job (see Table 6.1, p. 94), especially when compared with other jobs that require some kind of professional certificate (see Table 6.2, p. 94). Still, every year many people decide that they want to teach. Some decide they want to teach physical education and coach a team too. Let us briefly examine what that means and describe some of the positive and negative aspects involved in teaching/coaching.

What does the teacher/coach do?

To be a professional in today's schools involves a number of tasks. The purpose of this section is to identify those tasks and, in so doing, alert you to the complex and potentially demanding roles in which teacher/coaches find themselves. The following tasks are the most common ones that a teacher is typically expected to fulfill throughout the school year.

- *Teaching:* Teachers usually teach from four to eight classes per day, with class size anywhere from 20 to 60 students. Within the teaching function are tasks such as attendance taking, record keeping for purposes of

Table 6.1 Average teacher pay by state for 1984

State	Average Pay	State	Average Pay
U.S. and D.C. average	$23,546	Missouri	$20,452
Alabama	20,209	Montana	21,705
Alaska	39,751	Nebraska	20,153
Arizona	23,380	Nevada	22,520
Arkansas	18,933	New Hampshire	28,577
California	26,300	New Jersey	25,125
Colorado	24,456	New Mexico	22,064
Connecticut	24,520	New York	29,000
Delaware	23,300	North Carolina	20,691
District of Columbia	28,621	North Dakota	19,900
Florida	21,057	Ohio	22,737
Georgia	20,494	Oklahoma	18,930
Hawaii	24,628	Oregon	24,889
Idaho	19,700	Pennsylvania	24,435
Illinois	25,829	Rhode Island	27,384
Indiana	23,089	South Carolina	19,800
Iowa	20,934	South Dakota	17,356
Kansas	21,208	Tennessee	20,080
Kentucky	20,100	Texas	22,600
Louisiana	19,690	Utah	21,307
Maine	18,329	Vermont	19,014
Maryland	25,861	Virginia	21,536
Massachusetts	24,110	Washington	25,610
Michigan	28,401	West Virginia	19,563
Minnesota	25,920	Wisconsin	25,780
Mississippi	15,971	Wyoming	26,709

SOURCE: National Education Association, *Today's Education*, 1985–86, Annual Edition.
Note: Average teacher pay rose an estimated 7.3 percent from $22,019 in 1984 to an estimated $23,546 in 1985.

Table 6.2 Differences among starting salaries for 1984 college graduates in different fields

Field	Starting Salary	Field	Starting Salary
Electrical engineering	$27,000	Finance	$18,200
Chemical engineering	26,200	Agriculture	17,600
Mechanical engineering	26,000	Marketing	17,500
Computer science	26,000	Social Science	16,700
Physics	22,852	Communications	15,600
Civil engineering	21,200	Education	14,780
Mathematics	19,500	Liberal arts	14,179
Accounting	18,700	Home economics	13,917

SOURCE: National Education Association, *Today's Education*, 1984–85, Annual Edition.
Note: This data was originally derived from the 1984 Recruiting Trend Survey, Michigan State University.

grading, equipment supervision, and locker room supervision during change times, as well as the many instructional functions.

• *Planning:* Teachers are expected to plan for their instruction and often are provided with a planning period each day (or several each week).

This period is often used for functions other than planning lessons. Regardless, it is tough to face 30 eighth graders without having a careful plan for how you want them to spend the next 45 minutes.

- *Supervision:* Teachers are often required to supervise halls (hall duty), study periods, and lunchrooms. The primary role in these tasks is to maintain student discipline.

- *Administration:* Teachers often have to order equipment, maintain records, schedule events, secure permissions from parents, prepare reports for school administrators, and perform other administrative functions.

- *Committee work:* Schools are bureaucratic and often involve faculty on committees. There may be a physical education committee to plan the overall program, while other committees may be formed on an ad hoc basis for school purposes (discipline committees, personnel committees, etc.).

- *Student organizations:* Teachers are often asked to provide guidance for student organizations (yearbook, school paper, spring party, etc.) and to chaperone student events (proms, hayrides, trips to amusement parks, etc.).

- *Teachers' organization tasks:* Most teachers belong to professional organizations (the National Education Association and the American Federation of Teachers being the two largest). These organizations negotiate for the teachers with local school officials for provisions in a master contract. Professional organizations also provide other services to members and often require some teacher participation on committees.

- *Coaching:* Teacher/coaches often coach two of the three major seasons of the school year with responsibilities of either head coach or assistant coach. Coaching not only includes the planning and conduct of daily practices but also the preparation and conduct of teams at home and away competitions. Coaching also includes administrative functions such as ordering equipment, supervising the locker room, scheduling contests, securing officials, planning for home contests, securing transportation to away contests, and other such duties. Some of these duties may be performed by a school athletic director.

- *Professional coaching organizations:* Coaches often belong to local, regional, or national coaching organizations that provide in-service education on current techniques and strategies. They also have certain responsibilities with the state high school athletic association to plan for end-of-season competitions and to update rules. Coaches whose schools belong to an athletic conference have similar responsibilities with the conference coaches' group.

- *Professional teaching organizations:* Teacher/coaches often belong to a state and/or national teaching organization such as the American Alliance for Health, Physical Education, Recreation and Dance (AAHPERD). They devote time to reading the publications of these organizations and attending state, regional, and national conventions to learn of new techniques, strategies, and equipment.

- *Informal work with students:* Teacher/coaches are inevitably counselors to students. Adolescent students are in a developmental stage where they need to learn to relate to adult figures other than their parents. They often have social, emotional, and/or educational problems, and they are often not shy in bringing these problems to their teachers and coaches.

- *Formal/informal work with parents:* Teacher/coaches are often required to interact with parents at parent-teacher functions, at parents' days or evenings at school, in conferences requested either by parents or by school officials, in discipline hearings, and in other such events. Coaches are often involved with parents in booster clubs for school athletic teams, which often raise money that is of critical importance to the athletic budget. Teacher/coaches also are called upon to interact with parents in a host of informal settings that reflect upon the school and the reputation of the teacher/coach.

One cannot read through the list of tasks just described without coming to one conclusion: teacher/ coaches do a lot! The school day is often long; the opportunities for tutorial contacts and individual guidance are few and far between. These many different tasks and the roles they require teacher/coaches to adopt sometimes result in role strain and role conflict, important issues that are discussed later in this chapter. Obviously, however, a teacher/coach does not do all of these tasks every day. And professional teachers do find ways to balance the many demands placed upon them, do a competent, professional job, and still have time and energy for a satisfying personal life.

How a teacher/coach learns to handle these multidimensional tasks is most often a function of the school within which the teacher/coach works. Each school is a minisociety with a life of its own (Bain and Wendt 1983). Within each school there is a formal power structure and an informal power structure. New teachers need to understand both the formal and informal systems if they are to cope successfully with the demands of this system. No two schools are exactly alike. And research is absolutely convincing that new teachers quickly adapt to the social/professional norms of the schools within which they teach. Teacher/coaches can exert influence themselves and help to change the social/professional norms of the school, but this process takes time and is especially difficult for a new teacher. Patience, perseverance, and sensitivity to the forces that potentially affect your behavior as a new teacher are likely to be the strategies that allow you finally to exert influence to move school programs in new directions.

Conflicts in the teacher/coach roles

Physical education has one seemingly unalterable stereotype. The physical education teacher—often called "coach"—begins a class with a few calisthen-

POWER AND AUTHORITY

Teachers have certain powers. Power refers to control over others that is due to a position in a power structure which reflects rewards and punishments. How power is used is crucial to a school's success or failure. A teacher/coach has certain amounts of power in each of the roles he/she occupies. How the teacher/coach utilizes power is often crucial to his/her success.

Authority refers to power that is made *legitimate* by being accepted by others. While power is often vested in a role (the head coach has a large amount of power), the authority of a person typically needs to be earned. It is tremendously important that teacher/coaches have authority (that is, they need to have legitimate power). Teachers who lack authority often have to resort to threats and punishment to assert power. Teachers with authority find it much easier to gain student compliance with behavioral norms and also to allow for more student involvement and decision making.

Authority is earned. Students must gain respect for your authority. How is this accomplished? There is no magic answer but some guidelines are helpful. Teacher/coaches who exhibit *expertise* or *competence* in their subject matter and in their primary roles gain authority. Teacher/coaches who are *fair* and *consistent* gain authority. Teacher/coaches who demonstrate *emotional control* in tough situations gain authority. Teacher/coaches who demonstrate *caring* for their students/athletes gain authority. Teacher/coaches who are willing to exercise their authority in situations which call for it gain further authority. In short, teacher/coaches who behave professionally, fairly, consistently, caringly, and in a controlled manner will have their power accepted as legitimate. The teacher/coach is an adult in a special role vis-à-vis students/athletes—the importance of that relationship should not be forgotten.

SOURCE: Based on Bain, L., and J. Wendt. *Transition to Teaching: A Guide for the Beginning Teacher.* Reston, Va.: American Alliance for Health, Physical Education, Recreation and Dance, 1983.

ics (typically led by a student), organizes the class into teams for a game (football or field hockey in the autumn, basketball in the winter, and softball in the spring), gets the game started, and then retires to the side of the gym or the field, where he or she spends the rest of the period working on plays that he or she hopes to practice with the team that afternoon. Have you ever seen this stereotype in real life? The roll-out-the-ball teacher who is really more interested in coaching than teaching is the image of physical education that is most widely presented to the public in books and films and on television. Think for a moment of all of the times in books, films, or on television that you have seen a physical educator/coach portrayed. Was the portrayal flattering? Was the person an admirable person? Far too often, the answer is no! But that is the stereotype that we all live with and that we badly need to change in the public's perception.

Although stereotypes are seldom true representations of what exists in the real world, it must be said that substantial evidence has been developed to suggest that far too often physical educators do put less into their teaching than they should in order to put more into their coaching. Most of us have

Careful planning is the foundation of an effective PE program.

either known, worked with, or played for a person who fits this general description. In the research world, the phenomenon is known as *role conflict*. It is a real and serious problem for men and women who desire to teach physical education and coach school teams.

Role conflict: Language and basic concepts

To better understand what is known about role conflict, it is important to be able to use the language and concepts with which the problem is investigated and discussed. A *role* can be defined as a pattern of expected behaviors for a specific position. A teacher has a certain role to play in the school instructional program. A coach has a certain role to play in the interscholastic sports program. *Role conflict* occurs when the expectations for two or more roles are incompatible. For example, a teachers' meeting is called for 4:00 P.M. on an important professional issue, but the coach has to attend practice. He or she cannot meet the demands of both roles at that point. Obviously, we each have other roles to play also: wife or husband, son or daughter, father or mother, friend, etc.

Role strain exists when the demands placed on a person require more energy or time than the person has to give. Role strain can occur either in the teaching role or in the coaching role. For example, implementing an entirely new curriculum in physical education (during the time when one also has coaching commitments) can produce a strain on the teaching role. The kinds of strains that are almost endemic among coaches are well known and perhaps more obvious than those experienced in teaching.

Intrarole conflict occurs when a person occupying a role must respond to incompatible expectations from people or groups. A teacher may be under pressure from some sources to be more innovative in his or her curriculum and instruction and also under other pressure from different sources simply

Table 6.3   Differences between the roles of teacher and coach

Role Characteristic	Teacher	Coach
1. Relevance of role to career advancement	Low	High
2. Technical preparation required for successful entry	Low	High
3. Need for continuous upgrading (clinics, etc.)	Low	High
4. Requirements for daily preparation	Small	Large
5. Frequency of public evaluation of performance	Seldom	Often
6. Emotional involvement of evaluators	Low	High
7. Consensus about desired outcomes of performance	Low	High
8. Extent and intensity of contact with students	Low	High
9. Homogeneity of students worked with	Low	High
10. Degree of voluntarism among students	Usually low	Always high
11. Motivation of students worked with	Differs greatly	Mostly high
12. Skill level of students worked with	Differs greatly	Highest in school
13. Intensity and intimacy of contacts with students	Mostly low	Often very high

SOURCE: Siedentop, D. *Developing Teaching Skills in Physical Education.* 2nd ed. Palo Alto, Calif.: Mayfield, 1983.

to keep the classes well disciplined and provide them with a good daily work-out. A coach may be under tremendous pressure from certain sources to win while other sources, still wanting a winning effort, are much more concerned that many players get to compete and have a rewarding experience as team members.

Compatibility refers to the match (or mismatch) between a person's abilities and interests and the demands of the various roles he or she must fulfill. Some evidence suggests that teaching and coaching require somewhat different talents and abilities, and there is no doubt that the two roles have some markedly different characteristics, as Table 6.3 suggests.

Is role conflict and strain a real problem among teacher/coaches in schools? Every objective piece of evidence collected over the past several decades suggests that it is and that it deserves to be taken very seriously simply because the personal and professional consequences of conflict and strain are real and substantial.

What do we know about role conflict and strain?

Evidence about role conflict and strain comes from different sources. Some of you may have your own experience as an important source of evidence. Some may also have seen other teacher/coaches trying to deal with these issues. However, the kind of evidence referred to in this section is objective evidence developed through research done by physical educators.* The story it tells is both interesting and troublesome.

It appears that most students who are preparing to become certified as physical education teachers have coaching as their main interest. Some are in-

*Interested readers are referred to Locke and Massengale 1978, Bain 1983, Chu 1981, Massengale 1981, and Seagrave 1981.

terested in both teaching and coaching; unfortunately, some enter teaching simply because it is the best way to get a good coaching job in schools. This predisposition to value coaching more than teaching becomes very important when one is actually on the job, where there is a very uneven set of rewards for the two roles.

Coaches are greatly in demand. Having many coaching vacancies creates problems for school administrators. Some physical education teachers feel that they must coach to maintain their teaching position, even though they may not want to coach (or to coach in more than one season of the school year).

Administrators who hire teachers are often as interested in what they can coach as in how well they can teach. When head coaching jobs become available, people are often chosen for their coaching skills, sometimes regardless of *what* they teach or *how well* they teach it.

Teachers are seldom fired for teaching inadequacy, but coaches are often let go because their teams do not win often enough. Being a competent teacher in no way makes up for a person's not coaching as well as parents or administrators feel that person should. This is in no way objective or fair! But then neither objectivity nor fairness is always part of the issue when coaching is in question.

Evaluation of performance in the teaching and coaching roles differs dramatically. Principals may do a teaching evaluation once or twice a year, and the evaluation is typically casual and not very objective. If students do not misbehave and are kept busy, the physical education teacher is often evaluated highly. On the other hand, the coach does his or her work in public. Not only is the win-loss record a major evaluation in itself but so too is the performance of the players. Parents judge this. The local press judges this. It seems sometimes as if *everybody* feels qualified to judge the coach.

When teachers and coaches are observed doing their jobs (that is, when the *same person* is observed in both his or her teaching and coaching), the resulting observations differ tremendously. Team practices are likely to be

Trying to help students improve requires the teacher's attention and effort.

highly organized, intense, clearly focused on skill development, strongly accountable, and performance oriented. Physical education classes are typically more neutral, less well managed, only marginally focused on performance and skill development, less individualized, and less accountability conscious. The fact is that when the same person occupies both roles, his or her performance does often differ from role to role.

The monetary rewards for coaching are incredibly low! Coaches are typically paid on supplemental contracts to the regular teaching contract. We have already alluded to the fact that teachers are not very well paid (see Table 6.1). But the evidence suggests that coaches make between $0.32 and $1.74 per hour! Perhaps coaches put more time into the role than they need to, but all of the other pressures of the job and the natural rewards of it produce that kind of devotion and commitment. Nevertheless, we believe it is a fact that low pay eventually drives many competent coaches out of that role.

The nonmonetary rewards associated with teaching and coaching are extremely unequal. Some say that almost nobody cares what goes on in the gym during the day. Very few teachers, administrators, or parents show any interest in what physical education teachers are doing. It is almost impossible to pick up a newspaper and read what went on in a physical education class. But what about the school sports teams? They are not only covered by school papers but by local papers and television. Students talk about the upcoming game or last week's game and so do teachers and parents. This entire scene creates a set of rewards for coaching that are simply unavailable in teaching. The attention (both positive and negative), the constant interest, and the rewards for success in coaching have no counterpart in teaching.

It appears that the most common response to role conflict or role strain is to adopt one of the roles as a major role and to devote most of one's energy and enthusiasm toward that role. Of course, this means that the tasks demanded by the other role are completed with less energy and enthusiasm, if at all. When role conflict exists between teaching and coaching, most people adopt coaching as the major role. As a result, their teaching tends to suffer.

Part of the reason why coaching is so often adopted as the major role when conflict occurs is (as indicated earlier in this section) that many physical educators feel their skills and interests are more compatible with the demands of coaching than with the demands of teaching. Therefore, they tend to have very high commitments to coaching and lower commitments to teaching.

When role strain (simply too much work) is the major problem, teacher/coaches tend to cut back on their teaching effort. At least they report feeling as if there is a negative impact on their teaching when role strain becomes a problem. This series of influences may be responsible for the throw-out-the-ball stereotype described at the beginning of this section.

There is some evidence that in certain schools, administrators tacitly approve of the choice teacher/coaches make to devote more time to coaching and less time to teaching. Coaches are sometimes given a slightly lighter teaching load and a "planning period" as the last period of the school day. The planning period is intended to be used in relationship to the instructional duties of a teacher, but it often allows the coach to prepare for practice.

The teacher/moonlighter

It would be inaccurate for us to convey the impression that the only kind of major role conflict among physical education teachers is that produced when the teaching role is combined with a coaching role. Not all physical educators coach! Many coach during the early years of their teaching careers only to give it up for one reason or another. Does this mean that the potential for role conflict is eliminated? No! The fact is that the vast majority of male teachers and a high number of female teachers hold second jobs; in other words, they moonlight. The jobs are far too diverse to catalog here, but selling insurance or real estate, working as a clerk in a store, and doing painting and construction work rank among the most frequent moonlighting occupations of teachers. Many women, of course, teach *and* raise a family, which is often more demanding than having a *paid* second job. The important point is that teacher salaries are so low that a majority of teachers find it necessary to seek second jobs.

A second job can produce role conflict just as surely as coaching can. Many teachers learn how to handle the conflicts and strain and still teach responsibly and effectively. The effects of role conflict and strain are not inevitable! Teachers who recognize that these phenomena exist are more likely to be able to protect themselves against the potentially debilitating effects they can cause.

Stress, coping, and teacher burnout

Resolution E-42 of the National Education Association's 1983–1984 resolutions states that public demands on educators and the changing dynamics of our society have produced school and classroom conditions that are extremely stressful, increasingly leading to emotional and physical disabilities among teachers and other school personnel (*NEA 1983–1984 Yearbook*, 149). Teacher stress, teacher burnout, and related problems have gradually become issues of significance in teachers' associations. Teachers often cite these issues when asked what topics they most want to have explored during in-service education programs. How can I cope better with the stresses? Am I suffering from burnout? Why does my job make me so tense and irritable? These questions need to be attended to, and new teachers need to be forewarned of the potential for such problems in their own teaching careers.

Many jobs have stresses. The stresses in teaching come from disruptive students, not enough time, parents who are not sufficiently supportive, administrators who create problems rather than facilitate education, and a host of other personal and professional sources. Stress management programs are now common in school districts. NEA Resolution E-42 calls for all school authorities to develop programs for the prevention and treatment of stress-related problems. Often these programs involve psychological coping mechanisms and a personal physical fitness program. Most physical education teachers are already fit and thus should be better able to withstand the stresses encountered in teaching.

There is no magic way to cope with job-related stress. The general procedure is similar to a problem-solving procedure:

1. Define the problem.
2. Work out alternative solutions.
3. Decide on a course of action.
4. Avoid decision by indecision.
5. Evaluate the results and make modifications.

(Bain and Wendt 1983)

Defining the problem is probably the biggest part of the solution. Once the causes of stress are identified, then it often becomes easier to develop a strategy for reducing or eliminating the effects of the stress. In general, an *active* approach to stress reduction is more satisfactory and successful than a passive one. Adopting a passive approach can cause a person to withdraw almost totally in the misguided hope that "things will get better."

Burnout

Have you ever known a teacher who is best described as tired—not from the kind of periodic fatigue that we all experience, but a person who seems to have been *defeated* in his or her job? Teacher burnout is among the most talked about professional phenomena in recent years. Because of high levels of unemployment, more teachers stay on the job and are less likely to look for other work when teaching no longer challenges them. Furthermore, teaching seems to have become more difficult. It appears that burnout is produced when job stresses become more consistent and difficult over time and there is less likelihood of being able to escape the situation by shifting to another occupation.

Burnout is a label used to describe a syndrome that has many different causes. Doing the same job day in and day out for 15 or 20 years is probably sufficient in and of itself to produce a certain kind of boredom and anxiety. Multiple stresses that accumulate over the years add to the problem. Unfortunately, it is easier to see that burnout *has* occurred than to understand *how* it developed.

The effects of burnout are reasonably predictable. Research (Mancini et al. 1983) has shown that teachers suffering burnout typically plan less carefully, are inflexible in how they behave on the job, tend to be inefficient and careless, offer little reinforcement or feedback for their students, tend to be overly critical of students, and have generally lowered expectations for both their students and themselves—not a pretty picture! Given that portrait of burnout, it is easy to see why it has become a major issue in school districts and among professional organizations.

What can one do to combat burnout? The suggestions are many and varied, but there is no simple formula. Clearly, maintaining one's enthusiasm for

---

AAHPERD RESPONDS TO BURNOUT ISSUES

The American Alliance for Health, Physical Education, Recreation and Dance has not neglected the problem of burnout, as the following publications indicate.

> AAHPERD. "Combating Teacher Burnout." *Journal of Physical Education, Recreation and Dance* 52, no. 2 (1981): 35–48.
>
> AAHPERD. "The Teaching/Coaching Challenge." *JOPERD* 52, no. 9 (1981): 15–25.
>
> AAHPERD. "Alternatives to Teacher Burnout." *JOPERD* 51 no. 9 (1980): 53–60.
>
> Sparks and Hammond. *Managing Teacher Stress and Burnout.* Reston, Va.: AAHPERD, 1981.

---

the job is a key factor in preventing burnout. Any opportunity to change routine, occupy a different role, and do a totally different job for a period of time probably helps to prevent burnout. Here are a few specific suggestions:

- Train for doing your job differently or doing a different job in the school by attending graduate school.
- Ask for temporary assignment to another set of duties.
- Ask for a partial change in teaching load to teach in a new field.
- Look for job opportunities in a school that may offer a new context or a different set of opportunites.
- Start a new program with different methodology that causes you to change your instructional role.
- Seek support from administration to attend professional meetings where you can learn new approaches.
- Develop some new interest in your leisure time.
- Explore what policies exist in your district for professional or sabbatical leaves of absence.
- Explore what opportunities exist for professional exchanges with teachers in other countries.
- Explore the possibilities for preparing for a new profession.

None of these suggestions will automatically produce a magic change in a person's professional existence. If burnout is occurring, it needs to be dealt with systematically, over a period of time, with a rational, problem-solving approach. However, many teachers do experience professional renewal through a variety of means, and school districts are increasingly sensitive to facilitating this renewal. There is every reason to expect that increased recognition of the problem will require districts to provide even more help for teachers to

BURNOUT: PART OF THE JOB OR
A SERIOUS PROBLEM?

There has been so much talk about burnout lately that when hearing about it teachers sometimes suggest that they felt pretty good about themselves and what they were doing until they got informed about burnout—and then they realized they were suffering from it too!

But were they? Every job has its difficult moments and its difficult periods. It is important to distinguish between *real* burnout and just a difficult class, day, or semester. The following information might help.

Levels of burnout: *First degree (mild).* Short-lived bouts of fatigue, frustration, and irritation.

Second degree (moderate). Same symptoms as above but they persist for several weeks or more.

Third degree (severe). Physical ailments such as ulcers, chronic back pain, and/or migraine headaches.

Symptoms of serious burnout include depression, insomnia, impotence, high blood pressure, chronic colds, headaches, and other such physical responses to prolonged stress. The potential consequences of prolonged, severe burnout are quite serious. Included among them are marital problems, alcoholism, drug addiction, obesity, and suicide.

Clearly, serious burnout is to be taken seriously. But it is also important to distinguish serious burnout from the short-term responses to job stresses that most professionals encounter.

SOURCE: Based on Iwanicki, E. G. "Toward Understanding and Alleviating Teacher Burnout." *Theory into Practice* 22, no. 1 (Winter 1983).

---

renew themselves over the course of their teaching careers. Stagnation serves no one well—neither students, nor the school district, nor the teacher. It is, therefore, in the best interest of all concerned to combat it wherever it occurs.

The other side of the coin

It is important that the *real* problems of teaching be recognized and dealt with in a professional manner. But in describing problems and discussing their impacts and possible solutions, we should not lose sight of the many, many satisfactions teachers derive from their work. Joy in our work does not often come in big bursts but instead occurs in day-to-day events that continue to enthuse and uplift our spirits.

Do not forget what a grateful smile from a young student who has just demonstrated some real improvement in a skill can do for you. Do not fail to recognize that the exuberance and joy of a group of teenagers who have just finished a closely contested game is a result of the instructional planning that you have done; their exuberance is a direct result of your educational efforts.

Do not underestimate the satisfaction that comes from knowing that you have helped an adolescent through a difficult problem. Above all, do not forget how important it is that students learn what it means to be fit, to develop skill, to compete fairly and vigorously, and to share memorable moments with one another within those contexts.

To teach well and to coach competently is to perform a service of enormous importance to students and the community. Take heart from the small returns that come each day: the smiles, the remarks of peer teachers who recognize and appreciate your efforts, the comments of administrators who admire professional competence. What a teacher does is important! The fact that phenomena such as stress and burnout are real and prevalent makes good teaching all the more crucial.

Distinctive physical educators

The public stereotype of the school physical educator/coach is not usually flattering. We have discussed some of the difficulties encountered by the teacher/coach, including role conflict, role strain, and burnout. But the fact still remains that men and women do become teacher/coaches and do continue to teach and coach competently year after year. Although we cannot afford to ignore the potential problems for the teacher/coach, we would also be remiss if we did not emphasize the qualities and characteristics of those who serve our profession with distinction.

Earls (1979) has studied distinctive teacher/coaches and his work forms the basis of much of what is included in this section. A *distinctive* teacher/coach is one whose colleagues (fellow teachers, administrators, teacher educators, etc.) agree stands out among his or her peers because of a sincere interest in teaching, a continued enthusiasm for teaching, genuine concern for students, and evidence of a continual attempt to improve in what he or she does. Earls studied male and female teacher/coaches who were identified as distinctive. What follows are some of the conclusions he reached about this sample of excellent professionals in our field.

Distinctive teacher/coaches derive their primary satisfaction from their daily interactions with students. These interactions, however, are not just social in nature. Distinctive professionals are rewarded when students achieve and enjoy their involvement. These teacher/coaches are also aware of the long-term impact they have on their students.

Distinctive teacher/coaches seem to maintain their enthusiasm for teaching in two ways. First, they are constantly searching for new and better ways to do their jobs. They tend to vary their programs and their teaching from year to year. Second, they get involved in summer activities that are *different* from their regular school employment. This brings them back to their teaching job each autumn refreshed and ready to begin anew.

Distinctive teacher/coaches tend to be honest and open, both with themselves and their students. Being honest and open, they tend to be more relaxed with their students. They can admit to mistakes when they occur and

---

THE BUCK STOPS HERE!

Do teachers make a difference? Research in schools in the past two decades has provided an affirmative answer to that question. However, many parents, teachers, and administrators have long known that teachers make a difference. Listen to what Haim Ginott says about the effects of a teacher.

> I have come to a frightening conclusion. I am the decisive element in the classroom. It is personal approach that creates the climate. It is my daily mood that makes the weather. I possess tremendous power to make a child's life miserable or joyous. . . . In all situations, it is my response that decides whether a crisis will be escalated or deescalated and a child humanized or dehumanized.

SOURCE: Ginott, H. *Teacher and Child: A Book for Parents and Teachers*. New York: Macmillan Co., 1972, p. 15–16.

---

are willing to discuss both their strengths and their weaknesses. These teacher/coaches also emphathize strongly with students and behave with impartiality toward all students. One of the characteristics that goes completely against most stereotypes is that these teacher/coaches are very aware of and relate well to students of all types, skilled and unskilled, well-behaved and poorly behaved. The "loner" or the "loser" does not suffer in the classes of these teachers. Indeed, these teachers seek out students who are different and try very hard to relate to them.

Distinctive teacher/coaches recognize the potential problems of role conflict and see it happening to many of their colleagues, but they find ways to handle it in their own cases. All of these people coach, and all manage to recognize the potential problems and adjust to them.

The classes of distinctive teacher/coaches are virtually free from discipline problems. These teachers have authority among their students (see "Power and Authority," page 97), and because of this they do not need to use their power in ways that detract from educational goals. These teachers demonstrate the management skills described in Chapter 20. They teach the rules and expected behaviors well and early. They do not tolerate disruptive or damaging behavior. They achieve consistency, and students respond to it positively.

These professionals recognize the individual needs of the students they teach and are bothered that problems of class size and time prevent them from meeting the needs of each student. This, their greatest dissatisfaction, no doubt has a positive side in that it provides a continued motivation to persist in their efforts.

In their own words

The information presented above is meant to portray distinctive teacher/coaches as a group; it explains what they have in common. But they are also individuals, and it is important to understand them in that light. Following are some of their thoughts and concerns in their own words, which represent a more intimate way of understanding them and the good work they do (Earls 1979).

Pam, a middle school physical educator and coach:

> It's the quiet little ones that just go through it doing what you ask them to do but hating every minute of it. Sometimes I think we are not even aware of those kids and that we are not really getting through to them.
>
> It used to be that students were taught respect for their elders at home and therefore automatically did things for you. Maybe that is why I feel that I expect more, because you have to expect more to get that same response.
>
> I really like people and really love kids. I think you have to be people-oriented.
>
> Kids know if you are just putting them on or if you really care. You have to take time to listen and to really be involved and think about what is important to them. It may not be important to you, but it is really important to them.
>
> Ten years ago, I would have told you that I would never coach anything, because I didn't believe in competition and didn't enjoy it. . . . Now, it is one of the most fun things I do all year long.

Walt, an experienced senior and junior high school teacher/coach:

> He's a kid that I just have not been able to teach, and the temptation is there to forget it. You're doing a good job with the majority. Why worry about the minority? The challenge is that you've got to concern yourself, especially since 90 percent of kids I don't even have to worry much about because they like it and can do fairly well. But it is the other kids you have to force yourself for.
>
> I honestly believe that it has become very difficult being a head coach, which I have been, not to be affected adversely. . . . There is a lot of pressure so it is very difficult to do well the teaching job that you are paid for. . . . That's why I like being an assistant coach. I can still spend time and still worry a little bit, but I can still do my teaching without being distracted at all.
>
> I didn't feel a need to get away when I started, but as you get a bit older and with three sports—it tends to burn you out a little bit. My feeling has always been that I don't want to get to the point where I don't want to be here because then it's over.
>
> I see somebody that I remember from junior high teaching or high school coaching now using something that they got an inkling of from me. I saw a guy the other day who I had to really work with to get him to participate. Now he is completely different and very active. I love to see that.

Donald, a teacher/coach who has taught and coached at the elementary, junior, and senior high school levels:

> When I came in I was coaching on the high school level. I was young and facing kids in grades four, five, and six. Maybe at that particular point in my career I thought I was God's gift to them and the kids were going to do as I say—step on the black line, sit there and shut your mouth—and stuff like that. I don't think that I liked it. They didn't like it. I was getting uptight all the time and this had to stop. It took me several years to learn it.
>
> I want to treat the kids like I would have wanted teachers to treat me. I wasn't outgoing and sometimes I got beat on for it. I got beat on quite bad. If I didn't rebound I got beat on, and if I didn't talk right in class I got beat on. I'm sick of seeing kids beat on.
>
> Coaching!—and teaching. It's very difficult to do a decent job teaching and coaching.
>
> I think that the poor physical education teachers are the teachers that think their subject is poor, that they are put in the school as an outlet for kids and nothing more. The old sweatshirt and whistle syndrome is how they view themselves. . . . I look around and wonder what could be a better job than what I'm doing. I could be challenged in the business world, but this is where I'm at, right here.
>
> A few years ago, Project Adventure was nothing to me but something that you laughed about; until I went to it, saw it, and took part in it. Then, gosh! A whole bag of just what I believe in—personal interaction with kids.

Jean, an experienced teacher/coach at the junior and senior high school levels:

> I know that every student is not going to like activities, but I want them to make the effort. If they can show improvement in their skills, that's important to me and I think it is important to them. I think it should be pointed out to them when you see them improve; encouragement should be shown to them.
>
> I think you have to keep up with the changing times. For example, I had to go out and learn disco dancing from the kids first. Either I'm going to do something well or I'm not going to do it. That's just me.
>
> I think you have to care, take time to get things done. You care about things and get things done, and I'm talking about getting prepared to teach a class and then teaching it.
>
> The biggest problem is that young teachers are not supervised—a supervisor should say either shape up or you are out.
>
> If they can come into my class, work hard, learn something that will help them to succeed, and leave with a smile on their face, then I think that makes me happy.

**TEN TRAITS OF SERIOUS TEACHERS:
HOW WILL YOU MATCH UP?**

One of the major ways to distinguish between more effective and less effective teachers is in the seriousness with which they approach their job. What
characterizes a serious teacher? C. M. Charles suggests the following ten
traits. Ask yourself how well you will match up against them. More importantly, how well will you match up against them after being on the job for five
years?

Serious teachers . . .
  value education
    value learning
      value the golden rule
        prepare adequately for instruction
          make a good effort in their teaching
            keep students on task
              follow up on task assignments
                take the extra step
                  persevere
                    communicate with parents.

SOURCE: Based on Charles, C. M. *Building Classroom Discipline*. New York: Longman, 1981.

They do make a difference

Research in teacher effectiveness during the past 20 years has confirmed
what most of us have always believed—*teachers do make a difference* (Siedentop
1983). Good teachers help students. Poor teachers retard students' growth in
ways that are both immediately harmful and have long-run implications. The
physical educator and sports coach can have a tremendously positive influence on young people, and they can have a tremendously negative influence.
To continue to exert a positive influence means to continue to be motivated to
teach effectively, to have strong, positive expectations for your students and
athletes, and to persist in making the day-to-day effort that results in good
teaching and coaching.

Summary

The teacher/coach must juggle a group of multidimensional tasks, some of
which necessarily conflict with others. These tasks involve both power structures within the school and relationships to groups outside the school, as well
as the primary tasks of teaching and coaching students.

Role conflict and role strain are endemic among teacher/coaches. Research indicates that most who experience the conflict eventually devote more
of their attention to coaching with a resulting loss of effectiveness in teaching.

Role conflict also occurs when teachers moonlight on second jobs, often as a result of the relatively low pay teachers receive. As in coaching, any other second job often ends up receiving more attention than the primary job of teaching.

Stress in teaching comes from many sources including too much to do, not enough time to do it, disruptive students, and the year-to-year sameness of the job. An active approach to dealing with stress involves defining the problem, seeking alternative solutions, and taking actions to counteract the problem.

Burnout has many different sources but a common result: Teachers either leave their jobs or they "retire" on the job. Professional organizations and school systems are developing plans for dealing with teacher burnout.

Distinctive physical educators are involved with the achievement of their students, constantly seek new and better ways to do their jobs, involve themselves in summer activities that are different from teaching, and relate honestly and openly to all of their students. Their own remarks indicate that they have struggled with the difficulties of teaching and resolved them so as to continue to be motivated to serve youth through teaching. They prove that physical educators do make a difference.

Suggested activities

1. Discuss the ways in which physical educators you have known who both teach and coach handle the two roles.

2. Develop a list of school problems that can create stress for a physical education teacher. Then discuss ways in which such stress might be reduced.

3. Describe a distinctive physical educator that you have known. From your description and the descriptions of other members of the class, collate a list of the characteristics that make physical educators distinctive.

4. Debate the following issue: Because of the well-known problems in role conflict, physical education teachers should not also be coaches. Have three students argue the affirmative and three the negative.

5. Talk to teachers you know and find out whether they have outside sources of income. If so, find out from what kinds of jobs. To what degree do the teachers feel their second jobs interfere with their teaching?

7

Students with Special Needs

"An equal opportunity for education" is a phrase that seems direct, succinct, and easy to interpret. Unfortunately, until a few years ago when Public Law 94-142 was passed, the message in this phrase had little meaning for handicapped youth. Their situation was much like that of girls and women who, until the passage of Title IX legislation in 1972, were denied the opportunity to participate in sports. They were in fact unequal.

Times have changed for the better. Young people with handicapping conditions as well as girls and women now have more opportunities. This makes the task of the teacher more complex and diverse, requires more imagination, but is also more rewarding.

A typical school today includes many students with special needs; they are handicapped in one sense but exceptional and special in a broader sense. This chapter includes answers to three basic questions regarding exceptional youth:

Why is there such current concern for students with special needs?

Who are the students with special needs, how many of them are there, and what characteristics do they manifest?

What physical education techniques are effective in teaching youth with special needs?

Westmoor Middle School has a student population of slightly more than 1000. Westmoor is a crowded school; all of the classrooms are occupied each period, and one class is even held on the auditorium stage. That is not a very good teaching station. Westmoor is an urban school that participates in a desegregation order, and about 35 percent of its students are from families receiving financial assistance such as aid to dependent children. The school is somewhat unusual in that although it is quite large it was constructed on a one-floor plan that created very long halls connecting various wings of the building.

The field-experience supervisor from the local college, who was interested in placing some of her education students at Westmoor for observation and tutoring experiences, noticed the length of the halls as she watched a series of students whizzing down the halls in wheelchairs pushed by other students on her way to the principal's office. At that moment the principal emerged from a doorway and hollered in no uncertain terms, "Slow down!" Then he turned to the supervisor and said, "There goes the 10:30 express, spina bifida students on their way to catheterization at this time every day. We have over 30 of these youngsters in school."

The supervisor concluded arrangements with the principal in a relatively short time and sat on a bench in the school lobby, a major crossroad of the hallways serving the different wings of the building. Soon the bell rang and classes changed. She noticed more students in wheelchairs. She also saw some students with canes being led by other students; obviously some of them were partially sighted or blind.

Generally, the change of classes was orderly if a bit noisy. The supervisor continued to sit in the lobby, now almost deserted, thinking about the changes in schools in the past few years. Wheelchairs, spina bifida children, incontinent students, and partially sighted youth were rarely present in public schools prior to the 1970s. The schools could not manage such difficult youngsters, or at least they maintained that they couldn't before this period. It certainly was different. Where were these children before the 1970s?

Just then a police officer entered the lobby with three boys in tow. The boys were surly and unhappy, and one was yelling obscenities about being back in school. Well, that had not changed. There had always been recalcitrants, tough kids, hard to reach and manage let alone educate according to school values. These young people were educated according to the rules of the street, which are not necessarily compatible with the standards of the school.

The supervisor was pleased with what she had seen on two counts. First, the school would provide a rich experience for her college students. Second, as a person and a professional, she was glad to see exceptional students interacting with regular students in school in such a spontaneous and natural manner; it was refreshing to know that schools can respond to students with special needs. In a sense this reaffirmed her belief in the dimensions and significance of public education.

Why is there such current concern for students with special needs?

Americans have over a period of time made a philosophical commitment to those considered less fortunate. One of the cornerstones of our society is to eliminate injustice in any form. Obviously, if we can accept the oppressed, the victims of fate, the poor, and the hungry from abroad, we must also respond to the needs of special people at home. There is also a wellspring of concern for those with exceptional needs. It is an imperfect concern, and this is still a society that often exhibits uncaring behavior. However, at certain periods in history, groups of people and persuasive leaders have produced impressive gains in efforts to improve the fate of the less fortunate.

Public Law 94-142

P.L. 94-142,* The Education for All Handicapped Children Act of 1974, is a very important, almost revolutionary legislative act of the federal government. It states that each child is entitled to an education that meets his or her particular needs. The result of this legislation is to introduce into the vocabulary of education concepts such as mainstreaming, least restrictive environment, zero reject, and progressive inclusion. Definition of these concepts will help explain the dimensions of the legislation.

Mainstreaming basically means that young people with handicaps—mental, emotional, or physical—must have the opportunity to mix with other students in public education. The concept is to move the handicapped person into the mainstream or flow of activity and communication in society. Mainstreaming is an effort to encourage those with handicapping conditions to join in an as close to normal existence as is possible.

Least restrictive environment, a phrase that represents a continuation of the mainstreaming concept, involves the realization that not all individuals can do all of the same activities in the same environment but that they probably can do some activities in the same environment. A youth with a cardiac disorder may not have the stamina to participate in a full day of school, but he or she can flourish on a half- or partial-day schedule. Before the passage of P.L. 94-142, such a youth languished at home all day. The burden is now on the school to meet the exceptional student's need rather than on the exceptional student to meet the school program as it is constructed for the totally able population.

Zero reject means that everyone of school age is entitled to some part of the school program. No one may be shunted aside and forgotten.

Progressive inclusion, which is based on the belief that individuals progress as a result of educational programs, means that youth with disabling limitations must be provided an opportunity to move to less restrictive environments in order to share in the mainstream for greater and greater periods of time.

Figure 7.1 shows a schematic view of these concepts and illustrates their potential significance to exceptional people.

In the majority of schools today, few students proceed in their education entirely through regular class placement. Almost everyone uses related services at some time. How many students have never seen a school nurse, a teacher's aide, an associate librarian, or the athletic trainer? Some have attended regular classes but for one or two periods been assigned to an ad-

---

* P.L. 94-142 stands for *Public Law of the 94th Congress and the 142nd act of legislation passed by that Congress.*

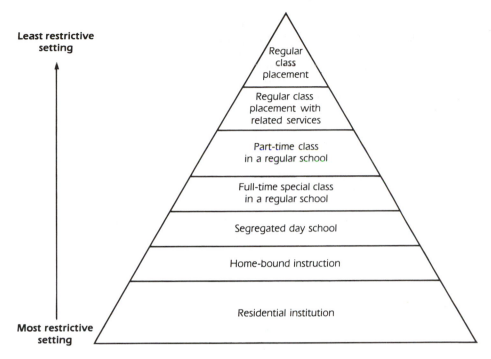

Figure 7.1 Progressive placement of handicapped youth for instructional purposes.

SOURCE: Adapted from French and Jansma 1982, p. 7.

vanced math class or a remedial speech class or a special computer class. The series of learning environments for exceptional students depicted in Figure 7.1 is only somewhat different from a placement pyramid used by schools for years with their standard student population.

The individual education program

The mechanism by which P.L. 94-142 is put into practice is the Individual Education Program (I.E.P.). The I.E.P. includes the following components (French and Jansma 1982, 42–43):

1. A statement of the child's present level of educational performance
2. A statement of annual goals, including short-term instructional objectives
3. A statement of the specific media, materials, and special-education and related services provided to the child
4. The projected dates for initiation of services and the anticipated duration of the services
5. The extent to which the child will be able to participate in regular educational programs

6. Appropriate objective criteria and evaluation procedures and schedules for determining, on at least an annual basis, whether the short-
term instructional objectives are being met

To develop an I.E.P. for an individual, the parents, the student where possible, the school administration, and the special educator must meet and
agree to the program. The school representatives to the agreement generally
turn to various teachers in the system for help in providing relevant information and appropriate educational objectives.

The only subject area mentioned in P.L. 94-142 is physical education. Students
with special needs must have an opportunity as part of an I.E.P. to participate, in an appropriate developmental and educational manner, in physical
education.

The revolutionary nature of this legislation lies not only in the concept of
individual planning but also in the recourse available to parents to challenge
the appropriateness of the I.E.P. in a court of law. The effect is to keep school
officials on their toes.

Other laws for the handicapped

Two other federal laws are also important to education for the handicapped. P.L. 89-10, the Elementary and Secondary School Act of 1965, provides billions of dollars to improve schools and programs. At least 15 percent
of the money is reserved for programs to help the handicapped. P.L. 93-112,
the Rehabilitation Act of 1973, is a civil rights bill for the handicapped. It provides protection under the fifth and fourteenth amendments of the Constitution for due process and equal protection. Title V of this legislation makes
specific reference to the right of the handicapped not to be excluded from any
program or activity receiving any form of federal assistance. Thus if a school,
public or private, receives tuition or transportation assistance or participates
in lunch programs or hundreds of other activities sponsored by the federal
government, then all of its activities must be available to the handicapped. If
you have noticed the construction of ramps or restrooms to accommodate
wheelchairs in schools, arenas, theaters, airports, and department stores in
the past few years, realize this is a response to P.L. 93-112.

Legislation as significant as we have just described does not occur spon-
taneously or even quickly. A strong grass-roots belief in the rights of the handicapped for the better part of a century stimulated the actions of Congress. It is
worth reviewing the philosophical or conceptual basis for these actions as we
seek reasons for the current belief in the rights of handicapped people.

Philosophical factors

Suppose you are a local superintendent of schools or principal and
your immediate supervisor (the board of education or superintendent) ordered you to send all children with freckles home for good—

no more school. Just suppose you followed that order. How long do you think the parents of more than 95% of the children would tolerate such action? (Wilson 1975, 69)

Not only is such an order illegal, but it also violates our sense of fairness and justice. Imagine depriving anyone of a chance to go to school because of freckles. It is unthinkable!

Minority recognition.   Now let's examine another situation. Suppose the principal ruled that all children who have freckles covering 99 percent or more of their body must be excluded from school. Such children would represent less than 1 percent of the total student population. Or suppose we decide to eliminate people in wheelchairs from school; they too represent about 1 percent or less of the population. Certainly parental and community pressure would not be as great to challenge such a decision simply because of the numbers involved. Yet the evidence of history supports the notion that eventually these few individuals would be represented by a ground swell of support that would seek to overthrow a rule deemed unfair and unjust. This is exactly the pattern followed to provide public education for handicapped children, voting rights for blacks, and health benefits for migrant workers in the United States.

Eventually the collective actions of the people serve to redress injustice or unfairness for a relatively small number of people. The system is slow, frequently uncaring, but eventually responsive. We operate in this fashion because our beliefs and laws emerge from the fundamental purposes of the society as embodied in the Constitution and Bill of Rights. These philosophical constructs include individual rights, equal justice, freedom of choice, and the dignity of the individual.

Exceptional people.   Consider for a moment these ten outstanding individuals, their roles, and their exceptionality.

- Franklin Delano Roosevelt, president of the United States, confined to a wheelchair as a result of polio
- Helen Keller, teacher of the handicapped, author, and lecturer, blind and deaf
- George Wallace, governor of Alabama, confined to a wheelchair as a result of an assassination attempt
- Bill Johnson, downhill skiing Olympic gold medal winner, delinquent
- Tom Dempsey, professional football kicker, right arm and kicking foot congenitally deformed
- Bobby Morrow, Olympic gold medal sprinter, March of Dimes poster boy as a result of polio
- Bobby Jones, professional basketball all-star, epileptic
- Scott Hamilton, world and Olympic figure skating champion, lack of any growth between the ages of three and seven

- Mike Levine, marathon champion, cerebral palsy victim unable to tie his own shoes
- Wilma Rudolph, Olympic sprint champion, told she would never walk again as a result of childhood trauma

It is exciting to review the accomplishments of these exceptional people. But it is even more important to think of the contributions each has made to this nation and its people. We would have been far poorer in fact and in spirit without them.

These people remind us of two other fundamental philosophical positions: First, we should conserve and wisely use our resources; second, we should remain optimistic about the future. This country cannot afford to exclude any of its people, women, blacks, or handicapped, from full participation. We need their energy and talent to prosper. In addition, each generation seeks to improve the human condition for the next. This is the ultimate optimism about life.

Positive elements.   In describing legal and philosophical reasons for the current effort to include those with special needs in all feasible programs and activities, we have used the terms *disabled, handicapped*, and *exceptional* interchangeably. In the broadest sense, every person is exceptional in some fashion and handicapped at some point in life. You are stronger at 20 than you were at 10, more independent today than you were as a child. So it is with the handicapped. Each of these individuals is able to perform to some degree and only disabled to some degree. The task of the physical education teacher in working with these individuals is similar to that described generally in working with adolescents: Work with the successful portion of each person's life.

Who are the students with special needs?

Marie, the Bowler

The high school bowling class was seated in the bus. Two students lifted Marie from her wheelchair to a seat on the bus while a third folded the wheelchair and placed it on the bus. The process had to be reversed at the bowling alley since there was no lift on the bus for handicapped students. Nobody seemed to mind the slight delay, however. Marie was 17, bright, vivacious, pretty, and confined to a wheelchair since an automobile accident five years earlier. As a result of traumatic injuries to her spine, she was unable to walk, stand, or use her right arm and hand. She wrote the best poetry in the school and had the highest bowling average in the class. All the heroes, the big, burly athletes, enjoyed the challenge of trying to beat Marie in bowling. She had a ramp attached to her chair at the alley that enabled her to bowl. A classmate placed the ball on the ramp, and Marie then maneuvered her chair with the ramp to an appropriate position and locked it in place. She then pushed the ball with her left hand, and the ball rolled down the ramp and the alley to the pins. Her class average was over 200! The ball rolled slowly in comparison to the power rolls of many of the other players, but it rolled to the same spot in the pocket almost every time.

Chuck, the Wrestler

The wrestling official was puzzled, in fact confused. He was a good official, selected to work at the state meet, and in the process of refereeing a bout at 138 pounds between two experienced boys, Chuck and Bert. Chuck was blind. The two boys were on their feet trying for a takedown in the first period. Bert was attempting to tiptoe around Chuck in order to secure a favorable position. A takedown was almost guaranteed if he could get to the rear without Chuck's detecting his position.

The crowd was wild—booing and hissing Bert for attempting a "sneak" move and also verbally abusing the referee for not preventing this activity. It was a full house, 800 or more people, and bouts were also in progress on five other mats. Ordinarily, Chuck would have wrestled in a gymnasium where the crowd maintained silence and his acute hearing enabled him to turn and face his opponent. This was impossible in the madhouse of noise and excitement.

Finally, the referee called time and brought the wrestlers and coaches to the scorers' table. He told them that because of the uncontrollable noise, he wanted the wrestlers to maintain contact in the standing position. Bert's coach screamed that was unfair to his athlete because his best moves were made while he was out of contact. However Bert himself seemed relieved at the decision; it isn't much fun to have 800 people screaming insults at you.

The bout resumed from a contact position. This really was against the official rules, but the referee believed his decision represented the spirit of the rules, fair competition.

Josh, the Softball Player

Josh maneuvered very well with his artificial leg. He had lost his left leg as a result of cancer when he was 13. Now at 17 he was a big, husky, strong young man. Much of his strength came from gymnastics. He had been a varsity team member for several years. He competed without the artificial leg, and some thought it an advantage since there was less weight to worry about on the horse, parallel bars, and high bar. No one thought much about balance problems.

The class was softball, and Josh could not run with his prosthesis. He played first base, batted, and had a runner substitute for him as soon as he hit the ball.

The teacher was delighted with the class reaction to Josh. There was never an argument from the other team about his having a runner. There was an argument about whether Jim's team had the right to choose the fastest member of the team to run for him, however. Some of the opposition would have chosen Bill to run since it was doubtful that he was faster than Josh to first base. Really it was a nice argument since for the teacher it represented an acceptance of Josh but the principle of competition remained as strong as ever.

Each of the three vignettes illustrates possibilities in physical education with regard to handicapped students. The greatest number of such students are assimilated into regular physical education classes with only modest requirements for adjusting the activities.

Numbers of handicapped

In the United States over 31 million people have some activity limitation caused by heart condition, impairment of back and spine, hypertension, impairment of lower extremities and hips, and several other conditions (*Statistical Abstract of the United States 1982–1983*, 121). The statistics do not include

Table 7.1 People 15 and under using special health aids

	Number of Persons × 1000	Rate per 1000
Special shoes	572	11.1
Leg or foot brace	76	1.5
Other braces	51	1.0
Wheelchair	47	0.9
Crutches	50	1.0
Artificial leg	13	0.3

SOURCE: *Statistical Abstract of the United States 1982–1983*, p. 123.

individuals sufficiently limited to be in institutional residential settings. Obviously, this is a very large number of people and in fact represents an increase of about 10 million people since the 1970 census. Probably the large increase is due mainly to an increased awareness and better reporting techniques today than in the past.

Some of the figures for people 15 years of age and under, the youth of school age, are truly revealing. Table 7.1 demonstrates this point.

Most sources indicate that approximately 10 percent of the school-age population has some kind of disabling condition. Disabling conditions can be categorized as follows:

- Mental retardation
- Emotional disorders
- Hearing and visual impairment
- Neurological and muscular disorders
- Cardiac and respiratory disorders
- Multiple handicaps

We shall examine these categories with regard to characteristics and acceptable activities. An important point to remember, however, is that students with special needs are individuals and do not fit neatly into categories. The categories of disabling conditions provide only a general starting point for program directions. It is also important to believe and act in a manner that assists students with special needs to achieve in areas such as strength development, stamina improvement, and self-directed leisure and sports skills—the same goals we have for students without disabling conditions.

Mental retardation

Individuals who fall two standard deviations below the mean intelligence norm of 100 are considered mentally retarded. Although these individuals follow the same developmental pattern as other people, they do so at a much slower rate and may not develop fully. Memory and attention span are deficient, and general physical fitness and stamina are frequently poor. Mentally retarded people have limited abstract powers, including vocabulary, and many times are easily frustrated and have a very poor self-image. A characteristic of the life-style of these youth is that since they are different in degree and slower than other young people, they are left out and ignored. Therefore, they lose the opportunity for stimulation to assist their developmental processes. The greater the lack of inclusion and participation, the more loss of stimulation and the greater the deficits as the years go by. Part of their lack of physical stamina may be explained by this pattern. If no one chooses or permits such youth to play childhood games, then the retarded child does not develop skills or fitness levels and subsequently will not be able to participate because of a lack of skill and fitness. Mentally retarded children need more, not less, attention and stimulation. Among the assets of these youth, particularly Down's syndrome individuals, is an affectionate nature.

For these young people it is important to emphasize strength and fitness and to maximize action without lengthy instructions or discussions. Initial success is important since they have experienced a lifetime of frustration. Change activities often, and be aware that inappropriate behaviors often stem from ignorance or a lack of understanding.

Judgment is not good among mentally retarded students because of a lack of concern for consequences or the realization of danger. The teacher's responsibility with such youth to avoid a negligent situation is therefore much greater. A structured environment is essential. Appropriate competition is excellent, as the Special Olympics has demonstrated over and over again.

Emotional disorders

Students with emotional disorders may not fit any single description, no matter how general. Such youth may be hyperactive or withdrawn; rebellious, loud, and aggressive or almost mute and subservient. Some even play both roles—one role for a fairly long period of time and then the opposite role.

Disturbed people are takers: They take teachers' energy and goodwill and expertise and affection, and they do not return them in kind. In fact many of them cannot, which is symptomatic of their disability. It is as if the self has run rampant, an extreme form of narcissism. For the most part, emotionally disordered youth have normal mental and physical abilities but are deficient in socially acceptable emotional responses. Some lack a desire to engage in competitive activities because a loss in such circumstances is too threatening to their generally poor self-image. As a result, many of these young people have poor skills and fitness levels.

Initially, individual sports with a focus on competition with the self rather than others may be helpful for emotionally disturbed students. A structured environment with clear-cut demands and goals is also helpful to limit their insecurity, and reinforcement of successful efforts and achievement is very important. In many cases motivation, not discipline, is the major problem for the teacher. Because judgment and self-control are often weak in these students, it is the teacher's responsibility to control the variables of the lesson and the environment and in a sense to protect such youth from their own poor judgment.

Hearing and visual impairment

Sensory impairment delays all other developmental processes. Therefore, the age at which a sensory disabling condition occurs is very significant to the educational program for students suffering from such impairment. For example, if a person loses her hearing after learning to speak, then talking is a far simpler task than starting the process without having heard the sound of a human voice, a situation in which pronunciation will be very difficult.

Hearing-impaired students frequently display faulty posture, make sounds at inappropriate times, have a poor sense of balance, and lack agility and the usual levels of fitness. These people are *not* retarded, merely delayed developmentally because of a lack of stimulation.

Partially sighted and blind students also display poor levels of fitness, lack of agility, and awkward movement. Much of this is due to insecurity, and the insecurity is frequently the result of a lack of exposure to and experience in motor activities.

> The official with his back to the crowded stands was puzzled. The students of the state school for the blind were cheering in unison, "Pin, pin, we want a pin!" Yet it was the 123-pounder from the school for the blind who was almost on his back, struggling against the near-fall hold being applied by the sighted wrestler from a local high school. Finally the buzzer ended the period, and the official awarded points for the near fall.
>
> The announcer relayed these activities to the crowd of over 300 students, almost all of them blind with a few partially sighted students among them. Another cheer began as the match continued.
>
> The referee finally realized that the entire event was a bit like watching a movie when the sound track is not synchronized with the lip movements of the actors and the sound effects do not correspond to the action in the film. The students' response was belated relative to the activities, but the enthusiasm and energy were even greater than at an ordinary wrestling match. It was an exciting event.

Students with sensory impairment do enjoy and learn through motor activity. With appropriate equipment and environmental modification any activity is possible for them. They need a chance and someone to care. Blind and deaf athletes compete in skiing, swimming, bowling, sailing, football, basketball, even golf.

Cardiac and respiratory disorders

Over 20 million Americans have some form of cardiac disorder, and many of them are of school age. The causes of cardiac malfunctioning include congenital defects, rheumatic heart disease, and hypertension. The important characteristic of cardiac disorder is the degree of incapacity associated with the problem. For some individuals, no restrictions on physical activity are necessary. For others—who will not attend school—total bed rest is required. The physical education teacher should insist on a proper activity prescription from a physician before initiating an activity plan for students with cardiac disorders. The teacher should also inform the physician of the relative strenuousness of various activities in his or her program. For example, some physicians may not consider swimming strenuous because they only swim recreationally; they may not realize that swimming in a school program involves an aerobic effect as part of an interval training program.

Asthma, the most common disease of childhood, is characterized by wheezing, coughing, rapid breathing, and obviously an interruption of activity during an attack. The teacher should know that excessive physical activity and fatigue may precipitate an attack.

Cystic fibrosis is a hereditary disorder that is incurable and leads to early death. Breathing is complicated by the excess production of mucus. Children with cystic fibrosis rarely come to school in earlier years, but improved medical practices continue to increase life expectancy and the quality of life for such youth and they will continue to appear in school programs.

Activity relative to the individual degree of handicap is appropriate for students with a cardiac disorder, asthma, or cystic fibrosis. Most of these people have been overprotected and denied the opportunity to develop appropriate skills or fitness levels. Many are on medication, and it is vital that the teacher learn from the physician the effect exercise may have relative to the medication.

Neurological and muscular disorders

Common neurological and muscular disorders include epilepsy and cerebral palsy. Epilepsy involves spontaneous isometric contractions of modest (petit mal) or massive proportions (grand mal). With the former, an individual may suffer a cessation of mental processes, minor twitching, and/or a loss of motor control for a period of not more than 30 seconds. With the latter, an individual may suffer a total loss of motor control, massive jerking and twitching, falling, perhaps loss of bladder control, and self-injury as a result of biting the tongue. The seizures can occur at any time and are frightening to observers and embarrassing to those afflicted, particularly adolescents. For many, it is a devastating disability.

SAILING COUNSELOR   Jan, you *must* wear a life jacket when you're in a boat even though you have a partner with you.

JAN   Even if I am only 14 I'm the best sailor in this camp—you know that. It's too hot to wear a life jacket.

SAILING COUNSELOR   You agreed to wear the jacket—it's for your safety regardless of how well you sail or ski or canoe.

JAN   You make me wear a jacket even in a rowboat, in the cove, 100 feet from the dock, and I'm an expert swimmer.

SAILING COUNSELOR   Everyone wears a jacket sailing and skiing in the lake. You wear one at all times in a boat, and you must always be with a partner because of your condition. That's our agreement.

JAN   My condition! I haven't had a seizure in three years; it's stupid to embarrass me.

SAILING COUNSELOR   You're still on medication. The doctor says precautions are necessary. You're making this worse than it is and only drawing more attention to the matter. No jacket—no boating!

JAN   Stinking rule, lousy place!

This is not an unusual reaction for epileptic adolescents. No activity is precluded, but precautions are absolutely necessary. A seizure can mean loss of motor control, falling, even drowning.

Cerebral palsy is a motor disorder caused by a brain dysfunction. In its most common form it produces unwanted movements, the appearance of spasticity, and the loss of gross and fine motor control. In extreme cases it leads to contractures, loss of joint movement, and paralysis of one or more parts of the body. It is the most common disabling condition among school-age youth (Sherrill 1976, 479).

Activities for epileptics are unlimited provided sufficient safety controls are in place to protect the individual if he or she is stricken with a seizure. People with cerebral palsy benefit greatly from learning motor skills. Again, however, the program must be patterned to their degree of disability. In almost every instance, the most effective technique involves training to eliminate unwanted movements via repetition and simple, slow exercises. We should also note that although people with cerebral palsy may demonstrate facial contortions, speech difficulties, body disfigurations, and strange movements, they are not necessarily mentally retarded.

Multiple handicaps

Some students may have more than one handicapping condition. For example, an individual may have learning and visual deficits or retardation in association with cerebral palsy or a physical handicap. In this case the teacher should usually combine the instructional strategy for each of the handicapping conditions.

Finally, we should note that the degree of appreciation expressed by students with multiple handicaps often exceeds that of the average student. Working with handicapped students therefore becomes an exceptionally rewarding experience for the teacher.

Effective techniques for teaching students with special needs

We implied in the preceding section that disabled young people usually participate in the regular physical education class rather than or in addition to a specially adapted physical education class. However, it is necessary to modify your teaching and their activities. Here are some suggestions for doing this:

1. Shorten time periods.
2. Shorten distances.
3. Change the types of signals.
4. Use guide wires, ground surfaces with different sounding textures, handrails, and similar devices.
5. Soften landing sports with mats.
6. Allow two hands instead of one where accuracy or power is involved.
7. Change the rules so that they do not contain as many limiting conditions that lessen success.
8. Lower nets, baskets.
9. Increase the size of striking implements and targets.
10. Increase or decrease the size of the projectile, such as the ball, discus, or javelin.

(French and Jansma 1982)

To involve handicapped and nonhandicapped students in a combined activity, use the following tactics:

1. Give different roles to the special student.
   Examples: a blind person paddles a canoe in the bow, and the person in the stern steers; a person with one leg plays first base in softball.
2. Assign different tasks to the special student.
   Examples: a cardiopathic student bats but does not run the bases; a paraplegic performs on the parallel bars and horse but not the vault.
3. Provide equipment that facilitates the task or role of the special student.
   Examples: provide larger bats, smaller balls, lighter weights, ramps for bowling.
4. Make the activity easier for the special student.
   Examples: increase the size of the serving area in tennis; permit returns to doubles boundaries rather than singles boundaries.
5. Ensure the safety of the special student.
   Examples: employ a partner system; use extra mats.

(adapted from Jansma and Wyatt 1977)

You may have to adjust environmental factors such as lighting, acoustics, water temperature, ventilation, and architectural features when teaching classes that include handicapped students.

You also need to avoid certain strategies. (1) Do not spread talent unequally between or among teams because of the special student. (2) Do not assign the disabled student continuous scoring or officiating functions. (3) Do not continually conduct elimination activities.

For a listing of agencies and publications available to assist the teacher with special students, see the Appendix, "Resources for Recreation and Competitive Sports for Students with Special Needs."

Summary

As the result of Americans' philosophical concern for those with exceptional needs, Congress has passed legislation, including Public Law 94-142, that defines the responsibilities of schools and teachers to handicapped students. Concepts such as mainstreaming, least restrictive environment, zero reject, and progressive inclusion, as well as the Individual Education Program (I.E.P.) are the result.

Among the disabling conditions of students with special needs are mental retardation, emotional disorders, hearing and visual impairment, neurological and muscular disorders, and cardiorespiratory disorders. It is imperative that physical education teachers work with the successful portion of these students' lives and assist them in such areas as strength development, stamina improvement, and self-directed leisure and sports skills within the parameters of their disabilities.

Happily, disabled young people generally participate in regular physical education classes rather than special ones. Combined groups of handicapped and nonhandicapped students require modification of teaching strategies and class activities. However, the teaching rewards—like the students—can be exceptional. Many agencies and individuals are available to assist the teacher in working with handicapped students.

Suggested activities

1. Arrange to meet one child from a local agency for exceptional children and to spend the day with this child. The day may include attending a sporting event, eating, talking, attending a class, and so on. Discuss the day's happenings with your classmates.
2. Discuss in class the educational consequences of preparing an I.E.P. for all schoolchildren, not just those with handicaps.
3. Attend a sports event involving handicapped young people. Record your observations and discuss them with the class.
4. Prepare a plan of activities for a physical education class of 25 middle school students, including one youngster in a wheelchair and one who is partially sighted.
5. Draw up a list of special teaching tactics to supplement those presented in this chapter. Share your list with classmates.

Part Two

Traditional and Alternative Models for Participation

8

Developing a Program Philosophy

The purpose of this chapter is to describe the potential scope of the physical education program, to examine various goals to which programs can be devoted, and to explain how the goals are brought to life through the curriculum. Here we analyze important issues to consider when developing a program and discuss the ways in which program elements can be combined in a total curriculum. Finally, we present and explain the language and concepts of curriculum development.

The major topics in this chapter are as follows:

The scope of the physical education program, including in-class and extraclass opportunities

The four important issues to consider when adopting program goals

The factors that contribute to the definition of a program once goals are defined

The process factors that enhance or limit goal achievement within a program

Ways to build a program from components

The language and concepts of curriculum building in schools

SCENE   BETH *and* MARY, *two young women who live in the same neighborhood, are at the community recreation center. This morning* BETH *introduced* MARY *to the beginning skills of racquetball, and then the two friends had a swim together.*

MARY   Gee, Beth, I'm worn out, and I didn't do half of what you did today. You're really in good shape.

BETH   If you'd come here regularly with me, you'd be in good shape in no time. I've done this regularly for so long now that a game of racquetball and a swim don't bother me at all; what does bother me is *not* getting a good workout!

MARY   You come here a lot, don't you?

BETH   Yes, it's one of the reasons we chose this area to live in. I wanted a place that I could get to regularly for both exercise and some organized competitions. The last place we lived had a terrific family YMCA program, but this rec center has even more.

MARY   Have you always been such a good athlete? What did they call you in high school, "Beth the superstar"?

BETH   No, not at all. Actually, I never was on any of the school teams, even though I was in high school when I became active on a regular basis.

MARY   But if you weren't on the school teams, how did you become so interested in sports and fitness?

BETH   You know, Mary, I've thought about that, and I guess we just had a very good physical education program. I know I learned a lot in the PE classes. And I was on an intramural team of one kind or another almost all the time. When I was a junior I joined the ski club, and when I was a senior I took a special elective course in fitness. I guess what I learned best was to want to participate regularly. And at least at my school, you could learn that and do it without being one of the top school athletes.

MARY   That doesn't sound like my PE program. The thing I remember most about high school PE was the awful uniforms they made us wear. And I hated the dirty showers and never had time to dry my hair. It was the pits! I don't think anybody took PE who didn't absolutely have to—except the jocks, of course.

BETH   It sounds like your program was as bad as mine was good. Maybe if you'd had a program like mine, you would've become a regular participant too.

Programs do make a difference

Physical education programs do have their effects! Sometimes, as in Beth's case, the effects are strong, positive, and lasting. At other times, as in Mary's case, the effects are also strong and lasting, but they are predominantly negative. Physical educators need to think seriously about what kinds of effects their programs have on students and how they can ensure that those effects are achieved with as many students as possible. In this chapter we explore the issues involved in developing programs in which students have strong, lasting, positive experiences.

The scope of the physical education program

There is a tendency to think only of the regular class structure as the total physical education program. Our notion of a program goes well beyond this important but limited component (see Figure 3.4). A program consists of *all* of the opportunities for participation in sports and fitness activities that a school provides its students. Instructional classes may occupy a central position in the program. But in many states, physical education is required only through the tenth grade. Does that mean there is no physical education program for eleventh- and twelfth-grade students? We hope not.

A school physical education program consists of instructional classes, intramurals, drop-in recreation opportunities, sports clubs, and varsity sports. The program operates within the school and also extends into the community. The program operates during the regular school day, after school, weekends, and vacation periods. The separate components of a program should not be viewed as discrete elements that bear no relationship to one another. This chapter is about a *program* philosophy. The implication is clear. The entire program must be devoted to achieving specified goals, and the various components within the program must be interrelated if the goals are to be achieved.

Surely the volleyball class that meets daily at 10:00 A.M. is an important part of the physical education program. Indeed, it probably represents the cornerstone of most programs. But a class curriculum, in and of itself, is not sufficient to accomplish all that physical education can and should accomplish in the education of youth. A noon-hour aerobics session, open to any faculty and students who want to attend, is also a program component. A weekend canoe trip, preparation for which may have taken place at the school site, is also a program component. A weekly evening ski session at a ski resort 25 miles from the community can also be a component. For many students, the interscholastic sports program is a component of major significance in their lives. For others, the intramural softball league may have a different, yet equally important meaning. The members of the strength club or the archery club may argue that their participation is of central importance. The point is that *together* the effects of these varied experiences constitute a real program influence on the lives of students. That is what a good program is all about.

With this notion of a program, it is clear that the role of the physical educator extends well beyond teaching. Teaching well is of great importance, and we have devoted several chapters in Part III to the skills that define effective

To develop good PE programs, physical educators must organize activities.

teaching. However, the scope of a total program in physical education also requires that the physical educator be an *organizer of activities*. Physical education teachers must prepare well for their classes, but much of what teachers do to develop a total program does not involve teaching. Instead, it involves the development, organization, and implementation of opportunities for students to participate. This role of organizer of good opportunities for participation is a key role if the total program is to be successful. It involves a set of skills that are quite different from teaching/coaching skills. It requires good administrative skills, proper planning, careful attention to details such as liability and safety issues, and strong, sound promotional skills. These issues are addressed in Chapters 4, 15, 17, and 22.

To what goals should a program be devoted?

Is there one set of goals to which all physical education programs should be devoted? The discussion in Chapter 3 (see pages 36–39) indicated that many different, yet seemingly valid goals have been suggested for schools. Diversity has been a tradition in American schools, and it is often cited as one of the system's greatest strengths. Someday, laypeople and professionals may come to an agreement on a common agenda for physical education in all schools. But that day is a long way off, and until it happens, physical education will continue to strive for a diverse set of goals.

We cannot and will not suggest to you what *your* goals should be. We will try to bring to your attention crucial issues about goals that you should consider no matter what goals you adopt for a physical education program.

Goals derive from beliefs. Goals are broad statements of intent that describe the kinds of outcomes that a program strives to achieve. Therefore, the first step in developing goals is to clarify important beliefs relative to students, the school, and the subject matter of physical education. We set forth our beliefs in Chapter 2 in order to clarify the basis from which we developed our perspectives. We also did this to stimulate your examination and clarification.

The physical educator must carefully consider four important issues when attempting to develop goals for a physical education program: (1) an emphasis on outcomes, (2) commitments to both equity and quality, (3) doing a few things well, and (4) socializing students into the role of participant.

Programs should demonstrate outcomes

Physical education cannot long survive as a school subject unless it can demonstrate tangible outcomes. Tangible outcomes are that students will be more fit, be able to shoot more arrows into a target, be able to rappel down a cliff, be able to lift more weight, be able to play soccer better, know more about football strategy, understand team play in basketball better, and be more eager to participate in activities as a result of the program. Somehow the experience

---

DON'T BE GUILTY OF PHYSICAL MIS-EDUCATION!

John Dewey has been the most important American educational philosopher of the twentieth century. Dewey argued that growth was the best way to judge whether any educational experience was valuable. *Growth*, in Dewey's philosophy, means that (1) an activity must be considered valuable and (2) the experience must lead to further experiences. A good educational experience, then, is one in which students participate in a valuable activity and the nature of the experience is such that students want to do more in the future.

If an educational experience is handled in such a manner that students do not want to do more, then it is not a growth-enhancing experience and not educational. In fact, Dewey described such experiences as "mis-educative." He recognized that many school experiences distort and arrest growth rather than enhance it.

Certainly, we all know of schools where students are required to engage in what can only be called physical mis-education! The programs in these schools turn students off to sport and fitness rather than turn them on.

Robert Mager, an educational technologist, took the Dewey notion and developed it more fully. He suggested that the *universal objective* of education is to treat students in a way that produces subject-matter approach tendencies rather than subject-matter avoidance tendencies. In this text, we have translated these ideas into an emphasis on helping students to learn to become regular participants.

---

in physical education has to *change the student*. We assume, of course, that the changes are positive (see above box).

We do not view "having fun during PE class" as a legitimate outcome! We are certainly not against having fun. Indeed, a long-term commitment to participation is impossible unless the participant derives satisfaction along the way. However, we rebel against the notion that having fun is, in and of itself, sufficient to justify physical education. Students can have fun without learning anything. Physical education can become a loosely supervised recreation period—a kind of recess grown up! In the long run, students tire of these kinds of programs and do not value them as learning experiences. Instead, students should learn the fun of being more skilled, the fun of being a better player, and the fun of being more fit.

Programs should be committed to equity and quality

We believe that equity and quality must always be considered together. A quality program for just a few students may be nice, but it doesn't fulfill the mission of education in a free society. Treating students equitably is nice too, but it does not mean much if all students have equal access to an inferior program. Equity, of course, does not necessarily mean that we should treat all students in the same way. The notion of equity implies that we will treat some students a bit differently from others because their needs are different. Equity means that we should provide all students with equal access to facilities, equipment, instruction, and participation.

One way of treating students equitably is to provide *quality* experiences for them. The less skilled students should have a quality experience at their level. In fact, in order for such students to move from being less skilled to becoming more skilled, they *have to have* quality educational experiences.

A quality experience also implies that students are held accountable for their performance. While teachers cannot demand as much of weak students as of strong students, that does not mean that teachers should place no demands on weak students. By modifying activities to fit the skill and fitness status of students, teachers can demand that all students improve and begin to achieve their potential in physical education. When teachers motivate all students to improve and stretch their potential, both equity and quality are achieved.

Programs are likely to achieve more by doing fewer things

It is difficult to achieve any important goals in a six-lesson unit. The skills and strategies of sport and fitness are not easily achieved. It takes time to improve sports skills. It takes time to learn group strategies. It takes time to learn the traditions and rituals associated with various games. It takes time to become more fit. Too many physical education programs try to accomplish too much in the sense that they seem to be forever *introducing* or *exposing* students to a different activity. With this strategy, students seldom get beyond the introduction stage. They seldom learn to be good players or to experience what it feels like to be fit.

Chapter 9 details the issues involved in developing a good multiactivity program. Generally speaking, programs tend to accomplish more when fewer activities are taught more thoroughly. However, no magic number of days, lessons, or weeks is "right." The best length of time for a unit depends upon the prior experiences of the students and the teaching skills of the physical educator. Many teachers suggest that long units in physical education are boring. The truth is that students often get bored because they get no instruction beyond the very basic fundamentals. Volleyball is not a boring game. Nevertheless, the way it is sometimes taught in short units, over and over again, can create boredom.

Programs should socialize students into the role of participant

We have already argued that achieving specific program outcomes is an important ingredient in building a successful physical education effort in middle, junior, and senior high schools and that participation is crucial to the achievement of outcomes. More specifically, students must learn the role of being a participant (Bain 1980). To be a regular participant in sports and fitness activities means to acquire the skills, knowledge, and strategies associated with the activities. It also means learning to value the rituals and

Activities during nonattached time can be fun and contribute to program goals.

traditions associated with the activities. Learning a *role* means that students begin more and more to see themselves as a certain kind of person, in this case a person who participates regularly in sports and fitness activities (like Beth in the opening pages of this chapter).

Regular participant is not the only role that can be learned in sport and fitness. Another role is elite performer and still another is spectator. The latter two roles are also learned, and although each has its place, neither is the role that the physical education program should strive to teach to its students. Research strongly supports the commonsense notion that young people who participate regularly and receive encouragement and support for participation tend to continue their involvement as adults. The family and community are major factors in this early socialization, but *so too can be the school program*.

Factors contributing to program definition

Most course requirements in schools, such as those for physical education, are determined at the state level. The actual program that a school provides is typically developed within a combination of influences and reflects national, regional, state, and local concerns. The purpose of this section is to describe some of those influences (Siedentop 1983; Taylor 1980).

Students

Who are the students being taught? Did they have a strong elementary physical education program? Are they fit? Do they have ample access to certain activities in the community? Are there many mainstreamed students? Are there special problems resulting from bilingualism, substantially different ethnic backgrounds, or racial composition? How many students take part regularly in the interscholastic program? What kinds of activities did they learn as children in the community?

The answers to these questions and others like them provide important information for building a sound physical education program. The program should be responsive to the specific needs of local students and to the differences among local students. It should both supplement and reinforce what occurs in the community.

Community

Community support for fitness and sports education differs tremendously from place to place. Community factors often influence school programs. To ignore the values and attitudes of the local community is a serious error. Teachers need the support of the community to develop a truly important program, especially parts of the program that are extended beyond the school and utilize nonschool personnel and facilities (see Chapter 4).

Some communities have well-developed emphases on aquatics, gymnastics, or soccer. Others have more balanced programs. Still others have never had a really good school program. Teachers need to consider these historical factors as they try to slowly develop a new program from the old or decide to break with the local tradition and recommend an entirely different effort.

Facilities and equipment

Facilities and equipment greatly affect program development and implementation. Unfortunately, they are also used far too often as an excuse for *not* doing something! The professional literature in physical education is full of examples of what energetic, creative professionals have done to develop and implement programs *despite* the lack of either natural or manufactured facilities. Climbing and rappelling walls can be built in schools where no mountains or cliffs are nearby. Expensive, high-technology strength development machines are nice, but a sound strength facility can be developed with far less money. Inadequate or old facilities can be modified to accommodate different activities. Likewise, activities can be modified so that they can be conducted with less than optimal facilities.

Professional trends

At the moment *fitness* is "in" with the general adult population. Several decades ago there was a major emphasis in professional physical education in *lifetime sports*. More recently, university physical education programs have had much success by offering courses in the *martial arts*. At all levels school programs are now beginning to offer more experience in *wilderness sports*. Each of these is indicative of a trend in professional physical education. Such trends are important, and teachers should consider them in program planning and development. Information on a currently popular activity is plentiful and can help one in teaching, developing, and preparing facilities for the activity. This information can help the teacher to include the activity even though he or she may not have ever learned it or performed it.

Personal interests

You are or will soon be a practicing professional educator; as such, you have a right to interject *your* points of view in the development and implementation of a school program. Teachers teach better and remain more enthused about programs when the programs reflect their interests and skills. Few things in professional life are more deadly than having to implement a program in which the teacher has little interest or skill.

Physical educators have too often felt a traditional obligation to offer all imaginable activities to all students in one program. In this tradition, teachers inevitably end up teaching short units in activities for which they are unprepared and uninterested. This lack of skill and interest is sometimes communicated to the student—the result of which is too predictable.

Teachers can and often do teach new activities for which they have little formal preparation, and they do so with enthusiasm. Few physical educators have had extensive preparation in team handball, fencing, or many wilderness sports. Yet they often teach units in these activities, teach them very well and with tremendous response from students.

There is no simple equation for bringing together the factors of student background, community issues, professional trends, and personal interests. Nonetheless, they are important to keep in mind as you read about the different program models described in subsequent chapters of Part II. You may want to adopt some or all of the models. You may want to modify one or more of them so that they better fit your specific situation. Or you may want to choose just one model and develop it fully for your entire program.

Process factors: Building in success

Sometimes programs fail not because the activities are wrong or poorly taught but because other aspects of the experience are so negative that students simply reject the entire program. Remember that a goal of all programs should be to teach students how to be participants and to teach them to want to be participants. This goal requires that process factors in the program contribute to program success and a positive program image among students, administrators, and parents.

As suggested on page 133, we should teach physical education in such a way that students develop approach tendencies toward physical education and toward sports and fitness activities in general. *Approach tendencies* are simply ways in which students behave that indicate that they enjoy, appreciate, and are interested in sports and fitness activities. Students are absent less often. They come to class early. They sign up for elective courses. They join intramural teams. They belong to sports clubs. They behave enthusiastically in class. All of these are behavioral indicators of approach tendencies. Avoidance tendencies have the opposite kinds of behavioral indicators, and we are all too familiar with them (absences, tardiness, poor behavior, griping, etc.).

Approach tendencies are developed gradually through good teaching and through a program in which there are high expectations and a great deal of support for students and in which many different kinds of success are achieved and recognized. Much of the material in Chapters 19 and 20 is relevant to these issues. Students should be treated in positive ways. Activities should be modified to meet student abilities. Success should be openly supported in a number of different ways, from the teacher's verbal reactions to formal recognition through awards. These strategies taken together create a positive climate within which students will grow, prosper, and eventually begin to see themselves as lifelong participants.

Other process factors that need to be considered are the locker room, shower, and dress arrangements within a program. As noted in Chapter 5, adolescent students are concerned about their appearance, often adopt a style of dress that sets them apart from others, and are very much involved in peer relationships. The physical educator should consider these concerns when developing a program.

Too often the physical education locker room is the dingiest place in the school. Too often students have only three to six minutes to shower, dress, and return to the school halls and other classrooms. The shower facilities themselves are often messy and unattractive. The physical education locker room does not have to be a country club, but it does not have to be a dungeon either. Students should also have the time they need to shower, change their clothes, and go on to other pursuits. *These factors have an impact on how students view physical education.* It does no good for adults to say that these factors should not matter so much. They do! And we must consider them if the program is to have a positive overall impact. On the other hand, students have an obligation to treat the facilities properly.

The same is true for dress. What do students most universally dislike about physical education? Typically, the answer is "those crummy uniforms we're forced to wear." One is never quite sure whether it is the uniform that causes the negative reaction or the fact that the uniform is required. Regardless, we would do well to have a student group help to choose a uniform for physical education if one is required. Or it would be useful to consider some *rules* about the types of shoes, shorts, shirts, and other items that are required but to allow students flexibility within those rules.

Students develop approach tendencies more quickly if they view a program as important. However they will not do this unless the teachers and school view the program as important. Ultimately, of course, students will not view a program as important unless *it is important*. The entire program effort must convey a sense of high expectations—for achievement, for enjoyment, and for effort.

If a program is to be important, then there must also be accountability. Adolescent students have already learned that when something important is happening, there is more likely to be accountability. Along with accountability, there must also be fairness and equity. That is, it must be an important program for *all* students, not just the best students and not just the athletes.

The major impetus for program importance must come from those who develop and implement the program. If they do not behave as if the program is important, why should anyone else? This sense of importance is made evident in a number of ways. Teaching must be prompt, vigorous, and effective. The places where the program is conducted (the gym, the fields, the pool, the weight rooms) must be attractive and conducive to an important effort. There must be frequent recognition of accomplishment. All of these things convey to students the sense that what is going on in these places really counts for something!

Finally, the importance of the program must be made clear to others—to faculty, to administrators, to parents, and to the community. These are the important *publics* to which the program must be explained and promoted. The materials in Chapter 22 are particularly relevant to this task.

Building a program from models

The remaining chapters in Part II describe several alternative models for physical education in middle, junior, and senior high schools. Each chapter contains a brief description of the model, a rationale for it, and examples of how it is implemented in various schools and at various levels. Many physical education staffs may want to combine several of these models as components in a total physical education program. The major models described are as follows:

- The traditional *multiactivity* model in which students take (either required or elective) a series of units aimed at accomplishing a varied set of fitness, skill, knowledge, and social goals. This model is described in Chapter 9.

- A *fitness* model whose major goals are strength and endurance fitness, particularly related to lifelong fitness. This model is described in Chapter 10.

- A *sports education* model in which students are organized into teams and have scheduled competitions in ways similar to the interscholastic program. This model is described in Chapter 11.

- An *adventure program* model in which students pursue wilderness activities and the program is extended into the community. This model is described in Chapter 12.

- A *social development* model in which personal growth and self-responsibility are the primary goals and activity goals are less important. This model is described in Chapter 13.

- A *concepts* model in which knowledge (of how to do and why to do) goals are foremost and a lecture-laboratory method is utilized. This model is described in Chapter 14.

- The *nonattached time* elements of intramurals, clubs, and drop-in recreation. These are described in Chapter 15.

Chapter 16 focuses on a few schools in which physical education is of *extra importance* to some or all of the students. In these schools you can begin to see the potential that physical education has in the education of youth.

We also want to make it clear that solid, successful school programs can be developed on the basis of only one of the models. In fact, each of the following chapters in this part of the text describes each model as if it were the only model utilized for the entire physical education program. The point is that whatever is done should be done well. Nonetheless, most physical educators believe that physical education is a tremendously varied field in which activity can contribute in many different ways to the education of youth. For people who hold this belief, a more varied program will be necessary to accomplish the broader range of goals. These people can develop a useful program by simply combining several of the models described in the following chapters.

The component approach to program development (using several models as components in a total program) can be used at one level (the junior high school, for example) or as a unifying theme to bring the total physical education effort together for a school district. Consider the following program as an illustration.

Junior High School

Seventh grade: physical education required for two terms	Term 1 Concepts model focusing on fitness and nutrition.
	Term 2 Sports education model with emphasis on team sports.
Eighth grade: physical education required for one term with health the other term	Term 1 Health.
	Term 2 Adventure skills program with a weekend trip.

High School

Ninth grade: physical education required for two terms	Term 1 Fitness model focusing on endurance and strength.
	Term 2 Sports education model with choice of team or individual sport.
Tenth grade: physical education required for two terms	Both terms are elective, and students can choose among fitness, adventure skills, and sports education opportunities.

| Eleventh and twelfth grades: no required physical education | Students are offered an elective program focusing on advanced instruction but for participation are programmed into clubs and intramurals. Regular drop-in activity time is available. |

This program uses four of the models described in the following chapters. The concepts model introduces students to fitness and nutrition in the seventh grade. This is followed up with a required fitness program in the first term of the ninth grade. Students are then given the option of pursuing fitness as an elective in the tenth grade and in clubs or on a drop-in basis during the eleventh and twelfth grades. Sports education is introduced in the second term of the seventh grade and appears again in the second term of the ninth grade, but this time with a choice between team and individual sports. Sports enthusiasts can join clubs, receive advanced instruction, or participate in intramurals and drop-in activity during the eleventh and twelfth grades. Adventure skills are included in the total program in a similar way.

Notice that the multiactivity model and the social development model are not used at all and the concepts model is used only as an introductory technique early in the program. Does that mean these models are less useful? No! It means only that the illustration reinforces the notion that programs should focus on fewer components and do them well; the social development model could easily have been substituted for the adventure skills model. We purposely avoided showing you a total program in which *all* models were utilized.

How much each program should try to accomplish depends on a number of factors, some of which we have already discussed. How adequate are the school facilities? How adequate are the community opportunities? How easy is it for students to get from school to the community sites? Do students have to catch buses right after school? Is the school district willing to provide supplementary compensation for faculty leadership in intramurals, clubs, and drop-in recreation? What is the state law regarding physical education? What support is there for going beyond the requirements of the state law with an elective program? *How motivated are the physical education teachers to build a program that really counts?* The answers to these questions will provide the background information for making decisions about how much a program can accomplish.

Our advice is straightforward: Use one component at a time and use it well. Start with a fitness term, or an adventure skills term, or any one of the models for that matter. But use it well. Use it in a way that will make students, faculty, and administrators recognize immediately that something important is happening. When that component of the program is in place and operating smoothly, then add another component. The addition of the second component will be easier. First of all, you will have been through the process once. Second, the program will have gained some acceptance within the school and be likely to get more support. Third, the students will have become excited and responsive to the program and more responsible toward it. Success builds success.

Curriculum: Its language and concepts

When teachers think about curriculum, it is most often in terms of a *course of study*. There is a biology curriculum, a mathematics curriculum, and a physical education curriculum. The focus of the curriculum is what goes on in the formal class structure of the school day. Perusal of a *curriculum guide* for a school district will reveal what that district expects will happen in the formal class structure of a particular subject.

Language of curriculum

We have already made the case for thinking about a total program rather than focusing only on instructional classes. We have avoided using the term *curriculum* simply because to so many people it is a term limited to the class program. But it does not need to be so limited. Indeed, as the following examples indicate, most current views of curriculum are quite similar to what we have described as a program.

> The curriculum is all of the learning of students which is planned by and directed by the school to attain its educational goals.
> Ralph Tyler, 1957

> The curriculum is now generally considered to be all of the experiences that learners have under the auspices of the school.
> Ronald Doll, 1970

> Curriculum is concerned not with what students will do in the learning situation, but with what they will learn as a consequence of what they do. Curriculum is concerned with results.
> Mauritz Johnson, 1971

> Curriculum is the planned learning experiences that a school presents to its students in order to socialize them into the prevailing culture.
> Leo Anglin, Jr., Richard Goldman, and Joyce Anglin, 1982

These points of view suggest that (1) the curriculum includes both in-class and out-of-class activities, (2) the activities are planned and directed to some purpose, and (3) outcomes are important to the definition of a particular curriculum.

This comprehensive view of curriculum (or program as we have chosen to call it) leaves no room for what used to be called extracurricular activities. An *extracurricular* activity was one that was outside the bounds of the formal instructional class program. Thus, school sports, intramurals, band, drama club, and other important school activities were considered to be *extra* to the main function of the curriculum. As such, they were seldom considered when teachers, administrators, and other interested parties met to consider curriculum issues.

Recently, the term *extracurricular* has been replaced by *cocurricular*, and even though the latter elevates certain activities to a more important status, they are seldom considered to be part of the *real* curriculum, that is, to what goes on in the regular instructional classes. These terms are counterproductive to the goal of viewing all planned school experiences as part of the curriculum. What goes on in a drama club, in the school band, or on a sports team is of major importance to the participants. It deserves to be considered just as fully and as contributing to the same overall goals as regular instructional classes.

Writing curricula has become an important part of the teacher's ongoing responsibility. Writing revised curricula can be a way of effecting important change in a school program. However, we would be less than honest if we did not admit that it often is simply a ritual, the result of which is a new document for the district but nothing new for the students. Regardless, it is imperative that physical education teachers be reasonably familiar with the major concepts used in developing or revising a curriculum.

Major curricular concepts

An *educational goal* is a broad overall statement of outcomes. Perhaps the most famous goals in American education were the 1918 goals defined by the Commission on the Reorganization of Secondary Education and known as the Seven Cardinal Principles: (1) health, (2) command of fundamental processes, (3) worthy use of leisure, (4) worthy home membership, (5) vocation, (6) citizenship, and (7) ethical character.

School district curricula begin with the goals the district has established for its students. These goals are typically too broad to provide sufficient direction for practice so they are given more substance by the establishment of general objectives. A *general objective* is a statement that is more specific than a goal and defines the activities that are thought to lead to the achievement of a goal. For example, if a district has the development of leisure skills as a goal, then a general objective related to that goal might be "students acquire a variety of sport skills."

General objectives provide direction for curriculum developers, but they are still too broad for evaluation purposes. Thus, a more *specific objective* is usually written to provide the clarity and specificity needed to decide what will go on and how it will be evaluated. Specific objectives are often written as behavioral objectives. *Behavioral objectives* state a learner activity in behavioral terms, describe the situation in which the activity will take place, and provide the criteria for evaluating success in the activity. This *situation-behavior-criteria* formula has become the standard method for defining specific objectives. (Goals, objectives, and task analysis strategies are discussed at greater length in Chapter 18.)

The specific objectives in a curriculum define the activities that will be utilized to achieve the general objective, which in turn contributes to goal realization. The amount that is taught in any given curriculum defines its *scope*. The arrangement of the various activities within the school year and across all school years defines its *sequence*. Scope and sequence projects are now common tasks for teachers. When both the scope and sequence of the curriculum have been defined, the curriculum developers are in position to produce a *graded course of study*.

If a graded course of study is developed with specific criteria that students need to achieve for the objectives at each level of the sequential curriculum, then it can be described as a *mastery curriculum*. The notion is that students must demonstrate certain abilities before moving on to new learning. The specification of explicit criteria that students should meet also provides administrators and teachers with a mutually agreeable means of evaluating program accomplishment. These specific objectives are often written as *competencies*, and the resulting evaluation takes the form of *competency testing*. Approaches to curriculum that emphasize mastery or competency models are part of a growing force in education most often referred to as the curriculum-accountability movement.

If *curriculum* refers to the planned experiences in schools, then how does one account for the many things students learn that are unplanned? This portion of school learning is most often described as the *hidden curriculum*.

EDUCATIONESE IS ALIVE AND WELL IN CURRICULUM DEVELOPMENT

In developing and promoting curriculum, educators sometimes slip into *educationese*, a language that is unknown to those outside the education profession. Recently, the parent of a high school student in Houston received a message from school announcing a special meeting about a newly proposed curriculum. The message read as follows.

> Our school's cross-graded, multi-ethnic, individualized learning program is designed to enhance the concept of an open-ended learning program with emphasis on a continuum of multi-ethnic, academically enriched learning using the identified intellectually gifted child as the agent or director of his own learning. Major emphasis is on cross-graded, multi-ethnic learning with the main objective being to learn respect for the uniqueness of a person.

The parent was so bewildered and angered by the jargon employed that the following note was sent to the school principal.

> I have a college degree, speak two foreign languages and four Indian dialects, have been to a number of county fairs and three goat ropings, but I haven't the faintest idea as to what the hell you are talking about. Do you?

SOURCE: Wiles, J., and J. Bondi. *Curriculum Development: A Guide to Practice.* Columbus, Ohio: Charles Merrill, 1979, p. 228.

Researchers have been particularly interested in sorting out the hidden curriculum of schools in terms of sex roles, racial stereotypes, competition, and other values that students tend to acquire in school but are not part of the formal agenda of the school. The hidden curriculum in a physical education program teaches values relative to important issues such as motor elitism, sports for girls, fairness in competition, ethical behavior in sport, risk, and relationship to authority. The formal program often teaches views on these issues too, but the program in action provides a powerful informal message to students. Physical educators need to examine their programs in practice to determine the degree to which the hidden curriculum promotes an agenda that is different from or similar to the formal agenda stated in the graded course of study.

Summary

A program consists of all of the opportunities for participation in sports and fitness activities that a school provides its students. The physical educator is the organizer of those opportunities and should utilize the instructional program, nonattached time, on-campus and off-campus programs, sports clubs, intramurals, and other opportunities to provide a total, coherent program.

When developing a program philosophy, physical educators should emphasize outcomes, focus on commitments to equity and quality, decide what things can be done well within the potential resource base, and make sure that the program will socialize students into the role of participants. These four features should be common to all physical education programs no matter what philosophy undergirds a particular program.

As a program philosophy is developed, physical educators should make sure that the philosophy and the program derived from it take into account the students served by the program, the nature of the community from which the students come, the facilities and equipment available (or capable of being developed), trends in sports and fitness education, and the personal interests and skills of the physical education teachers.

Programs often succeed or fail not only because of the substantive nature of the activities but also because of process factors such as the success orientation of the teaching, uniform requirements, and locker room conditions. These factors influence adolescent attitudes toward physical education and the activities themselves. The goal should be to increase the students' approach tendencies toward physical education; however, that cannot be accomplished if process factors are ignored.

Physical education programs can be built from the several models described in the following chapters in this part of the text. Programs can focus on one of many models. The component approach (using several models as components of a total program) is useful to unify a program within a school or as a means of ensuring total program coherence within a school district.

Teachers are inevitably involved in curriculum design and redesign. A knowledge of the language and concepts of curriculum is therefore basic to successful teaching.

Suggested activities

1. Develop a list of program goals in priority order and discuss it in class.
2. After the instructor assigns you one process factor, develop a plan for making that factor a positive force in a school physical education program.
3. Develop an in-class list of local constraints to building good physical education programs in area schools. Then discuss how those constraints might be overcome.
4. Debate the following issue: Physical education programs will achieve more if they attempt to do fewer things. Have three students argue the affirmative and three the negative.
5. Describe your view of what constitutes a *quality* physical education experience for an adolescent student. Discuss the similarities and differences in the various views of other members of the class.

9

The Multiactivity Physical Education Program

This chapter, which details the multiactivity physical education program, presents many familiar features of what is not only the most common program offered nowadays but is also probably the type of program you experienced. The major topics covered in this chapter are as follows:

The characteristics of a multiactivity program

How multiactivity programs respond to needs of students

Four programs that emphasize flexibility, variability, program-specific conditions, and administrative concerns about multiactivity programs

The constraints and pitfalls for teachers in multiactivity programs

SCENE   SUE *and* LAURIE, *who were neighbors before* SUE's *family moved to a new home in a nearby suburb earlier in the year, are both 16 years old and in the eleventh grade. It is Thanksgiving and their two families are spending the day together. After a turkey dinner,* SUE *and* LAURIE *leave the group and start to talk about school life;* LAURIE *mentions that there is one new PE teacher this year, but otherwise things are pretty much the same.*

SUE   Our PE program is elective. At the start of the year we were given a choice of activities.

LAURIE   You mean you could choose anything?

SUE   Well, there was a list with specific activities, but there must've been at least 20 to choose from.

LAURIE   And you could choose any of them?

SUE   Yes, but one of the four you choose has to be a team sport, another an individual sport, and another a recreational or outdoor activity.

LAURIE   Our new teacher is really good but, as you remember, our teachers decide what units we do. I don't mind it that way; at least they only teach what
they're good at. Can your teachers really teach all those activities well?

SUE   I guess they can. So far it's been fine. Anyway, what activities are you in this
year?

LAURIE   I'm taking volleyball now. I had field events—you know, shot put, discus,
and high jump—at the start of the year, and next I think I've got a personal
fitness unit, probably weights and circuit training.

SUE   I decided on aerobics, soccer, orienteering, and tennis. I think the variety's
neat. Next year we also get a chance to take PE if we want. It's not for credit,
but I hope I have the time for a few more activities that interest me.

LAURIE   Orienteering sounds interesting, but I wouldn't like to get a grade for it.
I'm hopeless with directions. Do they put you out in the wilderness for your
final exam?

SUE   No. It's all done on the school grounds and at the nearby golf course. Most of
the time you work with a partner. The activity outline made it sound neat. I'm
not sure how we'll be graded, but I know for the soccer unit we have to do the
skills well. Mr. Ashton, that's our PE teacher, always makes us perform well.
I don't mind that though; you learn better when you're expected to. I think
teachers teach better when they want you to learn.

Sue and Laurie have PE programs typical of many high schools. Activity
choices and a wide range of units have typified programs in secondary schools
over the last 10 years. The proliferation of activities, especially those of an individual and recreative nature, have been a curriculum response to changing
needs of adolescents and society. It may also reflect the changing emphasis of
professional preparation programs during the 1960s and 1970s. Traditional
team sports were deemphasized in favor of individual and lifetime activities.

Physical education programs in the 1960s and 1970s

In the 1960s physical education programs emphasized sports and typically fed
into intramural and varsity sports programs. Activities commonly included
basketball, volleyball, track and field, tennis, swimming, baseball/softball,
hockey (field and ice), and gymnastics.

By the 1970s physical education programs began to emphasize lifetime
skills. Activities commonly included archery, golf, tennis, badminton, canoeing, backpacking, hiking, softball, volleyball, and bowling.

We should also note that in both decades many of the activities were
taught to single-sex classes.

Defining the multiactivity program

Whether a multiactivity program is elective, required, or a combination of the
two, it will generally possess some unique characteristics. Rather than being

strictly governed by a particular focus or specific theme, the multiactivity program responds to the popular activities that exist in the local area. The diversity of the multiactivity program can readily be compared to the single-theme models described in the chapters on fitness (Chapter 10), sports education (Chapter 11), and outdoor pursuits/adventure education (Chapter 12). It is the specific activities themselves that give the multiactivity program its structure.

Multiactivity programs typically offer a wide variety of team sports, individual and dual pursuits, and outdoor and recreational activities. In principle, there is no limit to what activities can be offered. In fact, some exemplary multiactivity programs include unusual and rarely encountered activities (e.g., European handball, rugby), adding further to the smorgasbord of opportunities to entice adolescents to participate. Many different programs can be labeled multiactivity, reflecting teacher interest, student choice, the community culture, availability of facilities and equipment, and trends in the profession.

In Chapter 8 we emphasized the need for a program philosophy. Although typified by a wide range of activities, the successful multiactivity program nevertheless requires a sound philosophical base. It is important that the multiactivity program reflect a philosophy that is commonly shared by the physical education teaching staff and the broader school community. With a shared philosophy, rational decisions can be made for concerns such as what activities to include or exclude.

Flexibility and adaptability are two strong points of the multiactivity program. Both teacher expertise and current student interest can be accommodated in most programs of this type. A new community aquatic center or a recently opened racquetball center is sufficient reason for adding a specific activity to the multiactivity program.

The multiactivity program is primarily defined by the activities that it offers. The activities listed in Table 9.1 (p. 150), all of which have been successfully taught in grades 5–12, emphasize its potential scope. The activities are divided into the broad categories of team sports, individual/dual activities, recreational pursuits, and nontraditional activities. Our support for coeducation requires that these activities be offered to both sexes.

The list of activities in Table 9.1 is not exhaustive. Even so, you should quickly realize the enormous potential scope of a multiactivity program. There can hardly be an excuse for teachers to say, "There's nothing new to teach." The scope of activities does, however, illuminate the need for state departments, local school districts, colleges, and universities to provide programs of professional development and to inform in-service teachers in new and unfamiliar content areas that can improve programs with a multiactivity focus. Teacher-training programs cannot graduate physical education majors with the necessary personal performance skills to teach and demonstrate all of these activities. If a training program covers a third of these activities, it is doing extremely well. Therefore, professional development programs are an important adjunct to the physical education teacher's role. Nowhere is the need greater than for teachers implementing a variable and flexible multiactivity program.

Table 9.1   Content options for multiactivity programs

Team Sports	Individual/Dual Activities	Recreational Pursuits	Nontraditional Activities
Baseball	Aquatics	Angling	Equestrian
Basketball	Diving	Backpacking-hiking	European handball
Football	Swimming	Bowling	Korfball
Flag	Sychronized	Camping	Rhythmic
Touch	swimming	Canoeing	gymnastics
Hockey	Water safety	Cycling	Rugby
Field	Archery	Dance	Surfing
Floor	Badminton	Folk	Water polo
Lacrosse	Conditioning	Modern	
Soccer	Aerobic dance	Square	
Softball	Circuit training	Social	
Speedball	Jogging	Initiatives	
Volleyball	Slimnastics	Orienteering	
	Fencing	Rappelling	
	Golf	Sailing	
	Gymnastics		
	Tumbling		
	Acrosport		
	Handball		
	Paddleball		
	Squash		
	Martial arts		
	Aikido		
	Judo		
	Karate		
	Scuba diving		
	Skiing		
	Snow		
	Water		
	Skin diving		
	Table tennis		
	Tennis		
	Trampoline		
	Weight lifting		
	Wrestling		
	Yoga		

A rationale for the multiactivity program

Offering a multiactivity program in grades 5–12 seems very easy to justify. If such a program can be elective in nature, the justification is further enhanced. Adolescents have changing needs, so offering a wide variety of physical activities seems helpful in facilitating their growth. A wide variety of activities will enable them to test themselves and explore new interests during this often volatile time in their lives.

A multiactivity program can provide the appropriate settings for brief periods of experimentation. The lengthy list of activities detailed in Table 9.1 allows for interaction and confrontation for individuals, pairs, and groups. An individual can challenge the environment in a rappelling unit, individuals can pit themselves against other individuals in a game of tennis or in a fencing sortie, twosomes can cooperate together to race through the orienteering course, and groups can develop sophisticated strategies to defend the goal against another group who has a short corner in field hockey. Young men and women, together or separately, can develop social skills on their own terms when occupied in mutually attractive activities.

Multiactivity programs can offer diversity, novelty, and excitement not often possible in other more restrictive physical education programs. As mentioned in Chapter 5, educators should make every effort to focus on the possibilities for adolescence rather than the turbulence and problems of the period. The multiactivity program, if well taught and administered, can provide this focus. The number of changes that occur during adolescence is great. The multiactivity program can respond to these changes through its variety, scope, and flexibility. It can provide the necessary pathways for students to explore and gain competence in interesting activities.

Elective and nonelective multiactivity programs

SCENE   *The softball elective is in its second week, and* PAT, *one of the students, is bored and no longer willing to participate.* MR. FLACK, *the physical education teacher, notices this and takes* PAT *aside.*

MR. FLACK   Now listen, Pat, you made a choice two weeks ago to play softball. What's the problem?

PAT   Softball doesn't interest me.

MR. FLACK   Well, why did you choose it?

PAT   It was the one I thought I could do the least work in and pass.

MR. FLACK   Well, like it or not, you have to put in some effort, so get out there and practice.

Some students in secondary school are difficult to motivate, others will not work hard physically no matter what the activity, still others may make the wrong choice in an elective program and become disinterested, and even others will be happy whatever their choice. You were probably one of the last group as a secondary school student. Remember this when you are teaching in an elective multiactivity program.

Allowing students to choose activities can help them meet their variable needs, but teachers probably cannot keep all students happy all of the time. Offering a choice is no guarantee for stimulating student interest. The appropriateness of the activity and how well it is taught are what matter. Ensuring that students are held accountable for learning is also an important factor.

The multiactivity program and the beginning teacher

SCENE   *It is the week before the opening of school, and* JUANITA, *the head of physical education, and* RUSS, *a new teacher, are meeting to discuss the upcoming year.*

JUANITA   Well, let's consider our teaching duties for the first semester. I've given everyone the same duties they had last year, and you, Russ, will teach aerobic dance and gymnastics. Sally did a great job with those last year, and some of her ideas are in this folder. Any questions about what's happening?

RUSS *(hesitantly)* Ah, well, I've never taught aerobic dance, and really, I'm hopeless at gymnastics. Any chance of swapping with someone for basketball?

JUANITA I don't think so. Best if you give it a try—we'll help where we can. Anyway, you've come from a good university program; you ought to be able to teach everything.

RUSS Maybe it wasn't such a good program. I've got no idea what to do in those classes.

Beginning teachers are often given the activity units that none of the other staff want. Although this is not always the case, be prepared for it. Teachers put in a position such as this need skills in planning units and lessons (see Chapter 18). The teacher's reputation as a professional educator is on the line. Russ was committed to being an effective teacher, so he really had no chance but to put into practice all the skills he learned at college and a few new ones as well.

Russ acquired some music and videos to help him in the aerobic dance unit. He made the unit a little like exercises to music and made a point of integrating some basic exercise physiology principles (heart rate response, warm up, stretching, etc.) into each lesson. The gymnastics unit also represented a major challenge to Russ. He had completed one course in Olympic gymnastics in college and an elective in tumbling. He now realized that he had completed both of those courses without learning a great deal. The courses were not graded on skill achievement, so he never pushed himself. On reflection he regretted this. In college he was grade conscious, and if there were skills to be performed to get an A, he worked at them. He wanted to demonstrate the skills to his students so he began a self-directed crash course in basic gymnastics. His roommates thought he was crazy practicing neck springs on a mattress placed on the floor, but Russ was holding himself accountable. He wanted to be a good role model for his students; he believed good demonstrations were important for establishing his credibility as a teacher.

Russ made a fine effort to teach content that he was not familiar with. Maybe Juanita was a little insensitive to the neophyte and Russ was not typical of beginning teachers, but nevertheless, this situation emphasizes the scope of teaching expertise required in a multiactivity program.

One of the strengths of a multiactivity program is that teachers can teach in their area of expertise. If the focus of a unit is skill achievement, then a teacher's skill in teaching and understanding of the subject matter *should* promote greater learning. Note the emphasis on *should*. Expertise in the subject matter must be supported by effective teaching strategies if significant student achievement is to occur. A multiactivity program can be tailored to capitalize on the expertise of the teaching staff. With a multitalented staff, motivated and committed to making a difference, an excellent program can result.

Multiactivity program examples

In this section we present examples of four multiactivity programs. These examples provide insight into physical education programs that are coeducational, selective, elective, and responsive to adolescents' needs and desires.

Junior High School Coed Elective Physical Education Program*

Introduction

The entire junior high school operates on an elective basis. Every nine weeks students elect courses for the next quarter. There are no requirements in any area including physical education. The physical education program is arranged to enable each student to become physically educated through participation in six major areas.

Program Outline

1. The program includes six major areas:
   a. Team sports
   b. Individual sports
   c. Dance
   d. Fitness
   e. Recreational games
   f. Swimming
2. Thirteen to fifteen activities (at least one from each major area) are offered each nine-week period.
3. Performance objectives for each major area/activity clearly detail student requirements.
4. Data is recorded for each student on an individual evaluation form. Evaluation is based on improvement in skills, written tests, and use of skills in an applied setting (intramurals, athletic programs).

Program Description

Each student is given guidance to help coordinate his or her program to ensure a sound preparation for continuing physical activity and to facilitate the high school program. Counseling is provided to encourage students to become competent performers in one or two activities and then to encourage a diversity of experiences in the six major areas.

With 13 to 15 activities offered every nine weeks, students can elect a great variety of activities. For each course, the physical education staff has established specific requirements, including performance objectives. Skill acquisition is stressed.

Students are grouped on the basis of interests and skill level, not chronological age or year in school. Teaching is based on teacher expertise although new class offerings regularly appear each year.

Additional Feature of the Program

With the emphasis on skill development in this elective program, many students request more time to practice. As a result, a "study gym" time has been estab-

---

* This program example is based, in part, on the Coed Elective Physical Education Program at Theodore Roosevelt Junior High School, Eugene, Oregon. (AAHPERD 1976)

lished each day so that students can practice and refine their skills. One teacher and a student aide are available to offer assistance to those practicing a particular activity. The study gym has become a popular and busy place, quite a different scene from the study hall in the cafeteria.

Summary of the Program

With the wide offering of activities, teachers are motivated to be involved in curriculum development. Each teacher is asked to develop a new class offering (or a revised offering) each year. The coeducational courses promote greater care (increased sensitivity to learner need) in teacher planning, and students quickly accept the idea that boys and girls can happily interact and compete in physical education classes.

Selective Physical Education Program*

Introduction

The selective physical education program is arranged so that students may select from at least two activities every three or four weeks. Staff, facilities, and the marking period dictate the length and number of units offered.

Emphasis is placed on carry-over lifetime activities, with the traditional team sports always available. The structure is such that female and male students may take units separately or select the coed offering. The coed unit is usually a lifetime sport.

The philosophy underlying the program is to expose students to as many different types of activities as possible. This, in turn, will create the interest to pursue these activities on a more advanced level such as interscholastic sports, cross-country ski club, scuba diving, camp, and summer volleyball leagues.

Grading is unusual in the eleventh and twelfth grades because students are given "participation points" for each unit successfully completed instead of the traditional letter grade. At this level, students should enjoy activities from a recreational standpoint since they have acquired introductory skills throughout their earlier school careers. Local feeder schools provide curriculum details for all new students. This assists in the selective program's design. Some units still make instruction a priority. These units include golf, tennis, aerobics, skin diving, and cross-country skiing. At the end of the school year, juniors and seniors must have accumulated a predetermined number of credit points to complete the requirements successfully. At the ninth- and tenth-grade levels, however, it is still important to assign letter grades because more emphasis is placed on instruction, practice, and subsequent skill acquisition.

Program Outline

Units are added and deleted yearly, depending on their success and administrative functioning. Some changes that have been made from the original program include the following:

1. Bowling was dropped because of transportation costs.
2. Modern dance was dropped because of lack of trained personnel (teacher expertise).
3. Square dance was dropped because of lack of student interest.

---

* Based on a program developed at Lowville Academy and Central School, Lowville, New York. (AAHPERD 1976)

4. The following were added because of student interest:
   a. Coed volleyball
   b. Paddleball
   c. Indoor hockey
   d. Competitive swimming
   e. Water sports

Program Description

All juniors and seniors are grouped together in four blocks, each consisting of two 40-minute periods per week. All freshmen and sophomores are grouped together in a similar block arrangement with two 40-minute classes per week. Each class consists of 60 to 100 students. Three teachers are used per class, making an average class load of approximately 30 students per teacher.

This program has been designed to meet the needs and interests of the student body, to decrease the "cutting" problem, and to make the teaching of physical education more enjoyable by removing the boredom factor.

Conditions Specific to the Program

Facilities include two gymnasiums (what used to be called the boys' gym and the girls' gym), a pool, and a universal gym (the lobby between the pool and one of the gyms).

No special staff are used for the selective program. However, each teacher must be able to teach in the skill areas offered. Three teachers are required for every selective class: one for advanced skill, one for intermediate, and one for basic.

The funds for the program come from a budget submitted each year by the director of physical education. The selective program costs approximately $2,000 to $3,000. The money is used to replace worn or broken equipment and to purchase new equipment. Recently water sports were added to the program and water basketball backboards were purchased. The cross-country skiing and snowshoeing unit have been very successful, thus making it necessary to purchase additional skis, boots, poles, bindings, and showshoes. The program director makes a conscious attempt to spend equal amounts of money at each level of the program.

Summary of the Program

The selective program appears to have the following *strengths*:

1. Students like the program. Input from them is acquired by means of a yearly evaluation. The needs and interests of the students are identified and then the department attempts to adapt the program accordingly.
2. The cutting of classes has been reduced significantly.
3. Teachers are allowed to teach in their areas of strength whenever possible.
4. A greater number of activities is being offered.
5. All facililities are now utilized to their fullest.
6. The carry-over values are immediately evident. More students are playing tennis on weekends, buying their own X-C skiing equipment, requesting aerobics books from the library, and so on.
7. Teachers seem to be encouraged to teach in different areas, even some unfamiliar ones. This leads to research and professional growth.
8. Boredom is decreased because of the change of units every three or four weeks.
9. The program has aided in the developing of a skills course called Survival to Life, which one member of the staff has already planned. In addition, one of

the physical education teachers has teamed up with a teacher of anatomy and physiology to teach a unit on the physiology of exercise, using the aerobic approach to fitness. This unit takes up six 40-minute class periods.

Some weaknesses or problems in the selective program include the fact that students' dropping and adding classes through guidance personnel cause problems with the grade sheets and the fact that recording grades is time-consuming and often frustrating. A system for computerizing this area is presently being studied to eliminate these problems.

High School Elective Physical Education Program*

Introduction

This high school elective physical education program provides each student with a basic working knowledge of a variety of sports activities; creates a level of skill in each activity that will enable students to participate fully and effectively in carry-over activities; and gives students a thorough appreciation of these and other activities from a spectator point of view.

A stimulating educational experience is fostered by providing facilities, equipment, and a choice of 43 activities at a variety of levels. The physical education program culminates a well-balanced and organized intramural and interscholastic program. The interscholastic program consists of 23 sports for young men and women and has 49 teams at various competitive levels.

This program serves a high school enrollment of approximately 2,000 students for grades 10, 11, and 12. Students are required to participate actively in two 55-minute periods each week. Students wishing additional classes are accepted on a space-available basis. Eight full-time physical education teachers conduct this program.

The school year is divided into four quarters consisting of approximately nine weeks each. Students elect two different activities each quarter, one activity for each of the two days their class meets during the week. Students are not allowed to repeat activities over a single school year unless the nature of the activity requires repetition.

Program Outline

Students may choose from the following activities:

Fall (1st quarter)	Winter (2nd and 3rd quarters)	Spring (4th quarter)
Archery I and II	Judo	Archery I and II
Tennis	Volleyball	Tennis I and II
Golf I and II	Table tennis	Golf I and II
Horseshoes	Weight training	Badminton
Tetherball	Dance	Fishing
Badminton	Fencing	Fly casting
Flag football	Volleyball	Lacrosse

* Based on a program developed at Lexington High School, Lexington, Massachusetts. (AAHPERD 1976)

Fall	Winter	Spring
(1st quarter)	(2nd and 3rd quarters)	(4th quarter)
Soccer	Basketball	Track and field
Field hockey	Floor hockey	Softball
Speedball	Apparatus	
	Wrestling	
	Modern dance	
	Modern jazz	
	Movement for improvement	
	Self-defense	
	Floor exercise	

Program Description

At the beginning of each quarter, students select their physical education program for that quarter. Two different activities are selected, each meeting once a week for the entire quarter.

Two printed and color-coded data-processing cards are required for each student (one card for each period of physical education taken during the week). The instructor of each activity the student elects receives a card, which he or she uses to take attendance and keep cumulative evaluation records. At the end of each quarter, the cards are reassigned to the instructors of each student's new activities. The cards are filed by activity and gym class to enable easy accessibility in changing a student's gym class or activity. Also, all necessary records are readily available to any necessary substitute teacher. Colored bands across the top of the cards are used to identify the student's class period and year of graduation. The preprinted cards also contain the student's name, house, homeroom, and other pertinent information.

Conditions Specific to the Program

The program is essentially held outdoors during the fall and spring seasons. However, some activities such as badminton are held indoors to facilitate better utilization of space. The second and third quarters are held in the well-equipped gymnasium and field house, which accommodates six to seven teaching stations each period and contains a 160-yard, 4-lane running track with specialized areas for basketball, gymnastics, volleyball, etc.

The student-teacher ratio is one physical education teacher for every 250 students. The supply and equipment budget is allocated on the basis of $1.50 a year for each student in the high school. This budget is satisfactory and provides adequate funding.

Summary of the Program

Student interest in and general attitude toward the program are excellent. Few dress cuts occur, and systematic interviewing of students after a selection of classes also alludes to the success of the program. Since all students (including those participating in varsity athletics) are required to take physical education, the opportunity to select from a variety of activities allows for great flexibility in programming. The offering of two different activities each week allows more selection of popular activities and utilization of staff strengths.

The program requires a good deal of organization and can be time-consuming in terms of maintaining student accountability. Two teachers have some release time to work on specific organizational considerations. The total staff is involved with curriculum development and program improvement.

Physical Education Program Adapted to Student Suggestions*

Introduction

A series of meetings with students resulted in a list of "demands" that were fairly predictable and in some cases very constructive:

- A more flexible program from which to select activities
- A chance to spend more time on certain activities
- A chance to have some out-of-school activity count toward the physical education requirement
- Elimination of a specific required gym uniform
- Elimination of required showers
- A change in the grading system from letter grade to pass or fail

Staff members from the entire district, representing all grade levels, met in an effort to determine which suggestions were realistic and how, if at all, they should be implemented. The staff reaffirmed its belief that what was important for students was active participation in general rather than active participation in some specific activity. After all, if an activity helps a student develop skill, strength, agility, speed, endurance, etc., does it really matter which activity it is?

Changing the grading system from letter grades to a simple pass or fail caused the greatest consternation among staff members. However, when they agreed that most grades were subjective and were really not helping to accomplish the objectives of the program, and when they agreed that student participation was really the key to success, the members voted to give the pass/fail system a try.

Staff members also acknowledged that a strong elementary and junior high program existed. They agreed that by working together they could provide all students with a broad experience in movement and sports activities that would enable them to make more intelligent selections in senior high school. And so the present high school program evolved.

Program Outline

Students are required to participate in physical education for two and one-half periods per week or the equivalent thereof but elect the form of participation from the following program areas:

1. In the *"regular"* program, a maximum of 120 students are scheduled for a specific class period with four physical education teachers assigned to provide instruction. Usually, three or four student teachers from nearby universities are assigned to assist. The students can choose from a list of 6 to 10 activities for each of the 10-week marking periods.

2. An *individual development program* is offered for students who are in need of specific remedial help or who cannot participate in the "regular" program because of injury or illness. These students are assigned to a specific certified physical education teacher at a maximum ratio of 25 to one. Working together, the students and teacher arrange for a suitable program that meets

---

* Based on a program developed at Herricks Senior High School, New Hyde Park, New York. Adapted from Lovins, M. "Physical Education—Making Changes to Fit the Times." *NASSP Bulletin*, Spring 1978.

the specific needs of the students. Information from the family, school physician, and school nurse is encouraged by the physical education staff.

3. Students may also arrange for *independent study* for physical education credit. Here, too, a student who has a particular interest in pursuing an activity that cannot be offered at school because of facility or staff limitations can work out a program with an assigned staff member for the student to participate off campus. Procedures, objectives, and evaluations are arranged in advance, and student and teacher meet regularly.

4. A broad program of *intramural and interscholastic sports* is conducted for male and female students. All activities are assigned to physical education teachers and the emphasis is on participation. The needs of many students are met through the intramural program. However, some students seek the more intensive work that goes with interschool competition. This is not discouraged. Except for basketball, no cuts are made of candidates for interscholastic teams. If a greater number want to participate than the team or coach can handle, one or more junior varsity teams are organized to accommodate them. Having students participate under qualified leadership is the key to a successful program.

One value of multiactivity programs is the variety of activities offered.

Team teaching efforts in physical education allow some students to spend more time on certain activities. The ecology group, for example, teams the social studies, science, and English programs with physical education. In this way, students can integrate orienteering, canoeing, backpacking, and camping into a broader time slot than would normally be available.

Program Administration

Attendance. According to state law, all students are required to take part in a physical education program or instruction. The law requires attendance and active participation. The intramural and interscholastic programs, however, which are of great value to students, are offered on a voluntary basis.

Grades. Students receive a grade of P (pass), F (fail), or I (incomplete). In special cases, an M (medical) may be recorded when sufficient evidence is presented to and approved by the school health officers. However, the program is so broad that there are activities for *all* students.

Any student who receives the grade of I (incomplete) will not be given credit for the year's work unless he or she makes up the deficiencies. Seniors who fail to complete their requirements will not be granted a diploma until they have satisfied the requirements.

"Regular" Program Offerings. The following activities are typically presented during the class instructional period. These are also offered on an intramural or interscholastic basis wherever interest warrants.

Archery	Golf	Soccer
Badminton	Gymnastics	Softball
Basketball	Jogging	Speedball
Dance (modern)	Lacrosse	Team handball
Dance (social)	Paddleball	Tennis
Dance (square)	Paddle tennis	Track and field
Fencing	Personal conditioning	Volleyball
Field hockey	Recreation sports	Weight training
Flag football	Self-defense	Wrestling
Floor hockey	Slimnastics	Yoga

Each student in grades 10, 11, and 12 has the option of selecting one or more activities each 10-week marking period. Seniors will be given a preference when an activity must be limited because of numbers.

Summary of the Program

This program has been strongly endorsed and supported by the four principals the high school has had. Change has taken place over several years and through successive school administrations. Its success has been due, in part, to a willingness to listen and to clarify program objectives that best meet student interests and needs.

Common pitfalls in multiactivity programs

Many multiactivity programs offered in secondary schools fail to realize the goals that an effective program can achieve. The need for effective teaching strategies is no less true for this type of program than for any other. Far too often, under the guise of a multiactivity physical education program, we see only roll-out-the-ball supervised recreation. Such programs rate low in terms of teacher and student accountability. There is little or no emphasis on serious practice to develop and refine skills. There is little direct instruction. Seldom in such programs do we see appropriate activity and skill progressions between successive classes let alone between middle schools, junior high schools, and high schools. Often, popular community activities are ignored simply because they are popular.

Attention to these potential pitfalls can enhance the effectiveness of a multiactivity program. Never forget the importance of planning (see Chapter 18) when preparing to teach an activity unit. The activities themselves do not guarantee a successful program.

Teachers must also deal with the following possible constraints to the effective implementation of multiactivity programs:

- Lack of floor space and specialist facilities
- Teacher inability to teach effectively a wide range of skills
- Lack of administrative support in managing elective programs (which students are doing what)
- The time-consuming nature of maintaining student accountability
- Those students who may have difficulty operating in a freedom-of-choice environment

None of these possible constraints should jeopardize the implementation of a multiactivity program. Collectively, they present problems that may require some program modifications, but functional solutions are available. For example, some schools now use computer facilities to monitor which students are doing what.

Summary

Multiactivity programs, the historical backbone of physical education curricula, have changed over the past 20 years in terms of content offered. Recreational activities rather than traditional sports are more common now. Programs are typically diverse and offer a combination of required and elective activities. The activities that are offered give the multiactivity program its focus.

In offering a smorgasbord of activities for adolescents to participate in, the multiactivity program can, at least in part, meet the changing needs and desires of adolescents. It can provide diversity, novelty, excitement, and risk taking and really make a difference in young people's lives. This difference, however, like all other teaching-learning enterprises, requires the application of effective teaching strategies and nurturing and task-oriented administration.

The four program examples in this chapter provide details that allow us insight into multiactivity programs that are coeducational, selective, elective, and responsive to adolescent needs and desires.

Suggested activities

1. Reread Chapter 8 and then develop a program philosophy. Use this as a guide to design a multiactivity program of your own. With the permission of the instructor, you may work with two or three other students (as if you were members of a school physical education staff).

2. The content options for multiactivity programs detailed in the table on page 150 represent a broad range of activities. Using the following rating scale, rate yourself on each activity and then sum your score for each broad category, that is, team sports, individual/dual activities, and so on. Are you stronger in some categories than in others?
   0 = know nothing about
   1 = know some major skills
   2 = know most skills and could demonstrate them

3. Debate the following issue: Multiactivity programs should be eliminated. Have three students argue the affirmative and three the negative.

4. Imagine that you are a physical education teacher in a school that is in the process of implementing a multiactivity program adapted to student suggestions. Consider what the students wanted in the fourth example program in this chapter.
   a. Discuss the merits of these wants.
   b. Would you support changing the grading system from a letter grade to a pass or fail? Defend your answer.

5. Examine the course syllabi of local physical education programs to determine the degree to which they fit the multiactivity model. Report your findings to the class.

10

Fitness Models in Physical Education

Now, perhaps more than ever, families, communities, and even nations are espousing the value of physical exercise and subsequent improvements in health and fitness. The medical and economic benefits of a healthy life-style are proclaimed by industry, business, and social service agencies. Fitness has always been considered an integral part of physical education; yet today, with the support of the media, government, and popular opinion, it has the greatest potential ever, as a part of the school curriculum, to benefit young people. In light of this optimism, it is sobering to realize that the fitness goals of school programs are rarely met. The topics in this chapter address this and other important concerns in achieving fitness goals.

A basic description of fitness models

Various views of the different types and categories of fitness

A rationale for fitness programs

The significance of a fitness program for adolescents

Guidelines for the effective implementation of fitness programs

Examples of four school fitness programs

Fitness program constraints

Math class had just finished at Oak Park Middle School, and most of the students were off to the cafeteria for a lunch of pizza, salad, and a carton of milk. Glen was not joining his friends in the cafeteria; he was going to the physical education office to meet with Mr. Austin, his gym teacher. It was Wednesday and time for the weekly update on his individualized health fitness program.

At the beginning of the year all of the students were tested in an attempt to identify their levels of health fitness (i.e., fitness related to functional health). Glen, a

12-year-old, was in bad shape. When initially tested, he could only jog/walk 800 yards in 9 minutes, had a triceps skinfold measure of 24 mm, could perform only 14 sit-ups in 60 seconds, and on the sit-and-reach test recorded a score of plus 3 cm (his fingers went 3 cm past his toes). With the exception of the sit-and-reach flexibility test, Glen's results placed him at the tenth percentile in terms of the national norm. Mr. Austin was concerned about Glen's low health fitness and decided that the problem was serious enough to warrant his talking with Glen's family.

After three long months, Glen and Mr. Austin were starting to see some improvement. In fact, Mr. Austin had called Glen's father the previous night to inform him of Glen's improved performance at the latest testing session. When the program began, Glen, his father, and older sister had joined forces to initiate a home-based activity program with the specific goal of improving Glen's level of health fitness. Mr. Austin had decided on a combined school and home approach because he realized that physical education classes could not fully meet Glen's needs. After much initial planning and communication during the first month, Mr. Austin now met with Glen once a week to graph the activity data and answer any questions. Apart from this meeting, the program was now totally home-based; in fact, Glen's father and sister had it running very smoothly. Glen had systematically increased his activity level for six consecutive weeks.

Can you imagine an innovation such as this happening in a middle school or high school as a result of a fitness testing program at the start of the school year? Can parents or siblings really manage a remediation program such as this? In fact, it has been attempted and the results are encouraging. Many parents do believe that a satisfactory level of health fitness is an important objective for their child to achieve, and they are prepared to support a teacher in the initiation and development of a home-based fitness program. The situation we have just recounted helps to emphasize that there exist new and enlightened strategies for dealing with the achievement of important fitness objectives.

Physical education is much more than fitness education, of course. A physical education program that only focused on the achievement of fitness objectives would, for many students and teachers, be dull, restrictive, and boring. If physical educators continue to make grandiose claims regarding the fitness benefits of our programs, then we must do more than simply test all our students at the start of the year and then leave the improvement or maintenance of fitness to typically low-intensity skill classes. The time, effort, and administrative expertise involved in the fitness testing of students deserves more action than the mere filing of results in the coordinator's office. Awareness of the health and fitness needs of students too often begins and ends with a biannual fitness test.

Anyone who has attempted to get fit after a few months of too much eating and too little activity knows all too well that there is no easy way. Just as Glen's program was not easy for him to complete, this chapter on fitness models in physical education does not offer any easy solutions in terms of program implementation. It offers practical intervention strategies to enable students to achieve some of the fitness goals that school programs can realistically set for them.

The practical intervention strategies introduced later in this chapter need to be considered in the light of a clear understanding of how fitness relates to adolescence. The basic description of fitness models that follows attempts to enhance this understanding.

A basic description of fitness models

Physical education curricula almost always state fitness goals. Here are just two examples.

- Physical education should provide *knowledge and experience in activities that will encourage and assist the student to maintain fitness throughout life.*
- Physical education should develop *appropriate strength, endurance, and flexibility of major muscle groups.*

Such goals are remarkably consistent across a wide range of programs in physical education and appear to be almost totally independent of any particular philosophical base.

Most physical education programs provide a unit of instruction once, or maybe twice, each year to facilitate the achievement of fitness goals. Typically, in middle school or junior high school, a two- to four-week unit is devoted to physical fitness. In such a unit students may be introduced to a variety of fitness activities and training techniques. Interval training, circuit training, jogging, and aerobics seem to be the most popular. It is also common for units to include some important knowledge objectives emphasizing the value of exercise in today's sedentary society. In high school, students may elect to take a unit on weight training or sports conditioning or participate in a diet and exercise class. A small number of high school programs offer a knowledge-oriented course that focuses on basic physiology as it relates to exercise. Some secondary schools, particularly those in which teachers maintain a strong fitness orientation, attempt to include fitness activities in every physical education lesson. Vigorous warm-up sessions, exercise drills, calisthenics, and running activities in each class are evidence of this.

Different types of fitness

The variety of approaches to the fitness unit reflects the differing views teachers have about fitness. In this regard, it may be useful to outline briefly the accepted understandings of the different forms of fitness. Thirty years ago physical fitness was push-ups, straight-leg sit-ups, pull-ups, sprinting a short distance, and running a long distance. Perhaps it should have been called military fitness, from which the tests originated. Today, when discussing fitness, we need to distinguish its various forms, which include *health fitness* or health-related fitness, *physical fitness* or athletic fitness, and *motor fitness* or motor skill fitness. We need to understand these three categories of fitness if we are to plan programs to achieve the fitness goals specified.

A useful way to conceptualize the fitness categories is to look at them in terms of their degree of remoteness from basic physiological functioning.

Health fitness is concerned with cardiovascular function.

Health fitness is a relatively new concept in physical education and is the category of fitness assessment that most closely monitors basic physiological functioning. Health fitness is concerned with cardiovascular function, body composition, and musculoskeletal factors. Health fitness is particularly oriented to the health problems that afflict the adult population yet have been shown to have their genesis in childhood and adolescence. Test items for health fitness include an endurance run of approximately 9 minutes, skinfold measures of body fat, number of bent-knee sit-ups in 60 seconds, and the sit-and-reach flexibility measurements.

Physical fitness is further removed from basic physiological functioning than health fitness and not as skill oriented as motor fitness. Physical fitness focuses on broad categories of physical performance that go beyond health-related concerns. The behaviors typically measured in a physical fitness test include cardiovascular endurance, strength and endurance of major muscle groups, and speed and power. Test items that reflect this emphasis include the mile run, pull-ups, sergeant jump, sit-ups, 50-yard dash, and standing long jump.

Motor fitness is even more remote from basic physiological functioning. Motor fitness reflects a measure of skilled performance. Test items for motor fitness may include the softball throw, an agility run, a climbing test, various speed and accuracy drills, and activities related to hand-eye coordination.

Regardless of the fitness category being emphasized in a school program, teachers must provide a clear focus for all student activities related to the achievement of fitness goals. Without this, students will not practice fitness skills, and without practice, students will not acquire or maintain physical skills. It is crucial that students experience the benefits of physical activity firsthand; simply knowing about the benefits is not enough. Fitness programs cannot be judged as successful by a favorable assessment of student attitude and knowledge alone. The demonstration of a student's fitness skills must be the major determinant in judging the success of a school's fitness program.

We believe that health fitness should be the initial focus for a physical education fitness program. That all students achieve a basic level of health fitness as a result of participation in a physical education program is as important as those other basics so often espoused, including literacy. To ensure that this occurs, physical educators should keep the following points in mind when planning a fitness program.

1. Valid and reliable data must be collected to determine program effectiveness.
2. Fitness skills need to be taught and practiced.
3. Adequate time for improvement must be allocated on a long-term basis.
4. Understanding and knowledge related to fitness, at best, can only supplement a fitness program.

A rationale for fitness programs

Most young children are naturally physically active; they are inclined, however, to become sedentary as society and the environment make it increasingly difficult for them to remain active during late childhood and adolescence. As a result of investigations detailing the possible pediatric nature of coronary heart disease, an enthusiastic emphasis has been given to the study of fitness in school-age children. This emphasis has, in part, promulgated the health fitness concern evident in physical education. Fitness problems in youth are often manifested in adults as degenerative diseases and chronic ailments. These problems are displayed in poor cardiovascular endurance, high levels of body fat, abdominal bulge, poor lower-back strength, and deficient lower-back flexibility.

The social relevance of a fitness model takes on new meaning when physical educators consider the foregoing evidence. The need for new fitness programs in schools is further emphasized when one realizes that very little student time is spent in health fitness activities in physical education. Students cannot achieve fitness goals when they spend as few as 2 or 3 minutes of a 30-minute class participating in fitness activities. Drastic changes must occur in physical education classes if students are to achieve higher levels of fitness.

Can fitness ever be achieved in school physical education programs? This is a realistic concern, especially when one considers the exercise science principles that must be adhered to if fitness improvement is to occur. Although we will present several strategies for achieving fitness goals, the reader must realize that systematic fitness improvement is difficult to achieve as it has traditionally been taught.

What fitness programs mean to students

Fitness itself means many things to students in secondary school. Some see it as a part of athletics and something that only gifted athletes should strive for. Others view fitness with fear and anxiety. For still others, it represents hard work to be avoided at all cost. However, given a health fitness ori-

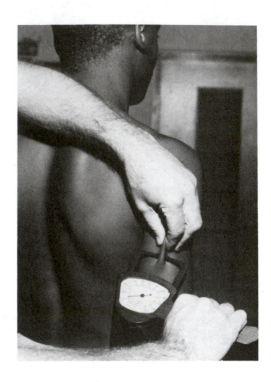

Fat composition is one indication of level of fitness.

entation, it is possible that adolescents will come to understand the meaning and relevance of fitness to their lives.

Adolescents are very conscious of their bodies. Sexual characteristics and physical appearance are of great concern and significance to them. To this end, the importance of their cosmetic fitness is continually preached in the media. Although overblown to promote commercial products, this emphasis on "looking good" presents the physical educator with a wonderful opportunity to promote involvement in fitness programs. For the 14-year-old frail, skinny boy and for the 14-year-old tall, obese girl, cosmetic fitness means a great deal. A tactful, enlightened physical educator can react to such students in ways that are beneficial to both the students and the fitness program.

By offering a fitness program that focuses on lifetime health and fitness, a school program can make an important educational contribution. But to do so, students must achieve a satisfactory level of fitness while in the program and the skills (psychomotor, cognitive, and affective) to maintain an ongoing commitment to personal fitness.

Guidelines for fitness programs in physical education

The criteria for fitness emanating from the literature on exercise science are clear: regular participation, a minimum of three 20-minute sessions each week, and progressive overload with respect to either intensity or duration. As outlined earlier, very few physical education classes have a total fitness emphasis; hence achievement of the exercise science criteria is rare. Research has shown that many physical education classes have a negligible effect in terms of fitness development. In fact, the summer vacation seems to have a greater impact on fitness development than does participation in physical education classes.

So what needs to be done? Several strategies are available to rectify the situation. The most fruitful approach would be to institute a special fitness class that meets at least three times a week, with a minimum of 20 minutes of activity that is monitored in terms of intensity, frequency, and duration. Recent innovations in Australian and Canadian schools have implemented daily fitness programs with encouraging results to support the continuation of such programs. Another approach would be to accept the fact that 50 to 90 percent of secondary school students (the percentage varies from school to school) maintain a satisfactory level of fitness and to design special remediation programs for the others. We consider examples of both approaches and several other innovative programs in the next section.

Before moving on to those examples, it is necessary to translate the exercise science fitness criteria into teaching practice. The summarized teaching activities represent a direct-instruction approach to teaching fitness. Fitness-direct instruction can bring about fitness improvement and then fitness maintenance if teaching activities reflect the following:

1. *Goals are clear to students.* For example, you must jog/walk 1200 meters in 9 minutes to achieve the minimum level of cardiorespiratory endurance.

2. *Time allocated for instruction is sufficient and continuing.* For example, you must perform 20 minutes of extended endurance activities three times each week throughout the year.

3. *Coverage of content is extensive.* For example, when planning activities teachers must attend to the essential components of health fitness, namely, cardiorespiratory endurance, body composition, lower-back flexibility, abdominal strength, and endurance.

4. *Performance of students is monitored, and feedback is provided.* For example, someone must accurately monitor physical performance on a regular basis to provide meaningful knowledge of results.

5. *Students can produce many correct responses.* For example, repetition is a key ingredient in any fitness program; therefore, students should be able to master easily activities that are offered.

The five parameters outlined for fitness-direct instruction (after Rosenshine 1979) represent guidelines that physical educators should follow if skill development is the teaching focus. Remember, fitness behaviors are skills, and you should consider them in the same way as motor skills when you are teaching a unit. That is, practice, repeated practice is necessary for improvement.

Physical education classes in general rarely reflect the characteristics of fitness-direct instruction. If such instruction is practiced, however, the achievement of fitness goals is possible. Teachers must decide whether to wave the fitness banner or not. It is hypocritical to wave it and then fail to provide appropriate activities in classes.

Fitness program examples

In this section we present examples of five fitness programs. The models focus on fitness remediation, daily fitness activities, circuit and weight training, and a comprehensive high school fitness program.

Health Fitness Remediation Program

This program can be incorporated at any school level. Its focus here is on health fitness for an entire eighth grade of 140 students. Its concern is with basic physiological functioning as it pertains to a healthy life-style.

Initial Diagnosis

For any remediation program, initial diagnosis is essential. In this model, diagnosis is based on performance on the AAHPERD Health-Related Physical Fitness Test (AAHPERD 1980). All students are assessed on the following items:

- Cardiovascular endurance: 9-minute run
- Body composition: skinfold measure (triceps and subscapular)
- Abdominal endurance: modified sit-ups (60 seconds)
- Lower-back flexibility: sit and reach

Those conducting the tests determine cutoff levels on the basis of the size of the sample. The idea is to think small and initially to identify those students in really bad shape. Based on the national norms (tables are provided in AAHPERD 1980), students who score at or below the tenth percentile on any test item receive 2 points, and those who score between the tenth and twentieth percentile receive 1 point. A student who scores at or below the tenth percentile on every item would, therefore, receive 8 points and be a prime candidate for the remediation program. A student who scores at or below the tenth percentile on one item and between the low 10 percent and low 20 percent on the other three items would receive a total of 5 points and should be considered for the remediation program. The actual size of the remediation group in this case was 14, that is, 10 percent of the eighth grade students. The cutoff mark was 4 points; that is, students who received 5 points or more were included in the remediation program. Two PE teachers and two classroom teachers were given the entire second day of school to conduct the test. The teachers, with student aides, recorded the results on each student's card.

The Remediation Process

Once identified, the 14 students were required to meet individually with a physical education teacher. At this meeting, the teacher worked to build the rapport necessary to promote a trusting relationship. He or she stressed the importance of health fitness and related specific feedback to the test performance of each student.

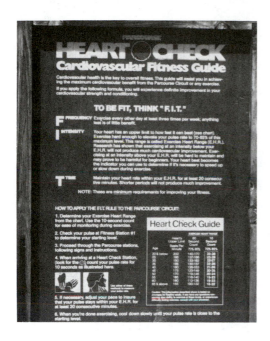

Frequency, Intensity, and Time are important in being F.I.T.

The school informed each student's family about the program and explained how the family could promote its success. In this program, all students followed the same procedure. Alternative procedures are possible, and we will briefly discuss these at the end of this example.

The goal for each student was to score fewer than 5 points on the diagnostic test. That is, the teachers specifically informed them of what they had to do to get out of the program. Three of the students immediately demanded a retest, and upon subsequent testing two of the three improved their performance sufficiently to be removed from the program. These students had not magically improved their health fitness but had tried harder and achieved a more accurate measure of their fitness. Teachers should always be aware of how motivation can effect performance in testing situations, especially in a test such as the 9-minute run.

With the number now down to 12, all students were scheduled to take three 40-minute health fitness classes each week. One physical education teacher took responsibility for this class and developed a series of lessons that maximized activity time and placed the necessary physiological demands on the students. The teacher included games, drills, and activities to promote a positive physical experience for the students, and the teacher was an active participant in many of the activities.

Evaluation of the Program

The remediation classes lasted 12 weeks. After each 4-week block, students took the test again. The first 4-week block emphasized aerobic exercise and caloric expenditure, the second muscular strength and endurance, and the third flexibility and aerobic exercise (repeated). Once in the program, all 12 students stayed with it for the 12 weeks. Those who were still eligible for the remedial group at the end of the 12 weeks (that is, those who continued to score more than 5 points on the diagnostic test) were presented with alternative strategies to bring about the desired change. These strategies included a *home-based activity program* in which parents monitored and controlled the health fitness program from their own home. (See pages 163–164 for an example of this strategy.) Another strategy was the *integrated faculty program* in which the school nurse, home economics teachers, and physical education teachers pooled their expertise to offer a more specialized program—with an emphasis on diet, exercise, and health practices—for each student.

Daily Fitness Program

This example is best suited to a school program where the classroom teacher concept is practiced. If there are only two physical education teachers in a school, they cannot teach a daily fitness program for all students and also a normal physical education program. In this model, the physical education teachers must sell their fitness innovation and then canvas both the administration and classroom teachers for support of a daily 20-minute exercise program. Perhaps the best way to do this is for the teachers to point out poor fitness test results collected at the beginning of the school year. A daily fitness program for the entire school will be successful only if a schoolwide commitment prevails. Administrative support is essential in such an endeavor.

Planning

The two physical education teachers, who are responsible for the planning and organization of the program, scheduled four 24-minute time blocks when indoor and outdoor facilities would be available. In our example these time blocks were immediately before the first class of the day, before lunch, during lunch, and after the final class of the day.

The PE teachers and administration provide classroom teachers with a great deal of support to encourage their commitment to the program and to help them feel comfortable with the task at hand. Regular faculty meetings are used as part of an in-service program. At these meetings, the participants discuss the meaning of the fitness test results, and the PE teachers explain the principles of exercise/fitness programs and fitness-direct instruction. This enables the classroom teachers to respond to many student questions. The in-service program concludes with a series of three model fitness lessons taught by the physical education teachers. Each lesson is identical to one that the teacher will teach in the actual program.

Themes for Daily Fitness

The teachers prepare daily lessons and repeat each lesson for an entire week. These lessons reflect a major fitness theme that lasts for a minimum of three weeks, that is, for 15 lessons.

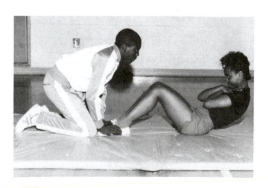

Fitness involves strengthening the abdominal muscles.

Possible themes are listed below; these will vary, however, according to a school's facilities, teacher expertise, and geographical location.

1. Walking and jogging
2. Abdominal strength and endurance
3. Upper-body strength and endurance
4. Circuit training
5. Jogging
6. Flexibility
7. Calisthenics
8. Fitness games
9. Interval training
10. Jogging

Note that each lesson reflects physical activities related to the three-week theme but is not restricted to those activities alone. Activities from the first theme will logically extend into the lessons reflecting the second theme and so on. If possible, teachers allow students to choose certain themes for each three-week period, thus building into the program greater student involvement. They also try to allow students to devise exercises and activities for the different themes.

Monitoring the Program

The physical education teachers monitor the program by rotating to different classes each day. Occasionally, they teach a class to reinforce fitness-direct instruction principles. By the end of the first three-week period, they have observed or taught every class. At monthly faculty meetings, the PE teachers inform the classroom teachers of progress and problems. Initially, the lessons are tailored to the needs of students with very low fitness levels; however, the demands of the lessons gradually increase as the program progresses.

The physical educators assess the program's effectiveness by observing a class, randomly selecting one or two students from each class, and monitoring their level of activity by collecting data on several physiological parameters. Heart-rate response is the most accessible measure for teachers to monitor. Teachers also conduct end-of-year school testing in order to compare preprogram and postprogram scores. The test items on the AAHPERD (1980) Health-Related Fitness Test represent the most functional parameters for pretest and posttest comparisons. However, if testing time is limited, teachers may wish to omit the time-consuming body-composition measure.

Circuit Training/Weight Training Program

This program is best suited to a high school physical education class. The circuit training/weight training example discussed here is for a class of 20 students with one teacher. The class meets three times each week, and the unit lasts for four weeks.

Circuit training is a frequently used strategy in fitness units. It has the potential to place great demands on the muscular and circulatory systems of the body and hence can bring about improvement in general fitness in a relatively short period of time. Combining weight training with circuit training strengthens particular muscle groups and enhances student motivation. Weight training equipment such as Universal or Nautilus is ideally suited to supplement a circuit training program. The ability to use weights quickly and safely is crucial in circuit training. If a teacher wants students to use free weights, he or she should set barbells with a poundage that suits all students. If enough free weights are available, the teacher can set up barbells to reflect different weight divisions. For example, for the bench press exercise, a heavy bar may be 160 pounds (level 1), a moderate bar 120 pounds (level 2), and a light bar 80 pounds (level 3).

Developing the Circuit

On the first day of class, the physical educator teaches students the correct form for each activity and then tests them for the maximum number of repetitions (RM) at each activity station. One minute is a standard time to allow for maximum repetition testing. Activities such as the shuttle run over 10 meters, sit-ups, burpees (squat thrusts), skipping, star jumps, and push-ups are suited to this form of testing. A partner records each student's maximum repetitions on the student's personal card (see Figure 10.1). The partner is responsible for counting repetitions and ensuring that all safety rules are followed and that the student completes the appropriate form of each exercise. The partner must closely monitor several exercises, such as push-ups and squat thrusts, to ensure appropriate form. One calculates the training dose (TD) by taking two thirds of the repetitions maximum (RM). A half RM can be used as a TD for beginners. Partners should also indicate the level of difficulty of an activity on the student cards. For example, students may complete sit-ups on the floor (level 1) with a sit-up board elevated one foot (level 2), and so on. The amount of weight a student lifts can also be categorized by level.

On the second day of the unit, students complete one set of all nine exercises listed in Figure 10.1. On the third and fourth days, they complete two sets. This gradual approach ensures that students perform the exercises correctly, that the rotation system of moving from station to station runs smoothly, and that the students do not overexert themselves. The concept of pacing oneself should be emphasized at this time; that is, it should be taught and practiced.

The nine-station circuit outlined on the card in Figure 10.1 is designed so that neither a particular muscle group nor the cardiovascular system is stressed more

Name: Anna Cobbin **Date:** 5/24 **Program Focus:** General Conditioning **Body Weight** 124 lb.

Exercise	RM₁	TD₁	Level	1	2	3	4	5	6	7	8	9	10	11	12			RM₂	TD₂	Level
1. Bicep curls	12	8	2																	
2. Shuttle run	18	12	1																	
3. Bench press	12	8	2																	
4. Sit-ups	36	24	1																	
5. Jump rope	75	50	2																	
6. Push-ups	21	14	1																	
7. Squat thrusts	36	24	1																	
8. V-sits	27	18	1																	
9. Half squats	24	16	2																	
10.																				
11.																				

Figure 10.1 Student record card for circuit training.

Aerobic dance workouts are fun and can contribute to fitness goals.

than once in succession. The sequence of exercises on the card stresses each of the following, in turn:

- arms and shoulders
- cardiovascular system
- arms and shoulders
- abdominals
- cardiovascular system
- arms and shoulders
- cardiovascular system
- abdominals
- legs and lower back

Physical educators can tailor individual circuits for particular student needs and for conditioning for a particular sport.

Implementing the Circuit

Completion of a multistation circuit by a large number of students requires both prior organization and high levels of on-task behavior. The teacher must actively monitor these aspects, as well as teach the rules governing safety and movement and see that students adhere to them.

The circuit we have been describing is set up as indicated in Figure 10.2 (p. 176). Each student works with a partner. Initially, one student rests while the other performs. Toward the midpoint of the circuit training unit (week 2), they can perform together. This promotes healthy competition, which often motivates students. When all students are active, the teacher sometimes includes a tenth station to

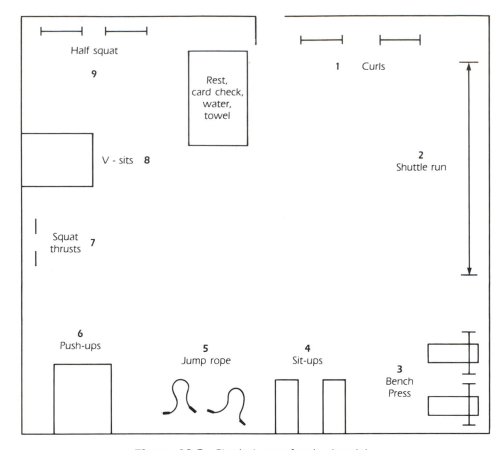

Figure 10.2 Physical setup for circuit training.

allow for a brief rest period, a drink (and towel), and reference to their cards. Each group of two students commences the circuit at a different station and progresses clockwise. The teacher can control this progression with rules governing movement—for example, "move to the next station only on the whistle." With high levels of on-task behavior, an automatic timing device or student gym helper can control progressions.

The physical educator monitors and evaluates performance in this circuit training unit by having each student complete the test for repetitions maximum on one of the last two days of the unit. A comparison of test scores before and at the end of the unit shows which of the students who were initially at a low fitness level have worked hard. Students who were fit before the unit began are best assessed by comparing times taken to complete the entire circuit on the second day of the second week and the third day of the fourth week.

Maximizing Use of a Weight Training Facility

Riverside-Brookfield Township High School (Illinois) has gradually developed its weight training facility. The project was initiated in 1973 with a gift of a multi-station weight training machine by the school's Booster Association. The local

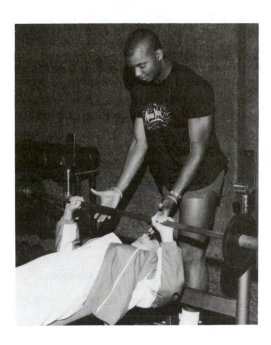

Students working together in weight training.

Kiwanis Club donated money for the purchase of Olympic weights, and the Booster Association quickly purchased another set. However, the most important step forward came in 1979 with the addition of Nautilus equipment, purchased through student fund raising and the generosity of local merchants. The equipment allowed Riverside-Brookfield to begin a research study on the rehabilitation and prevention of athletic injuries. The two physical educators most involved with the program's development, Anita Krieger and Duane Buturusis, were not satisfied with just having a first-class weight training facility and an important research program. They wanted the facility to serve more students and the community better.

Now several years later, their dream has been realized (Kneer and Grebner 1983). Not only does the facility serve the athletes at Riverside-Brookfield, but the physical educators have developed several important courses for students and a large community program.

An elective physical education course in individualized weight training is tremendously popular among students. Like many fitness courses, this individualized program aims to educate students about fitness as well as to make them more fit. What is most intriguing about this innovative course is the teaching aides who have made it truly individualized and efficient.

Students in the weight training course are preassessed and provided an individualized training program to meet their special needs (see outline of program in Figure 10.3, pp. 178–79). Available for each apparatus and each exercise are loop films, videotapes, and written materials that describe the purposes and techniques necessary for the student to use the exercise appropriately at the apparatus. These teaching aids also stress the safety issues involved in the weight training facility. Recently the school purchased a microcomputer for use within the facility, and software allows each student to track his or her own progress through an individualized program.

Two special physical education classes have also developed around the weight training facility. One class focuses on rehabilitation following injury or surgery.

I. Student weight training assessment

II. Introduction to weight training
   A. Grading procedures
   B. History of R-B Strength Fitness Facility
   C. Weight training terminology
   D. Safety procedures associated with weight
       training

III. Beginning phase
   A. Three modules required
       1. Isotonic exercise
       2. Isokinetic exercise
       3. Variable resistance exercise
   B. Module requirements
       1. How to do each exercise--refer to posters
           (learn by)
       2. How to practice each exercise--refer to
           Evaluation Checklist (practice by)
       3. Test over materials--refer to Evaluation
           Checklist (prove by)

IV. Intermediate phase
   A. One of three modules required
       1. Circuit weight training
       2. Isometric training
       3. Training for powerlifting
   B. Module requirements
       1. How to do each exercise--refer to posters
           (learn by)
       2. How to practice each exercise--refer to
           Evaluation Checklist (practice by)
       3. Test over materials--refer to Evaluation
           Checklist (prove by)

V. Advanced phase--training for personal goals
   A. Identify training goal(s)

Figure 10.3 Outline for individualized weight training course at Riverside-Brookfield Township High School.

B. Utilize the "Personalized Strength Training"
    microcomputer program

    1. Read the text on the disk concerning weight
        training theory and advanced terminology
    2. Take test covering advanced weight training
        concepts
    3. Proceed to practice by section of computer
        program
    4. Select whether the individual or the
        computer should format the workout
    5. If the individual, then:

        a. Make selection(s) from the body part
            list
        b. Choose specific exercises based on
            previous experience and/or preference
        c. Select the type of training program and
            degree of difficulty
        d. Hard copy of suggested workout will be
            printed including:

            (1) List of exercises and station numbers
            (2) Exercise prescription
            (3) Sample format

        e. Individual is to write out his/her
            suggested workout on "Personalized
            Workout sheet" (green form)

    6. If the computer, then:

        a. Make selection(s) from the body part
            list
        b. Select the type of training program and
            degree of difficulty
        c. Hard copy of suggested workout will be
            printed including:

            (1) List of exercises and station numbers
            (2) Exercise prescription
            (3) Sample format

C. Secure instructor's approval (before beginning
    workout)

The other focuses on adapted weight training programs for students who cannot participate in the regular program. In this class the activities are modified to meet the even more special needs of handicapped students.

In addition to these regular curricular offerings, the facility is open four nights per week for community use. An extensive adult fitness program provides individualized fitness prescriptions for each adult. These prescriptions involve the adults in the weight training facility and also in lap swimming, dance-exercise classes, and injury rehabilitation. The adults pay a minimal fee to cover costs of upkeep and personnel. Thus, the same facility that serves students during the school day serves the community in the evenings. More than 200 adults are enrolled during each fitness session, and many repeat sessions during the school year.

The experience at Riverside-Brookfield shows clearly the degree to which expertise and enthusiasm among physical educators can, over a period of time, develop and sustain important programs for students and the community.

A Total Fitness Effort at the High School Level

Lyons Township High School, located in a western suburb of Chicago, has an exemplary total fitness effort in its physical education program. The Lyons Township program recognizes that all students need to have a fitness orientation, that fitness needs to be attended to regularly throughout the school program, and that there are different kinds of fitness beyond the basic health-related fitness that is important for all students. The Lyons Township program, therefore, has several fitness components.

Freshman Fitness in the Core Program

All freshmen take a fitness course as part of a physical education core program. This course stresses concepts about fitness, skills in fitness-related activities, and a beginning involvement in fitness activities. It is similar to many of the concept approaches described in Chapter 14. A topical outline for this course is shown in Figure 10.4 on pp. 182–83.

Daily Fitness in Physical Education Classes

Students take physical education five days per week. Regardless of what physical education activity they are engaged in, they begin each class period with a 12- to 15-minute fitness emphasis. While activities vary, all instructors do similar activities every day. The daily fitness program features flexibility, muscular strength and endurance, and cardiovascular fitness.

Students do flexibility exercises each day; these include bending, stretching, and arching exercises. Students do strength exercises two days per week; these include push-ups, pull-ups, prone trunk lift, shoulder raises, abdominal exercises, and leg training. Students do cardiovascular exercises three days per week; these include jogging, aerobics, water activities, and circuit training, depending on where students are gathered for their main physical education activity. Their comprehensive fitness is tested each spring toward the end of the school year.

Fitness Elective Courses

During their junior and senior years at Lyons Township High School, students may elect to take additional physical education courses. Some of the more attractive offerings are in the fitness area: A figure fitness course emphasizes strength development, weight control, nutrition education, and analysis of various "popular" fitness programs in the private sector. A weight training and conditioning course focuses not only on improved strength through individualized programs but also educates students about weight training, care and use of weight training equipment, safety issues, and testing procedures. The newest offering is an elective course in exercise physiology for students who have achieved a B average or better in biology. This course is staffed on an interdepartmental basis with faculty from the science area. It focuses on topics such as anthropometry and body composition, respiration, the cardiovascular system, muscle physiology, diet, and nutrition. Much of the work takes the form of laboratory investigations (see Chapter 14 for more information on this teaching approach within physical education).

The Lyons Township program provides a basic fitness education in the freshman core course, provides for daily fitness activities within the daily fitness effort in regular physical education classes, and then provides attractive elective fitness options for juniors and seniors. This total effort ensures that all students become more educated about fitness and that many have the opportunity to continue fitness activities throughout their high school years.

Fitness constraints

Fitness programs that demonstrate important outcomes are difficult to develop and maintain within physical education. First, physical education in schools today is not considered to be a vehicle purely for the development of fitness. Many other outcomes are important, and these too take time and program resources to achieve. The second major constraint on achieving fitness goals is time. Improvement in cardiovascular fitness requires a minimum of 20 minutes of sustained aerobic exercise at 70 percent of maximum capacity at least three days per week. Strength and flexibility goals add to that time demand. Gaining adequate time for fitness and then using that time efficiently remains the most important ingredient in developing and maintaining good fitness programs.

Nevertheless, this chapter has revealed several different approaches that can and do work. Schools have developed fitness programs that achieve important goals. These programs are obviously the result of motivated and competent planning and development by physical educators who value fitness and are determined to do something about it. Such programs require teachers with ambition, good planning skills, efficient organization and instruction, effective management of student time, and accountability for student performance. In short, they require effective teaching.

Summary

Although the program examples presented in this chapter are different in terms of teaching strategy and organization, they have one crucial feature in common: Each is designed to bring about changes in the fitness skills and behaviors of adolescent students.

Health fitness is concerned with cardiovascular functioning and is the closest fitness concept to basic physiological functioning. Physical fitness focuses on broad categories of physical performance that go beyond health-related concerns. Motor fitness is even more remote from basic physiological functioning and reflects measures of motor skill performance. Teachers must

I.   Differentiation between skill-related and health-related fitness components

    A.   Health-related fitness components

        1.   Cardiovascular fitness
        2.   Body composition
        3.   Flexibility
        4.   Muscular endurance

    B.   Skill-related fitness components

        1.   Speed
        2.   Agility
        3.   Balance
        4.   Coordination
        5.   Reaction time
        6.   Power

II. Cardiovascular fitness (track)

    A.   How this transport system is organized
    B.   Pulse taking and interpretation
    C.   Step test (indoor conditioning)
    D.   12-minute run test
    E.   Training effects and benefits of exercise
    F.   Jogging principles
    G.   Threshold of training
    H.   Training prescriptions and terminology

        1.   Aerobic
        2.   Anaerobic
        3.   Intensity
        4.   Duration
        5.   Progression

    I.   Blood pressure (indoor conditioning)
    J.   Heart disease

III. Flexibility (indoor conditioning)

    A.   Function in fitness
    B.   Flexibility testing

        1.   Sit and reach
        2.   Shoulder
        3.   Back arch
        4.   Passive or static versus active or ballistic

Figure 10.4 Outline for freshman physical fitness core course at Lyons Township High School.

IV. Strength training (indoor conditioning)

    A. Weight room rules and safety
    B. Demonstration of lifts
    C. Muscle structure and function
    D. Identification of major groups
    E. Training systems

V. Body composition (indoor conditioning)

    A. Role and desired amount of fat
    B. Testing, use of calipers
    C. Fat control through diet and exercise
    D. Nutritional groups and diet
    E. Fallacies of weight control

        1. Fad diets
        2. Vibrating belts
        3. Impermeable sweat clothes, dehydrating

VI. Stress and relaxation--posture analysis (during wrestling and badminton)

    A. Lab on feet and legs
    B. Lab on back
    C. Problems
    D. Care of the back

VII. Skill-related test items

    A. Power--vertical jump test (volleyball)
    B. Agility--Illinois Agility Run Test (flag football)
    C. Speed--50 and 100 in track
    D. Strength--grip dynamometer (weight training)

determine which type of fitness they are attempting to affect and then go about it in ways specific to that type.

Health fitness is the most basic fitness goal, and teachers involved in programs designed to achieve it should collect reliable and valid data, teach fitness skills, provide adequate time for improvement on a long-term basis, and supplement the program with an understanding of fitness concepts.

Fitness-direct instruction is a model in which goals are clear to students, time allocated for instruction is sufficient, coverage of fitness content is extensive, performance of students is monitored, feedback is provided, and students can produce many appropriate fitness responses.

Fitness program examples include a health fitness remediation model, a daily fitness program with the homeroom teacher playing a pivotal role, a circuit training program, the total use of a weight training facility, and a comprehensive high school fitness program.

Suggested activities

1. Assessment of fitness has been considered important for physical educators. Consider the different fitness orientations of the following tests by comparing them to the AAHPERD Lifetime Health-Related Fitness Test (AAHPERD 1980).
   (a) Kraus-Weber Test (Krause and Hirschland, 1954)
   (b) AAHPERD Youth Fitness Test (Hunsicker and Reiff 1976)
   (c) Motor Fitness Tests for Oregon Schools (Oregon State Department of Education 1962)

2. On the basis of the test items of the AAHPERD Lifetime Health-Related Fitness Test, design a set of minimum requirements for physical education majors to achieve.

3. Discuss the notion of mandating fitness requirements for graduating college physical education majors. Compare this with requirements for graduating music majors.

4. Debate the following issue: Students should be required to achieve a cardiovascular fitness level each year in order to graduate. Have three students argue the affirmative and three the negative.

5. Visit local fitness centers. Report on what activities they provide, who goes to them, and how much they cost. Also try to find out the qualifications of the people running the programs. Report your findings to the class.

11

Sports Education

The purpose of this chapter is to describe and explain a curriculum model for physical education in which the primary objective is to help students become skilled sports participants and good sportspersons. To this end, we discuss what sports education is and present a philosophical rationale for it. Then we introduce a range of program models, beginning with the single-class format and extending to a complete, schoolwide model, including one or more examples of each. The major topics in this chapter are as follows:

The major characteristics of sports education

The role of competition in sports education

A rationale for sports education

Characteristics that differentiate sports education from traditional physical education

Four sports education models of differing levels of complexity and five examples of sports education programs

The importance of practice sessions

The physical educator's role in promoting the values and attitudes of a good sportsperson

Jean went to bed a half hour early last night. She told her parents that she wanted to be rested for her volleyball game today. Her team had not done very well at first, winning only three of their first six games. However, after that the team began to improve. Their practices paid off with better serving and blocking, and Jean and her three teammates seemed to play together better.

Since then they had won three straight games and now were playing for their league championship and the chance to meet the first-place team from the 10:00 league for the overall championship. Jean felt that she had really improved in her game, especially her serving and setting. She also felt good about her role on the team and the camaraderie that had developed among her and her teammates. Their coach seemed quite pleased with their progress and had commented just the other day on the important role Jean had played in their success.

Jean did not feel a lot of pressure going into this game; after all, she would be on another team next season and get another chance in a different sport. Yet she wanted to do well—for herself and her teammates. The game was at 1:15 P.M., and she felt excited about it—nervous, but in a way that she felt would help her to play better.

What does this short description remind you of? It sounds more like an interscholastic experience than anything else. There is mention of teams, schedules, conferences, practices, games, and championships, as well as a reference to a coach. Could this be a description of a physical education class experience? It certainly does not sound like most physical education classes. But that is exactly what it is—a description of the experience of a girl in a volleyball class in a sports education program. Perhaps it is really not correct to call it a class because the experience is obviously so different from most classes. Can physical education be conceptualized and implemented as a sports education program so that the experience of the student is similar to the experience students get in interscholastic sports programs, except on a smaller scale? The answer is yes, and it is the purpose of this chapter to describe the sports education model, to provide a rationale for the model, to show examples of how it can be implemented, and to address problems and constraints and how to overcome them.

What is sports education?

The purpose of sports education is to educate students in various sports—to teach them to be players, in the fullest sense of that term. Students cannot learn to be good sportspeople unless they participate in sport. However, the traditional way in which physical education has been conceptualized bears very little resemblance to sport. *Sport* is here defined as occurrences of playful competition in which outcomes are determined by combinations of physical skill, strategy, and chance (Loy 1968). Sport derives from play, and sports are institutionalized forms of motor play.

What characterizes sport as an institutionalized form of motor play, and how does sport differ from the ways in which physical education is typically organized and implemented? First of all, sport is typically done in a *season*. There is a basketball season, a hockey season, and a golf season. Physical education is typically done in *units*, and these units are often very short in duration. Sport typically involves an *affiliation*—players are members of a team or a club, and they retain that membership at least for the length of a season. In physical education it is more likely that affiliation changes from class to class, and sometimes students can be on different teams even within one class.

Sport typically involves a *formal competition*. It may be a conference season with a round-robin format. It may be a series of dual meets with a culminating championship event as in tennis or track. It may be a series of larger competitions such as is now common in collegiate golf. There is a schedule for these events, and it is fixed prior to the start of the season; that is, in sport, players usually know who their opponents are and in what order they will compete against them. In physical education it is common to have some competitions, but they are irregular and there is seldom a schedule. Since affiliation changes from class to class in physical education, a schedule would not mean much.

In sport, a season typically closes with a *culminating event*—a conference championship, a state tournament. This is because it is in the nature of sport to find out who is best in a particular season. In physical education, a culminating event is rare because there are seldom teams and schedules.

Another characteristic of sport is the keeping of *records*—scoring averages, hitting averages, kicks on goal, shooting percentages, and defensive averages. The records provide feedback for individuals and groups, and they become an important part of the tradition and ritual associated with sport. In physical education such record keeping is rare.

These characteristics—seasons, affiliation, formal competition, culminating events, and records—are typically present in sport and typically absent in physical education. Sports education seeks to incorporate these characteristics within the physical education program. It aims to develop sports programs for all the students within a school. This chapter presents a number of alternative ways in which sports education can be implemented within the school program. At this point keep in mind that in sports education there are seasons rather than units, there is team membership or some other kind of ongoing affiliation within each season, there is scheduled formal competition, there are practices and competitions, a season culminates with some event that defines who was best within that season, and records are kept and made available to competitors and other interested parties.

In sports education, students practice and compete as a team.

Sports education is *not* interscholastic sport. Interscholastic sport is usually for the best athletes, who want an extended experience competing against the best athletes from other schools. Sports education is for all students and is carried on within schools not between schools.

Does sports education overemphasize competition?

Upon first learning about sports education, many people react negatively to it because they perceive it to be an overemphasis on competition. They see in it the potential for all of the abuses that plague professional sport, intercollegiate sport, interscholastic sport, and even youth sport. We must face this reaction and criticism as straightforwardly as possible. Clearly, there are abuses in sport at all levels from the NBA down to youth sport. But sport is an extraordinarily valuable part of our culture, and professional physical educators need to be in the forefront of those who are trying to make sport as good as it can be, to remediate current abuses, and to prevent future ones. One cannot improve sport by disavowing it!

A major problem in sport at all levels is that parents, alumni, coaches, and players sometimes want so badly to win that they are willing to bend rules in order to gain a competitive advantage. Surely there is improper competition in sport at many levels. However, this does not make competition itself bad or inappropriate for the general student. Appropriately conceptualized and implemented competitive experiences have educational value. Physical education should not deemphasize competition. It should provide *good* competition. It is our contention—which we will explain more fully in the following section—that competition is fundamental to play and that it forms the very core of the sports experience. One of the major problems with motivation in school physical education at the middle and senior high levels is that it so often is devoid of competition and when competitions do occur they are too often trivial and uninteresting.

Thus, physical educators can embrace the good competition that sports education can provide for the general student. Good competitive experiences can go a long way toward improving the general sports culture of society. Good competition makes sports education an attractive curriculum model.

A rationale for sports education

The rationale for sports education rests on a few very basic and important assumptions. The first is that sport derives from play; that is, sport represents an institutionalized form of competitive motor play. The second is that sport is an important part of our culture and that sport occupies an important role in determining the health and vitality of the entire culture; that is, if more people participate in good sport, then the culture is stronger. The third assumption follows from the first two. If sport is a higher form of play and if good sport is important to the health and vitality of the culture, then sport should be the subject matter of physical education. The development of good sportspersons and the development of a better sports culture should be central to the mission of physical education. In fact, it would make sense, as is done in this chapter, to describe the subject matter as sports education. Let's examine these assumptions further.

All people everywhere play. Play appears to be a fundamental form of activity and a fundamental motivation in social groups at every level of development. As individuals mature, their play forms become more organized and predictable. As societies mature, their play forms become institutionalized. In developed societies, one of the major functions of education is to transmit the culture to the young. One of the aspects of culture that is transmitted is that of play, in all its various forms (see Siedentop 1980 for a more complete explanation of play and physical education), including art, music, drama, and dance. Clearly, the band or the drama group at school has much in common with the sports teams. They each derive their fundamental motivation from play.

Play is defined as activity that is voluntarily entered into, is separate in the sense that the time and space elements are defined especially for the play event, is uncertain as to outcome, is economically unproductive, and is either regulated by special rules created for the play activity or is fictive, that is, dominated by fantasy or make-believe (Caillois 1961). These characteristics do not represent either-or possibilities in the sense that an activity is either playful or not playful but instead represent ways in which the play element in an activity can be enhanced or diminished, made more or less playful. For example, if an outcome is fairly certain because of uneven competition, it tends to diminish the playfulness of the event, but it does not necessarily eliminate the event as play. When teams or individuals are closely matched and the outcome is therefore maximally uncertain, the playfulness is maximized and more pleasure and excitement are derived by the participants. Likewise, getting paid to perform, as in professional sport, tends to diminish the play element, to make the activity less playful for the participant (it still may be very playful for the spectator), but it does not necessarily eliminate the play element.

The play of little children is spontaneous, turbulent, and dependent upon immediate gratification. It is typically organized in a loose fashion, and whatever simple rules exist tend to change constantly. However, as people develop and mature, the nature of their play changes. Mature play is characterized by practice, the subordination to rules, the adoption of more specific roles, an appreciation for difficulty, increasing complexity in strategy and performance, the observance of rituals and customs, and an appreciation for tradition. Mature play forms become institutionalized; that is, they become organized in very specific ways that breed traditions, rules, and governing bodies. Golf, badminton, basketball, and a host of other sports are institutionalized forms of motor play. An activity such as frisbee or skateboarding is much less institutionalized; whether it becomes a sport depends on how it develops in the future.

The important point is that mature forms of play require practice, sustained involvement, the learning of specific skills, the understanding of rules and strategies, and an appreciation for the customs and traditions of the play form. *This is why they require education!* Practice, rules, strategies, and customs do not diminish playfulness. Quite to the contrary, they are exactly the characteristics that make play more meaningful for adults. This is why we have art education, music education, and drama education. It is also why we have sports education. Mastery and commitment are important to playfulness, and they can be acquired best by most people through a systematic educational effort.

Evidence that sport is important to culture is all around us. Sport has also been important to many other cultures, most notably those of ancient Greece and Rome. Sport tends to dominate weekend television. Pick up any newspaper and you can find a daily section devoted to sport. This tends to be the first section read by many people. When you next walk by a newsstand, take a careful look at the number of sports magazines on sale, not just the familiar general ones but the highly specific sports magazines that focus on individual sports from acrobatics to yachting, from specialized forms of martial arts to waterskiing. Sport is seemingly gaining in importance in our culture. It is being taken seriously in films, literature, and drama.

As sport grows more important in a culture, the danger that perverted forms of sport can weaken the culture also increases. When athletes take drugs to enhance performance, it perverts sport and weakens the culture. When television celebrities compete in pseudosports activities under the guise of celebrity sport and people watch them on television, it perverts real sport and weakens the culture (this form of sport is often referred to as trash-sport). When athletes behave poorly during competitions, it perverts the sport and weakens the culture. When young children are forced into mature sports forms too early, it perverts sport and weakens the culture.

What is clear is that sport is important in a culture and that it has the potential for good and for bad; that is, sport can contribute to the strengthening of the culture, to its betterment, or it can contribute to the weakening of the culture, to its decline. This is yet another reason why the notion of sports education is so important. Physical educators need to take some responsibility for the future of the sports culture, and they can do so by educating students in sport so that they become good sportspersons. Good sportspersons can participate in sport in skilled, appropriate ways and experience the tremendous pleasures that derive from participation. However, they cannot do so unless they are educated into the role, and they cannot be so educated unless they participate in sport.

This leads to the third assumption of sports education, which is that sport should be the subject matter of physical education. The sports culture is so important to the future well-being of our society—and there is currently much evidence that it is too often being perverted—that society needs to ensure that future generations are educated in sport, and the schools appear to be the best place to accomplish this. Educating in sport means participating in sport, not just sports activities taken out of their natural contexts but sport that involves seasons, affiliations, schedules, culminating events, and records.

The goal of sports education should be to involve all students in sport so that they not only improve as sportspersons but also gain an appreciation for *good* sport. "Sport for all" should be the motto of sports educators, who have the potential to be the grass-roots guardians of a healthy, sane, competitive sports culture.

Why physical education is not sports education

Physical education has traditionally been conceptualized as a school subject in which a variety of educational goals are achieved through a variety of activities. Motor skills, physical fitness, cognitive development, social development, character development, and emotional stability have all been suggested as goals for physical education. These goals, it has been postulated, are to be achieved through experiences in motor activities. Although many of these motor activities have typically involved sports activities, *these sports activities have typically been utilized without reference to the dimensions and characteristics that give sport its meaning*! To be sure, students in physical education have volleyball units in which they perform skills such as serving, passing, setting, spiking, and blocking, and they most often will have a few volleyball games in such a unit. But is it like volleyball as a sport? Very seldom. There is no team affiliation, no schedule, no formal competition, no culminating events, and no records are kept. By divorcing the activity of volleyball from its natural expression as a sport, physical educators have too often made it a boring, trivial activity that does not capture the imagination and enthusiasm of the students.

As pointed out earlier, a mature involvement in play is characterized by commitment, practice, the adoption of roles, an appreciation of skillfulness, increasing complexity in strategy and performance, and participation in the rituals and traditions of the play form. This kind of behavior is often found among those who participate on a school team or in a sports club (or in a band or a theater production for that matter). However, those characteristics are typically lacking in physical education, and it is clear that students tend to react to the two differently. Sports teams and clubs tend to breed intimacy, dedication, socialization, competence, and commitment. These qualities are often lacking from school physical education programs. Sports programs are often vital and full of meaning for the participants. Physical education is too often viewed as unimportant and trivial by the same students.

Sports education is a model through which we can change that attitude. In sports education we can give all students the opportunity to experience the meaning to be found in an appropriate involvement in sport, one in which their abilities are well matched to the demands of a sports activity but in a way that still preserves the important characteristics of sport as an institutionalized form of motor play.

The developmental nature of sports education

Sports education aims to allow people to enter the many worlds of sport in ways that tend to optimize their opportunities to find meaningful ongoing commitments to participation and, in so doing, to improve the conduct and practice of sport within society. In this way, sports education not only contributes to the growth of the individual but also to the growth of the culture.

We will not achieve these important goals, however, by imposing mature sports forms on young learners. Ability in sport, like any other form of higher playful activity, is acquired gradually. We must introduce it properly and then implement it in a developmental model so that students move along gradually into a more mature relationship to sport.

Sports education does not mean that middle school students participate in adult forms of the major sports, and it does not mean that a senior high school student who is learning a new sport is introduced to its adult form during his or her initial experience. Seventh graders who do not have the hand size to skillfully manipulate a full-sized basketball or the strength to shoot from 20 feet at a 10-foot high basket should not be learning the adult form of basketball. It is better to adapt the sport to their developmental status, to have them utilize a junior-size ball and have a 9-foot high basket. In this way, they can learn the appropriate skills and develop a commitment to the game rather than be turned off by the failure that is inevitable if they are thrust into situations for which they have neither the skills nor the developmental status to acquire the skills.

Likewise, sports education is best pursued when students are optimally involved. They not only learn more quickly when they get more opportunities at the skills and strategies, but they tend to like it more too. Therefore, activities such as six-on-a-team soccer or three-person volleyball are no doubt better for sports education than are the more adult forms of the activities. Maximizing participation is a major strategy of good sports education. Many sports require a modification of the parent activity so that more students can participate.

Thus, the examples we present later in this chapter are all *modified* sports activities. The activities are modified in two ways. First, they are modified to be developmentally appropriate for young learners or beginning learners. Second, they are modified to ensure optimal participation in learning the skills and strategies of the sports.

Major characteristics of sports education models

Sports education models share at least six characteristics that differentiate sports education from more traditional approaches to programming and teaching physical education. We present these characteristics to help you refocus your thinking about physical education and begin to see it from the sports education point of view.

1. *Sports education involves seasons rather than units.* A season encompasses both practice and competition, ending with some culminating event. Seasons in sports education often require longer time frames than do units in traditional programming. A touch football *season* must last longer than three weeks. An archery season or a golf season cannot be completed in 20 lessons. Therefore, we must begin to think of activities in terms of larger chunks of time. Of course, this means that there are fewer activities in the total yearly program. Many critics over the years have suggested that physical education units are typically too short to accomplish any real goals. The trade-off of longer activity seasons for fewer activities throughout the year is a good one. If more than one teacher or an entire staff is involved in the sports education model, then students can select from more than one sport in each season.

2. *In sports education, students quickly become members of teams.* Once team membership is established, it is retained for the entire season unless there is a specific provision for changing teams (an arrangement akin to trading period, for example). There are three general methods for establishing team membership. First, teachers can assign students to teams on a basis of their own choosing. Second, students can in some way select their own teams. Third, teachers can assign students to teams on the basis of a pretest. Because pretesting often takes a great deal of time, time that can better be used in instruction, practice, and competition, we favor teachers' choice of selection and/or student selection.

Naturally, a teacher must be very careful that student selection schemes do not create resentment and become traumatic for less-skilled players who might be picked last. Until students have some experience in sports education and learn how to handle the selection process, teacher assignment is probably the preferable strategy. A good way to bridge the gap between the two methods is to appoint (or have the students elect) a "board" for each sport. This board works with the teacher to make the assignments and may eventually be able to take over the task.

In a single class with 24 students, selecting teams is difficult because of the problems of ensuring equal competition. However, if two teachers have ninth grade classes at the same time and participate in a sports education season together, they may have as many as 50 to 80 students from which to assign teams. They could, in fact, develop two leagues within the combined classes, allowing for further differentiation for the purpose of equalizing competition. An elective program for students still further eases the problems associated with ensuring more equal competition.

3. *Sports education provides a formal schedule of competition.* In organized sport, the beginning of a season is typically dominated by practice sessions. After a period of practice, games or matches begin, but they are interspersed with practice sessions as players and teams continue to try to improve their performance. As the season develops, there are fewer practices and more competitions. That is exactly the model for arranging time within a season in sports education. For example, if a teacher arranges a softball season of nine weeks and has the students three times per week for classes, he or she has a

Game competition takes on new meaning in sport education.

total of 27 sessions (this is an example of the single-class model with competition only within the class). During the first couple of weeks the teams would practice, developing their skills and deciding who would play what positions and what their batting order might be. During the third week, the first game might be played. In each of the next two weeks, the students might have one game day and two practice days. In the next two weeks, they might have two game days and one practice day. In the final two weeks, all days would be game days. The teacher would arrange the formal schedule for the season ahead of time, and each team would know the schedule and plan accordingly.

4. *In sports education, there is often a culminating event.* One of the features of organized sport is the season-ending competition that is seen as the culminating event. It might be a one-day track and field meet. It might be a double elimination volleyball tournament. It might be the champion from one class meeting the champion from another class. In sports education, the culminating event should involve *all* the participants (simply because total participation is a goal of sports education even though it is not always a goal in other forms of organized sport).

5. *In sports education, records are kept and publicized.* Sport has rituals and traditions that provide a great deal of meaning to the participants. There is no reason why students in sports education should not have the same opportunities to participate in this aspect of sport. Sports education is important to the participants to the degree that it is made to seem important by those who plan and implement the program (see page 381). Teachers should publicize league or match standings, as well as the schedule for the next week, perhaps highlighting last week's play. It is useful to emphasize *team* performances rather than the individual performances.

6. *In sports education, teachers assume the role of coaches.* If only one teacher is involved in sports education, then he or she is the coach for all of the teams. If two teachers are sharing the responsibility, then one may coach half the teams and the other teach the other half. Coaches are responsible for basic instruction in skills, for the development of strategies, and for feedback about both during the season. In sports education, it is obviously helpful for teams to have student captains too (appointed, elected by teammates, or assigned by a student board). While the coaches (teachers) provide overall instruction and strategy, the teams can work to improve themselves within those guidelines, with the student captain acting in a leadership role.

In many sports it is tremendously helpful to develop rules that guide the teams in their selection and practice of skills and strategies. For example, a rule prohibiting zone defenses in basketball might be included for a basketball league. Or coaches might teach two basic offenses (one attacking and one more defensive) in soccer and have the teams choose which one they will attempt to perfect.

As sports education develops within a school, students can take on more and more responsibility within their teams. As is obvious in some of the examples that follow, students can eventually assume very important roles in both administration and coaching in sports education. Fulfillng these roles is not only educational for the students but also guarantees their commitment to the program and helps them to see that it runs smoothly and well.

Examples of sports education models

In the following pages we present four sports education models of varying levels of *administrative* complexity, ranging from the simplest model administratively to the model that requires the largest change in the administration of the physical education program. The first model can be used by any teacher anywhere, simply as a different approach to conducting his or her classes. The other models require more cooperation among teachers, adoption by a physical education department or staff, and support from the school administration to use the available time normally given over to physical education and intramurals in a somewhat different manner. The models are as follows:

1. *The single-class model with competition within the class.* This is the "beginner's" model. It does not involve other teachers or other classes and does not require different scheduling than ordinarily exists.

2. *The multiple-class model with competition within periods.* Many schools have more than one physical education class per period. Often teachers combine some classes for team teaching or differentiated teaching. This situation is appropriate for combining the classes and (a) have one sports season with one large league competition, (b) having one sports season with two league competitions based on skill, or (c) having two sports seasons with students selecting which sport they want to participate in. Again, this model of sports education requires very little change from the status quo in most schools.

3. *The single/multiple-class model with competition between or among classes.* This version of sports education uses time outside class for further competition, typically time that is ordinarily assigned to intramurals or some other form of nonattached time. Students practice and compete within their assigned class periods and also during the extended time. This version of sports education requires some administrative changes in most schools.

4. *The complete sports education model.* In its most mature version, sports education would become synonymous with school sport; again, this does not mean interscholastic sport but rather sport within the school. In physical education, time is typically arranged for instruction (in periods), for intramurals, and often for some nonattached, drop-in time. In the complete sports education model, the total available time is devoted to sports education. During the season, teams might practice during the school day or after (or before) the school day in time that used to be intramural time. When competitions begin, teams might have games during the school day or after or before it. The time is used flexibly to create *more total time* for sports education. This version of sports education requires drastic changes in the way in which physical education is ordinarily conceptualized and programmed in schools.

Three-Person Volleyball

This model is for a middle or junior high school setting in which two teachers share classes that total 50 to 70 students. Three-person volleyball is played with a junior-size volleyball, with a 7-foot high net, and a 15-by-40-foot court.

The class meets four days per week, and the volleyball season is designed for eight weeks or a total of 32 sessions. With 64 students, this class has two volleyball leagues. One league is for skilled players, and the other is for less-skilled players. (Note that there are other legitimate ways of dividing students for competition.)

The first week is devoted to practice and instruction. Four students of varying levels of skill are selected to assist the teachers in assigning students to teams. After three days of observation, the students are assigned to teams, four students to each team. The teams are then assigned to two leagues of eight teams each. On the fourth day of class, students begin to receive instruction and practice as a team. One teacher takes administrative responsibility for each league.

During the second week, the students have two practice days and two scrimmage days. Scrimmage days allow teachers to make sure that rules are understood and to teach refereeing as a skill. During the third week, a double round-robin league play begins for each league; there are two match days and two practice days. From the third through the seventh weeks, students have three match days and one practice day per week. During the eighth week, there is a championship tournament involving all 16 teams.

During match days students participate in a warm-up period followed by a timed match (the duration of the match is determined by the length of the teaching period), for example, 22 minutes. All matches start and stop at the same time. There is a signal every 5 minutes for substitutions. Students referee their own games, with referees being those students not playing at the moment. Referees also keep score. The winner of each match is the team with the most points at the final time signal. Standings can be kept in terms of total points scored or win-loss records (or some combination of the two).

The teachers observe games and make notes for individual players and teams in terms of skills and strategies to be worked on at subsequent practice sessions. Team captains are responsible for seeing that a certain portion of practice sessions is devoted to those notes. In other practice sessions, all teams and players practice certain skills and strategies as directed by the teachers.

Students get to choose a name for their team and adopt a uniform (as long as it meets the standards set by the teachers for physical education clothing). Each Monday the league standings are posted along with other items concerning the league. If team play in any league is very unequal, the teachers and the four student representatives can, at the end of the first round of play, make personnel changes in teams so as to equalize competition for the second round.

Softball

This model is for a senior high school setting in which one teacher has a class of approximately 70 students. The class meets three days per week, and the softball season lasts nine weeks.

The school in our example has space for three fields. A large (14- or 16-inch) softball is used so that gloves are not necessary and the space needed for each field is less than standard.

The first two weeks are devoted to instruction, practice, and organization of the competition. Six students are selected (or assigned) to act as student representatives, all students are assigned to teams, six teams are selected with 10 to 12 players per team, a double round-robin league schedule is arranged, and students are taught how to umpire.

In the third week of the season league play begins. Games are played on Mondays and Fridays with Wednesdays used for practice sessions. Rules are modified so that each team bats for 20 minutes. All games begin and end at the same time, and teams change the field at a midway signal. Total number of runs scored determines the winner of each game. The pitcher is a member of the batting team. This ensures speed of play and more strikes thrown. All members of the team bat in order regardless of how many are on the team. Nine players play in the field. A signal is given every five minutes for defensive substitutions.

During the final week of class a tournament is held. Teachers try to schedule out-of-class games with teams from other periods. They also arrange a Saturday tournament with teams from other classes at the end of the season.

Students umpire their own games. Teachers make sure that games move along quickly (the rules are designed to minimize wasted time between innings). Teachers also provide feedback and make notes for conducting subsequent practice sessions.

Gymnastics

In this example one physical educator teaches 25 students gymnastics five days a week for six weeks from the sports education perspective. During the first week students are checked on five drills: floor exercise, beam, rings, vault, and bars. The teacher provides beginning instruction, and students have a chance to practice each event. Five students are chosen as captains and together with the teacher select teams of five students each. Instruction continues with captains taking more responsibilities with their teams, especially in establishing which students are best suited for each of the various events. During the last part of the second week, students hold a scrimmage and perform under meet conditions.

During the third and fourth weeks meets take place on Tuesdays and Thursdays with practices on Mondays, Wednesdays, and Fridays. For the first several meets, team members select one event in which to compete. For subsequent meets, teams perform at each event and rotate as a team from event to event. All scoring is done on a graded point system. Cumulative points are kept for individuals and for teams. At later meets, teams compete in two or three events per meet. During the fifth week meets are held on Monday, Wednesday, and Friday with practice on Tuesday and Thursday. During the final week there is a practice on Monday and a final culminating meet for the remainder of the week. During each meet, members of one of the five teams act as judges and recorders. Students are provided both instruction and practice in judging and recording. The responsibility for this is rotated for each meet. The teacher monitors the performance of the judging teams and adds or takes away points from their team totals on the basis of how well they perform as judges. Thus, students take the judging task seriously as part of the total competition, and fairness in judging is reinforced.

Doubles Tennis

In this example two high school teachers run a sports education tennis program with competition within and between two classes with 35 students in each. Intramural time is used for between-class competition. The season is four days per week for nine weeks. A period is 50 minutes long, and six tennis courts are available.

During the first two weeks, the teachers teach tennis fundamentals, students learn rules, scoring, and officiating, and each class elects a student governing board. The governing board, along with the teacher, divides each class into five teams of seven students each. A double round-robin is set up for competition within each class. A match in the within-class leagues consists of one boys' doubles, one girls' doubles, and one coed doubles. On each match day one team has a bye. The bye team is responsible for refereeing, scoring, and retrieving, with a bye-team student assigned to each of the six courts. All matches begin and end at the same time on a common signal. All winners are determined by total points (each time a serve is made a point is contested and either won by the serving team or the receiving team). Matches are 24 minutes long. A serving order is established, and each server serves three serves before the serve passes to a player on the other team.

From the fourth week onward, matches are arranged between classes during the intramural time. Players from one class compete against players from the other class in boys' doubles, girls' doubles, and coed doubles (they do not have to compete as teammates as they do within their own classes). The game rules are identical as are the scoring rules.

During the last week, a play-off tournament is arranged within each class and also between classes. The within-class competition is on a team basis. The between-class competition is on an individual doubles team basis.

Three-Person Basketball

In the complete sports education model, the traditional distinctions among time for instructional classes, time for intramurals, and other nonattached time are eliminated. Time is available during school and after school. The time is used flexibly to accommodate each sports season.

In our example 100 high school students have elected to take basketball during the early-winter sports education season. Their electing basketball as their sport for this season gave them access to certain times within and after the school day. The 100 students begin their season by attending "tryouts" that are scheduled during the first week of the season, both during school and after school. The purpose of the tryouts is to allow the three teacher/coaches to evaluate student abilities. Three leagues are available. One is a girls' league, one a boys' league, and one a coed league, according to Title IX provision. Students indicate the league they are interested in and the tryouts are conducted by league.

Depending on the number of students indicating a preference for each league, the teachers select student respresentatives to sit on a governing board for each league. Each board, along with one coach, then selects teams with a view toward equalizing the competition. Each team has four players and is allowed to choose colors for its uniforms. Once teams are selected, there is a two-day period in which trading can occur within the league. All trades must be approved by the players involved and by the governing board.

During the second week of the season, each team attends a minimum of three practice sessions that stress individual fundamentals. The following week each team attends three practice sessions that stress offensive and defensive team strategies. At the end of this week each player must pass a rules test prior to the beginning of league play.

Each league has a double round-robin schedule, and games take place both during and after school. Practice sessions are also scheduled. Teams must identify to the coach in charge of their league the offensive and defensive strategies they plan to utilize. This forms the basis for further coach suggestions and feedback as the practice sessions continue and league play begins.

Games are of standard length, typically two 20-minute periods. Substitutions are allowed at each 5-minute point. The gymnasium can accommodate three games at once. All students have a certain number of refereeing assignments during the season but not in the league in which they are competing. A student is also assigned to keep the scorecard at each game, again not for the league in which he or she competes. Thus, in addition to learning playing and team skills, students also learn how to referee and score.

Each Monday morning a basketball news bulletin is released with scores and game highlights from the previous week and schedules for the upcoming week. This bulletin is administered by the league governing board.

Students both play and practice each week. Coaches for each league are responsible for assigning practice hints for each team and arrange time for several teams to practice together even though they may compete in different leagues. Coaches, aided by student coaches, are in charge of practice sessions.

Season-ending awards make team members proud.

A note on practice sessions

We must emphasize that sports education does not mean that students never practice but only "play games." Sports education is not just another excuse for supervised recreation in physical education. The clear intent of sports education is that students improve their skills, their abilities to play sports, and their attitudes toward sports participation. Practice sessions serve a very important purpose in this model.

We have already pointed out that in the sports education model practices occur often during the preseason and in the early part of the season and less often during the later part of the season. Coaches (physical education teachers) need to make very sure that the practice sessions are task-oriented and used to improve students' individual abilities and their group abilities to compete as a team. Throughout the season, practices can be devoted to specific improvement of various parts of the games as determined by feedback from the coaches who view the games.

Students take practice sessions more seriously when the sessions have specific goals; coaches should ensure that specific goals are made clear to students and that the students are held accountable for meeting them. Teams may work on specific aspects of their offensive and defensive strategies, or they may focus on improving individual skills. Obviously, more than one team will be practicing at a time, and different teams can help each other practice. However, coaches should make sure that this does not just result in "pickup games." Coaches should also encourage teams to get together in and out of school to practice their skills and strategies.

From time to time, coaches may want to bring all players together for a single practice session in order to (a) introduce a new skill, (b) introduce a new strategy, (c) refine skills or strategies, and/or (d) describe and demonstrate practice and training strategies. This kind of session is much like a clinic in which specific goals are to be achieved.

A note on developing good sportspersons

To be educated in sport means something more than being a skilled competitor. It means valuing the rules, the traditions, and the rituals of a sport. It means playing fairly. It means appreciating good competition and the efforts of teammates and opponents. These *values* and *attitudes* have behavioral dimensions that teachers can observe and teach to students. Students do not automatically know what it means to be a good sportsperson. They have to be taught—and that takes time and effort. For example, some teachers use an overall point system to determine the winner of a sports season. Part of the point system focuses on being a good sport. In this way students are rewarded and punished for good and bad actions during their sports performance; they are held accountable.

The sports culture grows better when more people have more skill and participate more fully. But it also grows better when the behavior of people in sport is better! Sports education should aim to teach that behavior in specific ways. This will not happen unless teachers discuss, model, teach, and reinforce good sports behavior.

Summary

Sport has several defining characteristics. Among them are features such as seasons, formal competition, affiliation with a group, a culminating event to determine a winner for the season, and records that become part of the traditions and standards that define a particular sport. These characteristics have often been absent in physical education even though sports activities are the focus of physical education units.

Sports education allows students to learn what good competition means and to develop an understanding of and affection for the rules and traditions that protect sport from abuses of competition.

Sport derives from play and its essential meaning is diminished when the play element is decreased. Adult play involves practice, skillfulness, traditions, and an increased appreciation for strategy. To become a *player* one needs to become educated in the skills, strategies, and traditions that define a particular sport. Good sport enhances the culture, but bad sport detracts from it.

Sports education is developmental in the sense that the student is gradually socialized into the mature form of a sport through a series of experiences in which earlier forms are adapted to his or her changing developmental needs. The games students play must be developmentally appropriate in terms of skills required, complexity of strategy, and opportunity for participation.

Sports education differs from traditional physical education in that seasons are used rather than units, students are members of the same team throughout a season, a formal schedule of competition is arranged, a championship is decided, and records are kept.

Sports education can occur within a single class, with multiple classes using competition within and between classes, or by using all instructional and nonattached time to form a single, overall sports education system.

Practice sessions are important in sports education just as they are in sport. Students practice in teams, and team captains play an important leadership role. As a season progresses, teams practice less often and compete more often, but the concept of practicing to improve individual and team abilities is central to sports education.

A good sportsperson is much more than a skilled competitor. This person values the rules, traditions, and rituals of a sport, plays fairly, and appreciates the efforts of teammates and opponents. Physical educators have an obligation to discuss, model, teach, and reinforce these values and attitudes.

Suggested activities

1. Discuss the major characteristics of sport. Provide examples from your own experience for each characteristic.

2. Divide into four groups. The instructor will assign each group a sports education program for one of the four models in the chapter. Prepare a written description of the program and present it to the entire class.

3. List the ways in which sports education differs from the more traditional physical education models discussed thus far.

4. Prepare a sports education program of your own choosing as if you were going to teach it during a student teaching experience.

5. Debate the following issue: For the sports portion of a physical education curriculum, sports education should take the place of traditional methods of teaching. Have three students argue the affirmative and three argue the negative.

12

Wilderness Sports and Adventure Education

Wilderness sports and adventure activities represent a form of risk and challenge to participants and, in a different sense, provide a strenuous test of a teacher's skills and dedication. Such programs generally require off-school trips, special financing, and full explanations to parents and other authority figures. Some adults who think little of students' banging heads in football or attempting giant swings on the high bar truly need reassurance when they see students dangling on ropes during a climbing exercise. The dangers seem too great although the safety records are exemplary.

Students' enthusiasm, interest, concentration, and desire to learn and achieve are worth the teacher's effort, however. This is an exciting program area. The major topics covered in this chapter are as follows:

The characteristics of wilderness sports and adventure activities and their relationship to physical education and experimental education

The potential values to students of participation in wilderness pursuits and adventure activities

Examples of exemplary programs in middle schools and high schools

Important factors related to the organization and administration of wilderness sports and adventure programs

Specific types of adventure activities

SCENE *Several European visitors accompany the school principal on a tour of the high school. The group has visited science rooms, a computer lab, industrial arts workshops, and the lunchroom, and sat in on several history and mathematics classes. They seem interested in the comprehensive nature of the U.S. high school, which is quite different from typical schools in their own countries. They enter the gymnasium and find certain unusual activities in progress. A group of about ten students are climbing the end wall of the gymnasium. Three students, two boys and a girl, are supported by belay lines controlled by other students. The girl is searching for handholds and is almost 30 feet above the floor. At the other end of the gymnasium other students are rappelling about 40 feet from a platform near the ceiling. Once again students maintain control of safety lines attached to each student performing the rappel. In the center of the gymnasium a third group of students are in the middle of a pile of rope, nylon webbing, and metal carabiners. They seem to be learning to make seat harnesses.*

There are shouts of encouragement and instruction among the students at each of the three teaching stations. The instructor, along with student assistants, supervises the entire operation. The European guests seem startled at these activities in a physical education class.

FIRST VISITOR   What are these activities? I think I am in the Alps at a climbing school. Is this what you do in physical education?

PRINCIPAL   These students are learning to climb or at least they are learning some very basic skills of climbing in this unit of their physical education class. Eventually they'll take a trip to do some rock climbing and rappelling. They'll camp, cook their own food, learn something about interpreting the natural environment, and do some climbing according to their ability.

SECOND VISITOR   What about accidents? Who is responsible? Don't they learn games? Aren't you concerned about physical fitness? How much school do they miss on these trips?

PRINCIPAL   Yes, they play games—but in our school there's an opportunity to choose these activities as well as more traditional forms of physical education. We call these activities wilderness sports. Some people refer to them as outdoor pursuits or adventure education. Some students really enjoy physical activity associated with outdoor pursuits. They're noticeably unenthusiastic about more traditional athletics. But I'm surprised that you ask. The whole notion really came to us in America through Outward Bound, which began in Germany and received its impetus in Great Britain. *You* should be telling *me* about the appeal of these pastimes.

THIRD VISITOR   Yes, but what about missing school and the risks?

PRINCIPAL   Students miss very little school because we use weekends or vacation periods for the trips. And the students spend many more hours in skill instruction on the school site in preparation for the trip than they do on the trip itself. That's really the culminating event, like a big game after days and weeks of practice.

There is a risk, but most of it is in the travel, not the activity. We use the best equipment—the walls of the gymnasium, for example, are constructed for different degrees of climbing difficulty—and the instruction is competent. Above all the students care! They pay attention; standards are very high. The student performs only to a personal level of competence. Our program has worked very well for several years.

The puzzled reactions of these European visitors to the activities in the gymnasium are similar to the reactions of almost any other visitor. The introduction of wilderness sports and adventure activities to the curriculum in physical education is relatively new. Some colleges and universities have offered such pursuits since the 1960s, when many young people developed a great surge of interest in ecology. However, similar high school programs did not start until later. Even though they are very popular, these programs are not common today in either colleges or secondary schools. Adventure activities and wilderness sports seem to be on the cutting edge in terms of physical activity interest in our society. More young people are skiing, taking bicycle trips, caving, scuba diving, backpacking, whitewater rafting, and participating in a host of similar activities to satisfy their recreational needs. We seek to provide appropriate instruction in physical education in order to capitalize on the interest of adolescents in such activities and make available to others the same opportunity for skillful and enjoyable physical experiences.

What are wilderness sports and adventure education?

The terms *wilderness sports* and *outdoor pursuits* can be used interchangeably, but *adventure education*, although related, is generally different with regard to purpose, activities, and practices. Wilderness sports include backpacking, kayaking, cross-country skiing, scuba diving, caving, and countless other activities. Conduct of the activities is related to the natural environment, and the activities take place in wilderness-type areas. The goal of wilderness sports education is the acquisition of skills necessary to participate safely, comfortably, and with the highest possible levels of competence. This is similar to the goal for volleyball, tennis, swimming, basketball, or any of our more traditional games.

Adventure education, on the other hand, involves activities in which we *create* an environment, such as a high-ropes course, or *contrive* an obstacle, such as a 14-foot wall, and present it as a challenge to a single student or a group of students. The goal is not skill but rather the personal or group challenge of overcoming anxiety and functioning under stress to solve a problem. The process of group involvement is usually more significant in adventure education than the acquisition of skill or even the successful completion of a task.

Obviously, there is a fair amount of stress, personal challenge, and group interaction in wilderness sports also. Paddling in fast water, stepping off a cliff to rappel, or exploring a cave creates anxiety and stress. Yet in these activities the feelings of tension and stress are by-products of the experience, not the principal focus. In a sense, the challenge of stepping backward off a cliff to rappel is similar to the basketball player's stepping to the foul line with the score tied and two seconds on the clock. Both are unique moments for an individual.

Characteristics of wilderness sports

Certain characteristics help define wilderness sports. These characteristics relate to the conduct of the program, and additional factors relate to the participant.

Program characteristics

Travel.   To engage in wilderness sports, participants must usually travel to a suitable location with natural features such as caves, white water, or a proper climbing face. Although in some activities, such as bicycling and cross-country skiing, participants may start from school in certain localities, the very nature of the activity involves travel. This is similar to an interscholastic team's traveling from its school to another school to engage in a hockey or baseball game.

Young people enjoy travel. It is a mark of contemporary society. We can use travel as an educational tool to promote interest, enthusiasm, and unique experiences.

Relationship to the environment.   Wilderness sports are creations of the environment; we need caves to spelunk, mountains to climb, and forests or open spaces to backpack. We also need technological equipment to engage in some wilderness sports. A classification of outdoor activities (Siedentop 1980) reinforces this point. Preindustrial activities include hiking, backpacking, camping, sailing, canoeing, kayaking, cross-country skiing, fishing, and caving. Postindustrial activities include scuba diving, hang gliding, dune buggying, sky diving, snowmobiling, and technical climbing.

Certainly specialized equipment has influenced our ability to participate in wilderness sports. Yet the major technological advancement is the ease of travel to natural areas. Good highways and reliable vehicles have brought most areas within our reach.

A more significant issue regarding the relationship of wilderness sports to the environment is the impact of the user on the resource. We need the environment to conduct the program, but if we mismanage our use of the en-

Adventure activities provide exciting alternatives to traditional programs.

vironment, we will destroy that which is essential for participation. Physical educators must make a significant educational effort to develop an appropriate land ethic among participants in wilderness sports in addition to their traditional emphasis on activity skills.

Competition with the self.   The great majority of wilderness sports emphasize competition with nature rather than with other people. The adversaries in canoeing are the wind, waves, temperature, and tide or current. These forces represent the obstacles to success or promote anxiety and create the stressful conditions.

> SCENE   *It is 4:00 A.M. on the shore of a very large lake. Two counselors and nine boys about 13 years of age, including a boy named* TIM, *paddle their canoes across a 15-mile stretch of the lake.*
>
> COUNSELOR   Let's go. It's dead calm out there. The longer we wait the more chance the prevailing wind will force us to follow the shoreline—that's 15 extra miles of paddling.
>
> TIM   I can hardly see. And a handful of raisins isn't much breakfast.
>
> COUNSELOR   We'll eat on the other side.
>
> TIM   Can we stop at Table Rock and jump from the cliffs into the water?
>
> COUNSELOR   We're leaving now to beat the wind and the six-foot waves. How can we stop and still do that?
>
> *Three hours later:*
>
> TIM   Well, here we are, back to where we started.
>
> COUNSELOR   You were very good out there—all of you. The wind just came up earlier and stronger than usual. I'm as sorry as you that we had to paddle 8 miles and then lock gunwale and drift back. We'll eat, go for a swim at Table Rock, and then try again tomorrow. Tomorrow we'll leave at 3:00 A.M.

This is not an unusual scenario in wilderness sports. The forces of nature are mighty, and they often conquer.

Time frame.   Students generally participate in wilderness sports on weekends, during interim periods, or during normal vacations. The pretrip training sessions and posttrip evaluations take place during regular school periods. In some circumstances, particularly when an interdisciplinary trip is scheduled, students may be gone for several regular school days. Such trips usually have multiple objectives. One school district in the Midwest uses a bicycle trip to visit Indian mounds, do gravestone rubbings at pioneer cemeteries, and participate in interpretive sessions at a conservancy center.

Time away from school is a sensitive issue with school officials and parents. We are still somewhat trapped in the notion that education only occurs in school, when surrounded by four walls.

Coeducation.   Both girls and boys participate in wilderness sports. There is no distinction in ability, interest, or enthusiasm for outdoor activities between the sexes. The 24-hour nature of wilderness expeditions means that teachers must make appropriate plans for sleeping, eating, use of facilities, and the responsibility for chores. Stereotyping tasks by sex role usually does not and certainly should not occur.

Leadership.   It is a rare school that has enough teachers with the necessary preparation to respond to the variety of interests of the student body. Wilderness sport is a perfect illustration of this point. Few physical educators are prepared by training or experience to conduct such a program. We can usually find one or more teachers in a system with a specific skill such as canoeing or backpacking, but we can rarely find someone broadly competent in wilderness sports and adventure activities. After all, for the most part physical education teachers are trained in more traditional sports and games.

This suggests that the teacher's energy in wilderness sports is spent to a greater extent in organizing experiences than in direct service to students. It is the teacher's role to probe the community and other teachers in the school to discover individuals with the capacity and willingness to lead wilderness sports experiences. This is exactly how many programs begin. A core of people emerge, some volunteers and some paid for specific assignments, to contribute direct teaching in this program area. Meanwhile, in-service experiences assist the regular teacher to develop competency. Newly prepared teachers seem to have training in this area not common to those prepared in earlier periods. The characteristic of leadership in wilderness sports is that many people contribute and these people have rich and varied backgrounds.

Program characteristics of wilderness sports include distinct patterns of travel, use of the environment, competition with the self, out-of-school time, coeducational activities, and broad leadership. Certain common factors also affect the individual participant in wilderness sports.

Factors that influence the participant

Risks and consequences.   A feature of wilderness sports is that risks are associated with the activities. Students can get lost in a cave, fall into a turbulent stream, freeze, slip on rocks. The risks are not risks of failure, such as

A horizontal climbing course built on a gymnasium wall.

missing the foul shot in the last two seconds of a game, but risks whose consequences can produce physical harm or discomfort. Yet another feature of the risks is that they are controllable for the most part. If students pay attention, use good judgment, respect the water and the rocks, and develop skills, then they minimize risks and control the situation. Being in charge of their destiny, so to speak, is a tremendous feeling. It produces great pride and a sense of self-worth. It is exactly the sort of thing that is important in adolescence. Fortunately, physical education offers many opportunities for a person to be in control of a situation. Wilderness sport provides one more vehicle.

Stress and anxiety.

JOSE   Jim, did you like the high ropes? I go next Saturday with the other half of the team. What's the course all about?

JIM   It's really different. It was good, but I didn't think so at the time. Some of the obstacles really scared me.

JOSE   What do you mean? You were never scared in your life. I saw you wrestle the state champ last year, and you didn't even blink.

JIM   This is different; I don't like heights, and everything happened 40 feet in the air. I almost froze on the flea jump.

JOSE   What's the flea jump?

JIM   You have to broad jump about four feet from one platform to another—only four feet, but there's nothing underneath you.

JOSE   Isn't there a safety harness?

JIM   Oh sure, you can't get hurt or fall more than a foot before the harness takes over, but wow, I almost froze; my pulse was pounding in my throat. The guy on the ground kept saying, "You can do it." I told him to stick it in his ear. But I finally did it.

JOSE   How did you feel?

JIM   Relieved, but also sort of good. You'll find out.

JOSE   That's what I'm afraid of!

That is one kind of anxiety—produced more or less deliberately on a high-ropes course. For some people a sufficient challenge is just to climb the ladder to the platform. For others the experience is a lark although that happens to very few people once they are 40 feet in the air.

Many stressful situations in wilderness sports are a product of fatigue in battling the wind, cold, heat, rain, or any other of nature's elements. Most people are just not used to being wet for long periods of time or not having electricity or other comforts. The wilderness is elemental, and society is technological.

If we place a person in contact with the forces of nature such as the weather or gravity and ask that person to accomplish some goal such as crossing a lake in a canoe or riding a bike from one town to another or stepping off a cliff to rappel, we generally introduce a measure of stress and anxiety as to the consequences. This sort of challenge seems to be necessary to an individual who seeks a full knowledge of self and acts as a participant, not a spectator, in life.

Apparel and the sense of belonging.   Apparel can be helmets for rock climbing, plus the rope and carabiners, tanks for scuba diving, helmets and life vests for kayaking, boots and backpacks for hiking. Apparel extends to a language vernacular and some courtesies and taboos associated with the activity. All of this contributes to a sense of belonging.

Wilderness sport is no different from any other aspect of physical education in providing apparel for participants. Common apparel promotes security, friendship, and intimacy.

Involvement and intensity.   It is relatively easy for a teacher to capture the attention of a group of students when explaining how to roll out of a kayak if trapped upside down or how to tie a knot correctly to secure a belay rope for a rappel. The consequences of error are so real that students do become involved. The glassy stare, the "Oh, no, not again" look, the deliberate avoidance, and the typical casualness and disarray are rare in wilderness sports education. Competence based on involvement is a normal attribute of young people involved in adventure and wilderness activities. This involvement is similar to the involvement, the tension, the enthusiasm students display toward interscholastic sports. The fifth and sixth grade students in one school get up at 5:30 A.M. during the winter months to catch a ride to the gym for biddie basketball. That is the only available time the gymnasium is available for their age group. These students are involved; they care about what they are doing. This is a tribute to sport and an opportunity for those of us involved to provide the experience.

Thus the factors that influence the participant in wilderness sports—risk taking, anxiety and stress, apparel and the sense of belonging, and involvement—coupled with the characteristics of the program help define a unique and exciting area in physical education.

The next logical step is to provide a rationale for including wilderness sports in the school and particularly in the physical education curriculum. The European visitors described at the beginning of the chapter sought just such an answer. In a period when accountability and back to basics are almost daily concerns, extraordinary activities such as high ropes and rock climbing deserve examination.

A rationale for wilderness sports

For years educators have asked why we insist that education only occurs when the class is seated and the door is closed, when students look at preserved specimens in bottles, pictures in books, or videotapes and films depicting social experiences or selected forms of plant and animal life. Perhaps we teach this way because it is simpler to do so. It is more complex to move out of the classroom and into the natural world. There are safety issues, discipline matters, expenses, travel arrangements, and probably a dozen or more other reasons why it is easier to have students sit and read or listen than have them moving to other environments for learning experiences. Elementary schools do better than most at providing a variety of opportunities for learning. Professional schools such as those of medicine and dentistry insist on practical or clinical experiences that are real. High schools are probably the least likely to respond to multiple learning environments. Only in art, music, and physical education, the "special subjects," do students generally have sensory rather than abstract experiences. In these subjects we seem to understand that young people have eyes, ears, a nose, muscles, and hands and like to use them, in fact, learn by using them.

"Rich in experience—short on information" (Siedentop 1980, 188) is a wonderful description of education in preindustrial times. Youth learned by working on the farm, in the mine or factory, at home, or on the trail. It was an education rich in experience but by the standards of modern society deficient in information. Then we reversed the matter; today education is long on information but very short on experience. We substitute abstraction for sensory learning. It is too bad that some children who read of cows and milk, cream, and cheese do not associate cows with milk at all. Cows are pictures in books, and milk comes in cartons from the supermarket, someplace in the back of the store. The loss of experience has meant a loss of association with natural phenomena—rain, heat, mud, walking long distances, thirst, the scent of flowers. We do not row or paddle very often—we use motors. Individuals seem to have lost the realization that they are part of the natural order, existing in a state of mutual dependency.

Two movements have developed in response to these changes in the education of youth. The first is Outward Bound, the second, a broader concept, experiential education.

Outward Bound

Outward Bound is a movement that attempts to challenge youth through intensive experience in the outdoors. A German refugee, Kurt Hahn, arrived in England with a notion that youth should be educated to develop character and to be of service to others. Eventually he established a school built upon that notion. The curriculum consists of classes in lifeboat rescue, kayaking, rappelling, rock climbing, first aid, and similar pursuits. Existence was Spartan-like, cold water, no heat, and a very demanding physical regimen. The school offered traditional academic classes, but the priority in its method was to test oneself through physical activities and to serve others in truly consequential ways, for example, lifeboat rescue. It was education for character and leadership. Test yourself, know yourself, meet the challenge! This was Hahn's response to a world bereft of experience. He manufactured it.

The Outward Bound movement came to the United States in the form of summer programs located in areas with natural features such as the mountains of Colorado and North Carolina, the ocean of Maine, and the canoeing lakes of Minnesota. The features of the environment were used to challenge people: challenge them to the point of physical exhaustion; challenge them to a sense of self; challenge their capacity for tenacity.

The typical experience lasts about a month. About ten days are spent in skill development, two weeks on a trek, and three to five days in a "solo." The motto is "strive, struggle, never yield." The skills portion includes great numbers of initiative problems and high-rope activities. The trek may involve paddling continuously for 24 hours during two weeks on the trail. The solo trip leaves the participant without food other than that gleaned from the land, and it is made alone. Those who complete the experience remember it. They may have been extremely uncomfortable, but the experience makes a lasting impression. It fills most people with a sense of pride that they made it.

Authorities suggest that Outward Bound is a survival experience, a physical challenge—but that is really an inadequate description. It is also a contemplative exercise, an opportunity to learn about oneself and about oneself in relation to others.

According to Edward Rhudy (1979, 26–27) five factors are essential to the Outward Bound experience.

1. Stress
2. Group-living experience
3. Success for the group as a whole and for the individual
4. A new environment
5. An individual experience—separated from the group—solo

It is a significant youth movement in this last part of the twentieth century, comparable perhaps to athletics at the beginning of the century. Almost every program involving adolescents and young adults reflects Outward Bound in terms of its curriculum; physical education is no exception. Wilderness sports and adventure activities relate to the Outward Bound program. Schools are a reflection of society and a significant portion of society now promotes physically challenging outdoor activities for youth.

Experiential education

The roots of the belief in experience as a form of education remain with us, reinforced by distinguished authorities such as John Dewey. Recently the Carnegie Council on Policy Studies recommended that junior and senior high school students attend classes three days per week and devote the other two days to education-related work or community service (Conrad and Heden 1983).

Experiential education evidences a concern for the total development of people—socially, psychologically, physically, and intellectually. This development is at risk today. Young people are shut off from encounters and challenges that promote health development. Some school officials are not interested in assuming experiential models of education. Others obviously are.

Generally, experiential education involves students in work experiences, community service projects, or direct investigation of a subject related to an academic enterprise. Students may attend school half a day and hold a job for the remainder of the day. Or a student or group may conduct an election poll or serve the community by working with senior citizens or handicapped people. Examples of these experiences are almost limitless.

Physical education has related to experiential education with a different focus. It basically attempts to promote experiential learning by means of group involvement, sensory experience, leisure skills, personal commitment, perceived risk, a unique environment, and social relationships. The means to such learning are in wilderness sports and adventure education.

This is not a new venture for physical education; rather, the current emphasis is a new model of a continuous use of the outdoors from organized camping, to outdoor education, and now to wilderness sports and adventure education. The schematic model in Figure 12.1 (p. 214) demonstrates the long-term relationship of physical education to three of the four major educational uses of the outdoors in this century. Note that the Outward Bound movement has had an impact on physical education instead of the other way around, as in the case of organized camping, outdoor education, and now wilderness sports. We are recipients of Outward Bound philosophy, method, and activities. That we are able at this time to promote wilderness sports and adventure activities in ordinary school settings is a testament to the persuasiveness of Outward Bound.

Individual development

One feature of wilderness sports is the notion of the development of identity and self-esteem as a result of participation. We assume that risk taking, stress, group relationships, perceived danger, and exotic environments lead to this development. This is similar to the claims we make for team sports; we build character, initiative, group cohesiveness, and deferral skills. There is a long-standing commitment in physical education to demonstrate concern for the whole person. This seems as appropriate today as in the past.

It is unfortunate that after all these years, a body of evidence other than the experiential is not available to substantiate our claims. However, such is the case, and this is also true for wilderness sports and adventure activities. The claims are there but not necessarily the evidence. In fact, the experiential nature of adventure activities has led to excessive claims for improvement in special population groups who participate in outward bound kinds of programs—that is, for delinquents who supposedly develop social rapport or model behavior as a result of a two- to four-week wilderness adventure. It is difficult for other child-care professionals to accept such claims without sub-

Organized Summer Camps, 1900–1940
1. Physical educators served as initial leaders and founders

2. Purposes
   • Fellowship
   • Leisure skills
   • Democratic values
   • Pioneer heritage

Outdoor Education, 1940–1970
1. Outdoor Education Project, AAHPERD leadership

2. Purposes
   • Sensory learning
   • Curriculum enrichment
   • School camping
   • Shared experience
   • Fishing, hunting, orienteering skills
   • Conservation

PHYSICAL EDUCATION

Outward Bound, 1950–
1. Curt Hahn, private school educators, business and social leaders

2. Purposes
   • Challenge
   • Stress
   • Group relationships
   • Self-awareness
   • Risk taking
   • Problem solving

Wilderness Sports and Adventure Education, 1960–
1. Physical educators promote programs in college and school

2. Purposes
   • Outdoor-pursuit skills
   • Challenge activities
   • Problem solving
   • Ecological awareness
   • Self-awareness
   • Stress and risk

Figure 12.1 Educational uses of the outdoors.

stantial evidence. After all, if problems in behavior take 15 years to develop, it is difficult to believe they can be corrected in two to four weeks.

Everyone has a tendency to justify a program by exaggerating its results. But this is unnecessary and even counterproductive. Wilderness activities produce skill development and are in the tradition of concern for the whole person. That is an acceptable goal of physical education. Our task is to measure outcomes more effectively and demonstrate actual results. Society permits us to do that and expects a fair evaluation rather than exaggeration.

In summary, the development of wilderness sport represents a contribution of physical education to the major effort in schools to promote experiential education. Furthermore, the tradition to use the outdoors for educational purposes and the nature of the subject matter, which emphasizes leisure skills, reinforces the role of this program in physical education.

Students learning to rappel indoors.

Purposes of wilderness sports and adventure activities

The characteristics of wilderness sports and adventure activities help to define their purposes, which include the following:

1. To learn outdoor sports skills and enjoy the satisfaction of competence
2. To live within the limits of personal ability related to an activity and the environment
3. To find pleasure in accepting the challenge and risk of stressful physical activity
4. To learn mutual dependency of self and the natural world
5. To share this experience and learning with classmates and authority figures

These purposes are similar to those a physical education program attempts to achieve within our schools. We have an opportunity to remotivate many young people through such activities and as a bonus introduce a new generation to the outdoor heritage of America.

Examples of programs in wilderness sports and adventure activities

This section will include descriptions of wilderness sports and adventure programs conducted by three schools. The examples include reference to instruction, schedule, and other administrative factors.

Dublin High School: Outdoor Pursuits and Adventure Activities*

Dublin High School in Dublin, Ohio, provides elective physical education experiences in order that students may meet state-mandated requirements for the subject. These experiences fall into the categories of (a) group instruction, (b) contract teaching, and (c) independent instruction. The last category, independent instruction, uses community personnel for direct instruction rather than the school physical education staff. Outdoor pursuits is a program within this category.

Outdoor Pursuits

Introduction. The outdoor pursuits activity is designed to give the students experience in outdoor living as well as exposure to activities that cannot normally be taught in the school setting. Three weekends per year are planned to include a variety of different activities: fall—camping, cycling, canoeing, orienteering; winter—skiing; spring—sailing, backpacking and hiking, camping, cycling.

A typical fall weekend schedule follows:

1. Pretraining schedule, prior to trip
   Monday: Cycling class
   (a) Safety
   (b) Cycle inspection
   (c) Trial run
   Tuesday: Canoe class, farm pond
   (a) Safety lecture
   (b) History and transportation
   (c) Skill development
   Wednesday: Orienteering class
   (a) Film
   (b) Compass and map experience
   Thursday: Camping class
   (a) Responsibilities
   (b) Campfire skits—planning
2. Trip schedule

Saturday	*Sunday*
Cycle 33 miles to state park	Breakfast
Set up camp in campgrounds	Orienteering class
Lunch	Lunch
Canoe classes	Take down camp
Dinner	Cycle 33 miles back to school
Recreation	
Campfire activities	

The outdoor pursuits program requires the use of a multitude of facilities, organizations, and personnel from the community.

Pretraining
Facilities: farm pond and school
Organizations: Boy Scouts of America—canoes
                  Department of Natural Resources—literature and safety talk
Local personnel: cycling lecture and practice session
                canoeing lecture and practice session
                orienteering lecture and practice session

* Based on Headlee 1978, 32–34.

Trip
Facilities: state park campground
              International Field Studies tent rental
Organizations: American Red Cross—canoe lessons and canoes
                American Youth Hostels—cycling and canoeing
                American Camping Association—orienteering
Local personnel: cook, nurse

The teacher's responsibility is to organize all of the community resources. Material to be covered in the length of time allowed must be discussed with the instructors. Facilities and equipment must be engaged and transported to the proper locations, etc.

During the spring weekend, sailing is substituted for canoeing, and backpacking and hiking for orienteering. During the winter, the students are taken to western New York for a skiing weekend. The format is the same on each trip.

Satisfactory completion of a weekend course permits the students to satisfy one of six requirements in physical education per year. Since the school offers three separate weekends with different skills included in each experience, students can satisfy half of the physical education requirement each year in wilderness sports.

Adventure Education

As a continuation of its outdoor programs, Dublin High School provides an adventure education experience, with a total of 44 hours of instruction, for interested and qualified students. The school is located within a 20-minute bus ride of an adventure center that has a series of group initiatives, a rappelling station, and a high-ropes course.

School Activities, regular physical education period, 20 hours:

Group initiatives, 8 hours

Ropes, harness, knots related to rappelling, 8 hours

Wilderness first aid, 4 hours

Adventure Center Activities, conducted on six Saturday mornings, four hours per session, or a total of 24 hours:

Group initiatives	8 hours
Rappelling	8 hours
High ropes	8 hours

Regular teachers conduct the instruction in school. Certified instructors teach the activities at the center. The school bears the cost of all instruction and transportation. A student qualifies for the class through outdoor experience on the weekend trips in Outdoors Pursuits, his or her general conduct in school and physical education, and a written report on why the student wishes to take the course. The selection process creates an aura of distinction about this course as something to strive to obtain (something similar to a place on the varsity team).

West Middle School: Backpacking for Inner-City Youth

A physical education teacher in West Middle School recognized the limited experience of her urban students and the need to try something different. She had to have some students on her side. The teacher received permission from the principal to take selected volunteer groups of students on weekend backpacking trips. A local philanthropic foundation helped to provide equipment and other resources. The students conducted several fund-raisers to secure additional supplies. The teacher was paid in one day of release time per trip plus a supplemental salary similar to the pay of coaches. University students participated in the trip for field experience credit. The middle school students knew of the trip about three months in advance. The teacher selected a larger group than could be accommodated because of possible dropouts, illness, behavior problems, and loss of interest. If for some reason a trip was oversubscribed, room was made on another trip for the young people. One afternoon per week for several months the middle school students met in the gym for pretrip instruction; information on tents, packing gear trail mechanics, safety, rules of conduct, sleeping arrangements, emergency procedures, orienteering, and preliminary rappelling skills was included in these sessions. Attendance was mandatory for those who signed up for the trip.

The trip schedule was as follows:

Friday

Depart school	2:30 P.M.
Arrive state park at trailhead	4:00 P.M.
Backpack to sleeping site	4:30–5:30 P.M.
Establish camp	5:30–6:30 P.M.
Dinner	6:30 P.M.
Campfire	8:00 P.M.
Bed	9:30 P.M.

Saturday

Breakfast	7:30 A.M.
Backpack	8:00–11:30 A.M.
Lunch	12:00 P.M.
Rappel	1:00–4:00 P.M.
Backpack	4:00–5:00 P.M.
Dinner	6:30 P.M.
Campfire	8:00 P.M.
Bed	9:30 P.M.

Sunday

Breakfast	7:30 A.M.
Orienteering	8:30–11:00 A.M.
Lunch	11:30 A.M.
Backpack to trailhead	12:30–3:00 P.M.
Arrive school	5:00 P.M.

This was a busy agenda, but it provided skills, adventure, an exotic experience for inner-city youth, and time to trust the teacher.

In West Middle School the backpacking weekend, including the pretrip classes, replaced the semester's physical education period for the participating students. That is, the experience met the physical education requirement for that one semester. Some schools use such an experience as a supplement to the traditional program. However, in those situations the program is frequently an extra and not a routine opportunity. Usually the program ceases when a particular teacher loses energy or interest or leaves the program because the school considers wilderness activities to be supplemental.

Lake Forest High School: Multiactivity
Outdoor Adventure Program*

A multiactivity outdoor adventure program is available to juniors and seniors at
Lake Forest High School in Lake Forest, Illinois. The students participate in physical education five days per week and have an opportunity to be self-directed in the
outdoors.

Sample curriculum for outdoor adventure education course

Weekdays		Optional Weekend Outings	
September			
2–5	Introduction to basic camping, backpacking equipment	19–20	Cycling overnight
8–12	Cycling		Ecology–biology
15–19	Cycling and camping		Light hike
22–26	Climbing		Sensory activities
29–10/3	Climbing		Star study
October			
6–10	Climbing and rappelling	17–19	Climbing
13–17	Climbing and rappelling trip planning		Canoeing, sailing
20–24	Climbing		Fishing
27–31	Orienteering		Belaying
			Rappelling
			Star study
November			
3–7	Angling and casting		
10–14	Backpacking and cooking		
17–21	First aid		
24–26	Water safety		
December			
1–5	Winter camping	5–6	Winter camping overnight
8–12	Shooting (riflery)		Star study
15–19	Shooting		Orienteering
January			
5–9	Cross-country skiing		
12–16	Cross-country skiing and snowshoeing		
19–23	Testing and wrap-up		
February			
1/31–4	Introduction and cross-country skiing		
7–11	Cross-country skiing		
14–18	Cross-country skiing and snowshoeing		
21–25	Riflery		
March			
2/28–4	Riflery and casting and angling		
7–11	Winter camping		
14–18	Conservation of energy and diet		
21–25	Backpacking and equipment		
28–4/1	First aid		

(continued)

* Based on Atwell 1983.

	Weekdays		Optional Weekend Outings
April			
4–8	No school		
11–15	Map and compass		
18–22	Climbing		
25–29	Climbing		
May			
2–6	Climbing	20–22	Climbing
9–13	Climbing		Rappelling
16–20	Climbing		Sensory activities
23–27	Cycling		Star study
30–6/3	Cycling	30–6/3	Cycling overnight
			Ecology–biology
			Sensory activities
			Light hike
June			
6–10	Wrap-up		

Sample day-to-day course outline and progression of activities

Bicycling
Sept. 2 Introduction, rules and regulations, responsibilities, requirements, equipment, schedule, discussion of schedule
3 Discuss equipment for those about to buy, collect permission slips, hand out material
4 Cycling introduction
5 Check bicycles for safety equipment and necessary repairs, start breakdown as follows:
8 Take apart a bike
9 Clean bike
10 Put bike together
11 Safety check
12 Camp-out organization
15 Safety ride
16 Community ride
17 Country ride
18 Town ride
19 Pack for trip

Backpacking
Sept. 20 Backpacking, hiking, backpacks, rucksacks, daypacks, boots
23 Tents and sleeping bags
24 Clothing
25 Foul weather—rain, wet, cold (hypothermia)
26 Cooking, stoves, fires

Climbing
Sept. 29 Introduction to climbing, equipment and safety
30 Knots and command
Oct. 1 Climb bleachers, belaying, falling
2 Climb wall, belaying
3 Climb wall, belaying
6 Climbing and rappelling
7 Climbing hazards—climbing
8 Types of climbs—climbing
9 Degrees of difficulty—climbing
10 Plan for trip

13 Climbing hazards—climbing, rappelling
14 Weather—climbing, rappelling
15 Climbing
16 Climbing
17 Pack for trip

Orienteering
Oct. 20 Introduction and compass—stride
21 Map types and legends
22 Map and compass together
23 Outdoor problems
24 Orienteering game

Archery
Oct. 27 Introduction to nomenclature, equipment, and safety
28 Short-range shooting
29 Long-range shooting
30 Short- and long-range shooting, field shooting, hunting and fishing with bow
   and arrow
31 Contest

Fishing
Nov. 3 Introduction to nomenclature, safety, types of fishing
4 Fly-fishing technique
5 Bait-casting technique
   Spin-casting technique
6 Conservation—outside speaker, movie
7 Game

Indoor Climbing
Nov. 10 Review of equipment, procedures, safety commands
11 Climbing
12 Rappelling
13 Technical-physical
14 Climbing
17 Rope work, challenges, introduction
18 Indoor climb
19 Indoor climb
20 Indoor climb
21 Indoor climb

Winter Camping
Dec. 1 Introduction to hypothermia, frostbite, movie on winter exposure, camping, etc.
2 Discussion of equipment, tents and sleeping bags
3 Plan for camp-out
4 Clothing
5 Prepare for camp-out

Shooting (Riflery)
Dec. 8 Introduction to safety, guns and shooting, nomenclature
9 Shooting introduction—outside speaker
10 Shooting, types and positions
11 Shooting
12 Match

Cross-Country Skiing
Jan. 5 Introduction to nomenclature, sizing, history; movie
6 Turning, kick turn, use of pole, diagonal stride
7 Straight running, use of pole
8 Uphill, straight herringbone, side step, downhill
9 Uphill, downhill, turning
12 Snowshoeing—types, uses, history
13 Hiking
14 Cross-country jogging
15 Cross-country trip
16 Cross-country trip

Number and type of outdoor education field experience

1. Devils Lake trip
   A. 3 days and 3 nights
   B. Curriculum
         Climbing
         Rappelling
         Obstacle course
         Caving
         Sensitivity work
         Camping and cooking
   C. Maximum 25 students
   D. 3 trip leaders, male and female

2. Winter mountaineering trip
   A. 2 days and 1 or 2 nights
   B. Curriculum
         Equipment preparation for winter camping
         Cold-weather camping and cooking
         Snow shelters
         Cross-country skiing
         Showshoeing
   C. Maximum 25 students
   D. 2 or 3 trip leaders, male or female

3. Bike trip
   A. 1 night and 1 day (students have requested additional time)
   B. Curriculum
         20- to 60-mile ride
         Bike preparation
         Camping and cooking
         Night sensitivity work
   C. 12 to 20 students
   D. 1 or 2 instructors (one to drive the car that carries equipment and supplies)

4. Canoe trip
   A. 1 or 2 nights and 1 or 2 days
   B. Curriculum
         Equipment preparation
         Canoeing instruction
         Canoe trip
         Camping and cooking
         Water safety
   C. Maximum 20 students
   D. 2 instructors

The example programs just presented are typical of wilderness sports and adventure activities in schools. In a few schools, usually residential or for students with special needs, the entire physical education operation is directed to this area. In such cases staff, facilities, transportation, and equipment are totally specialized for the outdoor programs. Regardless of the size and scope of a program, physical education teachers must consider several administrative factors, as we see next.

Administrative factors

Certain administrative matters are essential to safe, educational adventure activities and wilderness sports. These include the assessment of liability for risk activities, teaching schedules, student transportation, facilities and equipment, and the financing of the programs.

Risk liability

Any off-campus activities sponsored by schools involve some degree of risk. This is true of wilderness sports. The teacher's task is to understand the dimensions and the appropriate means to manage the risk. The major causes of accidents in adventure programs fall into the categories of unsafe conditions, unsafe acts, and judgment errors. See Table 12.1 (Meyer 1979).

To control or manage the causes of accidents, the head of a program must ensure that the program includes the following:

1. Published policies and procedures of operation
2. A continual analysis of trip goals versus the limitations or abilities of participants and leaders
3. Selection of participants
4. In-service training of staff
5. Inspections of equipment and facilities
6. Maintenance of safety records, including accidents and near misses
7. A program leader who provides direction to the enterprise

The programs that are most successful and have the best safety records demonstrate the following characteristics (Meyer 1979):

1. Consistent, directive, and nonpermissive management (someone is in charge!)
2. A carefully defined progression of activities
3. Repeated operations in known areas
4. Experienced and well-trained staff
5. An appreciation for the value of internal and external review
6. Commitment to readiness and rescue training

Wilderness sport has a fine safety record. On balance, such seemingly risky pursuits as rappelling and rock climbing are very safe when conducted

TABLE 12.1 Major causes of accidents in adventure programs

Unsafe Conditions	Unsafe Acts	Judgment Errors
Fast water	Poor position	Desire to please others
Loose rock	Lack of skill	Misperception
Unexpected weather	Unsafe speed	Distraction
Improper clothing	Unauthorized procedure	Fatigue
Poor or worn equipment	Inadequate water or nutrient intake	New, novel situation

under school auspices. Bicycling or vehicular travel to the activity site is the more dangerous aspect of the enterprise.

Liability is a product of negligence. If the appropriate procedures are violated and an accident occurs, a negligent situation may be declared. (See Chapter 21 for a thorough discussion of issues related to liability in physical education.)

Thus control regarding liability lies in the teacher's hands. Furthermore, insurance to protect even a negligent act is available. Today insurance companies charge reasonable premiums to protect participants, leaders, and institutions. This is the result of a good safety record in the field and insurance agents' increased understanding of the activities.

Teaching schedule

Outdoor pursuits are usually conducted on weekends, during interim periods, and during vacations. This extended time provides the opportunity for learning and savoring the experience. There is a sense of leisure in learning, which is more satisfying than the 45-minute periods usually associated with physical education in school. Perhaps 45 minutes is a maximum period of time for concentration in algebra or English or Spanish but not for sports activities.

For the physical educator involved in wilderness sports and adventure activities this requires an unusual teaching schedule. Perhaps even more than the coaching staff, the wilderness sports teacher is far removed from a typical eight-hour workday.

Transportation

Unless the facility or site for an outdoor activity is reasonably close to school, transportation by vans or chartered bus is superior to the use of a school bus. The typical school bus is designed for elementary-aged children, and trips of more than 50 miles are very uncomfortable for adolescents. The seats and leg room are simply inadequate. In some cases local car or van dealers offer schools rental or leasing programs tailored to their specific transportation needs. One absolute rule of transportation: Do not permit students to drive!

Facilities, equipment, and financing

Many public areas are suitable for outdoor activities. These include state recreation areas, national forests, and conservancy districts. Similarly, university land, power and light company landholdings, and even privately owned facilities are sometimes available for school programs. It is not economical at this time for schools to invest in their own wilderness sports facilities because so many sites are available at no cost. These facilities are also in proximity to major metropolitan centers.

Some older schools built of stone and double-walled brick are actually more appropriate for indoor climbing stations than modern high schools. In addition, high walls and sturdy construction permit the addition of facings that provide climbing practice at several levels of difficulty.

Much of the equipment used in wilderness sports and adventure activities is life-saving equipment. It is the teacher's responsibility to see that everyone involved treats it accordingly. For example, no one should be allowed to abuse a climbing rope by throwing it into a closet with the basketballs and softballs.

It is possible to rent equipment initially and to depend in part upon equipment that students already possess. Purchasing equipment for a program can extend over a long period of time until adequate supplies are established. One point of caution, however. No equipment should be purchased until adequate storage and security are available.

The school board is responsible for purchasing instructional materials and equipment for outdoor education activities. Different states and districts within states have various procedures for financing such activities. Almost all schools have established some plan to meet their financial needs for off-school activities.

Food, clothing and other personal matters are usually the responsibility of the participants. To defer the impact of these costs to participants, planners should schedule trips months in advance and devise ways for students to raise funds to meet these expenses as part of the trip plan.

SCENE   *Three commuters,* MAX, JACKIE, *and* DOM, *are on their way home from work at about 5:00 P.M. on a Friday in late May.*

MAX   Who are all those kids on bicycles heading north? They're strung out for two miles—must've passed 20 of them.

JACKIE   I think my daughter's one of them. Can't tell with the helmets. At breakfast she said goodbye for the weekend—an outdoor pursuits class including bicycling, camping, and canoeing. It's a physical education class. They stay at the state park about 20 miles from school.

DOM   That's right, my wife and I were chaperones last year. The gym teacher, Mrs. Gault, asked us. She really has great enthusiasm and energy.

MAX   My gym class in high school wasn't at all like this. We didn't accomplish much.

JACKIE   It's about time they did different things. These activities are great.

MAX   Did you ride a bike 20 miles when you did this last year? Do you still have a bike?

DOM   I confess—my wife and I drove the sag wagon; that's the van that brings up the rear and takes care of breakdowns or those who got too tired. Actually, everyone made it. We did canoe and do the other activities. If I go again, I'll ride a bike. I can make it—I think!

Adventure education

In 1971 the federal government supported Project Adventure to integrate the goals of Outward Bound into a public school setting, basically within the physical education curriculum. Most of the activities can be taught and experienced on school grounds; others involve travel. The purposes of adventure activities include a physical component but also involve social and emotional responses on the part of the student. The objectives in the adventure curriculum include but are not limited to the following:

- Developing balance, coordination, and agility
- Learning persistence, a willingness to try rather than achievement
- Cooperating in small group
- Learning new games
- Combating student passivity
- Sharing compassion, empathy, and risk with classmates
- Rediscovering oneself as a competent physical being

Adventure activities are generally divided into two categories: group initiatives and new or unfamiliar games.

Group initiatives

Initiatives are unusual group tasks that involve 8 to 20 participants and require a great amount of cooperative effort. Success is measured by group accomplishment rather than individual achievement. Here are four examples (the first three of which come from Rohnke 1977) that require little sophisticated equipment.

1. *The Clock.* All participants form a large circle and join hands firmly. (Males and females should alternate evenly throughout the circle.) After a marker is placed as a reference point, the entire group rotates first clockwise, then counterclockwise one complete revolution as quickly as possible. (The record is 17 seconds.)

2. *The All-Aboard.* All participants try to get on a two-by-two-foot platform at the same time. In order to succeed, everyone must have both feet off the ground for at least five seconds.

3. *The Trust Fall.* Approximately 10 to 12 spotters position themselves in facing lines below a four-by-five-foot platform. "Fallers" stand on the platform with their backs to the spotters, close their eyes, and fall backward into the spotters' outstretched arms. *Note:* Spotters' arms should alternate from one side to another; palms should be open and facing up, not grasped! Fallers should fall straight back with their arms at their sides. (Bending at the waist concentrates all of the weight at one spot in the line and spotters are not able to hold someone in this position.) Everyone gets a chance!

4. *High Ropes.* High ropes is a series of initiatives that takes place 15 to 50 feet in the air. The participant attempts to walk a balance beam and a swinging log, cross a fidget ladder, traverse a cargo net, jump a gap in the course, climb an inclined log, and descend via a zip line. The participant is secured by a belaying system that precludes any fall of more than one or two feet. The trouble is no one really believes this while attempting the obstacles so high in the air. As with other adventure activities the purpose is to attempt the unknown, to stress personal capabilities rather than achievement.

New games

Wouldn't it be different to play a game that is not only novel but by its very nature equalizes the competition? An earth ball, a ball that is six feet in diameter and covered in canvas, provides just such an experience. Superior players cannot dominate a game that involves an earth ball and 15 to 30 teammates. The objective is to move this huge yet lightweight ball from one end of a football field to the other against the opposition of another team. This is comparable to swimming against the tide, running in sand, paddling against the wind, or cycling uphill. Other "new games" that provide unique experiences include the following:

1. *Assembly Line.* Six people get down on their hands and knees and face the same direction. Six other people get on their hands and knees and face the opposite direction, alternating between members of the first line (i.e., every other person now faces the same direction). People facing the same direction look to their right and, as a unit, begin to rock forward and backward so that half of them are going forward while the other half are going backward. A "worker" lies down on one end of the assembly line and tries to make it to the other end without falling down. Everyone gets a chance!

2. *Catch the Dragon's Tail.* Eight to ten people line up, one behind the other, putting their arms around the waist of the person in front. The last person tucks a handkerchief in the back of his or her belt. At a signal, the dragon begins chasing its own tail, the object being that the person at the head of the line tries to snatch the handkerchief. When the head finally captures the tail, the head dons the handkerchief and becomes the new tail, while the person previously second in line becomes the new head. Another version involves two or three dragons trying to catch each other's tails.

3. *Lineup.* The problem is for the group to line up in a designated order while blindfolded. A number of situations can be used as the problem, but in all cases the participants are blindfolded. (a) Each member crosses arms over chest, and members line up according to height without talking. (b) Each member is assigned to be a specific animal. Animals must line up according to height by making only the sound of the animal they represent. (c) Members line up by shoe size. No talking is allowed.

The best source regarding the inclusion of adventure activities in the physical education curriculum remains Project Adventure. For further information, write to B. Simpson, Project Adventure, Inc., P.O. Box 100, Hamilton, Maine 01936.

Summary

An increasing number of schools have added wilderness sports and adventure education programs to the traditional physical education curriculum, thus allowing students to participate in activities such as backpacking, scuba diving, and cross-country skiing.

Many of these activities are conducted away from school, at times other than during the typical school day, and necessitate special arrangements related to travel, equipment, financing, safety, instruction, and liability. It is possible to provide adventure activities and the controlled risks associated with them on school grounds.

Adolescents enjoy participating in these relatively exotic activities. Wilderness sports seem appropriate at this developmental period and for some young people satisfy the need for acceptable risks, deferred goals, skill development, social opportunities, and self-direction.

Specific attention to teaching in an outdoor environment is central to a successful program. Safety factors, parent involvement, specialized equipment, and the effects of such activities on the school calendar are important considerations.

Many schools and agencies have established programs and provide information about successful practices that can help beginning efforts.

Suggested activities

1. Discuss in class Figure 12.1 on page 214, which describes the relationship between physical education and various outdoor programs. How might the information in the figure affect your future teaching?

2. Search the literature for physical educators prominent in the organized summer camp movement. Report your findings to the class.

3. Trace the leadership and program direction of AAHPERD's Outdoor Education Project.

4. Plan and carry out a weekend camping trip for approximately 12 people. Present a written critique of the trip, outlining strengths and weaknesses in your planning.

5. Prepare and present in class a report justifying to a school board a wilderness excursion for a class of eighth graders.

13

The Social Development Model

The purpose of this chapter is to describe and explain a curriculum model for physical education in which social development is the primary goal and to provide examples of program activities designed to achieve desired results. The major topics covered in this chapter are as follows:

A six-level hierarchy of social development through which students grow from irresponsibility to self-control

A curriculum designed to meet the demands of the social development model

A rationale explaining the importance of social development in the context of modern society, especially for troubled adolescent students

Examples of school programs and activities that have been used to meet the objectives of the social development model

Jan and Nate are two very different students. Jan has been in trouble with the law, has been suspended from school several times for disruptive behavior, is frequently truant, and has experimented with drugs. She seems to be headed nowhere—except for trouble. Nate is seldom in trouble; in fact, he is usually so passive and nonassertive that he seldom does anything! He is not a happy young man, and while passing most of his courses, he seems as uninterested in school as he does in social interactions.

Jan and Nate, although different in almost every aspect of overt social and academic behavior, share much in common. Neither has much self-control. Neither is a contributing member of a normal, healthy social group. Neither acts in a mature and responsible manner. And, perhaps most importantly, neither feels much control over what is happening to her or him right now or what might happen in the future. In a very real sense, the two are almost helpless to shape their futures.

Technically speaking, they are *alienated*; that is, they do not feel as if they are in control of their own destinies.

This year they have been in a different physical education program. They both hated physical education in previous years, but this year it has been different. Much of what they are doing is geared to their own needs. While providing a lot of support for them, the teacher really makes them take charge of some things themselves. At first, it was little things like paying attention and trying some new activities. However, as the year went on, without even realizing it some of the time, they gradually began to take responsibility for their own fitness program, develop some skills, and interact positively with the other students. On occasion they have even caught themselves being nice to other members of the class, encouraging them, and showing some leadership! And they like how that feels.

Neither Jan nor Nate is ever going to be a competent athlete, but that is not the purpose of their class. What they are learning is how to take care of themselves and to be responsible for their own choices, to show some concern for others with whom they are working, and to begin to think about doing some of those same kinds of things in other parts of their school life and maybe in their home life too. It has not been a steady uphill climb. There has been stumbling and backsliding. But they are certainly farther ahead than they were 16 weeks ago. Who knows if this will last. Perhaps it will if they can find another program that treats them the way this one has.

This brief vignette touches on some of the features of a social development model for physical education.* It is a straightforward model in that it

---

BEYOND BALLS AND BATS

Our profession needs to achieve some balance between helping people and developing and promulgating the subject matter (skills, fitness, strategies, etc.). However, I get my good feelings as a physical educator from helping students—especially struggling, hostile adolescents—feel good about themselves, become more aware of their motives, sort through the increasingly wide range of choices our society now allows, make some sense out of their identity and the world, and begin to reach out toward others. For me, the physical education setting—the gym—provides a potentially loose, open, hands-on, active, many-dimensional (not just verbal) place to conduct the search for self. . . . As we become more aware of ourselves—as we begin to get in touch with our own feelings and desires, our own potentialities, and some notion of the range of options open to us—we can begin the process of searching for and building our own identities, eventually freeing ourselves to really share and relate to the lives of others.

SOURCE: Hellison, D. *Beyond Balls and Bats: Alienated Youth in the Gym.* Washington, D.C.: AAHPER, 1978, pp. 1–2.

---

* The material for this chapter is drawn from the work of Dr. Don Hellison of Portland State University. In his work in schools, through his conference presentations, and through his writing Dr. Hellison has gradually developed this model over the past 10 years. His major work, *Beyond Bats and Balls*, and his recent book, *Teaching Ethics in the Gym*, present the model in its entirety. Those interested should consult Hellison's books for more detail.

does not claim to achieve a large number of goals in the skill area, the fitness area, or even the knowledge area—that is, unless one includes self-knowledge. In this program the social goals are foremost and the other goals are used as vehicles through which the primary social goals are attained. The purpose of this chapter is to describe this model and to provide a sense of how it works and how it might be employed as a unit within an overall program for some special students or as a central program.

What is the social development model?

As we have said several times in this text, one of the problems with physical education programs is that they are conceptualized to accomplish a wide range of goals but seldom are given the time or commitment to accomplish any of them very well. Clearly, it is better to make some real progress with a few goals than to flounder in an attempt to reach a number of goals.

The social development model is designed to help young people cope better with the difficult world they are entering, to respond to social change effectively, to achieve a sense of control over their lives, and to contribute in some positive ways to the wellness of those around them and to the world of which they are a part. It does all of this within the context of physical education activities, in the gymnasium, in the weight room, and on the playing fields.

Levels of social development

The social development model conceptualizes a hierarchy of six levels (0 through 5) of social development. Level 0 is characterized by irresponsible behavior and level 5 is characterized by behavior which shows that the student is ready to assume leadership for the class program. In between those two levels students go through a series of steps of progressively more mature social development.

Level 0: Irresponsibility. Students at level 0 often refuse to participate. They tend to blame others, make excuses, ridicule others, attempt intimidation, and occasionally even resort to abuse of other students and the teacher. Students at this level are extraordinarily difficult to manage, and the teacher can accomplish little until they move beyond this level.

Level 1: Self-control. Students at level 1 can control themselves sufficiently so as not to disrupt others, and this occurs without frequent prompting from the teacher or constant supervision. When students reach this level, they are at a point where they may begin to participate and learn. This level represents the fundamental level of self-discipline and the beginning of the acceptance of responsibility for one's own actions.

Level 2: Involvement.   Students at level 2 not only behave with self-control but participate willingly in activities. They exercise. They play games. They practice skills. They show progress in accepting the challenges that naturally occur when participating—learning a new skill, improving in a strength measure, being a member of a losing team. This is not the kind of involvement that occurs only under close teacher scrutiny but instead is shown enthusiastically and without prompting and constant supervision.

Level 3: Self-responsibility.   Students are at level 3 when they begin to make some of their own decisions; this means that they plan and begin to implement some of their own program and also take responsibility for the consequences of those actions. Students do not achieve this automatically; they require assistance in acquiring the behavioral skills necessary to think about their own actions, make plans, execute the plans, modify them if necessary, and accept responsibility for their actions.

Level 4: Caring.   Level 4 is characterized by behavior that goes beyond the self. While level 3 is characterized by an ability to deal with one's own life in physical education, level 4 behavior is demonstrated in how students react to their peers and to their teacher. The characteristics of level 4 are cooperating, expressing concern for fellow students, demonstrating a willingness to help, and providing support for others. This caring is conceptualized as an

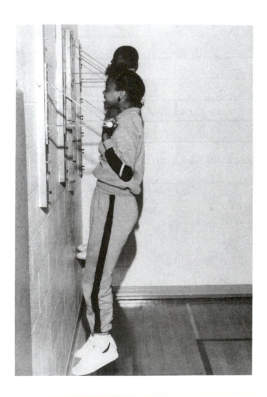

At level 3 students are responsible for their own fitness.

extension of a growing sense of responsibility—a responsibility not only for oneself but for the world around one. With students, this growing sense of responsibility first shows itself with the peer group in class.

Level 5: Going beyond. Students who have grown sufficiently to demonstrate level 4 behavior are often ready to begin to interact with the teacher in such a way that they begin to evaluate and suggest changes in the strategies being employed in the class, not only for themselves but for other students as well. Students at level 5 have grown sufficiently to become true co-workers, willing to accept the responsibility of leadership.

Certainly not all students enter a physical education class at level 0, and the model is not only for alienated and disruptive youth—any young person can profit from it. Therefore, this model can be viewed either as a "special" physical education program for troubled students or as a regular curriculum model for general students.

A curriculum for the social development model

As we will see, the social development model can be accommodated within many different curriculum designs. As with any other approach, the degree to which it can be implemented will no doubt be determined by the degree of control the individual teacher can exert over his or her own program and schedule. Like many other school-based changes, a shift to the social development model is probably best made by doing it individually within one's own classes and letting other staff and students see the good results rather than waiting until the entire staff is convinced before embarking upon the change.

Hellison (1978) has developed a curriculum to meet the demands of the social development model. This curriculum represents one way of meeting the goals of the model and assumes a five-day-per-week program. Each week is divided into three parts: two days of skill development and play, two days of fitness activities, and one day of activities designed to facilitate sharing and cooperation.

The implementation of this design requires that the physical educator get to know his or her students quickly. To that end, Hellison suggests that the teacher set aside time at the beginning of the course for diagnostic testing in skill, fitness, cognitive, and affective domains and use the resulting information quickly to individualize his or her attention to each student.

Hellison further suggests that the teacher use the early part of each period (five minutes) to direct and heighten student awareness of the day's activities. If students are eventually to gain self-control and exert responsibility, they need to become more aware of what they are doing and why they are doing it.

The skills/play days are devoted to the improvement of skills and the joy of playing. As many have suggested (Siedentop 1980), skill and enjoyment are intricately related and one is unlikely to occur without the other. The fitness days emphasize individualized activities designed to improve appearance and fitness and to ensure a noncompetitive atmosphere.

The day devoted to cooperation and sharing is designed to help students begin to make connections between themselves and the immediate world around them, that of their peers and teacher in the context of physical education. Cooperative games are very useful in this regard as are certain teaching strategies such as reciprocal teaching, a technique in which students in pairs or small groups help each other learn new activities and/or games (see page 385).

After 10 weeks of the program (or whenever students reach a level where they can take on some responsibility), the teacher can modify the one day each week that was previously devoted strictly to fitness so that students make and carry out their own plans for the day. Individualized contracts are typically used at this point.

Later in the term, students take over two days a week, and eventually they plan four days of their own program and carry it out, often reporting to the teacher by means of a daily journal. The fifth day continues to emphasize level 4 characteristics, which help students to make connections between their growing sense of responsibility for their own lives and the extension of that sense to those around them.

Clearly, teachers cannot implement this model without being committed to acting in certain ways with their students. Teachers must show a great deal of support and also take some very tough stances. More specific teaching strategies are described later in this chapter.

A rationale for the social development model

A number of arguments can be made in favor of a social development model for schools in general and for physical education specifically. We shall provide three such arguments—perhaps you can find others.

At the most general level, a number of scholars from diverse fields have suggested that life has become extremely complex during this century and that one of the negative side effects of the complexity is a general breakdown in social mores and a resultant increase in general levels of anxiety. Life is uncertain! Technology is rapidly changing our lives, and the future is full of perplexing questions. To be sure, the future may also be full of promise, but it is the uncertainty that gives rise to anxieties. Uncertainty also tends to lead to a general disruption in social mores—that is, the generally accepted rules by which we live, rules that give society a structure and that enable people to understand how they should behave and how others should behave toward them.

The young person coming of age today has more choices than ever before and, as a result, faces a less certain future. Many social norms have changed in the past several generations. Attitudes towards careers, life-styles, sexual practices, family obligations, and a host of other matters on which clear expectations and guidelines existed a century ago are now considerably more open.

Activities involving risk offer personal growth potential.

In many respects, this openness is good. Diversity is more acceptable. Discriminatory practices are less evident. However, there is always a price to pay for social change. In this case the price has been a weakening of the unifying customs of society.

Many psychologists and sociologists also believe that the anxiety created by the constant presence of nuclear annihilation has produced an underlying sense of insecurity that while not at a conscious level on a daily basis, tends to disrupt the social structure of society. There is no sense in overdoing this kind of analysis in a physical education methods text, but there is also no sense in ignoring its presence (see page 8).

What this argument adds up to is the fact that specific educational emphasis on social development is warranted. Schools have always included social development among their goals, but perhaps the time has come to give it a more central focus.

A second argument for a social development model stems from what has happened to schooling in the past several decades. Nothing seems clearer than that teaching is a more difficult job today than it was in the past. Let's examine a few of the many reasons for this.

Virtually everyone inside and outside of education believes that students are more disruptive today than they were in the past. Discipline has been the single most important issue in the minds of both parents and teachers over the past decade. Keep in mind, however, that we have no compelling evidence that students behave more poorly today than they did one, two, or three generations ago. It is difficult to make these kinds of comparisons simply because there is little evidence from earlier generations. Nevertheless, teachers, administrators, and parents *believe* that students are more disruptive, more difficult to manage, and more in need of disciplinary training; that is, these groups believe that students need better school training in social development. For a more detailed account of this issue, see the data in Chapter 19.

Regardless of what previous generations of students were like, it seems clear that the current generation needs to learn to behave better in school. Although school vandalism and assaults are down slightly from their previous highs of a few years ago, it is still true that a middle or junior high school student is more likely to be assaulted within school than outside it—and as long as that statistic remains valid, people will continue to show concern for the social development of students.

Along with the widespread concern about disruptive behavior, there is a related belief that the schools should do more to teach students appropriate social and ethical behavior. The Gallup Poll on public attitudes toward education has reported for a number of years that parents want schools to teach ethical/moral behavior to students. The deep and continuing concern about the social development of students makes the model described in this chapter particularly relevant to the current scene.

A third argument for this model can be traced historically to the tradition of concern in physical education for what used to be called character development. Professionals and laypersons alike hold the long-standing belief that in sport and games young people can learn valuable lessons pertaining to rules, authority, perseverance, courage, and responsibility. American physical educators inherited this tradition from their European counterparts. In early defenses of physical education as a school subject, character development occupied a significant role alongside physical fitness.

Over the years, as educational jargon changed, it became more common to describe this objective as social/emotional development rather than character development, but there is little doubt that the two mean essentially the same thing. The progressive education movement in the early part of the twentieth century served to emphasize even more the importance of the social development function of schools, and many important physical educators (including Hetherington, Nash, and Williams) placed great importance on social development outcomes in physical education (for a more detailed analysis of these movements, see Siedentop 1980, chs. 3 and 4).

As many have argued over the past quarter century, there is little evidence that school physical education has made any distinct contribution to character development in students. However, one reason for this lack of evidence may be that *it has very seldom been approached as the major goal of a program!* If social development is just one goal among many, it is not likely to be achieved to a degree that it becomes noticeable. With the model described in this chapter, however, there is good reason to believe that physical educators can achieve

social goals such as perseverance, self-responsibility, more appropriate behavior, sharing, and cooperation among troubled students and the general
student population.

Do parents simply want schools to do what they are no longer willing or
able to do in the home? Is it reasonable for schools to have the major responsibility for teaching social/ethical behavior that is vital for full, mature social development? Or is this all simply a dodge? Is the real issue that parents want
youth to be less rebellious, to be more respectful of traditional forms of authority? These are difficult and complex questions, and we have no simple answers. It is clear that the three arguments provided here as a rationale for the
social development model are valid.

Implementing the social development model

Physical educators can implement the social development model in many different ways. They can tailor specific activities to the kinds of students in the
program. The six levels of social development described on pages 231–233 are
sometimes reduced to five or even four, depending on the situation. One
middle school teacher uses the following levels (Hellison 1983):

0   Little self-control, verbal and physical abuse of others, not involved, often puts down those who are involved, irresponsible,
blames others, feels powerless

1   Under control, not involved but doesn't interfere with others' right
to learn or teacher's right to teach

2   Under control, involved in subject matter but only as directed by
teacher

3   Self-responsible and self-motivated, able to work independently,
able to take responsibility for actions and attitudes (accountability
accepted and acted upon)

4   All of the above, plus caring about others, involved with others in
a helping way, sensitive to the needs of the group or willing to put
ego aside to assist someone else

It is important that the progression from one level to the next is clear and distinct. The teacher should gradually make students aware of these levels and
the way in which the program is developed around them. The teacher should
encourage students to think about the levels, to begin to analyze their own
behavior in terms of the levels, and to compare their own perceptions with
those of others. Figure 13.1 (p. 238) shows a checklist of social development
levels; students use this to compare their own ratings with the teacher's.

A major aim of the social development model is for students to begin to
take over control of their own program. The behavior necessary for a student
to plan, implement, and evaluate his or her own program is indicative of a

Name _____   Adviser _____

Social Development Levels Checklist

Definition of Ratings	Period	Student Rating/Date	Teacher Rating/Date	Comments
0 Little self-control Not involved Uses put-downs Irresponsible Disruptive	1			
1 Under control, not involved	2			
Not participating	3			
Not prepared Nonproductive	4			
2 Under control, involved when teacher directed	5			
Frequently off task Needs prompting Needs frequent reminders	6			
3 Self-responsibility	7			
Works independently Self-motivated Positive attitude	8			
4 Self-responsibility and caring	Adv.			
Cares about others Involved with others Sensitive to needs of others				

Figure 13.1 Checklist used by students to compare their perceptions with those of teachers.

SOURCE: Jeff Walsh, Gregory Heights School, Portland, Oregon.

developing sense of responsibility and self-control—working at level 3 on the social development scale. However, it is important that students consistently achieve the status of level 2 behavior before embarking upon self-management projects.

Contracting appears to be the strategy most often used to develop level 3 self-management skills. At the outset the teacher encourages students to earn their way into a contracting situation one or two days a week. One way to do this is to distinguish between "teacher time," when the teacher directs and controls activities (level 2) and "student time," when students choose their own activities, engage in them, and evaluate them (see Figure 13.2). Often this entry into level 3 behavior takes place on fitness days. Figure 13.3 (p. 240) shows a 30-minute fitness contract that students can use to begin their entry into level 3.

Personal Program Contract

Name _____

Period _____

Date _____

My activity _____

In order to

_____ improve my health
_____ improve my physical appearance
_____ improve my personal safety
_____ win more often
_____ improve my talents
_____ have fun
_____ be with my friends
_____ help other students

My plan   **Teacher time**

Warm-up: 1–5 minutes with the group _____

_____

Skills	*Drills*	*Evaluation*
1. _____	1. _____	1. _____
	2. _____	2. _____
2. _____	1. _____	1. _____
	2. _____	2. _____
3. _____	1. _____	1. _____
	2. _____	2. _____

Your time: (If you check on me, you see me doing these things.)

1. _____

2. _____

3. _____

Figure 13.2 A program contract divided between teacher time and student time.

SOURCE: Jeff Walsh, Gregory Heights School, Portland, Oregon.

Directions: Choose one or more of the following goals. Only pick goals you are sincere about working on.

1. ____ Cardiovascular endurance   6. ____ Losing weight

2. ____ Muscular endurance   7. ____ Gaining weight

3. ____ Strength   8. ____ Toning muscles

4. ____ Flexibility   9. ____ Relaxation

5. ____ Other _____   10. ____ Other _____

On the basis of these goals fill out a fitness contract that will last for 25–30 minutes.

Exercise	How much	For which goal	Dates			
1.						
2.						
3.						
4.						
5.						
6.						
7.						
8.						
9.						
10.						
11.						
12.						
13.						

Figure 13.3 Short-term fitness contract.

SOURCE: Gayle McDonald, Jefferson High School, Portland, Oregon.

Contracting continues to be a useful strategy for achieving higher levels of social development. The teacher should keep contracts simple and short-term at the outset. He or she cannot expect students to work for many days or weeks for a deferred reward when they are first acquiring self-management skills. Gradually, the teacher can increase the length of the contract and its complexity. As the contracting proceeds, students can gradually take over more and more responsibility for the details in the contract; that is, they can choose the goals and the activities to achieve the goals and also the means by which the contract will be evaluated.

Figure 13.4 shows a fitness contract in which the activities are already prescribed and the student is responsible for implementing them. Figure 13.2 shows a contract divided between teacher time and student time. This example is typical of a midway point in the process where the student is given some but not all of the responsibilities for program design. Figure 13.5 (p. 242) shows a more advanced version, in which only a time division between fitness and skill/play is imposed on the student. Otherwise, the activities are to be

General Overall Fitness

Directions: You will do this entire contract for six days; as you do each exercise, either check it off or record the amount of weight you used or the number of repetitions you accomplished. Except for stretching, you may do the workout in any order. To progress to the next contract you must pass a written fitness-knowledge test.

Exercise	How much	Dates					
1. Warm-up	First 5 minutes						
2. Sit-ups	20–40						
3. Push-ups	As many as you can						
4. Bench press	1 set of 15 (1 × 15)						
5. Leg curls	1 × 15						
6. Pull downs	1 × 15						
7. Leg press	1 × 15						
8. Curls	1 × 15						
9. Leg extension	1 × 15						
10. Jogging	3 laps						
11. Stretching	Last 5 minutes						
12.							

Figure 13.4 A contract in which the activities are prescribed for the student.

SOURCE: Gayle McDonald, Jefferson High School, Portland, Oregon.

Name _____

Dates _____

You may now divide your time into two 15-minute segments and include a sport of your choice. In the circle to the right fill in the fitness activities and sport you wish to get better at.

Examples

Fitness: stretch 5 minutes, jog 10 minutes
Skill/Play: develop jumpshot, play basketball

Fitness
(15 min)

Skill/Play
(15 min)

I. Fitness

What?   *Where?*   *Why?*

II. Skill and/or Play

What?   *Where?*   *Why?*

Figure 13.5 A contract in which only the focus of the activity is prescribed for the student.

SOURCE: Gayle McDonald, Jefferson High School, Portland, Oregon.

designed by the student. Figure 13.6 shows a skills contract and is a good example of how the system works in skills/play time as well as in fitness time.

In many implementations of this model, students are asked to keep a journal in which they record their thoughts and perceptions as they progress through the program. The journal serves several purposes. First, it helps the student to reflect on the model and on his or her own behavior, and it emphasizes the feelings associated with progress through the various stages. For the teacher, the journal is a way of keeping in touch with what students are thinking and serves as a valuable source of feedback about the program itself.

Obviously, the social development model does not present a "recipe" approach to developing and implementing the curriculum. Remember that *social goals* are primary in this approach and that the activities are a means to achieve those goals. Some other strategies that teachers have used to implement this model are described next.

1. *Clean days.* A clean day is a day when a student attends class and behaves decently. Some teachers use a certain number of clean days as a require-

Skills Contract

Remember the three things you have to do to learn a new skill or get better at an old one:
1. Get a picture of it in your mind's eye.
2. Practice the action over and over again.
3. Get feedback from someone on what you are doing right and wrong.

  I. What skill will I see you working on?

  II. How should it look if you are doing it right?

  III. How are you going to practice it?

  IV. What feedback did you get about what you were doing right and wrong?

Figure 13.6 A skills contract in which the student decides goals and the means to accomplish the goals.

SOURCE: Gayle McDonald, Jefferson High School, Portland, Oregon.

ment for students to move into a special program component. For example, a student may need five consecutive clean days before he or she can participate in a personal program fitness day.

    2. *Open negotiation.* Open negotiation is a period of time (from one day to an entire grading period) during which students can negotiate all parts of the program, including attendance and grades. Notice that this is a negotiation relationship between the student and the teacher. The purpose of this strategy is for students to think seriously about the relationship between tasks and consequences and to have to present a case, defend it, and eventually reach a compromise with an authority figure.

    3. *Counseling sessions.* Counseling sessions are personal communications between the teacher and the individual student. The teacher asks questions designed to elicit the student's feelings, views, and opinions about the program, his or her reactions to it, how he or she is feeling about his or her progress, and other pertinent issues. Teachers should keep records of when they counseled each student to ensure that they eventually get to all students.

    4. *Confronting.* Confronting is a strategy to help students face up to the level of behavior they are supposed to exhibit. For example, consider the following dialogue between a teacher and a student in a situation where nonparticipation was a penalty in the grading system (Hellison 1978, 29):

MICHAEL I can't participate today.

TEACHER Your choice. Have a seat.

MICHAEL But I forgot my clothes.

TEACHER You could go in street clothes today. Your choice.

MICHAEL But I'll get all sweaty.

TEACHER Your choice.

This strategy is necessary for students to learn lessons about rules and consequences and responsibility.

5. *Talking bench.* The talking bench strategy (Horrocks 1978, 61) requires students who get into an argument to go to an assigned place—the talking bench—and work out their differences, report the solution to the teacher, and then make up the time missed. The last part of the strategy is absolutely crucial because it encourages students to be serious and efficient about dealing with their differences.

Many other strategies fit well into the social development model. We have outlined these few to provide you with some sense of how teachers must operate to implement the model successfully.

Summary

The social development model takes seriously the goal of increased social competence, particularly in the area of self-control and responsible behavior. It is designed specifically to achieve this goal and makes no claim to achieve other, more broadly conceived goals in fitness and/or skill development.

According to this model, social development is composed of a series of six developmental levels. The lowest level, level 0, is characterized by irresponsible behavior. At level 1 students have self-control, while at level 2 students become involved and participating. At level 3 students begin to move toward self-responsibility, and at level 4 they begin to feel responsible for others. At level 5 students assume leadership and self-initiative and engage in self-directed learning.

Not all students enter the program at level 0, but wherever they are when they enter, they generally proceed through the remaining levels. The model is applicable as a unit for troubled adolescents and as a basic social development course for general students.

The social development model can be defended on several grounds, including the difficulties associated with adolescent development in a socially complex world, the belief that students today are badly in need of educational programs that focus on social development, and physical education's historic interest in what used to be called character development.

Many different kinds of activities can be used to implement the social development model, but they must be organized and presented so as to achieve the behavior specified at each level of social development.

Suggested activities

1. Discuss the importance of social development as an objective in physical education, including an analysis of how such an objective is met in traditional programs.

2. Divide into small groups. Each group is to design an activity experience in which the major goal is social development. Compare and discuss the suggested activity experiences with the entire class.

3. Debate the following issue: Social development is a more important physical education objective for adolescent students than physical fitness or skill development. Have three students argue the affirmative and three the negative.

4. Divide into five groups. Each group is to take one level of the social development hierarchy and describe the teaching implications for that level.

5. Discuss the strategies described on pages 237–244. Add other strategies that might be useful in a social development program.

14

A Conceptually Based Program Model

The purpose of this chapter is to describe and explain a curriculum model for physical education in which cognitive understanding of physical education is the primary goal. A rationale for the model is presented and several alternative ways of implementing the model are described. The major topics in this chapter are as follows:

The concepts approach from a historical point of view and in its most current popular forms

A rationale for the curriculum model and the philosophy underlying it

A fitness approach to the concept curriculum

A sports approach to the concept curriculum

A concept model based on the subdisciplines of physical education

SCENE *A family dinner during which a father is talking to his son about a recent weight gain.*

FATHER I guess I'll just have to try to lose some weight. I'm four pounds up from what I was just two months ago.

SON That may be true, Dad, but you're never going to be able to tell what kind of shape you're in by stepping on the scale.

FATHER What do you mean?

SON Well, how much you weigh just doesn't tell you much about your body composition; it's the amount of fat you carry around that's important, not how much you weigh.

FATHER But isn't my weight a good indicator of that?

SON Not nearly as good as knowing your percentage of body fat.

FATHER   How do I find that out?

SON   I guess the best way is to have yourself weighed underwater, but in P.E. class we did it with skinfold calipers. We took measurements of fat in two or three places with the calipers and then looked up the results on a chart that told us what percentage of fat we each had. Then we compared that to what was normal for our age group. The kids who were above normal had to design an exercise program and diet that would enable them to reduce their fat content. I was just below normal for my age group.

FATHER   You did this in PE class?

SON   Yeah; it's part of a new program.

FATHER   When I was in phys ed all we did was play softball and bombardment!

SON   Well, I guess that's the way it used to be here too. But this new program is neat. We learn a lot of things. We did that body measurement stuff in our fitness and nutrition unit last marking period. Now we're doing a unit on biomechanics. Today we did a kicking experiment with soccer balls. It's amazing how the spin of the ball affects the way it bounces off the wall.

FATHER   I guess physical education's changed a bit since my day.

SON   Lots of things have, Dad!

Physical education has changed a lot in some schools. And one of the directions it has taken has become known as the *concepts approach*.* The concepts approach began to appear regularly in physical education literature in the 1960s and has steadily gained adherents. The educational reform movements of the mid-1980s, many of which focus on a restoration of excellence in academic preparation, have further boosted the concepts approach to physical education. Many physical educators believe that school programs can survive only if they become more academically oriented. Writing in response to a report by the Commission on Excellence in Education, David Marsh, a physical education teacher in New Jersey, suggested that "secondary school programs must provide course offerings that require intellectual rigor as well as physical toil if we are to be viewed as worthy in the hierarchy of education" (1983, 9). This point of view is shared by many physical educators who feel that physical education may be left out in back-to-basics or academic-excellence movements in schools. However, we must point out that the concepts approach was advocated long before current reform movements in education began, and it is not simply a response to current concerns.

A brief description of the concepts approach

Physical educators have always been concerned that students learn *about* physical education as they learn *how to do* the various activities of physical educa-

---

* Although there are many references to the concepts approach in the physical education literature of the past 20 years, much of the material in this chapter derives from the concepts model developed by Hal Lawson and Judith Placek and described in their book, *Physical Education in the Secondary Schools: Curricular Alternatives.*

tion. Knowledge objectives have often been included among the major objectives of physical education, that is, those of fitness, skill, social development, and knowledge (Siedentop 1980). Nevertheless, knowledge objectives of physical education have seldom been defined specifically, and although they have been stated as equal to skill, fitness, and social development objectives, they have seldom been attended to with equal vigor. Too often, the "knowledge focus" was no more than a short rules test at the end of a unit.

The concepts approach to physical education emphasizes the objectives of knowledge and understanding. (See Figure 14.1 for an example.) Although fitness, skill, and social development may get some attention in the concepts approach, the knowledge and understanding objectives dominate. This approach to physical education first became popular in the late 1950s and was known then as the foundations approach (Johnson 1966). The term *foundations* was used because proponents felt that such an approach provided the base from which all other physical education experiences developed.

The concepts approach emphasizes the *how* and the *why*. Although activity is often used and time spent in the gymnasium, it is common for students to meet in classrooms for lectures, films, and discussions. Indeed, the concepts approach typically utilizes what has been called the lecture/laboratory model, a combination of classroom activities and problem-oriented activities in the gymnasium or on the playing fields.

The concepts approach to physical education in schools developed at the same time as did the discipline movement in college and university physical education. The discipline movement sought to define and develop the body of knowledge that was specific to physical education. Within this movement,

---

Experiment 1 Try serving the volleyball over the net trying to put spin on the ball as directed in the instructions below. Use either an underhand or overhand pattern.

1. Try hitting the ball straight over the net with absolutely no spin. Where do you contact the ball in order to do this?
2. Try hitting the ball over the net with spin to the right (clockwise). Where do you contact the ball in order to do this? Describe the flight of the ball in the air.
3. Try hitting the ball over the net with spin to the left (counterclockwise). Where do you contact the ball in order to do this? Describe the flight of the ball in the air.
4. Try hitting the ball over the net with topspin. Where do you contact the ball in order to do this?
5. Try hitting the ball over the net with backspin. Where do you contact the ball in order to do this?
6. Draw a conclusion or generalization about where force is applied to the ball in order to put spin on the ball.
7. Relate this lab experience to another game you have played that incorporates the use of balls. State similarities of how you applied force to the balls in order to get the effect you wanted. How did this help your play?

Figure 14.1 *Examples of questions used in a problem-solving approach in a concepts unit. The sport is volleyball, and the focus is on biomechanical principles.*

SOURCE: H. Lawson and J. Placek. *Physical Education in the Secondary Schools: Curricular Alternatives.* Boston: Allyn & Bacon, 1981, p. 217.

GOAL STATEMENTS FOR THE
CONCEPTUAL APPROACH

The following statements are intended to provide broad, potentially measurable goals that taken together define the physically educated student.

1. After experiencing learning in physical education under a variety of environmental conditions and with numerous types of teaching-learning methodology, students will be able to solve problems on their own.

2. Students will be afforded the opportunity to pursue excellence in the physical and ludic activity or activities of their choice.

3. Students will be able to identify the ways in which the following variables influence their potential preferences for and capacity to engage in physical education activities: biomechanical variables, structural-infunctional variables, sociocultural variables.

4. Students will be able to distinguish fact and fancy regarding the physiological, prophylactic, and sociopsychological effects of exercise.

5. Students will be able to design home exercise programs that are based upon known principles of training and conditioning.

6. Students will be able to describe the components of the contest ethic in sport, including the necessity of honoring one's opponent, the obligation for playing fairly, the need for conditional equality between and among contestants, and the meaning of victory.

7. Students will be able to identify the functions and significance of participation in physical and ludic activities in their own and foreign cultures.

SOURCE: Lawson, H., and J. Placek. *Physical Education in the Secondary Schools: Curricular Alternatives.* Boston: Allyn and Bacon, 1981, p. 81.

---

subdisciplines began to develop. Among these subdisciplines are exercise physiology, kinesiology, biomechanics, sports sociology, sports psychology, sports philosophy, and sports history. As knowledge in these subdisciplines developed in the university, it was quite logical to begin to find ways to pass on the knowledge to students in K–12 schools. That point of view is still quite strong among current physical educators.

> Underlying all else is the need to clarify the body of knowledge of physical education within the context of the cognitive, as well as the psychomotor and affective domain. Just as the body of knowledge is consumed by the individual preparing to be a physical educator, it should be consumed by the secondary school students as a primary component of being physically educated. (Mancuso 1983, 9)

The subdisciplines of physical education often provide the framework for the curriculum in the concepts approach to middle, junior, and senior high school physical education. Although this is certainly not the *only* way to develop a concepts curriculum, it appears to be the most prevalent. Units are developed in areas such as cardiovascular fitness, sports biomechanics, and international sport. These units are designed primarily to increase the student's knowledge and understanding of the topics.

The teaching methods used in the concepts approach are typical of any laboratory-oriented subject. Teachers give students assignments that require them to *do* some activities in order to understand better the concepts involved. Often these assignments take the form of problems to be solved. Students work individually or in small groups. The problems are often small experiments in which students must engage in some physical activity in order to collect the "data" for the experiment. For example, students may practice kicking a soccer ball or hitting a volleyball in different ways to produce either no spin or different kinds of spin in order to understand how spin is produced in the striking action and what its effects are as the ball rebounds off the floor or a wall. In this example, skill in kicking is *not* a primary goal even though an understanding of spin and its relationship to rebound may eventually contribute to increased skill.

Evaluation in the concepts approach is based primarily on successful completion of assignments and on test results rather than on skill development or playing ability. This, too, tends to make the physical education class more like a regular academic class. The physical education class schedule for a week is often divided between classroom lectures and gymnasium activity.

School is a place where academic knowledge is valued. For many educators and more than a few physical educators, physical education has seemed a subject devoid of the kind of knowledge that is so highly valued in the rest of the school. The concepts approach to physical education teaching is a way to overcome that long-standing prejudice against physical education. The gymnasium, the swimming pool, and the playing field can become a laboratory in which students actively engage in the learning process and in which the outcomes of that process are similar to the outcomes that are produced in the physics or the botany lab.

A rationale for the concepts approach

The concepts approach to physical education curricula in the middle, junior, and senior high school is often undertaken for a variety of reasons. If one listens closely to physical education teachers talking about this approach, one can detect some of the reasons why they have adopted the model.

The kids really seem to get a lot out of this approach.

For the first time, we have gotten some support from the administration.

This is the only way that physical education can be respected in the high school.

I've gotten more positive reaction from parents on this program than anything I've done.

We believe the concepts model puts us on the cutting edge of what's going on in our field.

These reactions all point to *reasons* why a curricular innovation such as the concepts model is adopted in schools. The reasons have to do with important matters such as student motivation, administrative approval and support, perceptions of other teachers, parental reactions and support, and perceptions of being up-to-date within the profession. These are important reasons or motivations, and we can apply them to *any* of the curricular models presented in Part II of this text. That is, the same reasons might support a fitness model, a sports education model, or a wilderness sports model. However, none of them tell us much about the model itself or explain why the model is particularly good or timely; the reasons do not form a complete rationale.

The concepts model is typically based on a particular view of human beings and the role of education in the development of human beings. Sometimes that view is stated quite explicitly, and sometimes it is only implied by the way in which the model is explained. This view of human beings and the role of education in their development has several significant features.

1. Human beings should move from states of dependence to states of independence.
2. Each person has a unique set of talents and abilities.
3. A primary human motivation is to develop those talents toward competence.
4. Competence involves being able to *do* and knowing *how* and *why*.
5. Education must be liberating in the sense that human beings gain competence to be adaptive problem solvers.
6. People who are so educated will be able to control and direct their own lives in relation to health, fitness, and leisure activities.

The goal of this set of rationale statements is the self-directed, self-educating individual who is in control of his or her own existence and also takes responsibility for it.

This point of view most often underlies the concepts approach to the physical education curriculum. From these assumptions the *methods* and *purposes* of the concepts curriculum develop.

According to this view, individuals are in a process of development from a state of dependence to a state of independence. In the initial state, they have few skills, know little about the issues involved, and do not know why things should or do happen. People need to move from this state and become involved in experiences that help them to become more fully educated. At the outset, these educational experiences may be very directive, but they must move toward problem-solving experiences if the human beings are to be educated properly. Educators develop independent learners only by putting people in positions where their independent learning skills are tested, improved, and refined.

Each person has a unique set of talents and abilities. A goal of education must be to develop these talents and abilities toward *competence*. This requires some kind of understanding of the differences among people, and this, in turn, requires some kind of assessment at the outset. Diagnostic testing is often a major element in the concepts models. Students begin to understand themselves as individuals and in relationship to others by completing assessments that are diagnostic in nature. These may be skill assessments, knowledge assessments, fitness assessments, or attitude assessments. This diagnostic feature remains important throughout the concepts program and is one of the techniques used in the development of problem-solving skills and strategies.

Many experts point to the desire for competence as a primary motivation in human behavior. Competence means that a person has the knowledge, skill, and understanding to remain in control despite a constantly changing set of conditions in life. This kind of competence is obviously *adaptive* rather than static. It is strongly related to problem solving. It is also important to note that knowledge and understanding are as crucial to competence as is skill. It is not enough for a person simply to perform well. The person must also know

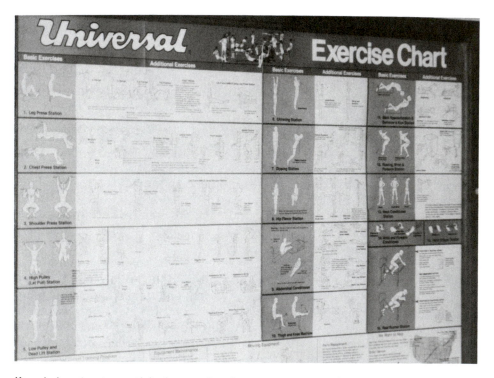

Knowledge about an activity is central to the concepts approach.

what factors affect the performance and when and why those factors become operational.

The importance of knowing *how* and *why* sets the concepts approach apart from other models that emphasize the *doing*. The knowledge of how and why requires an intellectual component to physical education. This requires methods and materials that are appropriate to cognitive learning. Thus, books, lectures, and films become tools for the physical educator just as they are for the classroom teacher. This affects the manner in which physical educators conceptualize and implement physical education experiences. It also seriously changes the manner in which they evaluate students in physical education. Physical educators who advocate the concepts model believe that students must acquire knowledge from the subdisciplines of physical education in order to be physically educated.

This knowledge is a necessary component in an education designed to result in critical problem-solving skills. The student is not viewed as a container to be filled up with knowledge but as a problem solver who needs knowledge in order to be better able to solve more problems and more complex problems. The goal of all of this is to produce an independent learner, one who can encounter new problems and solve them *without* the help of teachers and schools. The only way educators can fulfill this aim is to provide students with a great deal of practice in problem solving. Thus, problem solving becomes the primary educational method associated with the concepts model. This method has three main features (Lawson and Placek 1981).

1. Teachers arrange educational experiences that encourage and require problem solving.

2. Teachers gradually delegate more responsibility to students as their problem-solving abilities increase.

3. Teachers remain responsible for outcomes and therefore act to guide students in appropriate directions.

The role of the teacher is as a resource generator and behind-the-scenes guide to the learning process. Since students have differing talents and abilities, the learning process will have to be somewhat individualized in order for students to gradually acquire more responsibility for their own learning.

Students who have developed problem-solving skills in physical education and know the hows and whys of the subject matter will be better able to control and direct their future lives in terms of health, fitness, and leisure activities. They will be able to maintain their own fitness levels despite changing social conditions (a job downtown, rehabilitation of an injury, etc.) because they will know the hows and whys of fitness. The same is true for their health and leisure practices. In this sense they will have become physically educated and will remain so because of their adaptive problem-solving skills.

It seems clear that a rationale such as this one goes well beyond simply "knowing more" about physical education. The purpose is to help to develop a certain kind of person, one who has the competence to maintain a healthy, fit life-style and a meaningful leisure life. Such a person would be a knowledgeable consumer of fitness and physical education services in a modern society, able to detect the *real* fitness or recreation opportunity from the pseudo-opportunity. Such a person would be physically educated.

Concepts curriculum examples

The concepts model for physical education can be developed in different ways in the school curriculum. This section provides examples of three approaches: (1) the fitness approach, (2) the sports approach, and (3) the physical education subdiscipline approach. The method of the concepts model (to encourage problem solving) is used in all three. What distinguishes them from one another is the means for organizing the curriculum.

The fitness approach

The fitness approach to the concepts model is the oldest and most widely used. It has a strong tradition in physical education and for several decades was known as the foundations approach. This curricular model is often used as the first unit in a school program and is often considered to be foundational to other units.

The program at Westside High School, Omaha, Nebraska (Stewart 1983), is typical of the fitness approach. This tenth-grade program enrolls over 500 students per year. The students meet for one 60-minute lecture period and two 80-minute activity periods per week. Lectures focus on major fitness concepts, including cardiorespiratory fitness, strength development, stress, relaxation, drugs, alcohol, smoking, adolescent physical activity, and individual exercise plans based on diagnostic data, as well as the topics of health and nutrition.

The activity portion of the program includes a warm-up phase and an aerobic phase. In the aerobic phase students are introduced to a series of activities, many of them new to most high school students. These are activities in which students can engage for leisure reasons and also get a good fitness workout; they include water polo, handball, free-style wrestling, and floor hockey.

At the beginning of the program, students are tested and taught to understand their own fitness profile. The resulting information is used throughout the program to trace progress and for evaluation purposes. Although fitness performance marks are used partially for evaluation, the concepts model stresses student understanding of fitness as much as fitness itself. As in many concepts models, the fitness program is the first unit in physical education at Westside. The physical educators there believe this provides a foundation from which students can then make more responsible choices in the elective portion of the overall program in the eleventh and twelfth grades.

The lecture-laboratory approach to physical education is used often in the concepts model. The laboratory section is more than a typical activity period in which a warm-up is followed by skill drills and ends with some competitive activity. The term *laboratory* indicates a period in which students work to solve specific problems, often by collecting and interpreting data. The example of a cardiorespiratory laboratory session shown in Figure 14.2 is typical.

Name _____

Problems:

1. What effect does posture and speed of movement have on heart rate?
2. What is your minimum threshold of training?
3. What type of activities would best develop CR endurance?

Directions:

Work with a partner for this lab. Be sure to finish your activity near the clock so you can count your pulse for ten seconds. All the activities listed *except* calisthenics and volleyball can be done at your own pace. We will do calisthenics and volleyball together as a class.

Do each of the following activities and immediately upon finishing the exercise, take your pulse rate for ten seconds and record below. Multiply times 6 for your heart rate for one minute. Rest several minutes between activities.

Activity	10 sec HR	1 min HR
1. Lie down for five minutes. No talking, relax, make sure you can see clock.		× 6
2. Sit up (take pulse after 1 min)		× 6
3. Stand rigidly at attention for two min.		× 6
4. Slow walk (one time around gym)		× 6
5. Fast walk (one time around gym)		× 6
6. Slow jog (two times around gym)		× 6
7. Medium run (two times around gym)		× 6
8. Fast sprint (two times around gym)		× 6
9. Jump rope (1 min)		× 6
10. Calisthenics (10 min)		× 6
11. Volleyball (10 min)		× 6
12. Strength program (from other lab)		× 6

(continued)

Figure 14.2 Cardiorespiratory laboratory task sheet.

SOURCE: H. Lawson and J. Placek. *Physical Education in the Secondary Schools: Curricular Alternatives.* Boston: Allyn & Bacon, 1981, pp. 177–79.

| 13. Muscular endurance program (from other lab) | × 6 |

| 14. Run up stairs from basement two times and into gym by clock the second time | × 6 |

Questions:

1. What happens to heart rate as you change body positions (activities 1, 2, and 3)?

2. What happened to your heart rate from #3 (standing at attention) to #4 (slow walk)?

   Can you give a reason why this may have occurred?

3. Compare your heart rate during the activities with several members of the opposite sex. Is there a consistent difference? If there is, what is the difference?

The method for establishing your personal target zone is given below. Work out your own target zone.

Maximum heart rate × 70% = target zone heart rate
Maximum heart rate = 220 beats per minute − (minus) your age
220 − your age _____ = _____ (your maximum heart rate)
Maximum heart rate _____ × 0.7 = _____ (your target zone heart rate)

4. What would your target zone be if you were 45 years old? Show your work and circle your answer.

5. Compare your target zone heart rate you calculated with the average of 140. Is your threshold higher, lower, or about the same?

   _____

   Is the target zone for a 45-year-old person higher, lower, or about the same?

   _____

6. What conclusion can you draw about the target zone heart rate and increasing age?

Look back at the HR you achieved on the activities. Think about your *normal* daily activities.

7. Do you achieve the target zone HR during a normal day's activities?

   Yes _____

   No _____
   If yes, what activities produce this heart rate?

   If yes, do you do the activities long enough to develop CR endurance?

8. Which of those activities listed at the beginning of this lab would help develop your CR endurance if you just looked at heart rate?

Which of the activities you listed could you keep doing for at least fifteen minutes?

Therefore, which activities do you think would develop CR endurance *for you*?

9. List three or more sports or activities not listed at the beginning of this lab that you think will develop CR endurance.

Note that this laboratory session requires that materials be developed prior to the beginning of the session, including rather extensive written materials in the form of handouts. These materials are often put together in a laboratory book for the course so that each student has a copy. Notice also that, as in many laboratory situations, this cardiorespiratory lab utilizes peer partners in a problem-solving approach.

An important tool in the problem-solving approach is diagnostic assessment. Lawson and Placek (1981) suggest a six-period diagnostic assessment strategy as a lead-in to the physical fitness unit. During the six assessment periods, students learn (a) what the components of fitness are, (b) what good information is, (c) how good information is developed, (d) what the general parameters for each item are, and (e) how they stand as individuals relative to those parameters. The information is summarized on a physical assessment sheet (see Figure 14.3, p. 258). The assessment focuses on height-weight, body measurements, body composition, muscular endurance, flexibility, muscular strength, cardiorespiratory endurance, speed, power, dynamic balance, static balance, agility, and coordination (see Figure 14.4, p. 259, for an example). The information gathered here is then used in the laboratory sessions.

The sports approach

It is also possible to organize a concepts curriculum around traditional sports. In this situation, the physical education curriculum is still primarily a series of units of instruction in which a particular sport provides the organizing focus. However, the concepts model is implemented in ways that bear little resemblance to traditional ways of teaching sports in physical education. In the concepts model the sport is used to gain understanding of underlying issues such as biomechanical efficiency, strength development, the role of sport in culture, and the degree to which sports participation contributes to cardiovascular fitness.

Physical Assessment Sheet

Name _____ Male _____ Female _____

Doctor's name _____ Phone no. _____

List any medical problems under doctor's care: _____

_____

_____

Height _____ in   Height _____ in
Weight _____ lb   Weight _____ lb
Weight _____ kg   Weight _____ kg

Body Measurements (in inches)

	R	L		R	L
Calf	___	___	Calf	___	___
Thigh	___	___	Thigh	___	___
Waist	___		Waist	___	
Chest	___		Chest	___	
Upper arm	___	___	Upper arm	___	___
Forearm	___	___	Forearm	___	___
Other	___	___	Other	___	___

Body Composition: % body fat

Female (average 20–24%)

   arm _____   arm _____
   hip _____   hip _____
   % body fat _____   % body fat _____

Male (average 10–11%)

   arm _____   arm _____
   chest _____   chest _____
   abdomen _____   abdomen _____
   % body fat _____   % body fat _____

Muscular Endurance

Sit-ups _____   Sit-ups _____
Push-ups _____   Push-ups _____

Flexibility

Hamstring _____ in   Hamstring _____ in
Shoulder _____ in   Shoulder _____ in

Figure 14.3 Fitness assessment form used in the diagnostic phase of a fitness unit.

SOURCE: H. Lawson and J. Placek. *Physical Education in the Secondary Schools: Curricular Alternatives.* Boston: Allyn & Bacon, 1981, p. 149.

Muscular Strength

Isotonic (dynamic)

Quadriceps _____ lb   Quadriceps _____ lb

Hamstrings _____ lb   Hamstrings _____ lb

Bench Press _____ lb   Bench Press _____ lb

Isometric (static)

        R   L   R   L

Handgrip _____ _____   Handgrip _____ _____

Circle value of dominant hand

Cardiorespiratory Endurance

Bicycle Ergometer

Work load   Work load

_____ kpm/min   _____ kpm/min

HR _____   HR _____

O$_2$ uptake _____ l/min   O$_2$ uptake _____ l/min

O$_2$ uptake _____ ml/kg   O$_2$ uptake _____ ml/kg

Step test

HR _____   HR _____

O$_2$ uptake _____ l/min   O$_2$ uptake _____ l/min

Coopers 12-min. run

laps _____   laps _____

fitness level _____   fitness level _____

Procedure IV: Leg Adductors

Sit on floor, knees up.

Push knees apart while bringing *soles* of feet together (not side by side, but sole to sole).

Hold ankles with hands and pull feet in as close as possible to crotch.

Press knees toward the floor with elbows,

Your body should remain level and not tilt to one side.

Have partner measure distance of one knee from the ground. If both knees are touching, record distance as 0 inches.

Distance _____ inches from floor

What type of flexibility is being demonstrated by these last four exercises? _____

Look at your scores on the exercises. In how many joints are you. . . ?

flexible (more than 90° or + inches) _____

moderately flexible (90° or 1–2 inches) _____

slightly flexible (less than 90° or 3 or more inches) _____

(continued)

Figure 14.4 Laboratory task on flexibility.

SOURCE: H. Lawson and J. Placek. *Physical Education in the Secondary Schools: Curricular Alternatives*. Boston: Allyn & Bacon, 1981, p. 183.

Compare your partner's scores to yours. In how many joints is your partner. . . ?

flexible _____

moderately flexible _____

slightly flexible _____

Look at both your scores and your partner's. What conclusions or generalizations can you draw about the relationship of flexibility in different parts of the body? Hint: degree of flexibility in each joint. Consider your answers to the above questions to help in answering this question.

An example of this is the four-week volleyball unit taught at Lake Washington High School in Vancouver, British Columbia (Lawson and Placek 1981, 106–12). The unit uses volleyball to introduce important concepts in biomechanics and kinesiology and to reinforce fitness concepts that were taught in an earlier unit. The teacher administers a 40-question written test to determine how much students know about the subjects and also as a means for providing a baseline against which end-of-unit knowledge can be compared.

During the first week of the unit, students are introduced to the concepts of base of support and center of gravity. The set and bump task sheet shown in Figure 14.5 is typical of the kind of laboratory problem used to explore these concepts.

During the second and third weeks of the unit, the focus is on transfer of force and spin on balls. The volleyball skills used to explore these concepts are the block-spike and the serve.

During the fourth week, students play volleyball and take final tests. The tests show how much students have learned and also give the teacher some information about how effective the instruction has been.

Bump

Observe your partner and record good, ok, or poor after the questions. Or you may do the skill five times and then record the number of times the ball is hit correctly.

#1   #2

1. Player bends knees to lower center of gravity and use leg power.
2. Player uses forward stride position for more stability in absorbing force.
3. Player contacts ball on forearms so it will contact largest surface area.
4. Player positions body directly behind ball for best accuracy.
5. Player watches ball until it hits forearms (watch eyes).

Set

1. Player hits ball with thumbs toward face and has hands on outside of ball.
2. Player uses forward stride position.
3. Player sets ball at least three feet above head.

Figure 14.5 Bump and set laboratory task sheet.

SOURCE: H. Lawson and J. Placek. *Physical Education in the Secondary Schools: Curricular Alternatives.* Boston: Allyn & Bacon, 1981, p. 110.

What is important to note in this example is that biomechanical and kinesiological concepts can be taught through any sports activity. Softball can be as useful as volleyball. Track and field is an outstanding activity for exploring these concepts. The concepts approach lends itself very well to a physical education curriculum built around traditional sports activities.

In the sports approach to the concepts model most of the activity is likely to take place in the gymnasium or on the practice field. However the classroom can also be used for both instruction and enrichment activities such as films or discussions.

The problem-solving approach to sports instruction requires that students participate in an activity related to a sport and then try to understand that activity in relation to important underlying concepts. A brief lecture/demonstration and mere subsequent involvement in the activity cannot accomplish this. Instead, students must relate the concept(s) to the activity in a meaningful way. Teachers help them do this by means of lectures, demonstrations, discussions, and summaries. The examples in Figure 14.6 show how the biomechanical concepts of spin and rebound are taught in a soccer unit.

Spin

Activity:
(1) Have students hold ball at the top and bottom. Partner spins the ball to get it moving—spin around a vertical axis.
(2) Repeat, holding ball by fingertips on the sides—spin around a horizontal axis. Emphasize that depending upon the axis around which the ball is spinning you get a particular type of spin: top and back spin around a horizontal axis; right and left spin around a vertical axis.

Discussion: Review center of gravity of the ball; force application away from the center of gravity causes spin. Discuss what causes spin.

Activities:
(1) Have students kick black and white soccer balls (or mark an X for center of gravity on a plain soccer ball). To start, place the ball so that one of the black diamonds in the center of the side of the ball faces the kicker. This is the ball's center of gravity. Students should focus on this spot for kicking. Try to contact the ball directly through its center of gravity; above it; below it. Watch what happens to the ball. Can you kick the ball to your partner in the air without spin?
(2) Next, have students try to contact the ball away from the center of gravity—to the right of it and to the left of it. Which way does the ball spin? Does it go in a straight line to your partner? What happens to an aerial ball when it hits the ground?

Discussion: Emphasize how spin affects the flight of the ball—back spin allows the ball to stay in the air longer; a ball with right spin will have a curved pathway to the right in the air, etc. How can spin be an advantage/disadvantage in soccer? *Advantages:* Depending upon your purpose you can use spin in soccer to maximize performance. For example, in trying to project the ball for distance to a teammate down the field, back spin can be used in an aerial ball to keep the ball in the air longer (over the heads of opponents) and for greater distance. Spin also helps stabilize the flight of the ball so it doesn't waiver. *Disadvantage:* Spin makes the ball more difficult to control when receiving the ball, and spin affects how a ball will rebound.

(continued)

Figure 14.6 *Biomechanical concepts of spin and rebound taught in a soccer unit.*

SOURCE: H. Lawson and J. Placek. *Physical Education in the Secondary Schools: Curricular Alternatives.* Boston: Allyn & Bacon, 1981, pp. 128–29.

Rebound

Discussion: Illustrate the effect of spin upon rebound: Top spin makes ball bounce lower and longer on the rebound; back spin makes ball bounce higher and straighter on rebound. The illustration can be made very graphic here by the use of rubber playground balls and a hard or firm surface.

Activities:
(1) Have students face each other in 2's. *Toss* rubber ball back and forth with one bounce just before ball reaches partner. Vary the types of spin. Note the reaction as the ball rebounds from the surface.
(2) Have student receiving the ball try to adjust his or her position prior to receiving the ball so as to be in the correct position to receive depending upon type of spin.
Discussion: What is rebound? Return of the ball from a surface which has greater resistance than the momentum of the ball. What different surfaces can the ball rebound from in soccer? Ground, head, knee, shoulder, goalpost, etc.? Factors that affect the degree of the rebound include: (1) elasticity of the ball, (2) firmness of the surface, and (3) spin of the ball.

Activities:
(1) Partially deflate the class soccer balls. Have students experiment with kicking the ball to a partner (ball must be lofted). Note what happens on the rebound.
(2) Have students experiment with rebounding the ball off various surfaces—head, stomach, goalpost, etc. Note the strength of rebound and, depending upon spin, where the ball rebounds. Reminder: Have students take pulse before, during, and after classes. Ample practice time on pure kicking technique should be afforded students during the course of the section. A *summary* of the important elements should be given to the students at the end of the section elements that students should incorporate into warm-up times as mental practice.

The physical education subdiscipline approach

Most rationales for the concepts model emphasize the need to have students acquire knowledge and understanding related to the disciplinary bases of physical education; thus one popular way to arrange a concepts curriculum is to use the subdisciplines as organizing centers (rather than sport as in the previous example). An abbreviatiated form of the subdiscipline curriculum advocated by Lawson and Placek (1981) follows.

Unit 1   Diagnostic Assessments
Objectives: Students will

- understand their own backgrounds and interests in activity
- explain what factors to consider when determining their own level of conditioning
- explain how these factors can be assessed and make the assessments
- identify factors in motor fitness and assess their own abilities

Unit 2   Exercise and Fitness
Objectives: Students will

- identify and define aspects of fitness and principles of training
- design training programs based on these principles
- apply their knowledge by critiquing commonly advertised exercise programs

Unit 3   Nutrition, Exercise, and Cardiovascular Disease
Objectives: Students will

- determine weight loss/gain based on caloric intake/expenditure data
- identify factors in cardiovascular disease and weight control

- relate these factors in a way that explains their relationship
- critique exercise programs in terms of contribution to prevention or remediation of coronary heart disease

Unit 4   Biomechanics
Objectives: Students will

- estimate center of gravity in a number of varying bodily positions
- identify balance factors in various physical activities
- explain different spins as a result of application of force
- explain how spin affects subsequent action of ball
- apply Newton's Laws of Motion to force production in various activities
- analyze physical performance errors and offer solutions that reflect biomechanical principles

Unit 5   Play, Game, and Sport
Objectives: Students will

- identify motivations for participation, in themselves and others
- identify sociocultural factors influencing participation
- identify structural differences among play, game, dance, contests, and sport
- describe the nature and demands of the athlete's role
- explain the ethics of fair play and honoring one's opponent
- identify basic functions of sport in American society

Unit 6   Mind-Body Unity and Aesthetics
Objectives: Students will

- explain the fallacy of mind-body dualism in terms of their own participation
- identify factors that determine the degree of aesthetic satisfaction they experience in participation
- identify movement characteristics that contribute to judgments of aesthetic excellence

Unit 7   Motor Learning
Objectives: Students will

- describe and explain appropriate instructional progressions
- identify appropriate time allotments for presentation and practice
- identify common learning problems and solutions for them

Students work in small groups to solve exercise task problems.

These units represent *one* way of using subdisciplinary knowledge in physical education. The distinguishing feature of these particular units is the degree to which they use activity laboratories rather than classroom activities. One can easily envisage other subdisciplinary units that might use classroom activities—for example, a sports history unit or a kinesiology unit.

The three major examples shown in this chapter (the fitness, sports, and subdiscipline approaches) represent different curricular patterns for the concepts model. The examples differ in that each has a different organizing focus. However, even though these different focuses make the approaches appear to be different, they are in fact very similar. They all emphasize the acquisition of knowledge (rather than the acquisition of skill or becoming more fit). They all use a problem-solving approach to instruction. They all involve students in practical problems that lead students to underlying principles. In solving problems, students are required to *do something*. They may collect fitness data on themselves and classmates, participate in a discussion, bump and set volleyballs, or play in a softball game. However, their activity serves not only the immediate purpose of engaging in that activity but also the larger purpose of gaining knowledge and understanding.

Although homework is not commonplace in physical education, when physical education is conceptualized in a manner similar to other school sub-

---

Assignment Number Two

1. In the same way you used the unabridged dictionary to look up *play* and *game* before, look up the words that appear below. Remember to list both the root or original meanings and the more common meanings today.
   a. sport

   b. athlete

   c. ascetic

   d. hero

2. Go to a store that has a large inventory of indoor and outdoor games. Examine the various types of games which are on display at the store. In what ways can you classify (or group together) some of the games which you have discovered? List the categories you have picked and name at least three games in each category.

Figure 14.7 Homework assignment from a sports, play, and games unit.

SOURCE: H. Lawson and J. Placek. *Physical Education in the Secondary Schools: Curricular Alternatives.* Boston: Allyn & Bacon, 1981, p. 231.

jects, then homework becomes an obvious consideration. Figure 14.7 shows an example of a homework assignment from a unit on play, game, and sport.

Summary

The primary goal of the concepts model is cognitive understanding of physical education. The model has its roots in the "foundations" curriculum and more recently has been strongly associated with the movement to establish physical education as an academic discipline.

The rationale for a concepts curriculum is based on problem-solving approaches that help students to learn the hows and whys of physical education. By engaging in problem-solving activities, students not only become more competent in physical education but also develop adaptive problem-solving skills that will enable them to make wise choices about health, fitness, and leisure activities during their adult years.

Many concepts programs rely strongly on a fitness orientation, but a sports orientation and a subdiscipline orientation are also prevalent. The focus may differ, but all of the process approaches are similar.

Concepts programs use a lecture-laboratory approach as the primary teaching method. The approach is adaptable as an overall curriculum or as a component in a curriculum that also includes other approaches.

Suggested activities

1. Prepare a list of ways in which the concepts approach differs from traditional teaching in physical education. Discuss the list in class with special attention to what each difference means for the teacher and for the student.

2. Divide into small groups. Each group is to develop a unit of instruction based on the concepts model. Compare and contrast the units in class.

3. Debate the following issue: Physical education should include more academic content. Have three students argue the affirmative and three the negative.

4. Discuss the concepts approach from the students' point of view. What kinds of students would like it? What kinds might not like it?

5. Obtain some concepts laboratory tasks from one of the many texts that advocate this model. Take one class period to go through the tasks as if you were a group of high school students. Record your reactions to the experience.

15

Intramurals, Clubs, and Drop-in Recreation

The West Shore schools in Pennsylvania have a brochure that describes physical education activities in the district. Among these are class instruction three times per week, grades K–10; a daily morning exercise program, grades K–5; an adapted physical education program, grades K–12; a scoliosis screening program, grades K–8; a school-time and after-school intramural program; an individual and lifetime sports program, grades 4–12; and an aquatics program, grade 2.

What an exciting program! It seems to urge participation by young people and assumes community as well as school responsibility for physical activity. Intramurals, clubs, and drop-in recreation programs provide opportunities for students to play, to compete, to be physically active.

A school that directs its physical education energies only to instructional periods and varsity coaching does not serve youth fully. This chapter provides information and a philosophy regarding intramurals, clubs, and drop-in recreation in the total physical education program. The major topics covered in this chapter are as follows:

The significance of intramurals, sports clubs, and drop-in recreation as part of a school's informal curriculum

Structuring various types of intramural tournaments

The importance of creative ideas, proper scheduling, and awards

The genesis and characteristics of sports clubs

Unusual and interesting intramural-recreational examples and their effects on student participation

The benefits of drop-in recreation

SCENE *It is ninth period, and a guidance counselor is meeting with a group of five students—as she does with a different group each day—to help them complete their application forms for college and to prepare a résumé for possible employment.*

COUNSELOR It's usual to include your academic record on an application or résumé, but you should also indicate activities you participated in during your school years. Let's see what sorts of things you've done during high school. This may refresh your memory about activities. Frank, why don't you start.

FRANK I've been in varsity basketball and baseball for three years, and I'm captain of the baseball team this season. Oh, I've also sung in the school choir since I started high school.

MELISSA I've been in lots of theater activities—I've been an actress and a stage manager, and I ran the lighting panel in my sophomore year. I've even acted in community summer theater.

DAVE I've only played one sport, football, but during the winter since I've been in high school I've coached a kids' basketball team, part of the Athletes for Youth service club run by the physical education department.

JOAN I didn't do much of anything extra connected with school. I've taken riding lessons since I was little, and now I work at a stable whenever I'm not in school.

DAVE What kind of work?

JOAN I exercise horses, clean stables, ride other people's horses at shows, even help train horses. I do this before school, after school, on weekends—it's a career!

TOM My only school activities are with the Outdoor Club. I guess it's a community-school club since a lot of adults are also in it. We ski on Wednesday evenings during the winter, go on fishing trips, caving—we even went scuba diving in Florida over spring vacation. It's a great group. We're on the road a lot. I even received gym credit for some of the activities.

The informal curriculum

Although some students are not very active in or out of school, the vast majority participate in one or more extracurricular activities. Many of these are sponsored by the school, and a large number are associated with physical activity. The physical education program in its broad dimensions touches the lives of many students, even some of those who really do not like to participate in a formal physical education class.

The kinds of activities we are talking about here form the informal curriculum of the school. For many employers and college admissions staffs, these pursuits provide an important clue to the energy, enthusiasm, and social development of a prospective candidate. For students, participation is the thing; the activities are fun, exciting, and intimate, and they provide the opportunity for friendship as well as a good chance to excel and be self-directed.

Physical education should be an important contributor to the informal curriculum. Recall from Chapter 3 that, in our definition, physical education includes organized instructional classes but also sports clubs, varsity sports, intramural sports, and drop-in recreation. The sum of these elements provides a picture of a total physical education program. See Figure 3.4, p. 51.

The significance of intramural, club, and drop-in opportunities

SCENE *Two seniors driving to school.*

TONY We've got a big basketball game on Saturday. If we win, it means a chance to win the league championship.

DAVID I've got a big event on Saturday, too. It's the state slalom finals, and I have a chance at the championship. Only two or three other guys have a chance to beat me.

TONY I don't get it. You're one of the best athletes in the school, but nobody knows about it. Why don't you play on some school team?

DAVID I got started in skiing through the school ski club, but they don't have a team, a school team in skiing. Really, its not bad participating this way. No coach to set schedules, and other skiers know I'm good. Besides, Tony, it's a coed activity most of the time.

TONY Maybe I'm the one who should switch!

SCENE *It is a school night in March, and the stands in the high school gymnasium are crowded with students and a few adults who have come to watch the finals of the intramural boys' basketball tournament. Two students waiting for the game to start are chatting in the stands.*

SALLY Did you play in this tournament?

BILL Yes, our team played. Actually, there were over 30 boys' intramural teams. The teams were divided into five leagues, six teams per league, and each of the leagues played a round-robin. We played five games in the league, and then the two top teams played a single elimination tournament for the championship. We were knocked out in the first round of the elimination tournament. Most of the people, or at least the boys, in the stands played in the tournament at some point.

SALLY That's about how the girls play but not as many teams. Volleyball seems more popular with the girls than basketball.

BILL When do you play your games?

SALLY We have the gym for intramural basketball one night a week for three or four hours.

BILL Yes, that's our pattern; only with the number of teams we play, we get the gym two nights per week. I'm glad this school gives the gym to someone other than the varsity.

SALLY Me, too.

BILL   Here they come—that team's called Force Five. They'd give the varsity trouble. Three of their players work and can't take the time to be on a school varsity team.

SALLY   Oh, there's someone I have to see. Enjoy the game.

CHARACTERS

MR. TORRES   *a volunteer driver and adviser for the Outdoor Club*

RACHEL   *a member of the Outdoor Club*

SID   *a member of the Outdoor Club*

MRS. SMITH   *a trip chaperone for the Outdoor Club*

SCENE   *It is a late Sunday afternoon, a rainy, cold, dismal sort of day in early March. Three vans drive into the school parking lot loaded with high school students and a few adults. The Outdoor Club members, dressed in warm, rugged clothes, are returning from a weekend caving trip.*

MR. TORRES   Let's make sure all these people have their gear and a ride home.

RACHEL   We were in the cave on the wrong day. It was sunny all day Saturday but rainy and miserable for the drive down and back.

SID   Am I sore! Crawling in a cave is really a different exercise.

MRS. SMITH   I haven't done anything like this for 25 years. If you're stiff, think of me.

SID   Go on; you were leading the pack. I didn't think we would ever convince you to leave the cave and come back to the campsite.

MRS. SMITH   That's because I knew it was my turn to cook and then sleeping on the hard, hard ground.

RACHEL   We sure had plenty of food. Everyone's always hungry on these trips.

MR. TORRES   All the gear is out and everyone has a ride home. Don't forget our meeting next Thursday night. We have to plan for spring vacation.

SCENE   *A high school student is having his hair cut in the local barbershop.*

BARBER   I saw your picture in the paper, Gus. You had a big trophy for swimming in your arms.

GUS   What paper?

BARBER   The local paper, the *Clarion Call*.

GUS   Oh, I didn't see it; but you're the second person who's mentioned it.

BARBER   What was it for?

GUS   It wasn't really for swimming but a participation award for intramurals. I always take part and manage to win sometimes, but basically it's just fun to be doing something. I like sports, but I'm not big, strong, fast, or talented. Intramurals gives me a chance.

BARBER   That's great!

SCENE   *A mother and her son are talking in the kitchen before dinner.*

MOTHER   Why were you so late today?

SON   I worked out in the weight room. Rick and Walter were there too.

MOTHER   What is the weight room exactly?

SON   The school has a room filled with exercise machines and free weights. It's used for physical education class, varsity athletics, and rehabilitation by boys, girls, even some adults.

MOTHER   How can you use it if it's scheduled for all those other groups? You're not on a team this season.

SON   It's like the other facilities for sports in school; some time is reserved for drop-in use. So you don't have to be on a team to use the equipment. Lots of kids participate that way.

MOTHER   It sounds like a good idea.

In Chapter 2 we indicated the value of physical activities for *all* students: the importance of fitness, relationships with authority figures, skill, adventure, joy, rewards, and friendship. The preceding illustrations indicate opportunities to promote these values through intramurals, clubs, and drop-in recreation.

Organizing and leading intramural, club, and drop-in activities

A good informal physical education program does not just happen by chance or goodwill. In fact, it probably takes more energy and work to promote this phase of the total curriculum than instructional classes or varsity athletics. The mandate of state law supports the class program, and parents and community groups seem to provide a base of activity for athletics. No such power-broker is available for intramurals, clubs, and drop-in recreation. Therefore, it becomes very important to develop a table of organization that supports the notion of a sound informal program within the overall curriculum. (See Figure 15.1).

Explanation of organization

Note that the numbers in the following list correspond to those in the organization scheme presented in Figure 15.1.

1. The space and facilities committee schedules all activity space according to the priorities of the school and various departments. A representative of the principal's office is helpful to this committee since the office of the principal is the clearinghouse for all activities, requests, and complaints in the school.

2. The class program and varsity athletics program are more important than the organization scheme in Figure 15.1 indicates. The purpose here is only to show the relationship of these programs to intramurals, clubs, and drop-in recreation.

3. Faculty leadership of the informal program is important. Just as coaches are hired on the basis of training, experience, and enthusiasm, so must

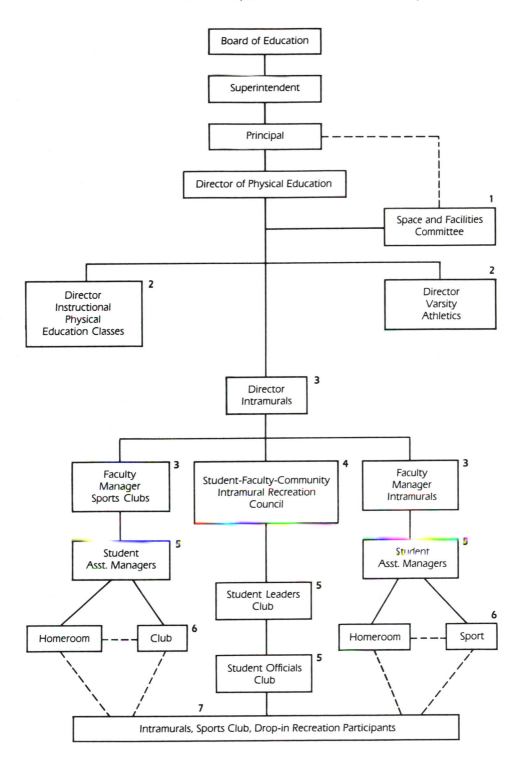

Figure 15.1 Organization scheme for intramurals, clubs, and drop-in recreation.

leaders of a well-run intramural club/drop-in operation. People who care and who bring consistency and stability to the operation generally increase its chance for success.

4. The intramural-recreation council acts as a clearinghouse for program direction. Note that this is a student, faculty, and community council, and it provides full information to those in authority. One of the features of intramurals, clubs, and drop-in recreation is the opportunity for choice and direction by students, not merely adults.

5. Students have the opportunity to become assistant managers who lead, administer, publicize, and generally participate in the conduct of these activities. These students are also trained as officials and conduct the tournaments and games of the informal program.

6. The organizing unit for activities can be a homeroom or a particular sport or club. In most high schools the best location for addressing students is the homeroom. This is the place where daily attendance is taken and significant announcements can be made. Thus it is important to announce information about intramurals and club and drop-in activities in the homeroom. It is preferable that a student leader rather than a teacher make such announcements.

7. The consumers or participants who engage in these activities on a voluntary basis support the organizational structure. If the physical educator forgets their needs, or ignores the fact that this is truly their program, the organizational structure will not matter very much. In time there won't be enough participants to justify a program.

This structure can be modified according to school size or to particular school conditions. One dynamic individual can create a program on the basis of the force of personality. However, if such a person leaves or loses enthusiasm, the program usually suffers or ceases entirely. Therefore, physical educators must help to translate the concept into an organizational pattern that makes intramurals, clubs, and drop-in recreation a standard, ordinary part of the school curriculum.

Generating creative ideas

One feature of a well-run organization is that ideas percolate in the system. Participants, faculty, community members, and administrators may all generate creative ideas. Here are just some examples adapted from Mueller and Reznik (1971).

1. Transport cross-country participants to the countryside and have them run back to school.

2. Take team photographs and present a print to each team member.

3. Present free movie passes to members of the winning teams.

4. Allow track-and-field letter winners to compete in intramural running events and vice versa.

5. Organize a system to draft and trade players in a manner similar to the pros.

6. Assemble a "picnic equipment list" that may be checked out over the weekend.

7. Provide junior-size equipment for junior-size participants.

8. Keep school activity space open 7 days per week, 24 hours per day, 365 days per year.

9. Develop an all-night intramural festival including breakfast.

10. Establish an endowment fund for intramurals from business and industry.

11. Assign some women officials for men's games and vice versa.

12. Require intramural officials to sign a contract for the days they are scheduled to work.

13. Identify a particular game as "game of the week."

14. Set up a tournament for last-place teams in a league.

15. Use a different type of tournament scheduling structure for every tournament.

16. Pay officials on a two- or three-step pay scale to create an incentive for improvement.

17. Use free-substitution rules in all intramural sports.

18. Have intramural winners conduct field days in an elementary school.

19. Spend an evening showing slides and films of a club outing to the student body.

20. Award a scholarship to an outstanding intramural participant.

Structuring tournaments

Competition is fun, and a tournament is the ultimate form of competition whether the final game is the Super Bowl, the last game of the World Series, or the intramural racquetball championship. Studying the draw, predicting the upsets, or determining who is the hot team or the player on a roll adds to the excitement.

A tournament has several goals beyond determining a winner. Frequently it is important to determine several place winners in addition to the champion. It is also important to promote fair competition and to provide opportunities for participation beyond a one-event elimination. All of these goals must be met in a manner that is consistent with space, facilities, equipment, and available time of participants.

Thus planners have developed several standard scheduling techniques to structure tournaments. These standard procedures are also useful for creative manipulation. Following are illustrations and analyses of standard scheduling and also an example of creative manipulation.

Round-robin

Simply stated, every team plays every other team in the round-robin system of competition. It provides maximum participation and also determines a champion as well as other place winners. The disadvantage is that the system is very time consuming and may have to be modified to meet the usual school situation. Round-robin is employed in the leagues of many professional sports to determine a league champion. The professional baseball leagues use this system, in fact a multiple round-robin, as each team plays every other team several times. At the conclusion of the season, an elimination tournament determines a World Series winner.

As an illustration, let's assume six volleyball teams are playing in the school intramural tournament. We shall number the teams 1 through 6 and develop a round-robin tournament. The task is to determine the top two teams in the competition.

Round I	Round II	Round III	Round IV	Round V
1–2	1–3	1–5	1–6	1–4
3–4	5–2	6–3	4–5	2–6
5–6	6–4	4–2	2–3	3–5

In this competition five rounds of games were played, the total games played equaled 15, and each team played five times. Let's assume a record in competition as follows:

Team	Won	Lost	Percentage
1	4	1	.800
2	1	4	.200
3	3	2	.600
4	1	4	.200
5	4	1	.800
6	2	3	.400

The ranking at the end of the tournament was as follows:

First	Tie between teams 1 and 5	4 wins and 1 loss each
Second		
Third	Team 3	3 wins and 2 losses
Fourth	Team 6	2 wins and 3 losses
Fifth	Tie between teams 2 and 4	1 win and 4 losses each

To determine the winner between teams 1 and 5, several options are available: (1) Since the teams played each other in the round-robin, the winner of that game can be declared the overall winner. (2) Teams 1 and 5 can engage in a one-game playoff. (3) The team with the greatest differential of points scored for and against during the competition can be declared the winner.

Formulas for rounds and games.   The formula to determine the number of rounds in a round-robin depends on whether there is an even or uneven number of entries in the tournament.

Even number of teams $= N - 1$

Uneven number of teams $= N$

Example: If 10 teams enter a round-robin, there are 9 rounds of games. If 9 teams enter, there are also 9 rounds of games.

The formula to determine the number of games in a round-robin is:

$$G = \frac{N(N - 1)}{2}.$$

Example: If 15 teams enter a round-robin, the number of games is as follows:

$$G = \frac{N(N - 1)}{2}$$

$$G = \frac{15(15 - 1)}{2}$$

$$G = \frac{15(14)}{2}$$

$$G = 105$$

Rotation of entries.   The rotation most often used for round-robin tournaments is clockwise. In our first example there are six teams (an even number) and no byes. Team 1 is stationary and all others rotate one position clockwise to start a new round.

Round I	Round II (clockwise rotation about team 1)	Round III
1–2	1–3	1–5
3–4	5–2	6–3
5–6	6–4	4–2

Round IV	Round V
1–6	1–4
4–5	2–6
2–3	3–5

The same clockwise rotation system is also employed for an uneven number of teams. The five teams in the following example rotate about the bye position in the round.

Round I	Round II (clockwise rotation about the bye)	Round III
1–2	3–1	5–3
3–4	5–2	4–1
5–bye	4–bye	2–bye

Round IV	Round V
4–5	2–4
2–3	1–5
1–bye	3–bye

Graphing a round-robin. Another method of planning a tournament and maintaining results is by means of a graph. Such a method ensures that each team plays the others and serves as a way to record the scores as well. See Figure 15.2.

The graph in Figure 15.2 indicates that team 1 defeated team 4 by a score of 15 to 8 but lost to team 5 by a score of 6 to 15.

A feature of the round-robin is the ability to divide an unusually large number of entries into two or more groups in order to manage the number of games more effectively.

Example: 16 teams enter a tournament.

$$G = \frac{16(16 - 1)}{2} = 120$$

Team	1	2	3	4	5	6
1				15–8	6–15	
2						
3						
4	8–15					
5	15–6					
6						

Figure 15.2 A graph of six teams in a round-robin tournament. Team 1 has defeated team 4 by a score of 15 to 8 and lost to team 5 by a score of 6 to 15.

If the tournament is divided into two 8-team sections, the results are quite different.

$$G = \frac{8(8-1)}{2} = \frac{28 \text{ games per section or}}{56 \text{ for both sections}}$$

This is a saving of 64 games and just might enable you to use a round-robin format to increase competition and participation while living within the strictures of available time and facilities.

Elimination tournaments

Single and double elimination tournaments provide a direct means to determine a champion, but unless they are coupled with a consolation or a losers' tournament, they limit participation. Frequently in school intramural programs, the elimination tournament is used after a round-robin to ensure maximum participation and a clear-cut champion.

As shown in Figure 15.3, the single elimination tournament (this one for 8 teams, A through H) does not provide much participation and, as presented, provides for only first- and second-place winners.

The double tournament ensures players at least two opportunities to participate and provides for a champion and runner-up. See Figure 15.4, page 278. A feature of the double tournament is that losers Art and Ed move to opposite halves of the bracket to avoid as long as possible playing the same opponent twice.

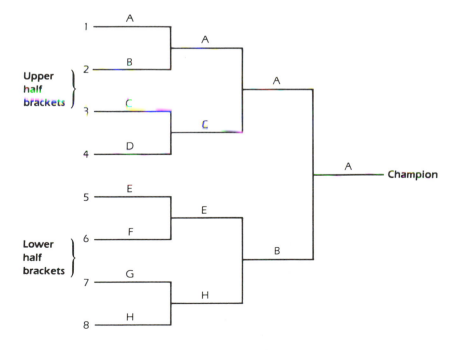

Figure 15.3 A graph of a single elimination tournament.

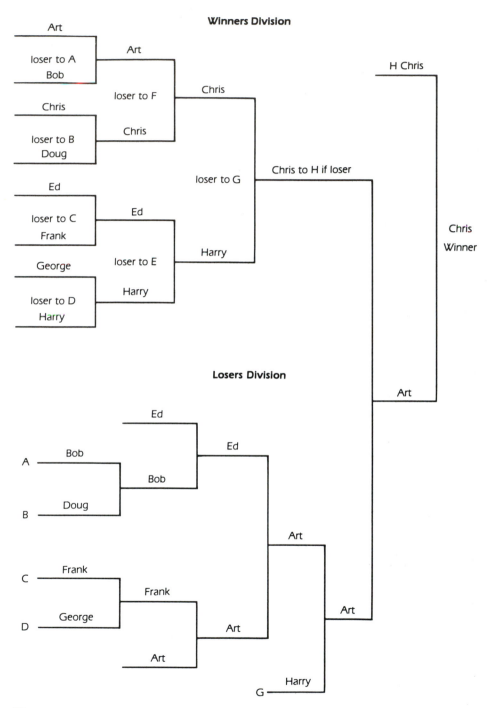

Figure 15.4 A graph of a double elimination tournament with eight contestants and a minimum of two games per contestant.

Power of 2 and byes. Since both of the elimination tournaments just described represent a perfect power of 2, no byes were necessary. The perfect powers of 2 include 4, 8, 16, 32, 64, 128, etc. Any number of entries other than these numbers requires one or more byes in the first round of the tournament. Byes should be placed in the first round and spread as evenly as possible between the upper and lower brackets. An exception occurs in the double elimination scheme, where a bye carries over to the first round of the losers' bracket.

To determine the proper number of byes, subtract the number of entries from the next highest perfect power of two. Here are a few examples:

Number of entries	Perfect power	Number of byes
7	8	1
9	16	7
22	32	10
5	8	3
4	4	0

In Figure 15.5, teams A, D, and E reach the semifinal round as a result of a bye. Placement in the tournament should be by random draw as it is usually an advantage to have a bye.

In a single elimination, the number of rounds equals the power to which 2 must be raised to reach the proper number that exceeds the number of entries. The number of games in a single elimination is one less than the number of entries. The double elimination tournament follows the same pattern with a

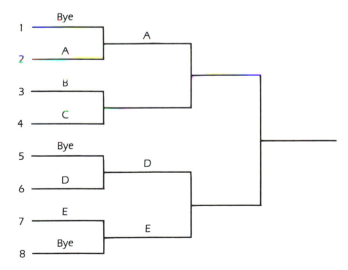

Figure 15.5 The placement of five teams in a single elimination tournament.

multiplier of 2. Here it may also be necessary to play one additional game since each team must lose at least twice.

Consolations. To ensure more participation and also to provide place winners in elimination tournaments, various consolation schemes are popular. An interesting system is the Mueller-Anderson Playback. See Figure 15.6.

Challenge tournaments

Challenge tournaments include ladders, pyramids, and many other configurations. See Figures 15.7 and 15.8. These tournaments are perpetual unless a time frame is included in the instructions for the event. Rules vary according to the type of challenge tournament, but certain guidelines are important to proper competition and participation.

1. Challenges must be accepted and played within a specified period of time.
2. Players randomly challenge any player on the board.
3. Players challenge one or two positions above or one row above.
4. Players must challenge someone in their own row before challenging above.

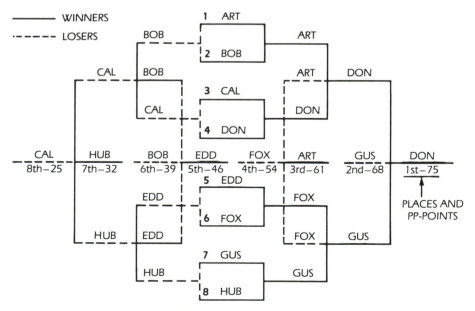

Figure 15.6 The Mueller-Anderson playback.

SOURCE: P. Mueller and J. W. Reznik. *Intramural Recreational Sports: Programming and Administration*, 5th ed. New York: John Wiley & Sons, 1979, p. 157.

	Tennis Ladder	
1	G	1
2	A	2
3	H	3
4	C	4
5	I	5
6	B	6
7	J	7
8	K	8
9	E	9
10	L	10
11	D	11
12	F	12

Figure 15.7 A typical ladder. Participants originally draw for a spot on the ladder; eventually, ability reorders the tournament.

Figure 15.8 A pyramid: Players may challenge in the row above them

5. Players challenge only those to their immediate right or left in the same row and the one above.

6. After losing, a player must accept a challenge from another contestant before reissuing a challenge to the player who defeated him or her.

7. A new player may enter the tournament by challenging a player in the lowest position on the tournament board.

The secret of success in designing a tournament is to use these basic schemes for competition to serve specific program purposes. Usually this means modifying a given system or using a combination of systems to ensure participation and clear-cut place winners. The students who participate are no different from the millions of people who watch the World Series or the Super Bowl or the United States Tennis Championship. They want a winner, determined in a fair manner. However, they also want to participate and have a chance at the prize.

Intramural scheduling is more difficult than that of varsity competition. Physical educators must be more creative to ensure good competition but also broad opportunity for participation.

Odd-ball competition

For some groups a taste of humility is worthwhile, and for others a chance to participate in a nontraditional manner offers greater hope for being a winner—at least once. Three ideas for odd-ball tournaments are a patch tournament, a one-point match, and a one-hand doubles game.

Patch tournament. Each participant places an eye patch over one eye and competes in tennis, foul shooting, or racquetball.

One-point match. Participants play a ladder tournament in tennis so that whoever wins a point moves up and whoever loses moves down. Conduct this in an afternoon or evening. Even John McEnroe or Chris Evert-Lloyd might have trouble reaching court one in this type of affair.

One-hand doubles game. For doubles tennis or table tennis tie the right arm of one partner to the left arm of the other partner and place a racket in the free hand of each partner.

Activities such as these provide a welcome relief from the routine. Almost everyone likes childhood games on occasion and odd-ball competition helps students revert to the spirit of simple games and competition.

Creative manipulation

Assume that 30 teams enter a basketball intramural tournament and your job is to provide as much participation for as many teams as possible and still determine the four top winners, places one through four. As usual, facilities are limited; only two courts are available for four hours per week for seven weeks. There are many ways to reach these goals. Here is just one of them.

Divide the 30 teams by random draw into five groups of six teams each. Each group plays a round-robin. The top four teams according to record and point differential enter a single elimination tournament with consolation to determine the four place winners.

Mechanics for the round-robin:

- 2 courts × 4 hours × 6 weeks = 48 hours of 2,880 minutes of available playing time.
- The number of games in the round robin is

$$G = \frac{N(N - 1)}{2}$$

$$G = \frac{6(5)}{2}$$

$$G = 15 \text{ per group}$$

- Since five groups are participating, 75 games (5 × 15) are necessary to complete the round-robin. This will provide at least five games for each team in the tournament.
- To estimate the time per game, divide total minutes (2,880) by the number of teams (75).

$$\frac{2880}{75} = 38+ \text{ minutes per games}$$

- Allow 30 minutes per game running time and 8 minutes to clear the court and start the next contest.
- The top four teams in the round-robin play the semifinals in one session and the finals plus consolations for third and fourth place in the remaining session. Each of these games can be as long as 45 minutes.

As stated, this is only one solution, and it has certain disadvantages although it does realize the goals. It is an example of manipulating time, space, and activity to foster the opportunity for intramurals. Those who complain about the bus schedule, lack of space, or too little time really beg the question and refuse to think in creative terms.

Awards

Recognition is a powerful stimulus to participation and achievement. Tenoschok (1981) suggests a wide range of awards that help create and sustain interest in intramural and club programs.

AAHPERD fitness award

Referee award

Appreciation award (for volunteers)

Honorary coaches award

Outstanding participant award

Intramural athlete of the week award

Ribbons and plaques (for participants in events who achieve)

Weight club award

One-hundred-mile jogging award

T-shirts (for service or achievement)

Photographs (of outstanding performances)

Newspaper articles (school and local papers, a regular column)

Trophy case (for outstanding participants)

Certainly you can add to these suggestions, but the point remains that it is important to recognize in a public fashion the many fine accomplishments of those associated with this phase of the physical education program.

Sports clubs

In a sense, sports clubs represent a European influence in the physical education program since most athletic participation in Europe occurs through the
club. Although sports clubs are less significant in the United States, they
share many characteristics of the European system.

- Members of a sports club are a mix of beginners, intermediates, and experts, females and males, students, teachers, and community members.
- Members drop in and out of participation on the basis of other commit-
  ments in their personal and professional lives.
- Members elect the leaders of the club, with a school faculty member
  serving as a liaison to the school rather than as a coach.
- Club activities are social and recreational as well as competitive.
- Instruction is a product of club membership. Advanced performers as-
  sist one another and train beginners.
- Schools provide only partial funding for club activities.
- During competitions, several teams of different levels of ability may
  meet counterpart teams from another club.

The ski club of a large midwestern high school illustrates these characteristics. The club receives some financial help from the school, generally for
transportation and a faculty adviser, a meeting room priority in the school,
and an opportunity to use selected club activities for physical education credit
on a contract basis. The members of the club—students, some parents, and a
few teachers—travel one evening a week to a nearby ski slope for an opportunity to participate. Members provide their own personal ski equipment, but
transportation is via school bus.

Members help teach one another, but they also participate in the lessons
offered by the ski center. The center organizes competition according to ability, but it is also possible to race against clubs from other schools. Twice a year,
during Christmas and spring break, members of the club go East or West for
skiing in more desirable locations. Each year an awards banquet caps off the
season and previews new ventures for the next year.

Some of the members are very active; others are more casual about participation. All must live by certain rules and regulations, some of which are related to school codes and some to the requirements of the membership. People
who violate the rules consistently must leave the club.

Sports experiences such as this are very attractive to students who seek
participation but with a qualified commitment compared to that required by a
typical varsity team. The opportunity is very important.

Examples of intramural-recreation
programs and activities

A middle school in Philomath, Oregon, uses several unusual activities to
increase participation in intramurals. These include tug-of-war, piggyback
scooter obstacle race, football-through-a-tire throw, caber toss, 37-pound stone

throw, and king of the horse. As a result, student participation in intramurals increased from 40 to 50 percent to 80 to 90 percent (Crass 1976, 58).

A school district in Greenfield, Illinois, uses novel competitive events to complement traditional forms of activity. These include a 1.7-mile cross-country race, punt-pass-kick contest, Yukon sled race, arm wrestling, cane wrestling, "dirty twenty-one" (combination of the NBA one-on-one and the 3-point play), 7.7-mile cross-country bike race, and slow-pitch home run contest (Tucker 1974, 63).

In the Newton, Kansas, school district athletics represent a threefold program: (1) basic physical education skills in elementary school, (2) intramurals in middle school, and (3) varsity play in high school. The middle school's concept of eliminating activities that are thought to be premature or precocious extends to athletics. The school has no varsity athletics but supports an extensive intramural program.

The director of the program is the assistant principal, and schoolwide announcements for intramural activities are made from the main office, adding authority to the program. The nine assistants who work with the director offer as many sports as possible, teach fundamentals, introduce strategies, and instill fun in the games themselves (Stineman 1979, 83).

In Parkersburg, West Virginia, a high school has responded effectively to space and time problems. Two nights per week, from 6:00 to 9:00 P.M., students return to school for intramurals, which include 22 different activities. Teams are established for the year, and cumulative records are kept. As a result, participation has increased dramatically (McCase and Hardin 1981, 64).

Finally, in Commack, New York, a well-conceived intramural program from elementary through senior high school looks like this (Tenoschok 1981).

Level	Fall	Winter	Spring
Elementary	European handball Flag football Physical fitness Soccer Softball Tumbling Volleyball	Basketball Dodge ball Floor hockey Gymnastics Volleyball Wrestling	Archery Basketball Cheerleading Floor hockey Gymnastics Handball Kickball Softball STX lacrosse Volleyball Wiffleball
Junior High	Bowling Field hockey Flag football Floor hockey Slimnastics Soccer Volleyball	Basketball Bowling Floor hockey Gymnastics Volleyball Weight training Wrestling	Badminton Basketball Fencing Floor hockey Gymnastics Softball STX lacrosse Track and field Tennis Volleyball Weight training

Level	Fall	Winter	Spring
Senior High	Basketball	Basketball	Archery
	Bowling	Bowling	Basketball
	Fencing	Box lacrosse	Bowling
	Flag football	Table tennis	Dance
	Floor hockey	Indoor soccer	Fencing
	Soccer	Volleyball	Floor hockey
	Weight training	Weight training	Gymnastics
		Winter track	Soccer
			Volleyball
			Weight training

Resources concerning tournament forms, ideas that work in intramurals, even new games and sports are available in national publications of the American Alliance for Health, Physical Education, Recreation, and Dance. In most cases the physical education teacher can use these innovative suggestions in the local situation with only modest adaptation.

Drop-in recreation

Both intramural activities and sports clubs represent organized forms of physical activity or sports participation. What of the student who seeks the opportunity to shoot a few baskets, take a swim, lift weights, or engage in an interval workout on the track? Shouldn't there be a place for someone who seeks activity but does not want to join a group or team to participate? Many students like to compete on a team some of the time but also to exercise or play in a less formal manner at other times. After all, much of life is structured, certainly school, yet one of the values of certain forms of play is spontaneity and informality. We are careful to provide opportunities for children to have some free playtime, but we somehow believe it wasteful to provide the same opportunities for adolescents.

To promote drop-in opportunities, those responsible for scheduling facilities can reserve a percentage of existing activity space for drop-in participants (e.g., reserve one lane of a swimming pool while the rest of the pool is used for varsity practice or class or intramural needs) and schedule and publicize drop-in facilities just as is done for other organized uses.

Even when areas scheduled for drop-in recreation are not being used, it is important that organized groups not be permitted to usurp the facility or space. This is a difficult task, but unless the principle of drop-in recreation is firmly established, it cannot be maintained.

Summary

Intramural athletics, sports clubs, and drop-in recreation are an integral part of the effort to promote physical exercise, leisure skills, competition, and sports for the general student body. Unless these forms of physical education are conceived as an integral part of the physical education curriculum, they generally suffer with regard to facilities, equipment, space, and leadership. It is the physical education teacher's responsibility to make certain this does not occur.

A principal feature of intramural competition is the wide variety of competitive tournament forms available to sustain interest in activity. Physical educators can manipulate time and facilities to ensure fair competition and to provide maximum participation for students. Modified forms of tournaments encourage less competitively oriented students to engage in activity. Publicity and appropriate awards heighten interest in intramural-recreation programs and are particularly attractive and significant to students.

Sports clubs are characterized by the diversity of their members; they are social and recreational as well as competitive. A faculty member serves as a liaison to the school, which only partially funds club activities, and instruction is a product of club membership.

Drop-in recreation affords students the opportunity to exercise or play in an informal and spontaneous manner.

Suggested activities

1. Plan and carry out a tournament for the class. See that each person participates at least three times and five place winners are determined.
2. Establish a plan to share and schedule space during an indoor and an outdoor season to meet the needs of varsity teams, instructional classes, intramural teams, and drop-in participants.
3. Outline and discuss a plan to finance a sports club program in a high school.
4. Write a paper defending the reservation of drop-in recreation time and space in a school with limited sports facilities.

16

Schools in Which Physical Education Is of Central Importance

This book has stressed the potential impact that physical education can have on the lives of adolescent students. If examples of superior physical education programs did not exist, we might reasonably be accused of mere daydreaming. However, as we shall see in this chapter there are programs in which administrators, teachers, and students have together built physical education into something very special and worthwhile.

Good physical education programs are most often found in good schools. While that may sound simplistic, remember that support and understanding of effective schooling can lead to improved physical education programs.

The major topics covered in this chapter are as follows:

The common characteristics of effective schools

The challenges physical educators face in planning and implementing effective programs

Core concepts and special components of three exemplary physical education programs

Effective schools

"Research on effective schools has done much to revive the optimism of practitioners that schools can be organized to enhance instructional effectiveness" (Rowen et al. 1983, 30).

With education now a common topic of conversation, it is not surprising that the school itself has recently become the focus of many research efforts.

Fortunately, a strong sense of optimism is emanating from this research focus, and those in the helping professions, including teachers, frequently need a sense of optimism to keep them going. Although the gloomy outlook toward school effectiveness that pervaded the 1960s (Coleman et al. 1966) may at last be subsiding, *A Nation at Risk* (1983) should remind us that many schools still have a long way to go.

Effective schools worldwide are reflected by the following statement.

> Successful schools emphasize high and uniform standards of academic achievement, but adopt multiple strategies in response to their particular needs and opportunities. Effective schools identify and acknowledge their own educational problems while acting firmly on the assumption that better schools can indeed be found. Such schools consistently communicate to staff, students, and parents that they are places for learning, and insist that this commitment be manifest in every classroom. (Mackenzie 1983, 5)

The dimensions of effective schooling detailed in Table 16.1 (p. 290) draw on many conclusions from current research. The dimension headings of leadership, efficacy, and efficiency parallel the path of effective schooling from the school and district level toward implementation in the individual classroom. Remember, too, that the ultimate determinant of school effectiveness is still what happens in the individual classroom or, in physical education's case, the gymnasium, playing field, and swimming pool.

When people discuss school effectiveness, they most often refer to standardized achievement tests or student performance in basic subjects such as mathematics and reading. Research also focuses on these "academic" outcomes in differentiating between more and less effective schools. Outcomes in physical education are not typically part of this differentiation.

Physical education outcomes will be considered more seriously within the overall school curriculum when they are considered more seriously within the physical education program. As we have emphasized several times in this text, physical education must accomplish tangible results in terms of student skill and fitness if it is to win acceptance and be valued within the educational community. To produce tangible outcomes, physical educators must set skill and fitness goals for their students and hold students accountable for reaching those goals.

SCENE *The principal of a suburban school that views physical education and sport as curricular priorities is talking with a university supervisor of student teachers.*

PRINCIPAL I'm glad I caught you. Have you got a minute?

SUPERVISOR Sure. I understand our student teacher is doing well. The cooperating teacher is giving some valuable feedback.

PRINCIPAL I really wanted to talk about our PE program. You know the PE teachers won't assess on skill or fitness. They base grades on participation and dress, not on achievement.

SUPERVISOR I've noticed that, and I think it's a real shame. In an environment like this, both the students and the teachers could achieve so much more if

TABLE 16.1 Dimensions of effective schooling

Leadership Dimensions

Core Elements

Positive climate and overall atmosphere
Goal-focused activities toward clear, attainable, and relevant objectives
Teacher-directed classroom management and decision making
In-service staff training for effective teaching

Facilitating Elements

Shared consensus on values and goals
Long-range planning and coordination
Stability and continuity of key staff
District-level support for school improvement

Efficacy Dimensions

Core Elements

High and positive achievement expectations with a constant press for excellence
Visible rewards for academic excellence and growth
Cooperative activity and group interaction in the classroom
Total staff involvement with school improvement
Autonomy and flexibility to implement adaptive practices
Appropriate levels of difficulty for learning tasks
Teacher empathy, rapport, and personal interaction with students

Facilitating Elements

Emphasis on homework and study
Positive accountability; acceptance of responsibility for learning outcomes
Strategies to avoid nonpromotion of students
Deemphasis of strict ability grouping; interaction with more accomplished peers

Efficiency Dimensions

Core Elements

Effective use of instructional time; amount and intensity of engagement in school learning
Orderly and disciplined school and classroom environments
Continuous diagnosis, evaluation, and feedback
Well-structured classroom activities
Instruction guided by content coverage
Schoolwide emphasis on basic and higher order skills

Facilitating Elements

Opportunities for individualized work
Number and variety of opportunities to learn

SOURCE: Mackenzie 1983.

student accountability were based on more than attendance and dress. The teachers would also have a real purpose in their instruction.

PRINCIPAL I'm really glad to hear you say that. I thought maybe I was the only one. The teachers won't have anything to do with assessment of skill.

SUPERVISOR You've discussed it with them?

PRINCIPAL Yes. They worry about PE's losing its appeal if students are assessed. I understand their view, but it's not right when a student can be class valedictorian and yet be seriously unfit. Such a person just hasn't achieved all the goals of the school. What do you think?

SUPERVISOR I think you're absolutely right. Either fitness and motor skills are goals of a secondary education or they're not. If we're going to state them as goals, our teachers have an obligation to ensure their achievement.

PRINCIPAL I'm glad you feel that way. I'll toss this around with a few other people over the next week or so.

SUPERVISOR Let me know what happens. I'd enjoy developing a case for skill and fitness assessment. Meanwhile, I'll send you and the teachers some materials on minimum health fitness.

The principal's comments reflect much of what we have been saying with respect to teacher and student accountability in physical education. A principal's concern is crucial when changes are made in the focus of a physical education program. Principals have by virtue of their authority the potential to improve program effectiveness.

Of course, principals need support at the instructional level, and that is where teachers come in. How would you respond to this principal? Would you be prepared to assess students on the basis of fitness and skill outcomes? How else can a school program demonstrate its effectiveness?

If the physical education curriculum were considered an integral part of overall school effectiveness more often, then more communities, administrators, and teachers would confront the real issue about any subject taught in schools, namely, "school effectiveness, if it means anything, comes down to behavior change in the classroom" (Tomlinson 1981, 48).

Physical education, in one form or another, has enjoyed moderate popularity in elective school programs. Now, with the back-to-basics push, there is a possibility that physical education, considered by many as an educational frill, will take more of a backseat in curricular priorities. Graduation requirements, instructional time, staffing allocations, facilities, and equipment may be further eroded.

The next decade may well take on some of the characteristics of a survival battle for physical education. If a battle does not materialize, then at the very least physical education will be faced with a need to continually justify its curricular role. We will need to convince students and parents that physical education makes a difference. Above all, we will need to convince students that in physical education that can acquire skills that will be valuable throughout their adult lives. Satisfied students are the best hope for the survival of physical education. Not only will they inform their parents of the value of physical education, but many will also eventually be parents of the next generation of students.

Sport and fitness are important to adolescents, and physical education can help them bridge the gap between childhood and adulthood. It provides the means for significant accomplishments. Physical education activities are concrete experiences, yet they allow for exploration and creativity. They are immediate in nature and challenging in process. Novak (1976) contends that sport for many adults is at the center of life, not at the periphery. Fitness and healthy life-style practices are developing in many communities. Physical education in secondary schools better than any other agency can respond to these new societal demands. We are moving to a more aged society, a technologically oriented society. We need to respond to the postindustrial values of the 1980s. Now more than ever physical education should hold a significant place in the school curriculum.

Effective physical education for adolescents

CHARACTERS

DIANE   *an elite-level athlete on the track, tennis, and basketball teams who is heading for college on an athletic scholarship*

GREG   *an outdoor pursuits enthusiast heavily involved in orienteering, rock climbing, and endurance cycling*

BRIAN   *a paraplegic who is restricted to a wheelchair but who has good upper-body strength and enjoys archery and weight lifting*

GAIL   *a student with poor skills and little motivation for anything physical*

SCENE   *Social studies class at a high school in which physical education is given equal emphasis, in terms of staffing and class time, with math, science, and English. After discussing the values of the community and how their school seems to complement these values,* DIANE, GREG, BRIAN, *and* GAIL *begin to discuss how the importance given to physical education in the school affects them as adolescents.*

GREG   Four hours of PE every week for the past three years works out to a lot of hours, but it's made a real difference in my life. In middle school, PE was supervised play. There wasn't any pressure to learn. I joined in and had a good time, but it just seemed like basketball, volleyball, and kickball over and over again. In high school I was forced to learn skills. I opted for outdoor pursuits most of the time and found that some of the activities really interested me. I had to work physically and mentally to get a decent grade. Who would've ever thought that my folks would be the ground crew for my 12-hour cycle race this weekend. I'm not going on to college, but high school physical education has given me plenty of *self-direction* for my adult life.

BRIAN   If I were talking about PE before eleventh grade, I wouldn't be saying much that was positive. It was really frustrating after my accident, and physical activity became a bore, maybe an embarrassment. Well, as you know, I want to be a dentist, so grades are important. I got a C in PE in tenth grade because I didn't improve on my skills in archery and table tennis. I complained that I was being victimized and had a meeting with the principal and the PE faculty. They made it very clear that in spite of my legs, I could still achieve and would be held accountable for achievement the same as all other students in the school. I wanted good grades, so at the beginning of eleventh grade I decided to bite the bullet. I chose the conditioning and advanced archery units and practiced every day. I made terrific improvements, got an A, and kept taking PE to develop my skills. I'm bench pressing more than some of the linemen on the football team, and if I can swim the 100-meter freestyle in less than 120 seconds this week, I'll have achieved every goal the teachers and I set.

   The PE program here held me *accountable*. In most other schools, I would've rolled into a corner and watched the world go by. It's made a heck of a difference to my life.

DIANE   I never realized you were made to do those things, Brian. The PE faculty and the principal must really *believe in the value* of PE.

BRIAN   Thank goodness!

DIANE   For me, sport has always been important. My mom and dad were college athletes, so I guess I followed their lead. The school athletic program has always been more important to me than PE, but I enjoyed the *variety and choice* in PE. Completing my Water Safety Instructor certificate was important though. Because of that and my tennis skills, I've got a camp job this summer that'll help me with the money situation before I start college in the fall. PE was fun. I guess I didn't have to work as hard as other people to get good grades, but I had to in math, so I guess that's a fair tradeoff.

GAIL   I'm the opposite of you, Diane. For me, math was easy and PE was hard. My athletic skills are terrible. I'm scared of balls and don't enjoy the yelling and screaming that always goes on in games. I guess if PE had been an elective, I wouldn't have taken it. But because I had to, I learned some useful skills. First of all, I know how to look after my health and fitness—now I walk to school rather than take the bus. I guess PE's made me aware of my body. Aerobic dance and synchronized swimming were the only activities I really enjoyed, but two is better than none. Maybe I'll use those skills after I graduate. If I don't, I know the teachers will be disappointed. They sure provided great *encouragement*.

With principals and physical education teachers who *believe in the value* of physical activity and who are prepared to hold themselves and their students *accountable* for learning while offering *choice, variety, and encouragement*, physical education can really make a difference in the lives of adolescents. We now turn to some programs that are making that difference.

Exemplary physical education programs

Wirreanda High School, South Australia

Wirreanda High School is a coeducational public school that represents the concept of a school within a school. The focus of the school is general education, yet a part of its staff, facilities, policies, etc. is specifically directed to the goals of physical education and provides specialized units to meet those goals.

The physical education program is facilitated by a supportive administration. The following details from a policy statement emphasize the importance of a coordinated planning effort in the implementation of a potentially effective physical education program. The staff handbook indicates the areas of importance, both from a school and a physical education perspective.

Statement of Purpose

Physical education is unique in its contribution to the preparation of students for life, as it aims to facilitate the physical, mental, and social development of each individual.

To allow such development, it is essential for physical education to feature significantly in the school curriculum at all grade levels. The faculty are committed to the promotion of physical activity on a daily basis and believe that commitment at this level is essential if students are to reach their full potential.

The physical education curriculum of Wirreanda High School has been developed after careful consideration of the outcomes believed to be attainable as a result of involvement in an effective program. These desired outcomes are that the student will

1. feel comfortable with and enjoy physical activity;
2. develop interpersonal relationships and socially acceptable behavior through physical activity;
3. develop a realistic concept of herself or himself and others;
4. experience a diverse range of physical activities within which there is the capacity for specialization;
5. attain a degree of mastery in a range of skills that will allow her or him to participate at either a recreational or competitive level;
6. develop and understand the nature of physical fitness and be encouraged to adopt a healthy life-style;
7. gain a level of appreciation and understanding of human movement through observation, experience, and analysis;
8. have normal growth and development facilitated by involvement in regular physical activity;
9. gain a knowledge of physical activity as it relates to social issues.

The success of any physical education program is largely dependent on the quality of teaching and the degree of encouragement given to students by parents. It is, therefore, essential that parents become aware of the contribution that physical education can provide in the development of the student.

The effectiveness of any educational course is often difficult to calculate, but if a single factor were to be used as a criterion for this subject, it would be the extent to which physical activity is adopted as part of the individual's life-style.

Program Administration

For students to achieve the desired outcomes, a substantial amount of time must be allocated on a weekly basis. In physical education, students choose either the specialist or general course, depending on skill and motivation. Counseling is available to guide their decision, and transfer from either course is possible, though not encouraged.

Grade 8	Specialist Course	480 minutes*
	or	
	General Course	100 minutes plus General Activities, 80 minutes
Grade 9	Specialist Course	500 minutes
	or	
	General Course	160 minutes
Grade 10	Specialist and General Course	80 minutes plus PE Electives, 200 minutes
Grade 11	General Course	80 minutes plus Recreation, 120 minutes
	or	
	Specialist Course	120 minutes plus PE Electives, 200 minutes
Grade 12	General Course	60 minutes
	or	
	Secondary School Certificate Course	300 minutes

* All times indicate number of minutes per week.

The specific aim of the specialist course is to enable students to experience an educational program in which the pursuit of excellence in both the academic and sporting fields is complementary. The specialist course curriculum provides study in the standard range of subjects offered but allocates enough additional time to the physical education/sports component to enable an in-depth study in both theoretical and practical areas. This section of Wirreanda's educational curriculum is divided into (1) *human movement studies*, an academic component based on human anatomy, physiology, and performance-related social issues; (2) *specialist skills development*, the development of highly specialized skills in the students' major sporting interest areas; and (3) *general activity sessions*, practically orientated sessions aimed at the development of fitness, general motor ability, and leisure skills. This course is demanding both academically and physically and is suitable only for students who are highly motivated in both of these areas.

The general course is a broad-based activity program offering systematic skill instruction for all students. It complements the standard range of subjects offered but does not provide for in-depth practical and theoretical study in physical education and sport.

The major aim of the secondary school certificate course is to familiarize students with the role that physical activity has to play in a modern technological society, both at the personal and community level. The foundations of the course are concerned with the physiological benefits of activity. These topics lead to the study of current life-styles and the sociological, physiological, and psychological factors that affect them. The practical material covered provides students with a range of skills and experiences that will enable them to put into practice concepts covered in the theoretical component.

Program Implementation

With a large physical education faculty and a variable program, specific implementation guidelines are needed to promote program continuity.

Professional development. Professional development is an ongoing process that can be achieved through experience and experimentation; reading of journals, books, and articles; attendance of workshops, conferences, seminars, etc.; and utilization of observation days. Professional development programs can aid the participant, the faculty, and students by providing valuable information for enhancing the quality of the education process. All staff members are expected to play an active role in professional associations.

Lesson procedure.

1. Lessons start on the bell or allocated time.
2. Students are to be let in by staff and encouraged to change as quickly as possible.
3. When changed, students are to wait quietly in designated areas.
4. Change rooms are then to be locked after lights are out and internal doors are closed. *No students are to use the change rooms during lessons unless under direct teacher supervision.*
5. Students must ask for permission to leave the class and are to use central toilets during class if necessary.
6. Staff to complete record cards in designated area.
7. The above procedures need to be carried out as efficiently as possible to maximize effective teaching time.
8. Lessons are to end five minutes before lesson change to enable students and staff to return equipment and prepare for next lesson
9. Last teacher is to ensure gym and change rooms are empty and locked prior to breaks.

Clothing requirements.

1. Students are required to be changed for all PE lessons except when they provide a note exempting them on medical grounds or by prior arrangement with their teacher. Staff are to use discretion and common sense when dealing with students who have injuries but do not produce a note. If in doubt, work can be assigned according to the criteria listed below, which can be waived if student produces a note explaining the situation.

2. All staff are to use the following guidelines for students *not changed.*
   a. 1st occurrence in term—no action.
   b. 2nd occurrence in term—1 page notes on current topic.
   c. 3rd occurrence in term—as above, along with letter home to parents (send to senior teacher along with record card for this).
   d. 4th occurrence in term—send to senior teacher, who will refer to deputy principal. (Staff are asked to use discretion when dealing with students who are usually reliable and bring gear regularly.)

3. Physical education dress requirements.
   The following articles of clothing will be required by all students to enable full participation in the physical education program (jeans are not acceptable).
   Boys: Summer—blue shorts; yellow, blue, or brown T-shirt.
              Winter—warm-up suit (preferably blue) or yellow, blue, or brown jacket.
   Girls: Summer—royal blue wrap-around skirt; yellow, blue, or brown T-shirt; blue or black shorts.
              Winter—warm-up suit (preferably blue) or yellow, blue, or brown jacket.
   Footwear: White-soled shoes must be worn in the gymnasium. Shoes will be required when using the tennis courts and field areas. Bare feet are an acceptable alternative for activities in the gymnasium.
   Showers: Available for student use.

Record cards.

1. All information to be completed during orientation lesson.

2. Ensure that students on probation are noted.

3. Comments need to be entered as often as possible and can be either objective or subjective, covering all aspects of the students' performance, e.g., behavior, skills acquisition, attitude, areas of concern, recommendations, areas of strength, and theoretical and practical assessment.

4. Attitudinal ratings can be allocated on the basis of the following guidelines:
                   A–Outstanding
                   B–Pleasing
                   C–Satisfactory
                   D–Below requirement
                   E–Negative

5. Overall topic grades are allocated by A, B, C, D, U, and + or − scores. *Term grades do not feature* ± *scores.*

6. Teachers are to assign final topic grades (attitudinal ratings can be considered when grades are borderline).

7. Attach all notes from parents, duplicate reports, etc. to back of record cards.

8. Record any additional work assigned on cards along with due date and other details.

9. Use code under attendance record regarding changing, etc.

10. Maintain cards in alphabetical order.

Homework and written assignments.

1. When making assignments, convey the following information to students:
   a. The required length, composition, and *quality.*
   b. The grading scheme that will be used.
   c. The class's homework.
   d. The due date.
   e. Standard project format includes a brief description of the game, field markings and positions, basic skills, drills (warm-up, fitness, skill), basic game tactics, and training programs.
   f. Late presentation: Extensions can be given under valid circumstances; however, the student must meet the new due date. Late assignments are penalized 5 percent of maximum mark per day.
   g. Assignments not completed:
      • If not presented after one cycle, refer to senior teacher. However, it is the obligation of the regular teacher to make every effort to ensure that work is submitted.
      • Standardized letter will be sent home outlining new due date and intention to detain the student on that day if the assignment is not forthcoming.
      • Refer matter to principal.

2. Written assignments/homework can either be in the form of a project or worksheets and written assessments.

3. Please note that the highest quality work is expected, and spelling, layout, comprehension, neatness, and so on are to be taken into account when marking assignments.

4. When practical homework is assigned, students are to enter the tasks in their PE book and have it signed by parents on completion.

Storage of equipment. Wherever possible, see that equipment is taken out in plastic tubs. Closely supervise the return of equipment to ensure that all materials are returned, the store is kept tidy and easily accessible, and any damaged equipment can be removed for repairs. It is the obligation of all staff to ensure that returned equipment is stored neatly to enable other staff to minimize organization time for their lessons. The store is to be locked at every break by the last teacher in from a lesson.

Lesson preparation.

1. All staff are to prepare written plans for all topics. Team-teaching situations may mean that comprehensive plans are not required for all lessons; however, lesson outlines and content are still required.

2. Lesson plans are to be completed on faculty planning sheets and maintained in a folder in teaching sequence and cataloged.

$$
\begin{array}{rl}
\text{Grade} & 8\text{--Yellow} \\
& 9\text{--Blue} \\
& 10\text{--Green} \\
& 11\text{--Mustard} \\
& 12\text{--Pink}
\end{array}
$$

3. The teacher evaluation section is to be completed where alterations to the lesson plans are necessary.

Discipline.

1. The booklet "Schools and the Law" covers a range of topics both directly and indirectly related to discipline, and we recommend that staff familiarize themselves with this booklet.

2. Set up teaching situations where students are aware of their responsibilities and standards of behavior.

3. Require a level of student discipline and behavior consistent with the expectations of the school at all times.

4. Act to avoid direct confrontation with students in the teaching situation.

5. If a student becomes rude or stubborn, refer the matter to the senior teacher; if he or she is not available, ask student to remain at end of lesson.

6. Make every effort to solve the problem amicably and within the faculty. It is wise to provide the student with an alternative that maintains class discipline but is reasonable and acceptable. The senior teacher is to decide whether or not further action should be taken.

7. It is preferable that students not be sent out of a lesson but remain under the teacher's supervision.

8. If written work is assigned, it should be constructive and relevant to the student's studies. Record on the student's record card the work assigned and due date.

9. Acceptable forms of punishment include a written assignment, a constructive manual task, yard duty, and detention (see guidelines in information booklet).

10. Please note that students are not permitted in the staff room unless specifically required by a teacher.

Assessment procedures.

1. The decision to use a grading system for all grade levels primarily arose out of the difficulties experienced in determining the direction senior school students should take in their next year at school. It was recognized then that some objective form of grading had to be applied to determine, and have reasonable grounds to justify to students and parents, promotions and course selection. As a result, the following procedures were instituted.

   a. All progress bulletins include the category "Achievement Grade," followed by the grade A, B, C, D, or U.

   b. In arriving at an achievement grade, *only* objectively assessable material is to be used (for example, tests, essays, homework assignments, exercises, projects). The grade is to be a reflection of the student's achievement and must be able to be supported by marks, grades, or percentages given during the assessment period.

   c. Other areas such as the student's attitude, cooperation, behavior, and punctuality are to be included on the progress bulletin but do not have a direct bearing on the way a teacher arrives at the achievement grade.

   d. An achievement grade should, at any stage of the year, be an indication of the student's *progress to date.* Continuing assessment is still State Education Department policy.

   e. Achievement grades are to be used along with other criteria to determine the direction a student should take the following year. This is particularly true for students in tenth and eleventh grades, where grades are given a numerical value and a minimum number of points is one of the criteria for promotion.

Some teachers believe that the above system is too narrow and does not take into account a student's total performance. That is to say, they find it difficult to fail a hard-working, cooperative student who has been unable to meet the academic requirements of the course. The system does make allowance for these students. It is the responsibility of the teacher to *modify* standard courses for those students who are not able to cope, thus giving them the opportunity to achieve success at their own level of ability. Naturally, this fact must be taken into account when determining promotions at the end of the year. For example, a tenth grade student who has reached a satisfactory level in a modified course might be promoted to a tenth grade standard course rather than an eleventh grade course. This would depend on the individual student, as several criteria are available to determine a student's future educational needs. Parents and students, as well as staff, need to be aware of the significance and use of achievement grades.

2. All results are to be recorded on the standard recording sheet and accompanied by a distribution scale. Consult the department head when allocating grade A or U.

3. All recording sheets are to be maintained in a springback folder with the record cards.

Summary of the Program

The details of the Wirreanda program may seem trivial, but remember that such details promote instructional effectiveness, which is the bottom line for any teacher's accountability. When schools have specific guidelines for physical education and they are followed carefully, physical education is taken seriously as a subject. When physical education is taken seriously by administrators and teachers, it will much more likely be taken seriously by students.

Many of the dimensions of effective schooling are apparent in this program outline. You should now be able to understand the significance of the leadership, efficacy, and efficiency dimensions from a practical standpoint.

All Saints' Episcopal School, Vicksburg, Mississippi

All Saints' Episcopal School is a coeducational boarding school for grades 8 through 12. The school is characterized by a strong emphasis on physical education in its general education program. The physical education program offers an extensive array of activities, 87 in all, with traditional sports, outdoor pursuits, recreational activities (active and passive), and numerous novel games serving as electives and required curricular components. A specialized aerobics unit is a significant feature of both the school and physical education program.

Statement of Purpose

At All Saints' Episcopal School we are committed to fostering the mental, physical, and spiritual growth and development of each person. We believe that each student is unique; therefore, each student's ability and previous experience should be taken into consideration, and all students should be placed in specific programs and classes that will meet their immediate educational needs and prepare them for postgraduate work commensurate with individual ability. This tailored program must not isolate or exempt the student from being a part of an interdependent community that stresses cooperation and mutual respect. We strive to equip each student with skills that will enable him or her to cope with a changing world and become a reasonable citizen in our society.

This commitment to individual growth and development governs all that we do at All Saints' Episcopal School. We believe that every student should be and is a "winner." That is, each individual has unique abilities and special value to contribute to the community. Our total program has been developed to identify these abilities and to allow the student to appreciate his or her special qualities as well as those of each member of the community.

Each student begins his or her association with All Saints' with a full day of testing in the school's Educational Evaluation Center. The center is staffed by two psychologists who administer a battery of formal and informal tests to identify the student's strengths and weaknesses. The results from this day of testing yield a profile of the student's needs and potential. The information is then used to determine the appropriate placement within each course and class.

A sign in the headmaster's office accurately expresses a major part of the school's philosophy: "You don't have to start all over here; you can start where *you* are!" That is the basis for the program at All Saints'. We begin at the student's level and help the student to grow to his or her potential. This applies to academics, physical education, recreation, dormitory life, and all aspects of the student's development.

Physical Education and Recreation Program

We feel that every child has the right to be physically educated. We want every boy and girl to learn at least one lifetime sport and to get started early thinking about physical activity as a part of his or her lifetime plan. At all levels, personalized learning and the individual's development of a positive self-concept are hallmarks of a quality program.

Our goal is for every child to be a winner—self-directed, resourceful, creative; aware of the body and what it can do; awake to the joy and value of physical activities and appreciative of his or her own contributions.

We do feel that we have a creative and unique program at All Saints'. We design activities, sports, and intramurals on the basis of the student's needs and interests. However, this program was not designed or implemented in one day; it has evolved and developed over a number of years and is a direct reflection of the changing needs and interests of our students.

In 1971 the Physical Education Department consisted of two instructors and several volunteers from the community. Physical education classes were required of each student, but no credit was given. The gym was actually the basement floor of the boys' dormitory. By 1975, a new gym was completed and there were four full-time PE and Recreation instructors and one assistant teacher. Students were able to earn full credit for participation in PE classes; and the total school became committed to individualized instruction. The schedule reflected the change by offering classes during lunch in traditional physical education and adding classes after school in interest-based activities. There are now six full-time instructors in PE and Recreation.

Physical education at All Saints' is a carefully planned sequence of learning experiences designed to fulfill the needs of every student in a variety of areas—growth, development, behavior, health, and play. The initial teaching methods used and student assignments made are based upon preliminary evaluations of the student's ability and skills. Then each student is taught according to his or her own ability to achieve. The extensive variety of our program through individualized activities in education, recreation, and competition allows each student to select from a broad range of courses. Programs are designed for students with unique interests so that they may be allowed to pursue those interests.

Students are encouraged and directed to reach their own potential by developing the skills of movement, the knowledge of how and why one moves, and the ways in which movement may be organized. Students also learn to move skillfully and effectively through exercise, games, play, and team and individual sports. Students learn to condition the organic systems of the body to meet daily and emergency demands.

Aerobics Program

Regardless of the number and variety of activities available to students, a period of continuous progressive cardiovascular-respiratory exercise is needed to ensure proper physical fitness. Therefore, an aerobics program was established at All Saints' School in 1982.

All students take an initial test to assess general fitness according to the distance covered in a 12-minute run. Based upon this information, students are placed in groups of similar fitness levels and needs. The activity of each of the 12 coeducational groups reflects the fitness level of the students. Most of the aerobic groups combine walking and running activities. Two groups contain students of excellent and superior fitness levels who participate in bicycling and cross-country running programs. There is one walking group and one group with specific needs.

In order to accommodate 187 students in the aerobics program, every inch of campus space is used. Students run on the fitness trail, on the driveway around the school, on Confederate Avenue, and around the nearby Vicksburg Hospital (this has been a source of curiosity and enjoyment for patients and doctors). Students walk around the soccer field and in the gym. A stationary bicycle is used for some aerobic activity.

Each group begins the 30-minute exercise period with stretching and concludes with cool-down activity. Students assess their own condition by taking an exercise heart rate pulse immediately after the aerobic activity and a resting pulse rate 5 minutes after the activity. A nutrition break of juice or fruit is provided at the end of the period. Students are able to continue the cooling-down process by walking to the serving area.

Continuous assessment is as important in the aerobics program as it is in any other individualized activity on campus. Ten weeks after the initial test students are reevaluated according to the amount of time required to run/walk one and a half miles.

Recently, a more complete assessment has been used to identify basic CVR data for each student. The information gathered includes weight, height, age, pulse rate, systolic and diastolic blood pressure, body measurements, percent of body fat, lung capacity, flexibility, and stress test results. The stress test uses a 3-minute step test to assess student pulse and blood pressure during exercise. This evaluation identifies any student who may need an adjustment in the CVR program.

Students have begun to be concerned with body appearance. Additional exercises are recommended as needed and a consultant for our aerobics program conducts a workshop for all students on nutrition and diet.

Aerobic activities are conducted four afternoons a week. This is the minimum amount of time to spend on CVR exercise to realize results. The physical program is supported by educating the students about their bodies and exercise. Each student has a book on CVR exercise that serves as a reference guide for all questions and concerns. Students are also able to share this information with parents, and thereby begin to reeducate the adults.

The goal of our program is for all students to be able to run/walk two miles within 23 minutes. However, the ultimate goal goes beyond immediate physical fitness. We want to reeducate students to achieve more enjoyment from life and a healthier life-style.

Summary of the Program

Physical education at All Saints' is not limited to one hour of instruction each day. The program does not function in isolation; it is an integral part of the education of the whole child. Each skill developed by the student is used, complemented, and refined in a variety of structured and unstructured activities. Classroom instruction gives the basic skills for afternoon activities, which also nurture skills for total community living and recreation. (See Figure 16.1, p. 302.)

This program and philosophy does not present a magic cure, but we do know that it is working for us and for our students! We begin with the student and identify strengths, weaknesses, needs, and interests through formal and informal testing and individual conferences. Then we create a program to meet the needs, use

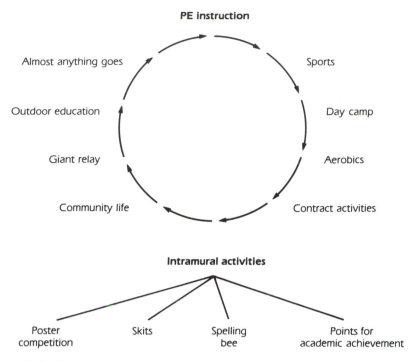

PE instruction

Almost anything goes

Sports

Outdoor education

Day camp

Giant relay

Aerobics

Community life

Contract activities

Intramural activities

Poster competition   Skits   Spelling bee   Points for academic achievement

Figure 16.1 Physical education and recreation program at All Saints' Episcopal School.

the strengths, remediate the weaknesses, and nurture the interests of that student. It takes a lot of work (*hard* work) and hours of planning and replanning. It involves a constant flow of assessment between the teacher and the students. However, it puts a new spirit and dimension in teaching because there is no set way to teach or work, but many different ways to achieve our goals—goals that we believe are very important.

Cincinnati Academy of Physical Education (CAPE), Cincinnati, Ohio

The Cincinnati Academy of Physical Education is a coeducational public school for grades 4 through 12. It is open to any child who is a resident of Cincinnati on a first-come, first-serve basis. There are no screening tests or procedures of any kind for admission. CAPE grew from 54 students to over 940 students in its first four years and now enrolls 1,600 students. Initially a middle school (grades 4 through 8), CAPE has extended its program through grade 12 as a result of its original success and enthusiastic parent support.

Statement of Purpose

Through a strong, basic, academic program and an enthusiastic program of physical development, the academy strives to develop an intelligent, healthy, vigorous person with a strict inner discipline to maintain the early Greek philosophy of a sound mind in a sound body.

The primary emphasis of the physical development program is on individual and dual sports. These sports provide a lifetime use of leisure time and help maintain physical and mental health.

Many children are physically able but not able enough to achieve success through organized team athletics. This program is for those children. Coordination skills, strength, flexibility, and body mechanics are part of the development program. Team sports such as football, basketball, and baseball are not emphasized. However, they are part of the program for those children who want and need them.

The physical education program is closely coordinated with all academic programs. For example, the outdoor education curriculum introduces and trains the child in the use of the natural environment and is closely correlated to the health, science, and mathematics programs.

The ultimate goals are personal motivation and self-discipline, stressing a high degree of social interaction. Physical and/or academic goals are developed for all courses, and excellence in achievement is stressed.

In an attractively presented folder available to prospective students, CAPE's rules and regulations affecting students and their parents are detailed as follows:

1. Attendance, including time of arrival, dismissal, tardiness, early excuses, class cutting, absence from school, and truancy

2. Code of conduct

3. Disciplinary actions and explanation of penalties

4. Grades and promotion requirements, including marking practices, exams, athletic/academic eligibility, honor roll

5. Helpful study hints

6. In-house regulations

7. Student activities

8. Student athletics

9. Student dress

Physical Education Program Components

The academy provides a structured physical education program with opportunities for individually prescribed programs for each student, a variety of intramural sports and club activities, an interscholastic sports program, a wide variety of high-interest, short-duration experiences with an opportunity for follow-up.

Students take eight periods each day; six periods are spent in academic areas and two periods are spent in physical education. One physical education class, *General Skills*, encompasses the vertical phase of the physical education curriculum. During this class students get a basic introduction to all areas of physical education. The other class is the *Skills Practice Program*. In this class, three or four activities are offered each quarter; the student selects one area and studies it for 10 weeks.

Activities offered in addition to the traditional team sports, individual sports, rhythm, aerobics, track and field, archery, golf, riflery, and wrestling include athletic training, body building, unicycling, physics of sport, outdoor education, recreation-camp counseling skills, sports photography, and leadership training.

Athletic Program

Continuity of the coaching staff from grade 7 through grade 12 is emphasized. For example, the head coach at the varsity level is responsible for the total athletic program in grades 7 through 12 in his or her area of expertise. This promotes the thorough development of each individual athlete's ability and means that students are spending time on skill development, not on adjusting to a new coaching staff every two years.

The counseling and athletic departments at CAPE work with students in making academic and physical talents known to colleges and universities throughout the United States to increase scholarship opportunities.

Selling the Program

CAPE believes it has a curriculum that offers academic excellence and an outstanding program of physical education. To publicize this, the academy reports special happenings and news in a publication known as the *CAPE Connection*. It strongly emphasizes the quality of its physical education program to attract interested students. CAPE encourages visitors to the school; it wants everyone to see a school in which physical education is central.

Summary

Research into effective schools is a relatively recent phenomenon in the area of educational research. The results, however, are encouraging when one considers the common characteristics that are consistently identified with effective schools: goal-focused activities, teacher-directed classroom management and decision making, high and positive achievement expectations, accountability and acceptance of responsibility for learning outcomes, effective use of instructional time, and a variety of opportunities to learn.

Many of the dimensions of effective schooling discussed in this book and collectively emphasized in this chapter are common to the three physical education programs we have detailed here. The basic core and special components of the Wirreanda program that permeate the entire high school physical education curriculum ensure adequate time and continuity to promote achievement in a variety of learning situations. The All Saints' program provides a great deal of variety and flexibility to meet individual needs. The integrated aerobics/fitness program, unlike most school-based programs, allows adequate time for fitness gains to be made, measured, and maintained. At the Cincinnati Academy of Physical Education, students receive two periods of basic physical education each day. In addition, students select one area of skill practice for each 10-week period. Again, time and practice allow for, and promote, skill achievement.

Suggested activities

1. Discuss ways in which a school physical education program can demonstrate its effectiveness. Be prepared to support your statements with facts.

2. Reread Table 16.1 (page 290). Meet with a local school principal or educational administrator to discuss the leadership dimensions outlined in

the table. Can you identify schools in your area that exhibit these dimensions? How do you know they exist? What characterizes schools in which such leadership dimensions do not exist?

3. The efficiency dimensions in Table 16.1 apply to implementation in the gymnasium. Much of your work in physical education should emphasize the core elements outlined. Based on your understanding of the teaching-learning process, develop an argument for physical education classes (a) being orderly and disciplined, (b) effectively using instructional time, and (c) utilizing diagnosis, evaluation, and feedback.

4. Obtain copies of physical education syllabi from local schools. Compare them to the details provided in the Wirreanda program.

5. Divide into small groups. Each group is to prepare a description of what it would consider the "ideal" school physical education program. Compare the programs in class.

Part Three

Implementing the Program

17

Managing the Physical Education Program

Middle, junior, and senior high schools often have two or more physical educators working as a *department*. The classes each teacher is assigned are meant to be part of an overall *program*. The program is supposed to work toward common goals. It is the purpose of this chapter to examine issues that relate to the development and maintenance of quality physical education programs. The following topics are covered in this chapter:

How programs differ from individual classes

Criteria for judging the quality of programs

The importance of departmental routines

Execution of the primary managerial functions

Understanding the formal and informal organizations

Building staff morale

Developing and maintaining a professional group

What was your physical education department like when you were in school? Almost all middle, junior, and senior high schools have physical education departments (or staffs or faculties or whatever label is used to describe the group of people who teach physical education). Do you remember your teachers? Were there major differences from class to class in the quality of instruction? Can you recall any objective that the department *as a whole* worked toward? Would it be fair to describe your physical education teachers as a group obviously working together toward common goals? Or was your experience more like the scene portrayed next?

SCENE *Two boys and two girls from the local junior high school have stopped for an ice-cream cone on the way home from school. The discussion turns to the experience one of them just had in physical education.*

SUSAN I'm already sore! We had a really hard physical fitness test in school today. I thought I was going to get sick after that 12-minute run. Mrs. Abbott was really on us to do well.

TROY Fitness test? We haven't had a test in PE all year. I don't think Mr. Williams knows what a test is—and I'm glad he doesn't.

WALTER Yeah, he's too busy thinking up plays for the team to have to worry about a test. If he gave a test, he'd have to pay attention to us for a change.

VANESSA Well, at least Abbot tries to teach us something. I've heard that Williams is pretty bad.

WALTER You can say that again! I'm so tired of dodge ball and softball, I can't stand it. I heard that the girls were going to do fencing next week. Is that true?

SUSAN Yes, Mrs. Abbott told us yesterday that we're going to have fencing right after the physical fitness unit. She even showed us the different swords we're going to use.

VANESSA You don't call them swords!

SUSAN I know that.

TROY Some of the kids say that Mr. Barnes at North Junior High teaches good stuff, too, just like Mrs. Abbott does. Anything would be better than Coach Williams. Is it hard for you to get a decent grade in PE?

VANESSA Not if you work hard and try to learn something. I mean you can get a B if you show any improvement at all.

TROY In our class all you have to do is show up and stay out of Mr. Williams's way and you've got an A.

VANESSA But what've you learned?

TROY Nothing.

WALTER You'd think two teachers in the same school would do things more the same way, but I guess not.

SUSAN I don't think they even like each other very much—at least she's always crabbing about the "other" PE teacher. We all know who she means.

VANESSA I wish they'd get their act together.

TROY Yeah, but don't bet on it.

From this conversation, we can draw several conclusions, at least for the school these students attend. First, instruction and grading are treated differently by different teachers. Second, the teachers evidently indicate, directly or indirectly, a lack of respect for each other. Third, the students understand these differences and react to them. Clearly, it would be inappropriate to talk about a physical education *program* at this school because there does not appear to be any overall direction or any concerted effort toward achieving similar goals. Regardless of the relative merits of the various teachers involved, we can legitimately conclude that this school physical education effort *is not well managed.* This chapter is about management of the physical education program; that is, it focuses on the kinds of *overall efforts* that physical educators must make to have an entire program work and to avoid any scenes such as the one described above. The remaining chapters in Part III explore in greater detail important facets and skills that contribute to a successful overall program.

The whole is greater than the sum of its parts

A physical education *program* will not succeed if only part of the teaching staff makes the necessary effort. In this sense, one poor teacher or one nonteacher can spoil the effort of others, can give the program a bad name among students, other faculty, and parents.

On the other hand, if *all* of the physical education teachers make an effort, the program can be successful. At least it can achieve a limited success that comes from each member's doing at least a minimally competent job. But what if a school wants to do more than the minimum? What if a group of physical educators wants to create and maintain a program that is really successful? How do they do it? The simple answer is that they all pull in the same direction! Not only do they each make an effort, but their separate efforts are directed toward similar goals. In that way, the sum of their individual efforts is greater than it otherwise would be. A successful *program* is not accomplished by having individuals work at their own goals, even though they may do that well! The consistency and support generated among a group of professionals working toward similar goals with similar methods yield results that go far beyond those that any one of them can achieve separately.

People in sport understand clearly how the separate skills and efforts of individual athletes in a team game do not necessarily add up to a good team performance. For a *team* to perform well, each member must do his or her share and direct his or her effort toward the team goals. Building and maintaining a successful physical education program in a school is a *team game*.

Would you know a good program if you saw one?

What makes a good program good? What are its main characteristics? There are several ways to answer these questions, and each has its place in an overall answer. First, it is clear that a *good* program accomplishes *something*. We have repeatedly emphasized our belief that physical education must accomplish tangible outcomes to gain acceptance by students, faculty, administrators, and parents—and then to have that acceptance grow into continued support. A second suggestion is that a good program is a program that students value. This means that students not only acknowledge the importance of what they can learn in the program but also appreciate the manner in which the program is conducted; that is, they appreciate the *outcomes* of the program and the *pro-*

cess by which those outcomes are achieved. Valuing one of these without the other sadly defeats the overall worth of the program. A third way to answer the question is to say that the teaching staff must also appreciate the program and support it actively through their behavior both in class and outside class. That is, in class teachers convey the fact that they value the program to their students, and outside of class they convey it to other teachers, administrators, and parents.

There certainly are other ways to characterize a good program besides the three broad perspectives we have just suggested. Here are some other indicators:

- Classes begin and end on time.
- Time within class is used wisely.
- The teaching/learning environment is physically safe.
- The teaching/learning environment is psychologically safe.
- Equipment is in good repair and available when needed.
- Student effort is required and supported.
- Students are held accountable for performance.
- Adequate, accurate records are kept.
- Students have input into ongoing program evaluation.
- High teacher morale is conveyed directly to students.

We would expect each of these characteristics to be present in a good program *no matter what the nature of that program.* In Part II we emphasized the many different program approaches available to physical educators, each of which can be successful if implemented in a manner consistent with the information in this chapter and the remainder of Part III.

The place to start: Departmental routines

Consistency is the hallmark of successful programs. Students should be treated similarly from class to class and year to year. Nothing destroys the credibility of a program more quickly than for students to experience inconsistency in treatment. In Chapter 19 we make a strong case for the need for physical education staffs to reach decisions on certain managerial and discipline issues and then to develop routines that are used *throughout* the program. A *routine* can be defined as a standard method of implementing some aspect of behavior within the program and then teaching this to students.

If students are treated similarly from teacher to teacher and class to class, they will begin to develop *generalized* patterns of behavior and will not need to be taught new patterns with each succeeding teacher or class. On the other hand, if teachers have different routines and rules (or worse, none at all!) then students will have difficulty figuring out exactly how to behave in any given situation. For example, consider the following seven areas in which overall departmental routines should be developed.

1. *Attendance routines.* Every teacher should take attendance in the same way. There are two main criteria by which we can judge attendance routines. First, they need to be highly accurate. Second, they need to take as little time from instruction/practice as possible. A third criterion might be that they should help students learn how to behave responsibly. It matters little what attendance procedure is used if these criteria are met. Teachers can take attendance by assigning each student a numbered "spot" on the gymnasium floor for warm-up and stretching exercises at the beginning of class and then checking the spots that are vacant. Teachers can require students to sign in before class begins. Regardless of the method chosen, every teacher should use the same method so that students become accustomed to it, thereby contributing to its efficiency and accuracy.

2. *Locker-room supervision.* Teachers should establish locker-room rules that include provisions for what to do with books, clothing, valuables, and towels, as well as for *expected and prohibited* behaviors. These behavioral procedures should be established early in the school year and supervised very carefully and consistently until they become habit. Each teacher should apply the rules in the same way.

3. *Absence policy.* The department should have a policy on what constitutes an excused absence, how absences are made up, and how interschool athletic absences are handled. Again, what matters is the fairness and consistency of the application of the policy, not its specific features.

4. *Safety routines.* The department should establish safety rules, especially as they apply to apparatus and equipment. Teachers should post the rules prominently, emphasize them to students, and enforce them strictly. *Adequate*

Locker-room problems need to be dealt with consistently.

procedures are the best way to guard against negligence! (See Chapter 21 for further discussion of the importance of safety procedures in legal liability issues.)

5. *Grading/evaluation.* As noted throughout this text, we believe strongly in holding students accountable for performance in physical education. We also believe strongly that evaluation of student performance should be fair and consistent and that grading procedures should be similar from teacher to teacher and class to class. Grades are important to students, and there are few procedures in the school to which they will react more adversely than inconsistent treatment in evaluation or grading. Our purpose here is not to suggest how students should be evaluated or graded but rather to emphasize that evaluation procedures must be fair and consistent and that grading procedures must be similar among the entire staff.

6. *Dress.* Few things have caused physical educators more problems than the enforcement of dress rules among their students. For some reason, the uniforms that physical educators choose seem to offend the sensibilities of adolescent boys and girls. If one teacher requires a uniform and another does not, then the problem escalates. Our suggestions are simple. The department should have rules about uniforms even if one rule is that students are allowed to wear whatever they like or even if a student group is allowed to choose a required uniform. Above all, do not let a seemingly silly issue like uniforms become a problem for the program. If you want to make a stand somewhere, do not choose the uniform issue as your "issue of principle."

7. *Discipline rules.* Chapter 19 stresses the need for basic rules of behavior in the gymnasium and on the playing field. Whatever the rules, they must be uniform across all classes and consistently enforced if consistently good behavior is to develop. Much of Chapter 19 focuses on how to go beyond mere conformance to a set of discipline rules to develop cooperative behavior among students.

Overall departmental routines are also useful and appropriate in other areas. The preceding examples are illustrative rather than definitive. A department that works together to develop and maintain routines in these and other behavioral areas will very quickly reap the reward of consistent treatment, which is consistent student behavior. Furthermore, a department that moves in this direction will have taken a major step toward developing a good program.

Executing the main managerial functions

If a department of more than two physical educators is to run smoothly and to accomplish its overall goals, some designated person must be responsible for certain important managerial functions. This is usually a departmental chairperson or a coordinator of physical education.

As departments grow in terms of faculty members and numbers of students served, the managerial dimensions grow accordingly. What follows is a very brief description of the important managerial functions that need to be attended to competently for a physical education program to work well.

1. *Planning.* There is always next term or next year. Certain things such as equipment acquisition and travel need to be planned well ahead of time. The more complex the program, the more difficult and time consuming the planning function. For example, planning an elective program for 2,500 high school students takes considerably more effort and time than planning a required program for 125 tenth graders.

2. *Budgeting.* School physical education programs spend money on equipment, travel, and extra personnel (for example, to pay for instruction at a local bowling alley or ski resort). Since only a limited amount of money is available, it needs to be budgeted wisely to achieve as much as possible.

3. *Staffing.* Who will teach the 10:00 A.M. class? Who will do the special unit on field archery? These are staffing questions and require managerial attention. Sometimes staffing is assigned by the central administration of a school, but in larger departments the physical educators are likely to have to provide staffing suggestions to the central office.

4. *Communicating.* One important and often overlooked managerial function is communication. We have emphasized in other places the need for teachers to communicate well with their students and the parents of students; Chapter 22 is devoted to ways in which the program can gain support through better communication. At the program level, messages need to be communicated among the staff, from the staff to school administrators, and from the staff to various outside constituencies such as parents, newspapers, and community recreation agencies. A clear, consistent, and positive flow of information is invaluable in developing and maintaining program quality.

5. *Reporting.* Schools have records. Student performance and attendance need to be reported accurately. Other departmental business needs to be reported to the school's administration. Many school administrators will quickly describe the crucial importance of filling out reports accurately and on time (they will also probably complain about the large number of them).

6. *Representing.* The physical education program needs to be represented to the central administration and on school committees, on community committees, and so on. The department chairperson does not necessarily always have to be the representative. The point is that "representing" is an important managerial function that should be carried out carefully and seriously. If the attitude is "whose turn is it to be on a committee?" then this function is unlikely to be carried out well.

7. *Coordinating.* Many things go on in schools. Many events are scheduled at the same time; many facilities have multiple uses. Someone (or some group) needs to coordinate these events and facilities so that they are used fairly and efficiently.

How these managerial functions get performed and by whom is really less important than that they are all taken seriously and performed well. If the department is large, it makes sense for *one* person to perform managerial functions and to be provided with some released time to do so. This role may rotate every several years, or it may be retained by the person who wants to do it and seems to do it well. Of course, the staff will feel more secure if they have had some say in who performs the managerial functions of the department.

Understanding the formal and informal organizations

Once education moved beyond the one-room schoolhouse, it necessarily became a more complex organization. Still, most American schools of 40 years ago had relatively simple organization charts and bureaucracies. Then came school consolidation. To develop a broader curriculum and offer more specialized teaching, small school districts were consolidated into larger school districts to create larger schools, especially high schools. The price that was paid for increased curricular flexibility and more specialized teaching was the creation of a larger, more complex organization and its accompanying bureaucracy.

Many suburban and urban schools today have large administrative staffs and enough bureaucracy to make life difficult at times for department leaders and faculty. By *bureaucracy* we mean an organization that has a defined hierarchy invested with relative amounts of power and a series of rules, practices, and regulations.

Bureaucracies are necessary for larger organizations to function, and they can be managed so as to make the job of the teacher *easier*. On the other hand, bureaucracies tend to be impersonal, authoritative, and resistant to change, thus often making the task of the teacher more difficult or at least more frustrating.

The *formal* aspects of an organization are defined by the relationships between and among elements in the organization and are typically portrayed on an organization chart. Thus, authority flows from the school board through the superintendent to the principals to the assistant principals to the department heads. When information flows up it should follow this defined set of pathways. (Every position in the organization has another position to which it reports and is responsible.) The nature of the formal organization is public and usually well understood. If a teacher violates this set of hierarchical authority relationships, he or she usually hears about it quickly and in no uncertain terms!

However, as organizations grow larger (and therefore more bureaucratic), they also tend to develop informal mechanisms for getting things done. The *informal organization* represents the channels among and between people and groups through which information flows and certain decisions are made. Now the actual decision appears to be made in the formal hierachy, but the groundwork for the decision is developed through informal networks of influence and power.

The informal organization does not show up on a chart. New teachers need to learn it as quickly as possible if they are to use it effectively and to avoid coming into conflict with it. Schools differ tremendously in terms of the relative power in the formal and informal organizations, but every school has some informal organization that makes an impact on decisions handed down through the more formal mechanisms of authority.

Staff morale

Physical education programs succeed as *programs* when the teachers are excited about what they are doing and when they strive constantly to maintain and further develop their efforts. This situation cannot be achieved without good staff morale. On the other hand, nothing can more quickly destroy the overall effects of a program than a disaffected staff, a group of teachers suffering from low morale.

Morale refers to an individual's attitudes toward the tasks expected of him or her within a group and his and her loyalty to that group. It is easy to discern high morale or low morale in a teaching staff as they go about their jobs on a day-to-day basis. One sees evidence of morale in the energy teachers expend in their teaching, in what they say to their students about the program, in how they talk to other teachers about the program, and in how they interact with other members of the physical education department.

Like most things in life, good morale is a quality that is typically *achieved* through direct efforts. Many of the suggestions made earlier in this chapter and throughout Part III of the text can help physical educators achieve better morale among a teaching staff. By attending to issues such as discipline, planning, and effective teaching as a group rather than on an individual basis, teachers bring the department together, contributing to a stronger sense of group purpose and, subsequently, to better morale.

Naturally, the department leader can help to promote better morale by working specifically to recognize and support the efforts of each staff member and to keep group morale in the forefront of each teacher's consciousness. Enthusiastic, competent leadership can also be infectious.

The peer panel. One method for developing and maintaining a professional atmosphere in which high morale can be sustained is the peer panel (Lawrence and Branch 1978). The notion of a peer panel grew out of teachers' efforts to cope with the many problems and changes that occurred in schools in the 1970s. A peer panel is a small group of teachers who give one another support and assistance. Successful peer panels seem to share the following characteristics:

- Membership is voluntary.
- There are no superordinate-subordinate relationships.
- Discussions are private except as agreed otherwise by all members.
- Members avoid evaluative judging of one another.
- Instead of evaluative judgment, members provide low-inference feedback to one another.
- The panel works only with an agenda that is on top of the table; no hidden agendas are pursued.
- The main tone of the group is built on empathy and mutual support.

Obviously, a peer panel meeting is not similar to a departmental meeting. The peer panel is for sharing and caring, for letting off steam, for discussing problems, and for getting help. It is a means for continued professional development and also provides a very basic group support system in which a member can get assistance when needed.

Members of peer panels avoid asking for assistance that is judgmental; that is, they would not ask, "What can I do to improve motivation?" Neither would others answer, "I think you should. . . ." Instead, they try to create low-inference feedback systems that still provide information. For example, one member may want to make sure that he is distributing his attention equitably among all students, so another member may go and code the interactions he has with students in an attempt to give him low-inference information relative to the teaching skill.

The privacy and intimacy of the peer panel allow members to express their frustrations and to help support one another in times of stress. The peer panel can also be a valuable mechanism for in-service education, as teachers try to program new activities, teach differently, or learn new skills themselves. Sometimes the discussion and effort will have a very personal focus, while at other times the focus will be instructional. Sometimes the task will be simple, while at other times it will be more complex. Figure 17.1 shows how these different issues can be categorized.

It is helpful for the members of the peer panel to be aware of the nature of the focus and the complexity of the issue before trying to address it.

Staying alive. In Chapter 6 we examined the problems of role conflict and teacher burnout. Many professionals are now beginning to focus seriously on the problems that are brought about by the lack of any career ladder in the teaching profession. (A career ladder exists when there are natural levels of advancement in which tasks may change and rewards become greater.) A first-year teacher and a 15-year veteran teacher may have exactly the same job description, and the basic job does not change from year to year. Clearly, it is difficult to do the same job year in and year out and still stay enthused and energetic in the performance of its tasks. Thus, it is of crucial importance to the ongoing vitality of the physical education program that we find ways to

		Instructional	Personal
ISSUES	Simple	A different way to teach the tennis serve	To increase one's knowledge about using praise effectively
	Complex	To plan, teach, and evaluate a unit on team handball	To change one's attitudes toward "culturally different" students

Figure 17.1 Examples of different issues for peer panel consideration.

SOURCE: Adapted from McNergney 1980.

help teachers stay alive, to remain involved with their teaching and continue to be energetic and enthused about their own work.

It may seem odd to delineate this issue in a chapter devoted to the managerial aspects of the physical education program, but the ongoing morale of teachers is an absolutely necessary ingredient in program success. There have been many suggestions for helping teachers to stay alive in their jobs, and some of these are mentioned in Chapter 6.

Telling teachers to read professional journals and attend conventions in order to stay involved is not a very powerful remedy for this very real problem. We believe that every teacher needs basic changes in routine. We believe that departments of physical education, in high schools particularly, would do well to develop some rotational scheme in which members have a different assignment every two to three years, one that allows them to do something new and challenging. We also believe that mechanisms such as the peer panel can help people to stay alive with their teaching. Most of all, we believe that teachers who become involved in attempting to sustain good programs in which students demonstrate improvement and performance are most likely to be rewarded by what they are doing. Providing custodial care for groups of adolescents five or six hours a day is not a task worthy of a professional person—and those physical educators who only provide custodial care are merely creating conditions in which they will grow increasingly disaffected themselves. It is a vicious cycle that once started is hard to interrupt. There are no "magic" formulas to prevent this from happening or to remediate it once it has begun. It takes effort and that effort has to be recognized and supported so that teachers making the effort are motivated to continue to do so.

Summary

In terms of the effects of a program, the whole is greater than the sum of its parts. When all teachers attempt to contribute to program goals, the result is more than simply the addition of individual efforts.

Good programs share several important characteristics whether they are fitness programs, sports programs, social development programs, or whatever. Good programs use time wisely, maintain physically and psychologically safe learning environments, maintain and make readily available appropriate equipment, require and support sustained student effort in classes, hold students accountable for performance, keep adequate records, allow students to have input into program evaluation, and communicate high morale to students through teaching that is enthusiastic and active.

To develop and maintain good physical education programs, members of the teaching staff need to attend to several important managerial functions. They need to plan carefully and well ahead of time, budget wisely to achieve optimum use of available resources, staff classes for the mutual benefit of students and teachers, communicate effectively among themselves and with their various constituencies, report accurately and on time, represent their program vigorously, and coordinate the use of facilities, equipment, and people to be both equitable and efficient.

Successful physical education programs utilize both the formal and informal organizations of the school. They discriminate accurately and professionally the kinds of issues and decisions that need to be attended to in the formal and informal organizations.

Finally, successful programs are the product of high staff morale. Although the peer panel is a useful strategy for developing and maintaining high morale, it is certainly not the only strategy available. Physical educators need to stay alive in their jobs. They need teaching conditions that motivate them to continue to want to teach well.

Suggested activities

1. Draw up your own list of the top five characteristics of good physical education programs. After all lists have been collated, discuss the characteristics in class.

2. Take the list of indicators of a good program on page 312 and visit a local school. Note the presence or absence of each indicator. Use the field results for class discussion.

3. Obtain an organization chart from a local school district. Examine the formal organization in terms of chain of command. Discuss where the informal organization might conflict with the formal chain of command.

4. Describe a situation of "high morale" in your school or sports experience. After other class members have described similar situations, try to generalize the characteristics of such situations. How might those characteristics be established in a physical education program?

18

Planning Units and Lessons

This chapter provides guidelines and suggestions to assist the teacher in planning effective instruction. One needs to practice the skills of planning, just like sports skills, to improve. People preparing to teach often become frustrated with the amount of time required for effective planning, but teaching is only teaching if students learn what teachers intend that they should learn. There is no better way to promote the opportunity for learning than by detailed planning.

This chapter initially focuses on planning a total unit of instruction and then addresses the matter of preparing and reviewing individual lesson plans. The major topics are as follows:

The importance of planning as a teaching skill

Preplanning considerations

Assessing student needs

Developing instructional goals for a unit

Task analysis and other concerns related to unit planning

Preparing and using lesson plans

The quality of teaching in physical education differs from school to school. Obviously, teachers do not all have the same motivation. Neither are all teachers held accountable in the same ways. Today more is known about effective teaching than ever before, and people both inside and outside the education profession believe that accountability for teaching performance needs to be sharpened. It is likely that student teachers will increasingly be held accountable by their college or university programs for good teaching performance. In fact, student teachers may experience stronger accountability measures during that experience than when they are on their first job. People should be required to show effective teaching performance *before* they are certified.

Planning is crucial to effective teaching, but it is not a panacea in and of itself. All teachers experience that rare moment when a well-planned lesson collapses! More commonly, however, a collapse is the result of inadequate planning.

Given a situation in which one teacher is asked to teach 50 students once a week, good planning will achieve only limited results. The constraints on student learning produced by large numbers and a small amount of time minimize what can be learned—although even in this poor situation, *something* can be accomplished.

On the other hand, when a teacher has 25 students and meets with them four times a week, we can reasonably expect a substantial amount of student learning to occur. If it does not, then both planning and other teaching skills should be called into question. The questions one might ask in this situation are similar to those teachers must ask themselves as they plan.

- What were the students supposed to achieve?
- What planning was done to secure that achievement?
- What strategies/activities were arranged to secure the achievement?
- How would anyone know if the achievement had occurred or not?

The importance of planning

CHARACTERS

CHRIS   *a student teacher*

MR. NICHOLS   *a cooperating teacher*

PROFESSOR ALI   *a university supervisor*

CHRIS   Mr. Nichols, here's my lesson plan for tomorrow's class.

MR. NICHOLS   *(quickly glancing at the lesson plan)* Looks great, Chris. Those professors certainly make you plan. Can't remember if I ever did that much planning. I do remember those behavioral objectives though.

CHRIS   Yes, they're tough to write.

MR. NICHOLS   Guess you're right. I wonder if you'll ever use them again once you leave college.

CHRIS   Do you think the lesson will work? Are the drills and activities appropriate for your class?

MR. NICHOLS   Should work all right. Just give it a try tomorrow, and we'll see. I don't find a lot of use for lesson plans nowadays, but I think you need them early on. In this school, things never seem to go as they're planned, so planning doesn't make much sense.

CHRIS   That's interesting. All I know is that the unit plan and these lesson plans take a lot of work. It makes teaching hard. You know, when I chose physical education as a major I made the choice because I thought teaching would be fun.

MR. NICHOLS   I know what you mean.

The next day, after CHRIS*'s lesson.*

PROFESSOR ALI   Well, Chris, you should feel pleased. The class went well. What did you think?

CHRIS   Thanks. I was a bit nervous when I saw you were here, but I knew what I wanted them to do, so I just stuck at it, and most of them did it.

PROFESSOR ALI   Let's have a look at your lesson plan *(pause)* looks good. The drills are clearly diagrammed and you set them up exactly as you planned them. The students enjoyed having to change hands—you could see them really concentrating, but after it was all done they smiled. They enjoyed being challenged. The transition time between the first and second drills was a little long but you can change that by setting up the cones while the students are checking off their scores. O.K., Chris, what comments would you like to make now that you've planned and taught a PE lesson?

CHRIS   Well, I'm glad it went well, but all that time and planning for one 40-minute lesson. I can't imagine doing that for six classes every day. And those behavioral objectives!

PROFESSOR ALI   Yes, they're a bit of a pain if you don't realize their significance. Remember when I asked what you thought about the class? You said, "I knew what I wanted them to do . . . and most of them did it." And that fact made you feel good. I think that's because you had an objective and at least partially achieved it. Your planning and its implementation enabled the students to achieve something.

CHRIS   Maybe you're right. I hadn't thought of it that way. It's interesting that Mr. Nichols never—*(Chris stops suddenly, as if biting his tongue).*

PROFESSOR ALI   Remember, anyone can wing a decent lesson once or twice, and you might have made it through today with less planning, but after a few unplanned lessons, physical education frequently becomes supervised recreation. Your lesson was much more than that. Your planning ensured that the students were required to practice and so they had a chance to learn. You won't always have to plan in such detail, but remember you're only a beginning teacher, and today, because you planned and the students learned, you felt like a teacher. It's hard to feel like a teacher if there's no learning going on.

Similar scenes take place every day as student teachers learn about the "real" world. It would be foolish to suggest that all physical education teachers plan extensively. However, it is clear that beginning teachers need to plan extensively if they want to teach well. Once a teacher prepares thoroughly and teaches well for a number of years, the need for extensive planning may diminish. Yet, even an effective veteran teacher will plan extensively when taking on a new activity.

Sometimes student teachers get caught between the demands placed on them by their college or university and a different set of expectations held by a cooperating teacher in a school. In the situation above, the expectations of the university preparation program are greater. But the opposite can also be true. Sometimes effective teachers serving as cooperating teachers are appalled at the lack of planning required by the preparation program.

Planning in detail is not always fun. But it does have a payoff, and it certainly appears to be a part of what effective teachers do!

Planning is a teaching skill that can be mastered by all physical educators, and when it is judiciously applied in the context of motor skills, it can really make a difference in student participation and achievement. Just as the exercise physiologist prescribes a specific exercise regimen for a cardiac patient and a physical therapist mandates an exercise program for the injured athlete, so should the professional teacher plan for optimal learning conditions in a physical education class. Both the exercise physiologist and the physical therapist set particular objectives and then plan interventions to promote the achievement of those objectives by their clients. Physical educators should also set learning objectives and plan interventions (lessons) to promote their achievement. Although adolescent clients may not be as compliant as the cardiac patient and the injured athlete, they are capable learners and teachers must provide them with the opportunity to learn. Planning avails them of this opportunity.

Unit planning

SCENE *An eighth-grade physical education teacher is instructing a tennis class.*

TEACHER   Today we'll begin our tennis unit. This is your third tennis unit, so I'm expecting to see some shots that Martina Navratilova would be proud of. It's good to see everyone dressed and ready to go.

Please pick up your rackets and form a semicircle in front of me. . . . Now let's begin.

Place your racket on the ground in front of you. Now, one person in each pair, pick up your partner's racket and offer it handle first. Next grasp the racket in one hand so that the V between your thumb and forefinger is on the top of the handle, like this *(shows grip)*. Repeat this four or five times. . . . Good job; it's going well. Place the rackets on the ground. Now let's see the other partner pick up the racket and repeat the same procedure. Remember to keep the V between your thumb and forefinger on the top of the handle. Always check this.

All right, let's practice these three drills for the next 10 minutes to make sure everyone can grip the racket correctly.

This lesson introduction, although very thorough, reflects poorly on physical education. The third tennis unit in physical education should be more than the shake-hands grip. If students learn tennis skills in the sixth grade and more tennis skills in the seventh grade, then why are they still being taught the basic shake-hands grip in the eighth grade? Unfortunately, other frequently taught units such as basketball and volleyball suffer the same fate.

If unit plans are thoroughly prepared, coordination and monitoring of all units taught in a particular program prevent the previous scenario. Figure 18.1 shows an activity card to monitor each student's progress in physical

Physical Education Unit Activity Card

Greythorn High School

Name:

Irene Phillips

Date of Birth:

April 16, 1972

	1983	1984	1985
Grade	6 ^{C}	7 ^{B}	8 ^{A}
Height	66"	67"	68"
Weight	118 lb	121 lb	126 lb
Fitness rating	top 10%	top 10%	top 10%

*Activity Unit**	*Level*	*When*	*Skills Achieved*	*Teacher*
1. Basketball	Basic	Fall '83	A	J. Sipman
2. Fitness	Basic	Fall '83	A	J. Sipman
3. Swimming	Basic	Fall '83	C	J. Sipman
4. Badminton	Basic	Winter '84	D	J. Sipman
5. Square dancing	Basic	Winter '84	C	D. Priestly
6. Fitness	Inter.	Spring '84	A	D. Priestly
7. Softball	Basic	Spring '84	A	D. Priestly
8. Cricket (2 weeks)	Basic	Spring '84	B	J. Sipman
9. Basketball†	Inter.	Spring '84	B	J. Sipman
10. Tennis	Basic	Fall '84	D	D. Priestly
11. Basketball	Adv.	Fall '84	B	J. Sipman

*All activity units are for 16 lessons (4 weeks) unless otherwise specified.
†Elective units

Figure 18.1 A cumulative activity card.

education. It offers a checklist for student performance that can be completed at the end of each unit. This type of data is essential when electives and forced-choice options are available to students.

Sound program organization, administration, and management can promote effective planning. Before pondering the actual content of a unit to be taught, physical educators should be aware of several preplanning considerations. It is to these that we now turn.

Preplanning considerations

In Chapter 8, we showed how the planning process relates to a program philosophy. If a program philosophy accurately reflects the needs of the students being taught, the local community, and the school, the choice of each unit of instruction will be soundly based. It is important that the choice of a unit of instruction be based on more than a passing whim of the teacher.

The content of physical education is extremely varied. As society changes, new activities are added—for example, the martial arts—whereas some activities are deleted—for example, folk dance. One would hope that such additions and deletions also reflect the program philosophy. Once activities have been chosen, the next planning step is to describe the *unit of instruction*, henceforth known as the *unit*.

The unit in a school physical education program can last for 2 to 10 weeks and include 4 to 40 lessons. For most units of instruction 15 45-minute lessons would appear to be adequate. In planning for a brief or extended unit, the teacher must take many considerations into account.

Teacher motivation, interest, and ability. Does the motivation of a teacher affect teaching performance? Do teachers do a better job when they have a personal interest in the activity? Obviously, the answer is often yes to both questions. Good planning is often the result of high motivation and interest. When planning assignments are made within a department, it makes sense to consider the interests of the various teachers.

Nevertheless, most physical education programs include many activities, and inevitably teachers must plan for activities in which they have less interest. While this chore may be harder, it still needs to be done well. It is a narrow physical education program when choice of units reflects one teacher's interest. The physical education staff cannot afford to lose sight of the program philosophy when choosing what content to teach.

The ability of a teacher to perform the skills being taught also needs to be rationalized when content is being adopted for the curriculum. Consider teacher A is a gymnast, teacher B is a volleyballer. If they know their particular subject matter well and teach it well, should their students have two or three units every year on volleyball and gymnastics? If a four-week unit on team handball is scheduled, what happens if the teacher has never played it? Teachers of physical education cannot be masters of all activities. However, they do have a responsibility to keep up-to-date and continue to develop professionally by attending in-service programs and conferences. Teaching and planning competencies are skills that can provide the necessary support mechanisms for teachers to introduce activities in which they are not experts.

Class time and season. Should basketball be taught before and during basketball season? What can my students achieve now that they have 80-minute classes? Is there any point in having a fitness unit when we have a 30-minute class each week? Time is a vital resource for teachers, and in physical education it is unfortunately one of the things that there is just too little of. (Sound familiar?) With time limited, planning well becomes even more important.

Facilities and equipment.   Whoever heard of teaching gymnastics without a balance beam? Why must I teach basketball in half a gym? These balls just don't bounce properly! Good facilities and equipment can add polish to a program, but they do not make or break a program. Many inexpensive, easy-to-make kinds of equipment are available to the resourceful teacher. Still, facilities limitations may make it necessary for two classes that meet on Monday at 2:00 P.M. to participate in different units, say, basketball in the gym and table tennis in a rarely traveled corridor, at one end of the gym, or in the weight room. Planning the yearly sequence of units is essential in this case.

Class size.   There are 64 students and just two teachers in the gym. Should they team teach or split the group? What about girls and boys in separate classes? Departments usually have rules about coed classes. If there is team teaching, planning must be a joint effort; too often it becomes the responsibility of no one.

With these preplanning considerations in mind, we turn next to the essential elements of a unit plan.

Essential elements of a unit plan

We recommend that you prepare a detailed unit plan as you read this chapter. You will need to attend to the following matters as you prepare your plan.

1. Planning for whom? A needs assessment
2. Developing instructional goals
3. Motor skills task analysis
4. Unit outline
5. Arrangement of resources
6. Motivation
7. Behavior management strategies
8. Monitoring and evaluating the unit

The needs assessment.   Physical education has a great deal to offer the developing adolescent. However, adolescent students are often at very different points in their physical, social, and emotional development. Thus, they have different needs, and physical educators must take these needs into consideration when planning activity experiences for adolescents.

The activity unit card shown in Figure 18.1 can provide an ongoing record of student participation and performance. Details such as this can limit the chance of students' being introduced to the shake-hands grip three years in a row. If the activity unit card is kept up-to-date during middle school or junior high and the information from it is given to high school teachers, they very quickly get an idea of the students' activity backgrounds. The high school teachers have some useful data to build a program that complements and develops the skills students have already acquired. Remember, however, that many students now take part in private-sector physical education. The information on the activity unit card will not tell it all.

SCENE PAT, *a student teacher, is discussing the upcoming seventh-grade gymnastics unit with* MS. KIM, *the cooperating teacher.*

PAT Ms. Kim, I'm starting to plan this gymnastics unit. What ability level can I expect?

MS. KIM They're only seventh graders, so you have to start with the basics. You know, forward rolls, backward rolls, dinner rolls—sorry—and maybe a few simple balances.

PAT Yes, I guess that's what I thought I'd do.

Third day of the gymnastics unit.

PAT Class, we've just completed our first week in the gymnastics unit, and it's obvious that we have a very wide range of abilities here. Several of you need some more advanced activities. Now hands up if you've belonged or do belong to a gym club. *(Of the class of 27, 10 girls and 2 boys put their hands up.)* I see. Would each of you 12 students take a copy of this checklist and indicate which skills you can perform. This'll tell me where you are and help me in my planning.

Pat showed insight, or rather professional skill, in determining that much of what she was teaching was too easy for some of the students. Pat did not want to turn off the good performers but to keep them active and to challenge them. Her decision to have them complete a needs assessment was a wise one. Ideally, students should have completed this assessment before the first lesson, but unfortunately the information given by the cooperating teacher suggested otherwise.

Pat showed that planning can be used to facilitate instruction even after a unit has begun. Again, the best time to complete a needs assessment is before the unit, but better late than never. Data from a needs assessment typically suggests the need for individualization. It is difficult for Pat to individualize with a class of 27, especially in an activity like gymnastics where safety is an important concern. Nevertheless, Pat has demonstrated professional competence by showing that individuals do matter in a physical education class.

Teachers can assess student needs in several ways. *First,* they can *ask students directly* about an upcoming unit. Secondary school students are capable of accurately reporting their skill status if they are given specific information about what the skill is and how well it should be performed. However, general questions such as "Can you play volleyball?" provide little meaningful data on which to base planning. Although informal questions may provide some interesting attitudinal information regarding an upcoming unit, a more thorough approach is recommended.

Second, teachers can *formally assess entry skills*; that is, they can have students complete a quick battery of skills tests. If students have the appropriate self-management skills, they can even check one another on the basis of explicit criteria provided by a teacher. Alternatively, the teacher can conduct an assessment for a seventh-grade volleyball unit for students who completed basic volleyball in the sixth grade by placing the students in a modified three-on-three game in which the volleyball can bounce once in each team's court. Within 10 or 15 minutes the well-prepared teacher with a checklist can assess the skill and strategy execution of each member of the class. This form of entry skill assessment also provides a useful orientation or scene setter for the new unit.

Third, teachers can *consult the physical education records*. Those who teach at schools that maintain reliable records of student skill levels may find it unnecessary to complete a formal needs assessment. The activity unit card is invaluable in this case.

Fourth, teachers can *refer to the curriculum*. In a physical education program that demands a mastery level of performance, teachers need only consult the curriculum or syllabus, locate the behavioral objectives, and identify the specific skills and how well they are to be completed to discover what minimal skills all of the students possess. The teachers then begin at the next level so that the next set of objectives can be achieved. That is what a curriculum is all about. It should indicate where the students are at any particular time.

Fifth, teachers can *confer with teachers at local feeder schools*. High school teachers should know what happens in the physical education program for middle school students in the local district. Similarly, middle school teachers need to be aware of the elementary programs that exist in the schools that feed students to their program. It is quite possible for junior high/middle school teachers to identify with an amazing degree of accuracy which students come from which elementary school. Many schools have particularly strong programs in specific areas, and this is reflected in both the performance and interest of their students. Communicating with feeder schools can further help to eliminate the syndrome of the shake-hands tennis grip.

With the needs assessment completed, teachers should have a sound idea of student entry behaviors for each unit of instruction. Given this important information, they can set an instructional goal and begin to analyze that goal.

Instructional goals. Physical education is more than just teaching motor skills. However, motor skills and strategies are what we try to teach most often, and they best represent the subject matter. The skills taught generally form part of an activity that combines many skills involved in the games, sports, and dance forms that characterize physical education programs in schools.

For every unit of instruction teachers must first determine *instructional goals* that anticipate what the students will achieve. That is, teachers must formulate a statement that indicates what the students can be expected to do at the end of the unit. Clear instructional goals allow teachers to hold students accountable and also to measure their own instructional performance. The unit plan should include clear instructional goal statements, and these should be communicated to students. Here are two examples.

1. Students will demonstrate basic forehand, backhand, and serving skills in a competitive game of singles tennis.
2. Students will participate in a modified game of basketball, performing passing, dribbling, and one-on-one defense and offense strategies.

An instructional goal is not a statement outlining the information that a teacher will convey about a topic. It is an indicator of what students will be able to do or have actually learned as a result of having received instruction. Remember, the more exact instructional goals are, the greater the chances of success. Teachers should establish goals that are achievable by most students who practice hard. Planning is all about promoting success; in fact, it makes success less of a chance occurrence. In this context, a functional instructional goal for a seventh-grade introductory volleyball unit might be "Students will successfully participate in a four-on-four game of volleyball, adhering to all rules and game modifications."

Many instructional goals for students reflect performance in a game or modified game situation. Teachers can quickly determine such goals once they have administered a needs assessment.

The task analysis process.   The real test of professional skills comes once an appropriate instructional goal has been formulated. The important planning skill of analyzing an instructional goal is known as an instructional or task analysis. The procedure involves considering the goal in depth and systematically breaking it down into a series of interconnected subskills commonly known as subordinate skills. The task analysis process is occasionally performed intuitively by some teachers and coaches. Once completed, it allows a teacher to organize activities that will advance students from the lower level (simple) skills to the higher level (more complex) skills.

In the task analysis (T.A.) process, the teacher asks the following question (the T.A. question):

In terms of my instructional goal, what would the learner have to do to perform this task?

The answer to this question is generally to master a series of subskills. Consider the example below.

Instructional goal: Students will demonstrate basic forehand, backhand, and serving skills in a competitive game of singles tennis.
Answer to T.A. question: Students will perform forehand strokes, backhand strokes, and serving and demonstrate scoring and knowledge of rules. (Note each of these is a subskill.)

To continue the task analysis, the teacher must ask the same T.A. question again, this time for each of the new subskills. Remember, the T.A. question is *What would the learner have to do in order to perform this task (the subskill)?* An instructional goal can be written for each of these subskills, and as the components of the initial goal are refined, more precise statements about each subskill are appropriate. Behavioral objectives for each subskill best meet the need for greater precision. Remember, all four of the subskills identified in our example must be performed by the student before the instructional goal is achieved. Note that the instructional goal does not demand performance of the overhead smash, so this is not identified as a subskill in the task analysis. The instructional goal does, however, demand performance of the skills in a competitive game; therefore, scoring and knowledge of rules become a relevant subskill.

When the first T.A. question is posed, it sometimes identifies subskills that are not but should be included in the goal statement. When this happens, the teacher needs to alter the instructional goal, that is, broaden its focus so that it includes all essential subskills.

Task analysis is not just identifying the common skills and then planning to teach them. This becomes apparent when the teacher asks the T.A. question for each subskill and, if necessary, for each subsubskill. The T.A. question can be asked again and again; in fact, some preschool and kindergarten teachers who teach motor skills do just that. One of the skills identified when the T.A. question is asked again and again is the demonstration of basic hand-eye coordination. Fortunately, secondary school physical education teachers rarely have to teach for skills at this low level, but the value of a detailed task analysis is that it can take the skill analysis this far if the learners require it.

Dick and Carey (1985) have introduced several ways to diagram a task analysis. A tennis example is shown in Figure 18.2 (p. 332). Note that the T.A. question is only asked twice. If the question were repeated, more subskills would be systematically identified. How many times one needs to ask the T.A. question is determined by the data from a needs assessment—that is, where students are in relation to the instructional goal the teacher sets before teaching the unit. Note that each subskill box in the task analysis diagram is stated in behavioral (observable) terms.

A task analysis diagrammed in this way is referred to as a *hierarchical analysis*, and each subskill in level 1 must be performed before the instructional goal can be achieved. Similarly, each subskill in level 2 is an essential component for the performance of its corresponding skill in level 1. A hierarchical analysis is appropriate when it is impossible for students to learn the components of one skill without first learning those of a preceding skill. We can show the significance of this form of learning dependence more clearly by asking the T.A. question again. This time we ask the T.A. question for only one of the subskills in level 2, performing forehand ground strokes. See Figure 18.3, page 333.

A hierarchical task analysis for a fitness unit (circuit/weight training) is diagrammed in Figure 18.4, page 334.

If the skill to be learned involves a step-by-step series of subskills that must be performed in an ordered sequence to achieve an instructional goal, then a *procedural analysis* is appropriate (Dick and Carey 1985). The best way to perform a procedural task analysis is to "walk through" all the steps required to perform the task. A motor skill well suited to such an analysis is the for-

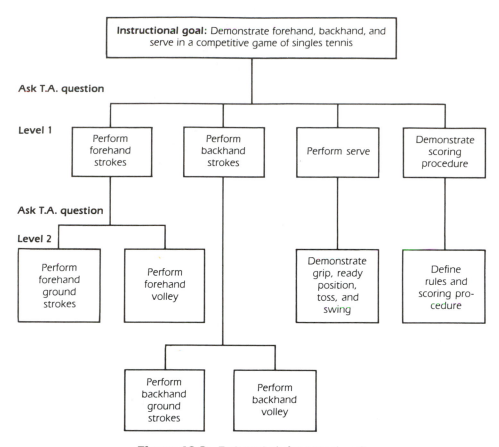

Figure 18.2 Task analysis for a tennis unit.

ward roll in gymnastics. See Figure 18.5 (p. 335). Note that each subskill iden-tified in Figure 18.5 is independent of the other skills for its own completion. The sequential completion of skills 1 through 8 is, however, crucial.

Remember: In a procedural analysis each subskill can be viewed as a sepa-rate (independent) skill not consuming the previous subskill but adding to it; in a hierarchical analysis each lower-level subskill is consumed by (part of) each higher-level skill.

Most task analyses can be diagrammed with either a hierarchical or a pro-cedural approach. However, it is sometimes appropriate to combine the two. This approach is logically called a *combinational task analysis* (Dick and Carey 1985). A combinational task analysis is diagrammed in Figure 18.6, page 336.

Completing a detailed task analysis is not an easy process; however, if teachers keep asking the T.A. question, they will eventually overcome the dif-ficulties. Remember that there is no one correct task analysis. Different sub-ject experts may analyze the same instructional goal in slightly different ways. But the differences are frequently only a matter of degree; that is, to what level does one need to go in a task analysis?

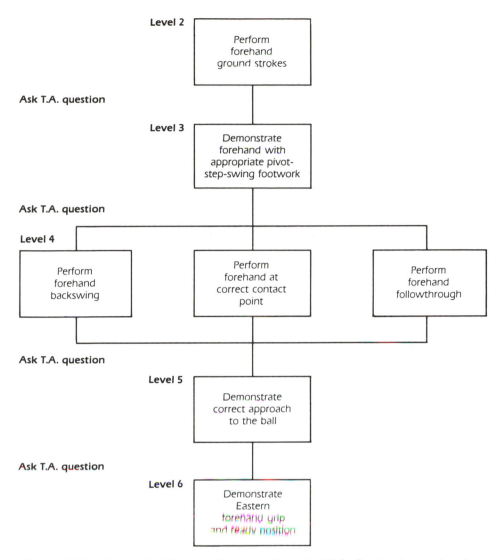

Figure 18.3 Task analysis for a tennis unit detailing subskills for forehand ground strokes.

The degree of specificity of a task analysis for a skill to be performed by handicapped students is much greater than that for nonhandicapped students. Development of an I.E.P. (individualized educational plan) requires that a very detailed task analysis be completed for every skill that is to be taught.

Task analysis skills are important in planning and when used consistently can help to promote more effective instruction. For activities with which the teacher is familiar, the task analysis of skills and strategies will come quite easily. However, many different activities are taught in school programs, and

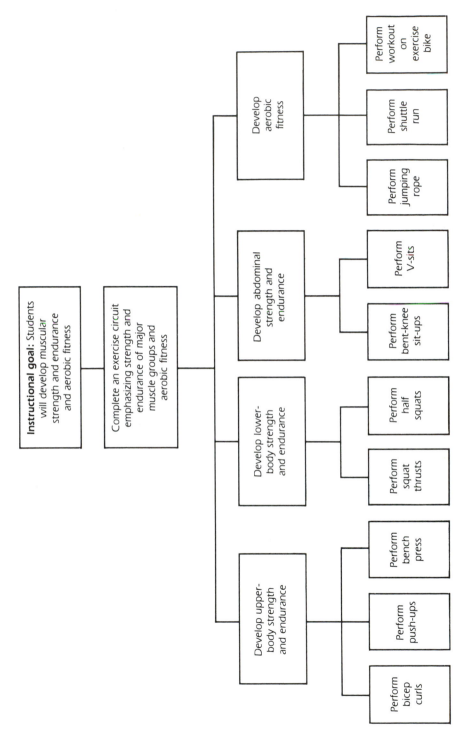

Figure 18.4 Task analysis for a fitness unit.

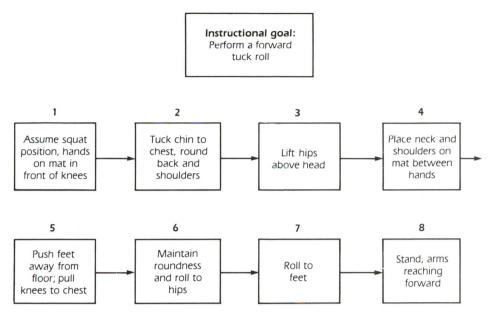

Figure 18.5 Task analysis for a forward tuck roll.

no one person can be accomplished in all of them. Therefore, the time will come when teachers need to do task analyses for activities with which they are much less familiar. In these cases, teachers should consult the many resources and books pertaining to those activities to develop realistic goals and acquire the information necessary to pose the T.A. question. In fact, there are few ways in which a teacher can get to know an activity more quickly than by doing a task analysis. Asking the T.A. question again and again will bring the teacher into contact with the skills and progressions needed to teach the activity to novice learners.

Behavioral objectives. Once the task analysis is completed and diagrammed, the next planning step is to write behavioral objectives for each subskill identified. The term *behavioral objectives* is equivalent to the instructional objectives, terminal objectives, consequence objectives, and skill objectives. The purpose of behavioral objectives is to communicate a precise instructional intent by describing what will happen as a result of the proposed instructional experience. Objectives are more specific than goals. They include details that make the reader understand exactly what the students will be able to do at the instruction's end.

Clear objectives have three components: the actual *task* or *behavior* to be performed, the *situation* or *conditions* under which it will be performed, and the *criteria* by which it will be judged. Consider the following behavioral objective for a tennis skill: "From the baseline after a self-drop, the student shall

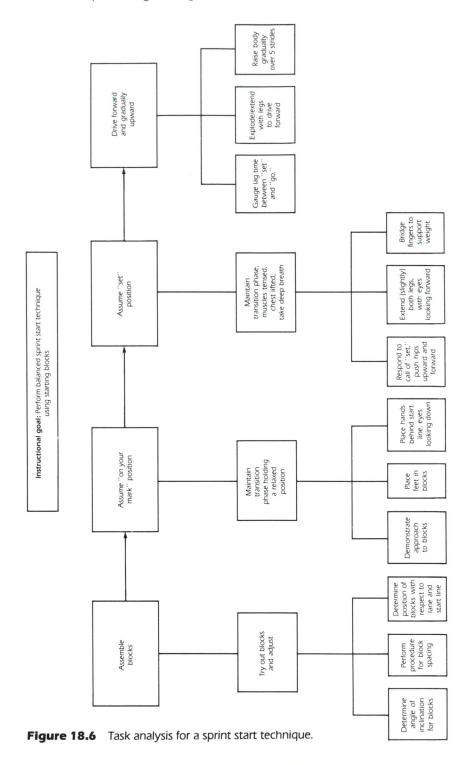

Figure 18.6 Task analysis for a sprint start technique.

stroke 10 forehands consecutively into the area marked on the fence." The behavior (task) is italicized. The *forehand stroke* is a clear, unambiguous, observable task. The situation or condition under which the task will be performed, "from the baseline after a self-drop," communicates all pertinent details. The criteria for task completion is that the ball must be hit 10 times consecutively "into the area marked on the fence," so there should be no problem in judging the performance.

Behavioral objectives that include task, situation, and criteria allow the planning process to proceed with purpose and direction. This, in turn, enables the accountability concerns for both teacher and student to be addressed. Behavioral objectives for motor, cognitive, and affective skills should all be written in this way.

Learning activities.   The behavioral objectives that derive from the subskills identified in the task analysis provide almost all the necessary ingredients for designing the learning activities that form a major part of most instructional units. For each objective or cluster of objectives, specific drills and modified games must be developed so that students are provided with ample practice of the skill being taught. If all drills and modified games have their origin in the task analysis, then systematic progress in terms of skill refinement is ensured.

Participation in modified games represents a crucial link in the development of skills. Teachers must design modified games so that the individual subskills students have already achieved are gradually incorporated into the more complex competitive situation. Drills that incorporate a competitive element can readily be transformed into modified games.

Putting together the essential elements.   The unit planning sequence of (a) developing an instructional goal, (b) completing a task analysis and identifying subskills, (c) stating behavioral objectives, and (d) designing learning activities outlines almost the entire planning process. The following example from a unit of basketball should make this clear.

(a) Instructional goal:	Students will participate in a three-on-three half-court game of basketball with an emphasis on defensive skills.
(b) Task analysis (see Figure 18.7):	Subskills shown in Figure 18.7, pp. 338–339.
Subskill from task analysis:	Perform boxing out skill.
(c) Behavioral objective for subskill:	In a mock rebounding situation (*situation*), students will box out an opponent (*task*) by making initial body contact, maintaining a low wide stance with arms in defensive position in preparation for rebound (*criteria*).

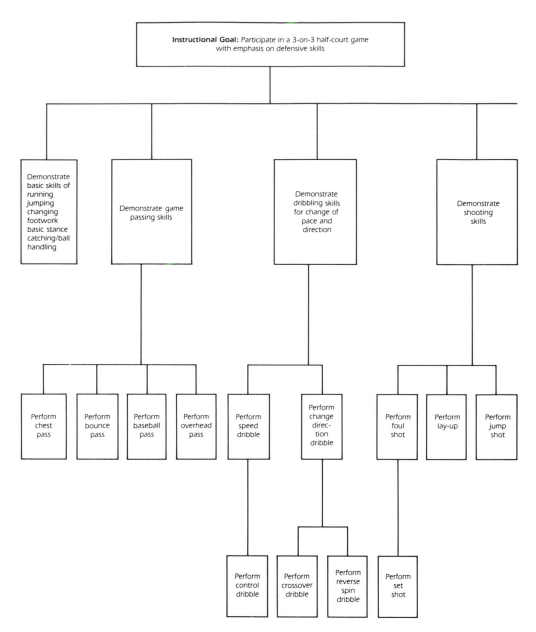

Figure 18.7 Task analysis for a basketball unit.

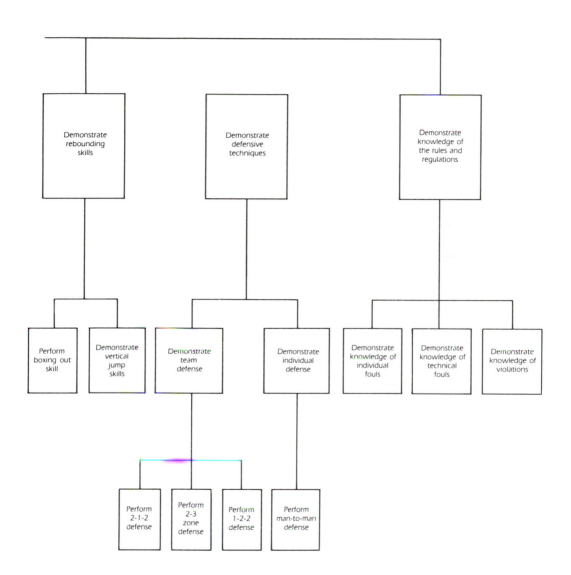

(d) Learning activity for subskill:

(1) Boxing out a partner; no ball. Partner (o) attempts to move in front of defender (x) on whistle or call of "shot's up." Defender (x) boxes out partner (o) to gain front rebounding position.

Basket

0

```
 x          x      x = defensive
 o  x  x  o        o = offensive
    o  o                player
```

(2) As in (1) above, with addition of each offensive partner (o) putting up a shot in turn.

After completing the unit planning sequence, the teacher prepares a unit outline/block plan for the basketball unit. The plan illustrated in Figure 18.8 shows the first 3 lessons of a 12-lesson unit for eighth graders; classes meet on alternate days for 40 minutes.

Chris and Pat, the student teachers who were concerned about the time and effort needed for planning units and lessons, may be pleased to know that after a year or two of detailed planning and diagramming task analyses, a teacher may come to rely on a block plan as her or his major guide. However, effective teaching for beginning teachers requires detailed unit and lesson planning.

Additional concerns related to unit planning

Good unit planning also involves the organization and management of resources, strategies for motivating students and managing their behavior, and monitoring and evaluating units.

Arrangement of resources. Teachers who plan generally focus on the motor skills to be taught. Planning for things other than content skills is rare. However, the organization and management of resources at a teacher's disposal have a more significant impact on the success of a unit than the organization of its content. That is, it is more important to arrange the marker cones for drills and the number of balls per student than it is to teach dribbling before passing or vice versa in a basketball unit. Teachers should direct all planning toward the optimal arrangement of their human (students), material (equipment), and temporal (time) resources. By considering the number of students in the class, the equipment available, and the amount of activity time allocated, teachers can increase the likelihood of achieving a well-integrated and cohesive unit.

Without detailing every specific strategy at a teacher's disposal, it is important that we identify areas worthy of particular attention in terms of optimal resource arrangement.

Monday	Tuesday	Wednesday	Thursday	Friday
Lesson 1 Introduction Practice self-management skills (relays, formations) *Basic skills:* running, jumping, footwork, stance, catching Drills (n = 33)	Same as Monday but with a different class. (n = 24)	*Lesson 2* *Passing:* chest, bounce, baseball, overhead Drills *Modified game:* introduce traveling and 5-second rule	Same as Wednesday but with a different class	*Lesson 3* Modified passing game *Dribbling:* speed, control, change of pace, crossover. Drills *Rules:* double dribble, palming, hacking, charging

Figure 18.8 A block plan for basketball.

Communicating what is to be learned. Consider the first day of a unit, each new subskill, and setting up drills and modified games.

Maximizing opportunities to respond. Consider equipment ratio, apparatus ratio, time occupied by instruction/demonstration, feedbacks and hustles, activity (number of trials per student), waiting time expected, off-task behavior, and changing activities (transitions).

Providing feedback. Consider clarity, frequency, form (information, hustle, behavior), who provides it (teacher, student), and whether it is artificial or intrinsic.

If a teacher carefully considers the arrangement of resources, it is unlikely that a class will ever be characterized by two lines of 15 students waiting patiently for their chance to try a lay-up or by 30 students playing dribble tag with one ball.

Student motivation strategies. "I just can't get these students going; they lack motivation when they get to the gym." Does that complaint sound familiar? It is true that adolescents are not the most predictable human beings and that in a confined environment like the school this unpredictability may be increased. Nevertheless, physical educators can motivate adolescents; in fact, many teachers do so consistently with the same activities that other teachers say will not motivate adolescents. How then can instruction, drills, and modified games be planned so that students run into the gym ready to get moving and work intensely on improving their skills?

Two major motivational issues need to be attended to in order to increase the likelihood that adolescent students will get turned on to physical education. First, it helps tremendously if the units and lessons are interesting and challenging to students and provide success for them if they make a decent effort. Adolescents enjoy success. Who doesn't! If teachers plan interesting activities and arrange them so that students are challenged by them but also achieve success in them, part of the motivational problem will be solved. Second, teachers need to build a positive climate in physical education. *Climate* refers to the social-emotional fabric of the class. A positive climate develops when teachers state high but realistic expectations for students, encourage them consistently in their efforts, and find many different ways to reinforce their accomplishments. Verbal praise, public recognition, wall charts, star boards, ribbons, and certificates of accomplishment are all techniques for increasing the number and frequency of rewarding events in the physical education setting.

Behavior management strategies.   Unit and lesson planning rarely takes into account the behavior management strategies necessary to ensure the smooth operation of a class. The details related to classroom discipline discussed in Chapter 19 emphasize the importance of effective behavior management for physical education teachers. Research on teacher effectiveness has similarly emphasized how functional management strategies typify the effective teacher, that is, the teacher who facilitates student learning.

Because of our emphasis on behavior management strategies in other chapters, our coverage here will be brief. To emphasize behavior management strategies, we present six management-related objectives that are important to effective planning and teaching.

1. Use appropriate management strategies to reduce *management time* (dressing, attendance, daily announcements, etc.) to no more than 10 percent of class time by the fourth week of teaching. (Note that 10 percent is only a guideline; this figure may vary depending on the school context.)

2. Establish and maintain an adequate rate of *appropriate student behavior* where the definition of *appropriate* is predetermined by teacher and supervisor (and students when possible).

3. Teach *self-management skills* to students so that when instructed, they quickly complete the necessary management tasks and teacher instructions do not need to be repeated.

4. Use *positive behavioral interactions* to accomplish management goals and to promote a positive classroom climate.

5. Cope with and *remediate unexpected classroom disruptions* by utilizing several behavior management strategies.

6. Use *students' names* in behavioral interactions.

These management objectives are not achieved without detailed planning. For example, attendance taking consumes an inordinate amount of potential instructional time in many schools. Since attendance does not get taken automatically, teachers must develop an efficient strategy for it. Using a sign-in sheet, taking attendance while students complete the warm-up, or having a reliable gym helper do the job can save valuable class time. The material in Chapters 19 and 20 provides appropriate strategies to achieve these six objectives.

Beginning teachers often make inappropriate assumptions about adolescents based on their perceptions of what physical education was like for them when they were students. Some such assumptions typically include the following (Siedentop 1983):

- Students will enter the gym quickly.
- Students are eager to begin the lesson.
- Students will be attentive to instructions and demonstrations.
- Students will organize and change activities quickly.
- Students will make an honest effort to engage in the planned learning activity.
- Students will behave in a way that is consistent with accomplishing the goals of the lesson and respect the teacher's authority.

Most physical education teachers probably enjoyed their gym classes when they were students. In fact, this positive experience probably colors their perception of the motivations other students bring to physical education; that is, their own positive experience causes them to assume the same motivations for other students. But some students do not like gym class. Some students do not like school! A teacher cannot assume that students will come to physical education ready to learn and motivated to do well. Here good management techniques become very important. One of the first management issues that should be dealt with is the development of rules for appropriate student behavior in physical education.

Rules placed on a bulletin board in big bright letters may not be appropriate for secondary school students, but rules still need to be communicated clearly and enforced consistently. The positive features of school rules are stated in Chapters 19 and 20. Teachers should take the time to develop appropriate rules for all classes. Discussion with students is often an effective way to promote compliance. Perhaps the best way to develop rules is to compile a comprehensive list of both appropriate and inappropriate student behaviors. This list may vary slightly from unit to unit. Some of the rules will pertain to individuals, others to groups, and still others to the class as a whole. They should reflect the school rules and be consistently applied by all physical education faculty. They should also be explained to students if they are to be accepted by students.

Once teachers have finalized the list of appropriate and inappropriate behaviors, they must develop strategies that will promote the appropriate behaviors. Again, planning is the key.

Unit monitoring and evaluation.   Monitoring and evaluation are necessarily the final element in the planning process, but they are crucial because they represent a potent source of feedback about the success of a unit. This element responds to the important issues related to accountability for student

Achievement of subskills can be monitored by student checklists.

learning. It also keeps the teacher informed of the student's progress throughout the learning experience.

Being a vigilant observer in the gymnasium or on the playing field is the most useful form of monitoring. However, in a busy class with 30 or more students actively responding, the teacher needs a monitoring system that will reliably indicate the current skill level of each student. Casual observation will never meet this requirement. Consequently, a built-in monitoring system is essential. Ideally, students can learn to self-determine when they are ready to move on after completing a task. A student-controlled checklist can monitor such progress, and step-by-step achievement of subskill objectives can lead to achievement of the instructional goal. Students can use the criteria set by the teacher for each subskill objective and related drills or modified games to monitor their progress.

However, students must have strong self-management skills if such a monitoring system is to be incorporated, and a teacher-controlled checklist is often needed. The skills identified in a task analysis can readily be transferred to this checklist. Figures 18.9 and 18.10 (p. 346) show two types of checklists.

Very closely linked with unit monitoring is unit evaluation. The major problems and concerns of evaluation in physical education are detailed in Chapter 21. It is important that a strategy for measuring student performance be developed for each unit so that performance can be meaningfully compared to the established instructional goal.

If student performance cannot be monitored on a continuing basis, then an end-of-unit skills test is necessary. Skills tests should be valid, reliable, and functional. For example, a soccer skills test for ninth graders should closely approximate game performance (*be valid*), should accurately assess, again and again, student skill performance (*be reliable*), and should be completed quickly and efficiently (*be functional*).

Clearly, it is easier to evaluate students on their attendance, whether they are in uniform, and on a subjective impression of their "effort" or "good behavior" than on increased skill, better game performance, better use of strate-

STUDENT RECORD: _____

Skill	Date Passed	Checker
1. Short serve		
2. Short serve to backhand serving right to left		
3. Short serve to backhand serving left to right		
4. Flick serve		
5. Long serve		
6. Long serve to backhand serving right to left		
7. Long serve to backhand serving left to right		
8. Drive serve		
9. Doubles serve		
10. Underhand defensive clear		
11. Underhand attacking clear		
12. Overhand defensive clear (5 to 5)		
13. Overhand defensive clear (2 to 3)		
14. Overhand defensive crosscourt clear		
15. Overhand defensive clear to backhand		
16. Overhand defensive clear with movement		
17. Round the head defensive clear		
18. Overhand attacking clear		
19. Backhand defensive clear (5 to 4)		
20. Backhand defensive clear (3 to 2)		
21. Overhand drop		
22. Overhand drop to backhand		
23. Round the head drop		
24. Overhand drop with movement		
25. Straight smash		
26. Smash for accuracy		
27. Smash for reaction to opponent's movement		
28. Passing smash		
29. Crosscourt smash		
30. Underhand net rally		
31. Sidearm forehand net rally		
32. Sidearm backhand net rally		
33. Combination net rally		
34. Push shot		

Figure 18.9 Checklist for completion of instructional objectives for advanced badminton.

SOURCE: D. Siedentop. *Developing Teaching Skills in Physical Education.* 2nd ed. Palo Alto, Calif.: Mayfield, 1983, p. 213.

Tasks	Students and Date Completed
Dribbling obstacle course	
Jump shooting	
Free throw shooting	
Driving lay-ups	
Defensive movement	
Passing	
Rebounding	
Strategy	
Game play	

Figure 18.10 Checklist for completion of tasks (clusters of objectives) in basketball.

gies, increased strength, and better understanding of rules and skills. Few issues in professional physical education are more serious than this one: Is learning and performance in physical education important? If so, it should be evaluated!

A unit evaluation should also include details of the teacher's grading scale or the standard departmental grading scale. High skill achievement should be rewarded with a high grade. Remember, evaluation also provides information to assess teaching performance. Having students learn as a result of teaching is a major source of teacher motivation.

Lesson planning

Unit planning in the manner described in this chapter is the best guarantee that students will achieve a unit's instructional goal. Detailed unit planning is not, however, the entire ball game. The implementation of the demonstrations, drills, games, exercises, and activities is still to be done. As mentioned earlier, sound unit planning will enable the experienced effective teacher to use a unit outline as the primary lesson guideline, and detailed lesson planning may not be essential. Daily lesson plans further enhance the teacher's effectiveness.

Beginning teachers must plan each lesson. Lesson plans not only function as an immediate point of reference during lesson execution but also reinforce the components of the unit plan. Lesson plans provide beginning teachers with a set of trainer wheels that guard against major imbalances. Lesson plans respond to the following questions on a daily basis:

- How will students know what to do and when to do it?
- How will students know how to do the task?
- What opportunities will students have to do the task?
- How will students get feedback about how they are doing?
- Why should students want to do the task?
- How does one task relate to another to form a lesson?

Lesson plans provide for the realities of day-to-day teaching. Yet school assemblies are called, band practice takes 20 students from class, and many other unexpected happenings can sabotage a lesson plan.

Lesson plan format

With a detailed unit plan completed, lesson plans need only be brief. The two-page lesson plan form presented in Figure 18.11 (pp. 348–49) outlines the major considerations to which we suggest teachers direct their attention.

The guiding principles for developing good lesson plans are the same principles that guide sound unit planning. Lesson plans are often developed with a particular framework in mind. One such framework requires that there be three phases for each lesson: (1) introductory phase—warm-up, skill orientation activities; (2) skill development phase—demonstration, instruction, drills; and (3) culminating phase—game, competitive activities.

Another framework, this one suggested by Dick and Carey (1985) for individualized instructional materials, can be translated to guide lesson planning. The considerations in this case are (1) preinstructional activities—organizational concerns (class size, etc.), motivation, student objectives, prerequisite skills, safety; (2) presenting information—teaching style (direct instruction, task cards, problem solving), lesson focus, precise content, teaching cues; (3) student participation—opportunity to respond, time organization, equipment; (4) testing—student outcomes; and (5) follow-up—review, what happened, what to do next time.

How to use a lesson plan

Whichever framework is used, the lesson plan must meet the teacher's needs while he or she is actually teaching. It must be *easy to read*. Do not feel that looking at a lesson plan during class is a sign of weakness. On the contrary, it reflects a commitment to follow through on what was planned. The lesson plan is there to guide teaching. Teachers should use it to do just that and not hesitate to refer to it. To ensure that it can be used during a lesson, they should put the plan in an *accessible place*. To enable ready reference, the plan should *not be too detailed*. Here *diagrams* representing drills or activities are a great help. If the content is arranged in a *time sequence*, the teacher can

Lesson Plan

Name _____ Date _____

Class _____ Date(s) to be taught _____

Unit _____ Lesson # _____ of _____

   I. Skills already developed by students _____

     _____

     _____

  II. Major skills _____

     In this lesson, the students will perform _____

     _____

     _____

     My goal for improving my teaching is _____

     _____

     _____

 III. Instructional/practice time/organization (over)

 IV. What happened last lesson? _____

     _____

     _____

  V. Equipment and resources needed _____

     _____

     _____

     _____

Figure 18.11 A sample lesson plan format.

Time	Activity development	Organization/Management	Teaching cues	What happened

quickly gauge how things are going against the clock. A sample lesson plan is shown in Figure 18.12 to emphasize these points.

Lesson plans complement unit plans. Teachers who are happy to supervise recreation and call it physical education rarely plan. Lesson planning represents a form of professional accountability. Although it may become less

---

Lesson Plan

Name___*Ian Miller*_____Date___*Feb. 11, 1986*___

Class___*7th grade*___Date(s) to be taught___*Feb. 12, 13*___

Unit___*Volleyball*_____Lesson #___*2*___of___*9*___

I. Skills already developed by students_*Pretest indicated*_ *v. low-level skills. No formal experience in elementary* *school. 4 students participated in summer recreation program.*

II. Major skills_*Basic set, bump*_____

   In this lesson, the students will perform_*the set and* *bump in a combined set-bump drill with emphasis on* *assuming correct ready position.*

   My goal for improving my teaching is_*to limit time* *spent in giving instructions (ensure all students are* *watching demonstration so I don't need to repeat myself).*

III. Instructional/practice time/organization (over)

IV. What happened last lesson?_*Students happy to use* *nerf balls. Bump needs more work.*

V. Equipment and resources needed_*8 volleyballs, 8 nerf* *balls, 16 cones, 8 rings (hula hoops)*

Figure 18.12 A volleyball lesson plan.

important after you have taught for three or four years, remember that plans are plans, nothing more, just plans; they continually need refinement, and they rarely function in the same way when repeated. Lesson plans allow teachers to revise, update, and most important, improve their instructional effectiveness.

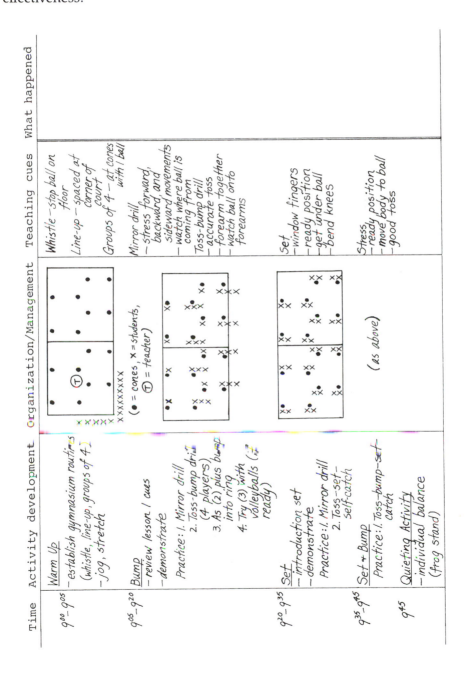

Time	Activity development	Organization/Management	Teaching cues	What happened
9⁰⁰–9⁰⁵	**Warm Up** — establish gymnasium routines (whistle, line-up, groups of 4) — jog, stretch	(● = cones, ✗ = students, Ⓣ = teacher)	Whistle – stop ball on floor. Line-up – spaced at corner of court. Groups of 4 – at cones with 1 ball	
9⁰⁵–9²⁰	**Bump** — review lesson/cues — demonstrate. Practice: 1. Mirror drill 2. Toss-bump drill (4 players) 3. As (2) plus bump into ring 4. Try (3) with volleyballs (if ready)		Mirror drill – stress forward, backward, and sideward movements – watch where ball is coming from. Toss-bump drill – accurate toss – forearm together – watch ball onto forearms	
9²⁰–9³⁵	**Set** — introduction set — demonstrate. Practice: 1. Mirror drill 2. Toss-set-self-catch		Set – window fingers – ready position – get under ball – bend knees	
9³⁵–9⁴⁵	**Set + Bump** Practice: 1. Toss-bump-set-catch	(as above)	Stress, – ready position – move body to ball – good toss	
9⁴⁵	**Quieting Activity** – individual balance (frog stand)			

Summary

Planning is an important professional function that is strongly related to effective instruction. The unit plan is the major element in a curriculum and the major tool used by teachers to prepare and implement effective instruction.

Planning is affected by teacher motivation and interest, teacher ability, time considerations, facility availability, equipment availability, and class size. While these are often constraints, they need not prevent good planning and effective instruction.

The unit plan includes a needs assessment, a formulation of goals, a task analysis, behavioral objectives, and learning activities. It must take into account the arrangement of resources, a plan for motivating student participation, strategies for managing student behavior, organizational strategies to ensure high levels of on-task behavior among students, and a system for monitoring student progress that will allow for end-of-unit evaluation. Each of these elements is important and must be planned for if intended outcomes are to occur.

Evaluation in physical education is a major issue because it so often focuses on aspects of student behavior that do not include learning and performing. Physical education will never be a serious part of the school curriculum unless student learning becomes a central goal. Student learning cannot be a central goal if it is not evaluated.

The lesson plan becomes the day-to-day vehicle through which the unit plan is translated into action. The lesson plan provides a "map" for the teacher to navigate the lesson, getting from start to finish smoothly and accomplishing established objectives.

Suggested activities

1. Develop a detailed unit plan for a 15-lesson unit. Attend to all of the unit planning elements discussed in this chapter.

2. Make a list of the activities you were taught in high school physical education and indicate for each one at what level the instruction was designed (that is, basic, intermediate, or advanced). Did any activity classes demand high levels of skill performance to merit a grade of A?

3. The following topics shape the subject matter in physical education: (a) teacher motivation and interest, (b) teacher ability, (c) time, (d) facilities and equipment, and (e) class size. Develop an argument to emphasize the importance of any one of these.

4. Effective teaching is rarely determined by facilities and equipment, although many teachers claim that they would teach a lot better if they had good facilities and plenty of equipment. Discuss this contention and suggest why facilities and equipment are so often used as excuses for poor physical education programs.

5. Determine an instructional goal and complete a task analysis for (a) a seventh-grade volleyball unit, (b) a backward roll in gymnastics, and (c) the cross-chest carry lifesaving rescue. Diagram each task analysis appropriately. Compare one of your analyses with an expert's.

6. Complete a lesson plan, paying particular attention to your lesson objective (what students will perform), the time frame, activity development, and organization and management.

19

Discipline: Developing Cooperative Behavior

The purpose of this chapter is to describe the procedures and strategies that lead to cooperative behavior on the part of students in physical education classes. It is our contention that effective discipline is the foundation from which effective instruction can develop. The major topics covered in this chapter are as follows:

Statistics and comments suggesting that school discipline is a major problem

Practices in schools where discipline is ineffective

Practices in schools where discipline is effective

Discipline as a systematic schoolwide strategy that can be implemented by the individual teacher and the physical education department

How to develop cooperative behavior among students, teachers, and administrators

Limits and guidelines for the use of punishment

General strategies for achieving effective discipline

Despite the issues of busing, budgets, and back to basics, the public's number one educational concern over the past decade has been school discipline. This concern does not merely relate to problems of misbehavior, fighting, and vandalism. People continue to express a concern that schools do more to teach moral and ethical behavior. Thus, the focus of this chapter is not solely on preventing and solving discipline problems but also on developing cooperative behavior among students, teachers, and administrators.

Nobody is quite sure whether today's students misbehave more often than their counterparts did two, three, or four generations ago. There is very little research on this. Nevertheless, most people, both inside and outside of the education profession, seem to *believe* that students are less respectful, less obedient, and less willing to live in accordance with rules.

The recent past is more easily documented. For two decades student achievement in school deteriorated, although it now appears to have stabilized and even turned slightly upward. During the time when achievement was headed downward, all data on school disruptions and forms of misbehavior in schools, including assaults, robberies, school vandalism, and other such acts, were heading upward. But those data too have more recently leveled off and are now beginning to head downward.

The sheer enormity of the problem tends to be overwhelming, especially when one considers that the estimates made by school authorities are extremely conservative: Only one of every six actual crimes committed in schools is ever reported! Still, as the data on page 356 show, the statistics, even when underestimated, are alarming. A fair conclusion of most studies has been that students have a greater risk of being violently assaulted in schools than on the streets and that the risk for junior high students is nearly twice that for senior high students.

This does not mean that in their first year of teaching all teachers will necessarily encounter numerous incidents of robbery and vandalism. School discipline problems are not distributed evenly across all schools. In many schools, problems such as smoking, showing disrespect to teachers, and cutting classes are still the biggest problems. Most studies of school discipline have agreed that a remarkably high percentage of students in most schools behave quite well, but some students have become so increasingly disruptive that the statistics look grim and the very stability and productivity of a school can be threatened (Feldhusen 1979). The motivations and values of these students seem to be so different from the norm that school efforts to control or modify their behavior show little success. Part of the reason why the trend in school disruptions has leveled off and is starting to get better is that schools have experienced serious disruptions and tried to do something about them. Along the way, a great deal has been learned about effective discipline at the school level and for the individual teacher. A major purpose of this chapter is to summarize the results of these efforts in ways that will help teachers to develop and maintain effective discipline and to learn some strategies by which they can construct a foundation of cooperative behavior so that learning and enjoyment can proceed without disruption.

We want to be very honest and straightforward about the purposes of developing and maintaining good discipline in schools in general and physical education in particular. Effective teaching and learning cannot be achieved in an atmosphere of constant disruption, chaos, and fear. Research on teacher effectiveness indicates that good teaching is built on the solid foundation of successful management. And successful management begins with effective discipline. Although helping students learn how to behave appropriately is a

SOME ALARMING STATISTICS ON SCHOOL VIOLENCE

In the 1970s, two major studies documenting the degree of violence in American middle, junior high, and senior high schools were conducted. Some of the data from those reports is presented here.

- Estimates indicate that throughout the United States 70,000 teachers are physically attacked each year.
- Each year 100,000 teachers have their property vandalized.
- Of all the robberies of youth at the junior high level, 68 percent occur at school.
- In any given month, 2.4 million high school students have something stolen, 282,000 are attacked, and 112,000 are forcibly robbed on school premises.
- At the high school level, 42 percent of all attacks are interracial, and 46 percent of robbery victims are likely to be a minority at the particular school.
- In the 1970s, seizures of weapons in schools rose by 54 percent, rape was up by 40 percent, and robbery increased by 36 percent.
- Researchers estimate that only one of six serious incidents is likely to be reported and included in official data.
- Larger schools and schools with larger classes suffer disproportionately more crime, violence, and vandalism than do smaller schools and schools with smaller classes.
- Since researchers estimate that only one of six serious incidents is likely to be reported and included in official data, it seems to follow that the school is a relatively safe place for students who commit what would be labeled as crimes if done on the streets.

SOURCES: Based on *Challenge for the Third Century: Education in a Safe Environment—Final Report on the Nature and Prevention of School Violence and Vandalism.* Report of the Subcommittee to Investigate Juvenile Delinquency to the Committee on the Judiciary of the United States Senate, Birch Bayh, Chairman, 95th Cong., 1st session. Washington, D.C.: U.S. Government Printing Office, 1977; and National Institute of Education. *Violent Schools—Safe Schools.* Washington, D.C.: U.S. Department of Health, Education and Welfare, 1977.

legitimate school goal, the major reason for the development and maintenance of good discipline is so that learning can occur!

Ineffective school procedures

Several factors that tend to prevent schools from dealing with discipline effectively have been identified (Duke 1977). These factors are not only indicative of ineffective school procedures but also point out the need for more useful policies.

- Discipline problems tend to be viewed as classroom problems rather than school problems. As a result, few schoolwide policies develop and *school* responsibility is lessened.
- Teachers and administrators rarely discuss discipline policies and/or problems. Overall issues are too often viewed as the concern of the central administration rather than teachers.
- No accurate data on misbehavior is typically kept. Therefore, administrators and teachers seldom work from a factual basis when dealing with discipline problems.
- School rules are fuzzy and not communicated clearly to students.
- School rules are enforced inconsistently. Inconsistency is of two types: first, inconsistency in treating the same behavior from time to time and, second, inconsistency in treating the same behavior from place to place or person to person.
- Minor problems are not confronted immediately and tend to become major ones; misbehavior is not dealt with promptly.
- Consequences for misbehavior are seldom made clear as part of the rules and tend to be applied with a great deal of inconsistency.
- Since school discipline is not viewed as a total staff issue, time is seldom allotted for discussion of policies or in-service training to create more effective use of policies.
- Parents are not often involved in the resolution of discipline problems.
- Students are seldom asked to be part of the policy-making or policy-enforcing process; they are typically left out and feel no ownership for the policies and little responsibility toward them.

The need for a systematic school approach to discipline

Discipline in schools is more effective to the degree that it operates on a systematic, schoolwide basis rather than on a class-to-class basis. That statement is consistent with research conducted in schools, and it is also consistent with what is known about how people behave. Behavior tends to be stronger, more predictable, and more consistent to the degree that it is treated similarly in different settings. If student behavior is treated differently from class to class, the result is often confusion and erratic behavior. If the *same* behavior is treated differently from day to day, then the results are even more disastrous, often producing not only unpredictable behavior but rebellion and counterattack. Individual teachers can do a great deal in their own settings, but their tasks will be easier to the degree that a systematic, schoolwide program is in place and operating reliably.

Some of the causes for misbehavior are beyond the control of the school. Administrators and teachers can do little about ineffective families, economic situations within a community, or the amount of violence on television. Nonetheless, schools must deal with the inappropriate behavior that occurs as a result of these cultural factors, and schools must also do as much as possible to eliminate potential causes of student misconduct within a school. Thus, the total approach to school discipline must initiate preventive measures as well as meet and deal with misbehavior as it occurs, no matter what its causes.

There is ample evidence that schools do not need to be battlegrounds, that effective climates for learning can be developed, even in situations that are difficult (see page 360 for two such examples). A major source for this evidence is research on what are known as "instructionally effective schools." Investigators have conducted a number of studies to determine the characteristics of schools in which students have higher levels of achievement *even though the schools are typically in low socioeconomic areas and are exactly the kinds of schools that have had disproportionately high levels of school violence and disruption.*

Characteristics of effective schools

One of the most revealing research endeavors of recent decades has been the study of characteristics of effective and ineffective schools (with effectiveness being defined by student achievement and lack of disruption within the school). The characteristics that tend to define the effective schools (Mann and Lawrence 1981) are both interesting and instructive.

1. *Principals* provide strong leadership, are assertive and directive, and yet provide strong support for teachers. They tend to have high expectations for both teachers and students.
2. *Teachers* are task oriented, feel responsible for the achievement of students, and show high expectations for learning.
3. The *school atmosphere* is orderly and highly disciplined. There tends to be a high level of structure and high morale.
4. The *instructional emphasis* is on clear learning goals, and there is pressure and support for excellence, especially the acquisition of basic skills.
5. *Student progress* is closely monitored and frequently evaluated.

Underlying these characteristics appears to be a set of beliefs that tend to influence the norms, attitudes, and behaviors of the entire school staff, thus creating a *school climate* that is favorable to learning and achievement (Lezotte 1981). Fundamental to this climate is the belief that all students can learn what is expected of them in the area of basic skills. The staff also believe that they can teach the students, that is, that the necessary competence and dedication exists to do the job. The staff believe that society wants them to do this job and that it requires a total team effort within the school. They look to and expect leadership from their principals and are committed to the notion that the school must be a businesslike place for these goals to be achieved. When beliefs such as these are given life in the daily behavior of administrators, teachers, and students, then schools tend to be effective in achieving their goals.

Schoolwide discipline

Most experts agree that major problems exist in many schools today because discipline is often viewed as only a classroom matter and not as a schoolwide issue. However, careful examination of schools that seem to "work" well as places for learning indicates that in these schools discipline is first of all a *school* issue, that there are clear schoolwide rules, and that the rules are enforced consistently. Duke (1977) has advocated a systematic management plan for school discipline (SMPSD) that brings together many of the successful strategies used in schools where discipline (in the sense of an absence of disruptive behavior) has been achieved and a positive climate for learning has been established. One of the most critical elements of the SMPSD is the development of the school as a *rule-governed institution*. It is in the development and enforcement of school rules that a schoolwide discipline program succeeds or fails. The following guidelines are suggested for establishing schoolwide rules:

1. Rules should be developed collaboratively—administrators, teachers, students, and parents should be involved.

2. Consequences for breaking rules should also be developed among the same groups.

3. Only those rules that can be enforced should be developed and these should be as few in number as possible in order to achieve the goals.

4. The rules must be publicized widely in the school and in the community. Parents must be made aware of them on a regular basis.

5. Procedures must be developed for the consistent enforcement of rules and the consistent application of consequences. These procedures should respect the students' right to due process.

6. The rules (and their consequences) should be part of the regular curriculum. Special orientation should be provided for incoming students and transfers.

If rules are to be taken seriously by students, they must be treated seriously by the school, that is, by the administrators and the teachers. Students might be tested once per year on the school rules so that no student could claim lack of awareness when a rule was violated. Parents should be notified at least once per year about the rules and the consequences for breaking them.

Once rules are well established, systematic efforts can also be made to reward students who obey rules. Many attractive activities are available within the school program and the school facilities, and free time to use them can be a useful and pleasant reward to motivate student behavior. Use of the gymnasium and its related facilities can be among the most popular "reward activities." A physical education program benefits when students view access to its activities and facilities as a reward for good behavior.

Within the SMPSD there is also a need for a mechanism by which conflicts can be resolved. Students must know and respect the procedure for resolving conflicts. Some schools have developed negotiation procedures involving the

---

TWO APPROACHES TO CREATING AN ORDERLY CLIMATE FOR LEARNING: THE PRICKLIES AND THE GOOIES

Many schools faced with high levels of student disruption have sought to create an orderly climate for learning. What is obvious is that there are many different ways to achieve this goal.

A high school in New York decided to do so by "cracking down." Teachers and administrators developed rules, clearly stated them to students, and then quickly and consistently enforced them. Basic skills and abilities were emphasized in classrooms. The principal took the leadership role in the entire program. The school had been racked with violence prior to the program, but within a reasonably short time it turned into a peaceful and well-organized educational environment.

A high school in Florida faced with similar problems chose instead a collaborative model in which students, teachers, administrators, parents, and community officials were brought together to develop a set of rules and expectations for the school. The rules were agreed to by all parties and communicated to students. The enforcement of rules was a task shared cooperatively by all parties. This not only created a better educational climate but increased respect and trust among students, teachers, and administrators. Complaints about misbehavior were drastically reduced.

The first approach appears to be a "tough" model while the second appears to be a "soft" model. Yet the two have much in common in terms of rules, expectations, and enforcement. The fact that the results of the two programs were similar is probably attributable to their similarities rather than their differences.

SOURCES: Based on Wint, J. "The Crackdown"; and Van Avery, D. "The Humanitarian Approach." *Phi Delta Kappan* 57 (November 1975).

---

offending students and teachers, whereas others have depended more upon administrators to solve the conflicts that inevitably arise in any rule-governed institution.

One very promising conflict resolution strategy is peer review (Bronfenbrenner 1973), a system in which an official student review board sits regularly to adjudicate problems that arise within the administration of school rules. There is much to be said for such a peer review system, not only as an effective mechanism for school discipline but also as a valuable learning experience for students.

The teacher's role in schoolwide discipline. An individual teacher can seldom exert sufficient influence to change the direction of a school's discipline program, but an individual teacher can do *something*! Every teacher within a school structure has a voice, even though it is a single voice and may represent a minority point of view. Our guess is that there will be many other teachers who feel that schoolwide discipline is important and would like very much to see an effective program put in place. The problem here is that individual teachers too often feel powerless and therefore do not make their views known; thus colleagues who feel similarly never learn what these silent teachers feel, and likewise, they do not learn that their colleagues share their views. So a first step is to speak up—not necessarily in a formal way, which is often difficult for a beginning teacher, but informally, during one of the many opportunities within schools to discuss discipline problems.

A second contribution that an individual teacher can make is to learn as much as possible about schoolwide discipline and discipline strategies. There are in-service education programs designed to help teachers acquire new information, and teachers often get to suggest topics for future in-service programs.

A third contribution is to take part in the collaborative processes described above—for example, to be willing to serve on a committee charged with formulating school rules and consequences. The time and effort put in by such committees can pay considerable dividends in the life of the school. And a school that runs more smoothly and is a more pleasant place makes a teacher's life considerably more pleasant.

Finally, the individual physical educator can be a strong spokesperson for developing procedures within the entire physical education faculty, an important issue to which we now turn.

Departmentwide policies. In middle schools, junior high schools, and secondary schools there are often several physical education teachers, members of a physical education department. Everything we have said thus far about the importance of schoolwide policies applies also at the departmental level. All of the students taking physical education will behave better if the entire department arrives at procedures and policies that are carried out in each class. If students are treated consistently from class to class and from teacher to teacher, they will quickly learn what is expected of them and their behavior will become more consistent.

Just as school rules are important, so too are departmental rules. These specialized rules should cover the major ways in which physical educators expect students to behave in the gymnasium, on the playing fields, and in the locker rooms. The guidelines suggested on page 359 for establishing schoolwide rules also apply here. The staff (together with students, if possible) should develop the rules and the consequences for breaking them. The rules should be made public and the behavior to which the rules refer should be systematically taught to the students early in the school year. We cannot overemphasize how important it is that rules and enforcement be similar from teacher to teacher. Inconsistency in application will undermine the program, and teachers will quickly lose their credibility among the students.

Department rules should be posted conspicuously in the gymnasium and referred to often, especially at the beginning of the school year and whenever a group of new students starts a class. Research indicates that what teachers do in the first several weeks of school concerning discipline and school rou-

Students who are on-task reduce discipline problems.

tines is fundamentally important to their effectiveness throughout the school year. The lesson is quite clear: Those teachers who take the time to establish effective rules and to teach specific classroom routines tend to be more effective teachers than those who do not. Their classrooms are much less disruptive and more pleasant, and their students also tend to learn more and to feel better about themselves and school (for a more thorough treatment of this subject, see Siedentop 1983).

Nowhere are departmental discipline policies more important than in those activities that take place off campus—in the local bowling alley, on a weekend bicycle trip, or on an overnight camping trip. The physical education department is in less control whenever students move off campus. Therefore, the rules for appropriate behavior become even more important. All those who work with students in physical education activities but are not members of the department need to be informed of the rules and also need to understand how important it is that the rules be applied consistently off campus just as they are on campus. It would be of great benefit to a department to develop a small brochure for this purpose so that the rules are made clear *before* the activities are undertaken.

Developing cooperative relations

The establishment and maintenance of rule-governed behavior form the foundation for discipline and learning in the school, but this does not represent the entire picture. Within the framework of the rules, it is equally important that students learn to behave cooperatively and that they learn to do so because of the important positive consequences that derive from settings in which people respect one another and cooperate in the achievement of goals.

If discipline in the middle and secondary school is conceptualized only as student obedience to teacher instructions, then the best that can happen is a kind of cease-fire atmosphere. The very nature of adolescence (see Chapter 5) is such that relationships based solely on authority are likely to be tested, to be resisted, or even when compliance is achieved, to be accepted only grudgingly.

We began this chapter with an emphasis on school rules because they do indeed form the foundation of an orderly school. We also made clear that rules developed and enforced cooperatively are better than rules imposed by teachers. But we must now go beyond the level of rules toward the social learning goals of the school, toward the development of cooperative relations.

The foundation for cooperative behavior in physical education is built on (1) the specification of group norms, (2) the strength of the teacher as a source of reinforcement, (3) gradually working toward improved relations, and (4) precise communication (Jensen 1975).

Specifying group norms

Cooperation is a set of complex relationships within which people work toward common goals; students cooperate with students, students with teachers, leaders with followers, etc. The best way to develop cooperative behavior is to specify clearly what it means! Adults may have some understanding of what it means to be cooperative, but they should not assume that young students have already learned cooperative habits. If teachers cannot specify for a group of students what it means to behave cooperatively, then perhaps they should not expect students to be able to do so.

Obviously, it is not enough to say, "be more cooperative," just as it is not enough to say, "be prompt." Neither is sufficiently specific to provide a group norm. "Be in your assigned place when the bell rings" is specific and can provide the basis for a group norm that represents promptness. Helping a student to practice a skill when the student is having trouble is a specific form of cooperation that can, if the teacher so desires, become an example of cooperative behavior in physical education.

As teachers attempt to develop group norms, they should expect students to test the rules and even to suggest counternorms—such as, "Oh, did you mean *that* bell?" or "Doesn't the bell mean to start talking?" Consistent reinforcement and enforcement of rules is necessary if they are eventually to become norms.

Reinforcing student cooperation

The teacher is the major person responsible for the development of cooperative behavior. The teacher can do a great deal if he or she is a source of reinforcement for the students, that is, if the students value the attention of the teacher. If the students do not value the teacher, then the chances for developing and maintaining cooperative behavior are slim. Notice we have not said that it is necessary for the students to *like* the teacher. It is nice to be liked and to be a popular teacher, and there is no doubt that being liked can be helpful. But what is necessary is that the students respect the teacher and value his or her attention.

Teacher attention in the form of feedback, praise, time to discuss, and simple forms of nonverbal attention such as smiling can be a powerful motivator for students. When students demonstrate cooperative behavior and the teacher responds favorably to it, then the cooperative behavior is strengthened. However, that formula does not work if the attention is not valued!

There are many, many ways in which physical education teachers can enhance the value of their attention. First and foremost, they can be good, serious teachers of physical education. Second, they can voice positive expectations for their students and what they will be able to do in physical education. Thus, being a competent professional educator is no doubt the most important general ingredient in being valued by students.

However, we can also offer some specific suggestions. One is to compliment and interact with students in basically "nonschool" situations. For example, compliments such as "You're looking very good today," "Those are great shoes you have on," "What fun things did you do this weekend?" or "I hear you're doing very well in your other classes," when delivered sincerely and in an appropriate context, can begin to establish the teacher as a positive person who is valued by students. When similar verbal and nonverbal rewards are made contingent upon acts of cooperative behavior, they are more likely to have a strong effect.

It is also very helpful if the teacher models cooperative behavior himself or herself, either with other teachers or with students directly. Whenever a teacher goes out of the way to do something in a cooperative manner, he or she acts as a model for the very norms that are being established with the students.

Similarly, it is important that teachers avoid situations in which the value of their attention might be diminished. Conflicts are inevitable and how they are handled will influence the degree to which the attention of the teacher maintains its value. Above all, teachers should avoid hostile encounters with students as conflicts are being resolved. Teachers should not get into verbal battles with students where the compliance of the student is seen as a victory for the teacher! The best way for a teacher to handle such situations is to refer to the rule or the norm with which the contested behavior is in conflict. If a behavior is against the rules or in conflict with a norm, the teacher can refer to the rule or the norm in desisting the behavior. Because rules and norms have both been defined in terms of consequences, it is also useful to refer to the consequences of the behavior in question—for example, "If you make that much noise, your classmates can't hear instructions or get feedback."

Another situation in which teachers need to be careful is when minor disturbances (ones that do not violate rules or norms) are occurring. The bottom line seems to be that if the behavior does not violate a rule or norm, does not present a danger, and does not interfere with others unduly, then it is best to ignore it and the only action warranted is to compliment those who are not engaging in that form of behavior.

Working gradually toward improved relations

Teamwork does not develop overnight. Young students do not learn all the subtleties of cooperative behavior in one class or one unit. This takes time. It takes specific attention. Perhaps most of all, it takes a clear understanding on the part of the teacher about what he or she is trying to achieve.

Whatever the final goals may be, it is necessary to start where the students are. The place to begin is with whatever cooperative behavior the students now exhibit or what the teacher can prompt them to exhibit. That behavior needs to be reinforced and the best way is to attend to it, either verbally with a compliment or nonverbally with a smile or a pat on the back. It helps tremendously if the reinforcement ("Thanks, Jim") can be coupled with some specific feedback about the cooperative behavior ("When you help to get the equipment ready, it gives us all more time to get the game started").

As students learn more about being cooperative, then gradually the teacher can differentially reinforce more mature forms of cooperation. And as students become more consistent in their acts of cooperation, the teacher can provide attention less frequently. This will occur simply because the consequences of acting cooperatively are also positive and the students will gradually come under the influence of those consequences rather than just the teacher's attention.

Communicating precisely

Cooperation is an elusive concept. How many times during your childhood and adolescence were you accused of "not being cooperative" only to wonder what you had or had not done to deserve such an accusation. Teachers who ask their students to be cooperative tend not to get very far. Their communication needs to be more precise. Precision is achieved by describing what is to be done or not to be done in behavioral terms. For example, when two games are going on in adjacent courts, it is inevitable that the ball from one game will invade the space of the other game. What happens? What would you like to have happen? Telling a group not to interfere in the other game is not quite good enough. A group norm has to be established in this case, one that describes what it means for classmates to cooperate in retrieving the ball and not disrupting an ongoing game. This might be achieved by designating one person to retrieve balls that stray and his or her doing so in a way that does not disrupt the game in the next court.

Precision is also enhanced when statements are direct rather than indirect and when they are not phrased as questions. When a teacher says, "Shall we get started?" inevitably one or more students will answer, "No!" Better to say, "It's time to begin the warm-up."

Precision in communication is often best achieved by *showing* along with the telling. If the teacher takes time to have a student actually demonstrate the behavior in question, other students have no doubt about what is expected of them. The time it takes to provide this kind of demonstration is well spent because it helps students to learn cooperative behavior more quickly and also because it will eventually save time. When cooperation is better developed, disruptions and conflicts are avoided, thus saving time that can be devoted to instruction and practice.

Punishment

The term *punishment* refers to strategies designed to reduce the frequency of inappropriate behavior by the application of consequences. Punishment is not revenge. Indeed, the emphasis in this chapter has been on positive strategies for developing cooperative behavior and compliance with school, departmental, and class rules. However, there are times when students misbehave and punishment is a legitimate and useful strategy *if it is used appropriately*. The problem with punishment in schools is that historically it has been used inappropriately far too often. As a result, it is still a common stereotype that teachers are often cruel people and schools are often punitive places.

Punishment in physical education typically takes several forms: being taken out of an activity, doing extra work (such as exercising or running laps), having a grade reduced, being reported to the principal's office, relinquishing privileges, or being paddled.

Corporal punishment is used less often than it used to be. Certain states have banned it altogether, and school districts commonly ban it even though state law may allow it. Even where legal, corporal punishment must be meted out according to very strict guidelines. It should never be applied in anger. The teacher who strikes a student in anger, shoves a student, pinches a student, or in any other way physically assaults a student is asking to be sued no matter what the provocation. Schools that still condone corporal punishment usually require a standard method of punishing (typically a paddle), a witness to the punishment (typically another teacher), and a specified amount of punishment that responds fairly to the seriousness of the offense (typically a certain number of blows). It is our judgment that corporal punishment is not necessary in schools, that it is far too risky, that it often results in legal action even when done according to policy, and that there are other, better methods for achieving the same goals.

The purpose of punishment is to stop a misbehavior. However, simply stopping misbehavior is not enough. Therefore, punishment should be used in combination with other strategies that redirect the offender's behavior in more cooperative directions. The following guidelines are useful for punishment strategies and the administration of penalties (Charles 1981).

1. The strategy should stop the misbehavior. It is not a punishment unless it works! If students run laps as a consequence of coming late to class and their tardiness does not decrease, then running laps is not effective as a punishment!

2. Punishment should be used in connection with some positive strategy through which the student can be rewarded for behaving appropriately. If a student does not share equipment properly and is punished, he or she should later be shown what "sharing" looks like and verbally rewarded when engaging in that behavior.

3. If possible, punishment should make right what was done wrong. It is useful if the punishment can include actions that remediate the original problem. This is often accomplished by means of "positive practice" wherein a student has to practice the correct behavior X number of times as a result of having done the incorrect behavior.

4. Punishment should not destroy the cooperative bond. It should never be applied in anger. Punishment that is the result of anger risks what is called the "spread of effect" where not only the behavior is called into question but also the worth of the student. Remember, the purpose is not to degrade the student but to correct the misbehavior. Punishment that is administered correctly allows good personal relations to continue and does not diminish the reinforcing power of the teacher. Put simply, you cannot expect your attention to be a reinforcer for students if you punish out of anger and degrade, embarrass, or ridicule students.

When punishment is used according to these guidelines, it becomes yet another skilled teaching strategy rather than a traumatic experience for teacher and student.

The most common form of punishment in schools is the verbal desist. When used skillfully, it can be an effective tool. Verbal reprimands should first of all be timed and targeted properly; that is, they should be delivered immediately after a misbehavior occurs, and they should be delivered to the primary offender. If they are delivered late, delivered after the misbehavior has spread, or delivered to a secondary offender rather than the primary offender, the teacher's credibility is diminished in the eyes of the student; the teacher is not considered to be "with it" (Kounin 1977).

Desists that are effective are clear, firm, and have some follow-through. First, a desist conveys clear information. Rather than say, "Stop that!" teachers should specify clearly what should be stopped. The desist should also be firm, which means that the voice should have authority and teachers should show that they mean what they say (this does not mean that teachers should shout, which conveys anger, not authority). The desist should also be followed through, which shows again that teachers mean what they say; ways of following through are maintaining eye contact, moving closer to the offender, and requiring the student to acknowledge the misbehavior.

General strategies for effective discipline

Good discipline is a *necessary* but not a *sufficient* condition for effective teaching and learning; that is, smooth management and a well-behaved class are necessary conditions for effective teaching but do not in themselves create effective teaching. Many discipline problems can be prevented (Siedentop

An effective teacher has the attention and support of the class.

1983). In fact, the preventive aspects of classroom management are probably more important than are the discipline strategies themselves.

Of particular importance to good preventive management is the development of gymnasium routines. A *routine* is any managerial/behavioral sequence that occurs fairly regularly and for which specific ways of operating are taught to students so that time is spent as efficiently as possible. Examples of routines are roll taking, ways of getting the first activity started, ways of changing activities, etc. Effective routines utilize time efficiently. Disruptive behavior in class often occurs during lag time. By eliminating lag time or waiting time, the effective manager eliminates the situations in which much disruptive behavior occurs (thus the notion of preventive management). More information about routines is presented in Chapter 20.

But the major focus in this chapter is on specific discipline techniques, and during the past 20 years, much has been learned about effective discipline in schools. Charles (1981) has reviewed the major theories of classroom discipline and identified strategies that seem to be common to all of them. In fact, we should point out that many of the approaches work very well, no doubt because they all contain basic elements necessary for an effective program even though the "packaging" of the approaches may look different. Thus, reality therapy, assertive discipline, behavior modification, and Adlerian discipline may look different upon first glance, but upon further study we can see that they embrace certain common principles. These principles are presented below. They form the basis for specific discipline strategies as well as effective discipline programs.

1. *Provide leadership in establishing and maintaining discipline.* All authorities agree that teachers should take charge of their classes. Student input, as we have often emphasized, is important but the teacher is ultimately responsible for what goes on and must act accordingly. Once rules are established, teachers must communicate them clearly and enforce them consistently. Consequences must be established at the time the rules are established and should be reviewed periodically. When students understand rules and consequences, then it is they who actually *choose* to violate them and suffer the consequences. Teachers should not ignore students who comply with rules but reinforce them frequently. Leadership in discipline requires persistence. Teachers should maintain poise and a professional manner in dealing with discipline problems. If they cave in, if they allow students to bend the rules, if they do not invoke the consequences, then they should not be surprised when their system fails and students do not view the system as having credibility.

2. *Deal with misbehavior immediately.* Teachers should deal with destructive behavior immediately and convincingly. No student should be allowed to disrupt the learning of the other students. Misbehavior must be confronted directly and forcefully yet within the guidelines suggested on pp. 366–67. If students learn that a teacher is willing to confront misbehavior directly, while still keeping his or her composure, then the teacher's prestige will be enhanced. Such a teacher will be viewed as a person who is tough but fair and who cares about students.

3. *Communicate effectively with students regarding discipline.* Much is to be gained from consistent and frank communication. If rules, norms, and consequences are made clear, then students have a choice. This choice forms the basis for a teacher's communication with students, helping them to make good choices by reminding them of the immediate, positive and negative consequences as well as those of longer-term importance. This frame of reference allows the teacher to talk with students about good and bad behavior without being either hostile or wishy-washy. The teacher earns and maintains respect by speaking frankly, simply, and forcefully. Teachers should meet with students periodically to review rules and norms and to allow student input into the process. Students feel involved when they are kept informed and allowed to comment; this involvement results in a loyalty not only to the system of rules and norms but also to the teacher. The result of this growing loyalty to the sytem and the teacher is that students will defend both to their peers.

4. *Set high but reasonable expectations for classes.* Teachers must both *say* and *show* that they expect students to behave well, and they must do this frequently at first and periodically thereafter. Cooperation is built slowly by developing a climate of expectation in which behaving well toward others becomes the norm. Setting expectations requires frequent prompting, reminding, discussion, and reinforcement of good examples when they occur.

5. *Reinforce good behavior.* Research shows clearly that there is far too little reinforcement of appropriate behavior in schools, especially in physical education (Siedentop 1983). Teachers tend to be stingy with their praise. Remember that good behavior is gradually shaped by rewarding the bit of good behavior that does occur and then developing more and more of it. According to Charles (1981) systematic reinforcement of good behavior works with all students at all age levels and "is the single most effective technique for building the kind of behavior you want to see in your students" (215). Too often rules and discipline focus only on inappropriate behavior. Cooperative behavior is not simply the absence of bad behavior. Teachers must do all they can to support the development of cooperative behavior by emphasizing it, prompting it, and rewarding it when it occurs. Teachers can also be a model for the kind of behavior they want their students to develop. By showing concern, being courteous, using good manners, and being helpful, teachers can draw students' attention to good behaviors.

6. *Build a success-oriented learning climate.* All students like to be successful, and they like to be recognized for their successes. This cannot happen unless the learning environment is geared for success. Teachers must reduce the chances of failure. Students who consistently fail often get frustrated and lose interest in the class. Such students often cause discipline problems. To be sure, activity goals have to be challenging, but they also have to be attainable by students who apply themselves. Teachers also need to find ways to let students see how they are progressing. These may include feedback, charts, contests in which there are many winners, and "success clubs." The application of this principle requires both careful planning and good instruction (see Chapters 18 and 20).

7. *Establish a good support system for the discipline program.* Achieving discipline is more easily accomplished with the support of administrators, parents, and other teachers. Parental support is particularly important. The first step is to inform parents about the program and the expectations for cooperative behavior among students. Parents should understand that the goal of good discipline is to ensure that students have a chance to learn more and to learn more efficiently. The support of administrators is necessary because they must back up the teacher when students behave so poorly that they need attention from the school level. Administrators can also contribute to the positive aspects of the program by occasionally visiting the classroom and the gym and expressing their expectations, which are in accordance with the teacher's, and verbally reinforcing appropriate student behavior.

Getting started on the right foot

As mentioned before, research on teacher effectiveness shows that teachers who take the time during the early part of the school year to teach students how to behave in their classrooms and gymnasiums tend to be the most effective teachers throughout the year. By taking time early to teach specific gymnasium routines and by establishing clear rules and consequences, teachers can often prevent disruptions throughout the year.

Typically the effective teacher not only describes the routines, rules, and consequences to his or her students but also provides opportunities for the students to practice the routines and rules and rewards them for improvement. When the teacher emphasizes rules and behaviors within routines frequently during the first several classes, students quickly learn the routines and rules and also that their teacher means business. They are less inclined to "test" the teacher, and classes begin to run more smoothly. Even though this takes some time at the beginning of the school year, the time is more than made up by smooth operations in classes throughout the year. When a physical education department institutes policies such as those we have been describing, then only new or transfer students will need to be initiated into the system, and returning students or those in new units or semesters will only have to be reminded of the rules and routines to behave more consistently. The payoff for the staff throughout the school year more than justifies the time spent during the first several class sessions to accomplish these behavioral goals.

Summary

School discipline has been a major concern for the past 20 years. School violence and vandalism data seem to support this concern, which is shared by parents, teachers, and administrators, as well as the general public. Good discipline is the foundation for effective learning. Thus, it is a problem of fundamental importance if schools are to improve.

Practices in schools where discipline is ineffective have been identified. They include failure to view discipline as a schoolwide responsibility, poor communication, failure to keep accurate data, fuzzy rules, inconsistent enforcement, unclear consequences, lack of parental involvement, lack of student involvement, and an unwillingness to confront minor problems. These ineffective practices indicate the need for a systematic approach to school discipline.

On the other hand, the characteristics of schools in which discipline is effective include strong leadership from principals, task-oriented teachers, an orderly school atmosphere, a strong instructional emphasis, closely monitored student progress, and a total school involvement in the making and enforcing of rules.

Rules are necessary for discipline. A great deal is known about how to develop good rules, how to teach them to students, and how to reward and punish students who are compliant and noncompliant. Rules are a major part of successful school discipline programs regardless of whether the school takes a "hard" approach or a "soft" approach.

Individual teachers can contribute to school discipline, but they do so most effectively within the context of a schoolwide program. The most effective physical education departments are those in which all department members teach common rules and enforce them consistently.

Schools should do more than prevent misbehavior. They should help students to learn cooperative behavior. Specifying group norms, using the teacher as a reinforcer, gradually working toward improved relationships, and being precise in communication are the major strategies for developing such behavior.

Punishment is a specific discipline strategy that is often misused. Corporal punishment is risky because of legal and ethical problems. Effective punishment redirects misbehavior into more appropriate channels without unduly harming the student.

Preventive management is the best way to reduce the number of discipline problems that occur. Teachers need to provide leadership in establishing and maintaining good managerial strategies and discipline programs. Misbehavior should be dealt with immediately, rules and consequences must be communicated effectively, and teachers should have high expectations for their students to behave well. A learning environment that is attractive and success oriented also contributes to the maintenance of good discipline.

Suggested activities

1. Describe two or three incidents of major school discipline problems from your own experience. How was each incident handled? What was its outcome? Discuss the incidents in relation to effective school practices.

2. Divide into small groups. Each group is to develop a discipline code for physical education as if it were the teaching staff in a physical education department in a high school.

3. Debate the following issue: Corporal punishment should not be used in schools. Have three students argue the affirmative and three the negative.

4. Obtain discipline codes from several local schools. Discuss them relative to the effective practices described in this chapter and compare them in terms of what student behaviors are considered to be important.

5. Draw up a list of strategies for developing cooperative behavior.

20

Effective Teaching Strategies

The purpose of this chapter is to explain how specific teaching strategies and various teaching models can produce effective learning environments. These strategies and models are applied to teaching physical education, and practical tips for each aspect of effective teaching are suggested. The major topics in the chapter are as follows:

Explanation of effective practices rather than emphasis on one particular method of teaching

Eight teaching strategies shown to be effective by research on teachers in actual educational settings

Popular models for teaching physical education and how they relate to teacher effectiveness

Important teaching tips for achieving results in physical education

Effective teachers are the backbone of education. They are not magicians; they are skilled professionals, and they work hard at what they do. Their effectiveness lies in their careful and skillful application of teaching strategies to ever-changing and complex situations. This chapter is about teaching strategies and how they are applied in different situations. But first we must take a moment to discuss briefly an assumption about the purpose of physical education.

As stated in Chapter 2 (see page 25), we believe that physical education, in order to survive as a school subject, must be able to demonstrate tangible outcomes and students must show recognizable achievement gains. Students must know more. They must be more skilled. They must be more fit. They must be better players. They must be more committed to an active, healthy, playful life-style. Although there are legitimately different ways to conceptualize and implement physical education programs for youth, to be successful the programs must accomplish *something*. In other words, we believe that the main business of physical education is for students to learn and that learning should be the central goal for physical education everywhere. We have reason to believe that this assumption about learning and performance is not widely shared in physical education. Surveys of grading practices (Morrow 1978) indicate that student subject matter performance is not among the major items that contribute to evaluations of students. If those data are correct, and experiences tell us that they are, then the right uniform, a good attendance record, and good behavior are all that one needs to get a top grade in physical education. Many physical educators feel that it is unfair to hold students accountable for performance. Others feel that physical education should be fun (we agree) and that any kind of grading on performance negates that possibility (we disagree).

The purpose of raising this issue here is to underscore the idea that *effective teaching can be judged only in terms of the goals of the teacher*. If student learning is not a teacher's main goal, then strategies that are specifically related to learning are not important. Our assumption is that learning *is* the main agenda of physical education and that "effectiveness" for teachers is related to student performance.

Teacher effectiveness and teaching methods

Research on teacher effectiveness in physical education (Siedentop 1980) and elsewhere has been a large and successful enterprise in education during the past several decades. This research has been done in schools, with regular students, under normal conditions. Thus the information in this chapter is not just someone's idea or theory about effective teaching but rather what research seems to support.

Another of our assumptions stated in Chapter 2 suggests that there is no best method for teaching physical education (see pp. 28–29). Research evidence strongly supports that assumption. Therefore, this chapter will not try to convince you that there is one best method for teaching all activities to all students in all schools. Many seemingly different methods can be effective. Under the right conditions, task teaching, contracting, direct instruction, and discovery teaching can each be effective—or ineffective!

Effective teaching is characterized by a predictable set of strategies that have little to do with "method." Effective teachers use these strategies; teachers who are less than effective usually do not. A *strategy* typically consists of several discrete teaching skills. For example, the strategy of active supervision consists of the teacher's moving in unpredictable patterns around the teaching space, frequently checking on students not in close proximity, prompting on-task behavior, desisting inappropriate behavior quickly and accurately, and providing academic feedback.

It seems to us that teaching skills are very much like sports skills. You can fairly quickly master the basics of tennis. You can learn how to serve, how to stroke forehand and backhand, how to volley, and how to smash. You can learn when each of these should be used. However, to be a good tennis player, you have to put the skills to use at the right time, in the right order, and in the right way. Learning to be an effective teacher is like that too. We will present the effective teaching skills as separate skills; they can be practiced separately, and this kind of practice is important. Gradually, however, you must bring the skills together to become an effective teacher. Doing this requires some serious practice under good conditions. People do not become good tennis players without lots of practice, some good help along the way, and the right conditions. And they have to want to be good players! The same holds true for learning to be an effective teacher.

Eight effective strategies

This section describes eight strategies that characterize effective teaching. These strategies, when used in proper combination, tend to promote student learning (Siedentop 1980) as confirmed by research both in the classroom and in the gymnasium.

Any teaching method that is characterized by these eight strategies can be highly effective. Any model that neglects them tends to be less effective. The literature on effective teaching holds little support for one best style of teaching for all subjects and all situations. Teachers should use their own style, but that style should incorporate the following strategies:

1. Devote a large percentage of time to content.
2. Minimize management/wait/transition time in class routines.
3. Devote a high percentage of content time to practice.
4. Keep students on-task.
5. Assign tasks that are meaningful and matched to student abilities.
6. Keep the learning environment supportive and set high but realistic expectations.
7. Give lessons smoothness and momentum.
8. Hold students accountable for learning.

Allocate a large percentage of time to content

Under appropriate conditions, students will learn more if they have more time to learn.

During the 1980s time-to-learn became a central issue in education. Is a longer school day needed? Is a longer school year needed? Is there a sufficient amount of time-on-task in classes? These questions have been debated widely for one simple reason: *Research has consistently indicated that quality learning time is the essential ingredient in effective schooling.*

There are several ways to examine the use of time in physical education classes. First, how much time does the teacher *allocate* for student learning? We can usually answer this question by examining daily lesson plans.

Second, for how much of that allocated time are students actually *engaged*? *Engaged time* is a better measure of student opportunity to learn than is allocated time. But what about the nature of the student's engagement? Is the learning time productive when a ninth grader is trying to high jump with the bar set at 5'2" when the student can hardly clear 4'2"? Is the learning time productive when a student is in a volleyball game but possesses neither the skills nor the strategies to play the game decently? Clearly, the answer is no! For the learning time to be productive, the learning task must match the student's present skills and abilities, the student must have a fair chance at being successful.

This is exactly the notion that led to the development of the concept of academic learning time (Siedentop 1980). *Academic learning time (ALT)* is a unit of time in which a student is engaged with a task at which he or she can be successful. ALT is *quality* learning time. Research indicates that ALT in physical education classes (ALT-PE) is typically quite low, often no more than 3 to 5 minutes per student per 30-minute class in the secondary school. The concept of ALT-PE provides a simple, convenient criterion by which to judge teaching effectiveness in physical education.

> Effective teaching means structuring the lesson so as to maximize the amount of time in direct practice by *each* individual at a level which ensures a continuing development of the skill. . . . It was our major conclusion that the ALT-PE system supplies the missing element, or indeed major component, needed to evaluate effective teaching in physical education. Time-on-task, academic learning time, opportunities to learn—call it what you will, and measure it if you can—this is the vital component of an effective lesson. (McLeish 1985, 84–85)

Notice that ALT-PE is a measure of time for the *individual student. Class* time allocated for practice needs to be translated into *individual* practice time. For the physical education teacher that becomes the main challenge—how to provide good learning time for 25 to 40 *individuals* in the same class!

Minimize management/wait/transition time in class routines

A *routine*, as we have noted several times, is any behavioral sequence that occurs regularly and for which specific ways of behaving are taught so as to minimize time and disruptions. According to descriptive research, in many classes students spend more time in management, transition, and waiting than they do in activity. Indeed, this nonactivity time often is two or three times as long as activity time (Siedentop 1980). Managerial time refers to non-content time that ranges from taking roll to collecting money for a school function. Transitions are episodes that take place within and between activities, such as changing teams, moving from one drill to another, moving from inside to outside, or changing equipment. What waiting means is all too evident! Students wait for class to begin; they wait for equipment to be put up; they wait for games to begin; they wait in line to have a turn.

Effective teachers minimize these time gobblers by developing routines and teaching them to students early in the academic year. In fact, a teacher's first order of business at the beginning of the school year should be to teach students important routines that can save time, create order, and minimize disruptions. Many of these time-saving routines have been described by Siedentop (1980):

1. Establish a time-saving method for taking attendance.

2. Control initial activity so that when students enter the teaching area (gym, pool, or field) they immediately get information, say, from a poster or chalkboard, about what to do and where to do it. Thus, when class officially begins, the students are already engaged in activity.

3. Use one signal to get students' attention. This needs to be a specific signal that is not used for any other purpose. When students hear it, they should stop what they are doing, put any balls or equipment on the floor, and face the teacher.

4. Establish a routine for quickly gathering students together. This is often necessary for instruction or feedback.

5. Establish a routine for quickly dispersing students. This is necessary when students are returning to an activity or beginning a new activity.

6. Establish a routine for invading space. Students often play games on adjacent courts and practice drills in confined spaces. When this happens, balls often move from one space and invade the space of others who are playing or practicing. An established routine answers the question of who retrieves the ball and when.

7. Establish equipment routines so that equipment-related time is minimized and the teacher does not have to be responsible for handling the equipment.

Routines save time and minimize disruption. They form the cornerstone of good preventive management in the gymnasium. Students should have a chance to practice the routines and to get feedback on how well they are performing them. Teachers should prompt students often when they are learning routines and praise students genuinely when they show improvement. Once students have internalized the routines, they will behave appropriately and predictably and be able to devote more time to learning.

Devote a high percentage of content time to practice

The first strategy we suggested in this section is to allocate a large percentage of time to content. A corollary to that strategy is to devote a high percentage of allocated content time to actual practice. Specifically, this means giving instructions and demonstrations quickly and efficiently and planning optimal time for students to actually practice the activities. By practicing and receiving good, accurate feedback, students progress. Students also enjoy physical education more when they are active more of the time.

Devoting a high percentage of time to practice is a strategy that teachers need to employ at the level of the individual student. For drills this means that small groups and more groups are better than larger groups in which less practice per student is achieved. It means that smaller-sized games are better than larger games; for example, three-person volleyball rather than six per side, and soccer with six per side rather than eleven.

Getting students involved in good practice situations is one of the most important teaching strategies for physical educators. We recognize that this

---

HOW STUDENTS SPEND THEIR TIME IN PHYSICAL EDUCATION

During the past decade a number of researchers in physical education have completed large descriptive studies that include observations of how students spend their time in physical education classes. The following data are from five major research projects and are expressed in terms of the amount of time students spend in various general categories as a percentage of total class time.

Where research was conducted	Management (including transitions)	Waiting	Receiving information	Engaged in motor activity
Victoria, Canada	20%	22%	22%	26%
Belgium	6%	32%	23%	30%
New York	13%	25%	25%	27%
Ohio	22%	24%	15%	21%
Quebec, Canada	18%	29%	17%	22%

The results appear to be fairly consistent from place to place. It is clear that students spend as much time waiting as they do engaged in the subject matter! The evidence also suggests that *classroom management* is a serious problem in physical education.

kind of total involvement can create managerial problems for teachers and that the potential for disruption may increase. However, the techniques for management and discipline described in this text should enable the serious physical education teacher to create situations in which all of the students get a high percentage of practice time and do so in ways that are not disruptive.

Keep students on-task

High rates of on-task behavior are extremely important if learning is to take place. And students who are involved appropriately with a learning task will not be disruptive. Students need to learn very early in the school year that the teacher both expects and supports on-task behavior. There are many different ways that teachers keep students on-task. Eventually, students can learn to stay on-task themselves, especially if they learn to like the subject matter. They can become more self-directed and less in need of supervision. What follows are some of the most important teaching strategies to keep students on-task.

1. Teachers actively supervise students. Physical education is typically taught in a large space. During practice sessions students are often dispersed throughout that large space. A teacher cannot be in all places at the same time. But by means of active supervision strategies, the teacher can make it seem as if he or she is everywhere. Active supervision means that a teacher moves about the space often and in somewhat unpredictable routes. In active supervision, teachers also regularly scan the space to make sure they know what is going on. As soon as students realize that the teacher knows what is going on, they will tend to remain on-task. In the early stages of a school year, active supervision is best accomplished if the teacher stays near the perimeter of the space so that most of the students are in sight at all times.

2. Teachers quickly respond to off-task students. Students who are off-task need to be directed back toward the task. Teachers can do this in a number of ways. They can issue a verbal desist. They can simply move closer to the students. They can provide an on-task prompt that redirects the students. If a teacher desists and redirects off-task students quickly, students will learn that the teacher is aware of what is going on in the space and will be less inclined to get off-task.

3. Teachers support on-task students. A kind word is important to students who are really trying to be on-task. Teachers can direct positive feedback to an individual or to a group. Teachers should do this frequently at the beginning of the year so that students realize that their efforts are appreciated. Teachers should try to provide two supporting, positive feedbacks for every one desist they need to give. Gradually, teachers who do this will discover that they need to desist less often and the ratio of positive feedbacks to desists will become much larger. It is important to understand that good behavior needs to be supported by teachers! Teachers should not hesitate to compliment students—genuinely and often.

4. Teachers have high expectations for on-task behavior. Most teachers do expect their students to stay on-task, but they seldom communicate that expectation to the students. It is important that students understand clearly that teachers expect them to be on-task and to make an effort to learn. Teachers can communicate these expectations in a number of ways. The most direct way is simply to tell students periodically that these are the expectations. A second way is to prompt often during lessons, especially at the beginning of the school year. Verbal prompts that keep students on-task and generally energize students have been called "hustles" (Siedentop 1980). Statements such as "Let's make an effort today," "Keep at it, keep at it," "Work hard now," and "Let's hustle on this drill" are examples of verbal prompts that keep students on-task. Teachers can also communicate on-task expectations when they provide skill feedback.

Assign tasks that are meaningful and matched to student abilities

Effective teachers do not ask their students to do trivial meaningless tasks; neither do they ask students to do tasks that are either much too simple or much too difficult. Effective teachers develop student activities that are both challenging and provide for a great deal of success. Obviously, as students improve, teachers should make the activities progressively more challenging while still allowing for high rates of success if students make an effort to learn.

It is also important for teachers to ask students to do meaningful tasks. Students in physical education are not experienced athletes. They have not always learned the perseverance necessary to work on an isolated skill. They do not always understand how the isolated skills are put together into meaningful wholes. Thus, it is better for physical education teachers to try to make each activity a meaningful unit of practice in and of itself. They can do this by turning drills into games by adding a clear goal, some rules, and a scoring system. Rather than just pass volleyballs, dribble basketballs, or kick soccer balls with no particular objective in mind, students will do better in a drill/ game that has a definite goal for them to achieve and a way for them to know if they have achieved it.

Games must be modified to match student abilities.

Matching tasks to student abilities is one of the basic teaching skills that physical educators need to acquire. The chapter on planning includes materials on task analysis, which is the basic strategy for developing activities that are both challenging and allow for successful participation (see pages 330–340). Very few middle, junior, or senior high school students have the skills or backgrounds to play the adult forms of most sports. These activities need to be modified to be appropriate to student abilities. The best modifications are those that teachers design to meet specific instructional goals.

Keep the learning environment supportive and set high but realistic expectations

One of the clearest, most consistent findings in research on teacher effectiveness is that negatively oriented climates are often associated with lower achievement. Classrooms in which teachers criticize a lot, are sarcastic, punish often, and provide mostly negative academic feedback are strongly related to lower achievement, poorer attitudes, and lower self-concept on the part of students. There is absolutely no support in either theory or research for the teacher who wants to be a "tough guy." Punishment is sometimes necessary, but teachers should use it skillfully and minimally. Teachers cannot expect students to learn and grow in educational climates that are negatively oriented.

Instead, teachers should strive to build a learning environment that is supportive and set high expectations for student growth. Teachers can develop supportive environments in several ways. First, they can support students with positive feedback and praise for staying on-task, for trying hard, and above all, for getting better. Positive prompts are also helpful. Providing meaningful tasks that are challenging yet allow for successful participation also contributes strongly to a positive learning climate.

Teachers can and should communicate high expectations directly. Students should understand very clearly that teachers expect them to improve. A climate of high expectation coupled with strong supportive comments from

---

GOOD AS GOLD

Sometimes the simplest advice, if it is based on real experience, is worth its weight in gold. The advice, if acted upon, can save time, trouble, and headaches. Here are three such nuggets that have been passed along for many, many years—evidence of the degree to which they still are true in schools.

- For routines to go smoothly at school, be on good terms with the school secretaries.
- For the gymnasium and locker spaces to stay in tip-top shape, stay on good terms with the maintenance staff.
- For help with student learning and discipline, stay on good terms with the parents of your students.

the teacher is contagious. Students will begin to understand that this is a place for learning and that the teacher supports and appreciates their efforts.

We are not suggesting that teachers have to be cheerleaders all of the time. There are many ways to communicate support and expectations that are quietly effective. What is important is that teachers recognize the importance of a positive climate filled with high expectations and then do something about it.

Give lessons smoothness and momentum

We often make the comment that the foundation of effective teaching is good class management. Good management is no guarantee of good teaching—sometimes classes are well managed but very little takes place in them. On the other hand, it seems impossible to teach well without good management. We have already spoken of the need for high percentages of practice time and for high rates of on-task behavior. We have also described the importance of class routines that minimize time used up in managerial events, transitions, and waiting. Once a lesson gets started (quickly, we hope), it is important that it move forward with a strong momentum and not be slowed down by interruptions. You have often heard sports commentators refer to the importance of momentum in a game. It is important in teaching, too. There are several ways that lessons can lose momentum and smoothness (Kounin 1977). A few of the more important ones follow.

An event intrudes on the lesson, and the teacher cannot handle both the intrusion event and the continuation of the lesson, thus causing a pause in the lesson that destroys its momentum! What if a messenger comes with a note from another teacher? What if a message comes over the loudspeaker? Every day events intrude on teachers' lessons. Teachers have to learn how to handle these events and still keep the class going smoothly. A teacher cannot afford to give complete attention to the intrusion to the complete neglect of the lesson. The teacher can give students a prompt "keep working," handle the intrusion quickly, and return his or her attention to the class.

Teachers sometimes interrupt ongoing activities at the wrong time and thus spoil the momentum of the lesson for the students. Often teachers need to change activities or to provide some further instruction or to give a group feedback. However, the teacher should wait for an appropriate moment to interrupt the ongoing activity.

Teachers sometimes dwell too long on an event or instruction. Most instructions, demonstrations, and feedbacks in physical education can be handled quickly. Too much information is hard for students to absorb. If a teacher dwells on a topic too long, she or he risks slowing down the lesson and will find it hard to regain lost momentum. The teacher's own behavior should be exemplary of a brisk yet complete pace.

Hold students accountable for learning

Research in the classroom (Doyle 1979) and in the gymnasium (Tousignant and Siedentop 1983) indicate that accountability is a crucial factor in student learning. It appears that physical education teachers often tend to hold students accountable for attendance, appropriate uniform, and appropriate behavior in the gymnasium, what Tousignant (1982) describes as "being a member in good standing" of the class. Beyond this, teachers often require little more than a minimal effort. It is little wonder that students do not progress under such conditions.

We want to confront you directly on this issue because you may not believe as we do. As we have said several times before, many physical educators believe that it is *unfair* to hold students accountable for performance, to grade them on how *well* they do. However, research, theory, and common sense suggest that lack of accountability will lead to lack of learning.

Doyle (1979) has suggested that the major agenda in many classrooms is for the teacher and students to agree to cooperate and then to fill the available time with some activities. Does that sound like some physical education classes you have seen?

Accountability systems can be formal or informal. Formal accountability occurs when teachers test, grade, or use task-oriented systems that rely on contingency management (Siedentop 1980). Informal accountability occurs when teachers provide feedback and encouragement for performance and let the students know that improvement is both expected and rewarded. This is a crucial issue that you should think about and discuss with others. (See page 384 to find out how supervision and accountability work together to define for the student what the *real* issues of the physical education class are about.) Regardless of what one *says* about performance, it is the accountability system one implements that will ultimately determine what students do. If the system does not require improvement and good performance, then teachers should not expect to get too much of either.

Models for teaching

A number of teaching models have been developed in recent years and applied successfully both to classroom teaching and to physical education. These models have much in common even though they may look quite different to the inexperienced observer. The models tend to define tasks clearly, provide for an ample amount of good practice, provide regular assessment and feedback, help to keep students on-task, and provide a solid accountability system. These features have allowed models to be successful in a wide range of school settings and in different subject areas. Let's turn now to six of these models.

Direct instruction

The most widely used form of effective teaching in American schools is direct instruction (Siedentop 1980). In this model, the teacher is the leader. In direct instruction, the teacher makes goals clear to students, plans a sufficient

HOW DO STUDENTS KNOW WHAT THE *REAL* TASK IS?

The student teacher organized the 26 students into four groups to practice a beginning bump pass skill in a volleyball unit. Each group was to form a circle and keep the ball up by bumping it to one another across the circle. However, 45 seconds after the drill began and with the student teacher at the other end of the gymnasium, one circle decided to see how often they could hit the ceiling with their bump passes. They modified the task to their own liking.

Teachers spend time each day explaining to their students what the activities will be for that lesson. They describe each task and disperse students to perform the task. But students often modify the task to make it either simpler or more challenging, or they try to avoid doing the task at all! What students end up doing is often very different from what the teacher asked them to do. The task *stated* by the teacher is often modified beyond recognition.

It appears that students learn the *real* tasks of the lesson when active supervision and accountability are present (Tousignant and Siedentop 1983). The cycle seems to go something like this:

> Teacher states a task.
> > Students make responses.
> > > Teacher supervises and responds to the modified responses.

The teacher's response (a form of accountability) to the students' attempt at the task defines what the *real* task will become. Often the *real* task becomes something quite different from the *stated* task because (a) teachers do not supervise actively and do not see the modification and (b) they see the modification but accept it. Thus, it appears that teacher accountability is primarily responsible for what the real task becomes in the gymnasium.

amount of time for practice, supervises student practice actively, gives supportive feedback frequently, and holds students accountable for their performance. The teacher is clearly in charge, the teacher controls the pace and direction of the lesson, the teacher chooses the activities and matches them to the abilities of the students, and while doing all of this, the teacher also creates a warm, supportive educational climate. Direct instruction is *not* a cold, authoritarian approach. The learning environment is highly structured and the teacher controls the elements of the lessons, but the atmosphere is one of high expectations and strong support for student efforts.

Direct instruction does not refer to "traditional" teaching or to "command" teaching. Direct instruction, as a teaching style, was identified through recent investigations of models of effective teaching in schools. The group of strategies that come together under the rubric of direct instruction *are those that effective teachers use in schools*! In direct instruction, teachers work hard and take responsibility for their students' learning. Their efforts and enthusiasm convey to students that the main agenda is learning and that their expectation is that students will pay attention to that agenda.

Task/station teaching

Task/station teaching is a model in which teachers create different tasks for students to practice, describe these tasks on cards or posters, arrange the teaching space with different tasks at different stations, divide the class into groups, and then have students work through the lesson by moving from station to station in some predetermined way. Task/station teaching is used widely in physical education and is especially suited to activities such as gymnastics.

Often the task cards are displayed prominently at each station. Sometimes students carry a series of task cards with them as they advance through the system. Each task card clearly defines an activity. Typically, the task card includes the conditions or situation under which the activity is to be done, a description of the activity itself, and information that will allow students to know when they have successfully completed the activity.

Students can progress through a task/station system in several ways. One way is to allow them a certain amount of time at each station. On a signal, students then move to the next station. Another strategy is to allow students to move through the system according to how well they can do the tasks. This kind of *self-pacing* is one of the attractive features of task/station teaching. Self-pacing requires only that students master the task at one station before moving to another station.

Tasks can be sequential and progressive; that is, they can be related to one another and made progressively more challenging. Or tasks can simply be different skills or strategies that later will contribute to some combined set of skills. For example, a task/station system in volleyball might include a serving station, a bumping station, a set station, a spike station, and a receiving station. These skills would then come together when students began to play a modified game of volleyball.

We should mention that task/station teaching cannot be done appropriately until students have learned to stay on-task and to use the task/station system. The teacher must teach students these behavioral skills. A teacher cannot simply expect students to use a task/station system successfully without instruction and behave well in doing so. The *freedom* of the task/station system is useful only if the students behave *responsibly*.

Reciprocal/group teaching

Reciprocal/group teaching (Mosston 1981) is a teaching model in which students are put in pairs or in small groups and the partner/group system is used to enhance the teaching/learning process. In this model, students can provide instruction for one another, provide feedback as practice goes on, and help one another to improve by providing encouragement and group support. Reciprocal/group teaching can be used in combination with a number of other models and is particularly appropriate with the task/station, contracting, contingency management, and PSI models (see page 389). The reciprocal/group approach is also useful in sport education models (see Chapter 11).

An assumption of reciprocal/group teaching is that positive socialization will occur within the group or between the partners. By helping one another learn, students will not only progress in their skill/strategy/knowledge development but will also experience positive social growth.

Use of this model requires several prerequisites. First, if students are to provide instruction and feedback to one another, the teacher must take time to teach them how to exercise these important teaching skills. Second, the teacher must instruct students carefully in what expectations he or she has for the nature of the interactions among members of the groups. If students are to act as peer tutors for one another, they must take the role seriously and behave decently toward one another. Furthermore, the teacher must convince students that helping one another is an important part of their responsibility in the class.

The teacher should arrange groups/partners so that total learning can be facilitated. The teacher should not place students of highly unequal abilities together because this prevents *reciprocal* interaction from taking place. If students are terribly unequal in ability, then the student with less skill will have little success trying to be a peer tutor for the student with greater skill, and an unequal relationship will develop.

Contracting

Contracting is a model in which students agree to complete a certain task at an agreed upon level of performance in order to receive some reward. Contracting can be used within regular classes, but it is most often used for independent study in physical education or for classes that take place off campus. For example, a teacher might use contracting for a bowling class that meets at a local bowling alley (see Figure 20.1).

Contracts can be short and simple, but they can also be long and involved. Teachers tend to get what they contract for, and it is therefore important that the contract have sufficient specificity to ensure that the desired outcomes will be realized. Contracts should specify what is to be done, how well it needs to be done, and the consequence of completing the tasks (in high school this is typically a specific grade). Teachers can make contracts more flexible by assigning criteria to multiple grades, for example, by assigning stipulated levels of performance to earn a C, B, or A grade for an activity.

Contracts can emphasize the *process* of practice, the *product* of practice, or both. In bowling, for example, if the teacher wishes to emphasize process, he or she words the contract to specify how many games students will bowl, how much time they must spend in practice on picking up spares, and the number of pages in a bowling book that students must read. If the teacher wishes to emphasize product, he or she specifies outcomes such as the scores per game, the number of spares converted, and scores on a test on the bowling book. Examples of contracts appear in Figures 20.1 and 20.2 (p. 389).

REQUIRED AND ELECTIVE CONTRACTS
BOWLING UNIT

REQUIRED

1. Bowl six games at any local bowling alley. Bring your scoresheet back as part of your report. On a separate sheet of paper list and define the symbols used in scoring. Also list the two basic rules for scoring.

2. Write a paper detailing the development of bowling as a sport. Use at least four library references and include them in a bibliography. The paper should be equivalent to two double-spaced, typed pages.

3. At a brief practical examination with the instructor, be able to demonstrate appropriate grip, correct hold of the ball, footwork for the approach, and proper form at release. Also, be ready to demonstrate how these features differ when the bowler wants to throw a hook ball, a straight ball, or a back-up ball.

ELECTIVE (complete any combination that totals 75 points)

1. Observe one complete session of any local bowling league for adults. Write a two-page, double-spaced paper on your impressions. (20 points)

2. At a brief practical examination with the instructor, be able to demonstrate the appropriate technique and strategy for picking up various splits and spares. (15 points)

3. Bowl three games with a friend or classmate. Describe in detail the technique used by the bowler including an analysis of the errors committed. Based on the analysis, suggest specific practice strategies to help this person improve. Prepare in writing both the analysis and the suggestions for improvement. (20 points)

4. At a brief practical examination, be able to explain to the instructor how to select a ball. Be sure to include information about weight of the ball relative to the bowler, fitting the hand to the ball, and what options exist for a person purchasing a ball. (15 points)

(continued)

Figure 20.1 Contingency bowling contracts.

SOURCE: Fast 1971, p. 32

5. Read any published instructional book on bowling. Write a brief review of the book including a review of the contents and a critique of how the information was presented. (20 points)

6. Practice bowling by completing an additional six games in addition to those in the required contract. Keep a journal of what spares and splits you had to pick up and how successful you were. Based on these games, analyze your strengths and weaknesses as a bowler. Turn in the journal and the analysis. (20 points)

7. Watch a professional bowling match on television. In a two-page, typed, double-spaced report, describe in detail how what you observed differs from your local league. (15 points)

8. Interview at least three bowlers from an adult league. Ask each bowler why they bowl, what pleasure they derive from the sport, and what they think is important about being a good bowler and having fun at it. Write a two-page paper on your interviews. (20 points)

Contracting is a useful strategy, but it requires teachers to hold students accountable for fulfilling a contract. Teachers must do everything they can to ensure that contracts are completed honestly and within the time specified in the contract. Not all students will have acquired the self-direction needed to make contracting work. However, they can develop these self-direction skills,

Name _____

Mark the date on which you meet each performance objective.

_____ 1. Insert the mouthpiece by placing the wide flange between the lips and teeth, and the smaller flange lightly between the teeth. Breathe through snorkel above surface until comfortable with mouth breathing.

_____ 2. Squat down until mouth and nose are submerged and breathe cautiously through the mouth. Repeat 5 times.

_____ 3. Squat under water until snorkel floods. Rise until eyes are above water and puff forcefully through mouth to clear snorkel. Do 4 out of 5 times successfully.

_____ 4. In shallow water, attach snorkel to mask and submerge with a clear mask and snorkel. Flood and clear the snorkel 4 out of 5 times.

_____ 5. Breathe with face submerged (snorkel above surface), flood mask and snorkel by submerging, and surface with mask and snorkel clear 4 out of 5 times.

_____ 6. Repeat no. 4 in 6 feet of water 4 out of 5 attempts.

_____ 7. Repeat no. 4 in 9 feet of water 4 out of 5 attempts.

_____ 8. Repeat no. 5 in 6 feet of water 4 out of 5 attempts.

_____ 9. Repeat no. 5 in 9 feet of water 4 out of 5 attempts.

Surface dives

_____ 1. Swim at the surface with face in water and pike at the waist and dive to the bottom. Clear snorkel as you surface 4 out of 5 times.

_____ 2. Start at shallow end of pool and begin on surface of water completing 3 surface dives before you reach the deep end. Snorkel should be cleared after each dive. Complete 3 lengths.

Figure 20.2 Items in a contract for the snorkel section of a skin diving unit.

and the option to use contracting greatly enhances a teacher's ability to provide a complete physical education program.

PSI/Mastery learning

PSI stands for personalized system of instruction and is also known as the Keller method (Siedentop 1973). Mastery learning is an instructional model that was developed by Benjamin Bloom and his colleagues. The two models have much in common. First, the total amount to be learned in any given unit of instruction is broken down into small "chunks." These chunks are often related to one another in that learning one is a prerequisite to attempting another. For example, demonstrating the ability to serve a volleyball overhand from midcourt might be prerequisite to learning how to serve overhand from behind the baseline. In other cases, the chunks are unrelated. The teacher provides instruction for each chunk and gives students the opportunity to practice it. Once students believe they have attained that level of performance specified by the teacher, they are tested. These frequent assessments of smaller units of learning are the major feature of PSI and mastery learning. *Students are not allowed to go on to the next unit until they have reached the mastery level for the previous unit.* If, when assessed, they do not reach the mastery level, the teacher provides new instructional feedback and requires them to practice more.

PSI/mastery models allow for substantial amounts of self-pacing and demand a certain level of performance. At the end of a PSI/mastery course, students will differ more in *how much* they have learned rather than *how well* they have learned it. PSI/mastery models tend to be highly motivating because each unit assessment provides a progress check for students. The major difference between the two models is that in the PSI tradition each unit performance contributes to an overall grade, while in the mastery learning tradition the unit progress checks are not formally graded, and only the final assessment at the end of the total unit is used for grading.

PSI/mastery models require teachers to develop instructional materials for students. They also assume that students have developed a good level of self-discipline and on-task behavior. Students are allowed to work at their own pace, and the teacher acts as a tutor, feedback agent, and evaluator. Obviously, these models also lend themselves to various forms of reciprocal teaching. For more information on PSI and mastery learning, consult Tousignant (1983) and Siedentop (1973). Figure 20.3 shows a portion of a PSI tennis unit.

Contingency management

Contingency management is a model in which a system of specific rewards is tied to a system of instructional goals. Students are provided clearly specified descriptions of instructional goals, and the accomplishment of each instructional goal is "worth" a certain amount of reward. The term *contingency* refers to the relationship between a task and a reward.

Perhaps the most widely used form of contingency management in junior and senior high schools is to provide points for completing specified learning tasks and to use the point system for grading purposes. In this way students know exactly how well they need to perform to earn certain grades. Differences among the various grades can be made in several ways. First, the teacher can assign a higher grade for the completion of *more* work. Second, the teacher can assign a higher grade for *better* work (performance). Third, the teacher can use a combination of *quantity* and *quality*. Examples of contingency management approaches appear on pages 387–388.

Although grades are widely used as rewards in the contingency management model, we want to emphasize the wisdom of using other forms of rewards too. Teachers can arrange many reward systems within the budget of school physical education programs. Simple certificates, brightly colored ribbons, and a host of other cost-effective rewards are available. The point is that

UNIT 4—Rules and Rally

Terminal Objectives

1. Student will demonstrate knowledge of tennis rules by scoring 80% or more on a written test.

2. Student will demonstrate the ability to move from a ready position to the forehand and/or backhand ground strokes so that a rally is continued for 6 consecutive hits, and the balls remain within a singles court.

Learning Tasks

Student will read handout provided and answer questions on a worksheet.

Student will participate in "home base" drill so that 6 consecutive balls are hit between singles boundaries.

Student will participate in "ground stroke" scramble until 6 consecutive balls are hit within singles boundaries.

Student will participate in "two-on-one" drill until the student can rally 6 consecutive times within singles boundaries.

Figure 20.3 *Objectives and learning tasks from a high school PSI unit in tennis.*

SOURCE: Tousignant 1983, p. 34

for contingency management to be effective, the reward system must motivate the students. Grades do not always motivate all students.

Another form of reward is public recognition of progress. Therefore, the physical education department might institute an "improvement" club and publicly display the names of students completing tasks each week. Public recognition of achievement is important to adolescent students, and physical educators need to be constantly aware of how rewarding their classes are for students. The "rewarding" nature of a class is determined at three distinct levels. First, a supportive, positive climate is important, as we emphasized in Chapter 19. Second, improvement and achievement are important because they are the aspects of student behavior that get rewarded. Third, a more formal system of rewards can serve to enhance the other two levels; and that is where the contingency management model is so effective.

Teaching tips

Teaching skills can be learned, practiced, and perfected. Just as in sport, where the development and refinement of separate skills does not necessarily add up to a competent player, the acquisition of separate teaching skills does not automatically add up to a competent teacher. The successful application of a large number of skills in the right combination at the right time tends to define both the competent player and the competent teacher.

This section is devoted to tips on using important teaching skills. Most of these tips are based on research which shows that when used properly, these skills are related to student achievement. The skills reviewed in this section are the most commonly used interactive teaching skills. Planning skills, instructional design skills, and classroom management skills are covered in other chapters.

Provide instructions. Teachers introduce skills, explain games, explain practice drills, and provide feedback to a group about their performances. Each of these situations requires the teacher to provide verbal instruction.

- Carefully plan what you want to say, make notes, and use them.
- Limit the information. Do not overload students with technical details, but be specific in what you say.
- Use language appropriate to the skill and the students' previous experience with it.
- Make sure that you use language properly. Do not embarrass yourself and the profession by having a student correct your grammar.
- Talk slowly and emphasize crucial points clearly.
- Try as often as possible to provide a demonstration (visual information) along with the verbal description.
- Make sure the students are paying attention. Check their understanding by asking questions intermittently.
- Speak up, be assertive, show enthusiasm and leadership in the way you talk.

Provide demonstrations. Students need to *see* how a skill looks, what a drill involves, and how a strategy is used. Each of these situations will require some demonstration. Done well, demonstrations can contribute strongly to more efficient learning. Done poorly, they probably retard learning.

- Be sure the demonstrator is an adequate model, that is, is able to do properly what is being shown.
- If equipment or materials are necessary, set them up beforehand rather than waste time while students wait.
- Show the entire skill/organization/strategy first. Give an overall understanding before focusing on details or parts.
- Do the demonstration at the place where the skill or strategy will be used.
- Direct the demonstration to the students. Let them see more than one view.
- Emphasize safety points if relevant.
- Organize the students in such a way that they can at least partially *use* the skill or strategy as you show it to them. This involves the students and directs their attention to the demonstration.
- Do not get too technical; limit information; be crisp and do not over-dwell.
- Check for understanding *before* you disperse the students.

Some activities are difficult to supervise.

Supervise student practice. Active supervision is one of the most important teaching skills (see page 379). It is important for keeping students on-task and also for your being in a position to see their performances and to provide them with useful feedback.

- At the outset, try to stay on the perimeter of the space so as to keep all the students in view.
- Do not get so caught up in watching one student that you do not glance often to see what the other students are doing.
- Try to avoid moving in predictable patterns.
- Do not hesitate to use your voice across the space to let students know you are supervising. This does not only mean stopping misbehavior; it also means providing supportive comments and positive prompts. The key point is that students have to learn that you are *aware* of what is going on.
- Stop students' unsafe or disruptive behavior immediately.

Provide behavioral feedback. Teachers need to provide students with feedback about their social and organizational behavior in class. This feedback, of course, should not always be in the form of critical, corrective, or punitive statements. Good behavior needs to be supported, too.

- Make sure that your feedback is specific to the class rules and expectations.
- Provide frequent feedback early in the school year or term.
- Try to avoid giving feedback only when you see some misbehavior.
- Support appropriate behavior with compliments.
- Provide personal feedback to individuals and also comments to the group as a whole.
- Along with feedback statements, try to provide the reasons *why* the good behavior is important. This helps to develop standards among the students.

Provide skill feedback. Most physical educators agree that the right skill feedback at the right moment can greatly enhance learning. This is no doubt true for individual skills as well as group efforts.

- Try to be in good position to see the performance so that you get good information.
- Make the feedback statement specific to what the instructional cue or prompt has been; i.e., do not tell a student to focus on one aspect of a skill and then provide feedback on another aspect.
- Try to give specific information with most feedback statements. "Nice going" and "well done" are positive comments, but feedback needs to have greater specificity.
- Try to provide as many positive feedbacks as corrective. Although corrective feedback is useful and necessary, it is also important that students learn what they have done correctly and well.
- When possible, tell students *why* a correction is necessary (bend more at the knees *so that* you can generate more power).
- Try to *show* as well as *tell*. Visual feedback information can be given more quickly and is more relevant to the learner than long, involved descriptions.
- Do not hesitate to use positive models to provide group feedback. Singling out a student who is doing something well not only provides recognition for that student but is a good source of feedback for other students.
- Try to stay with a student or group long enough to see if your feedback is *used*. It is important that students try to implement your suggestions.

Use questions. Teachers often ask questions of students as an instructional strategy or as a means for checking student understanding. Questioning is a skill that teachers do not often do well.

- Make questions brief and clear. Do not ask multiple questions in one statement.
- Try to distinguish between questions that have specific answers (convergent) and those that have many answers (divergent), and make sure that you use the type that is relevant to your purposes.
- Ask the question and then call for volunteers or name a student to respond. Avoid calling on a student and then asking the question.
- Allow time for students to respond. Do not answer for them if they are a bit slow.
- If you are concerned with facts and understanding, ask simple, direct questions that have simple, direct answers. Do not make a quiz show out of your questions unless that is your purpose.
- If you wish to involve more students, redirect your questions to elicit answers from several students. However, if you use the redirect tech-

nique, wait until several students have responded before you provide confirmation and feedback.

Provide accountability. Earlier we suggested that accountability was a key factor in student learning (see page 382). Formal accountability is provided by a grading system or some form of contingency management. Informal accountability is primarily provided by teacher interaction and basic teaching strategies. Students are not fools—they tend to adjust their performance and behavior to the expectations and accountability of the learning environment. In other words, teachers are likely to get just what their system requires!

- Make sure the accountability system is clear to students early in the experience.
- Be absolutely consistent in your application of accountability. Avoid changing the system for individual students; students view inconsistency as a major defect.
- Keep the group alert to your expectations by frequent prompting that involves information relevant to the accountability system.
- Make sure you communicate realistic, positive expectations about student performance. If you do not communicate that you believe students can do something, then do not expect them to believe they can do it.
- Give public recognition to achievement and progress; show students that you value both. And do not hesitate to praise good performance.
- If the accountability system involves recording results of student performance, make sure that the recording is done accurately. This is particularly relevant when students are recording one another's performance results or when they are recording their own results.
- See that formal and informal accountability systems reward consistent improvement in small increments. Do not arrange a system that requires months of improvement before recognition is provided.
- Be fair. Do not demand too much performance for too little reward; conversely, do not give too much reward for only minor improvement or performance.
- Persevere. Without standards, the educational environment will quickly deteriorate.

Summary

Effective teachers are the backbone of education. Being an effective teacher does not mean adopting a "magic" method that works in all places for all students; it means using teaching strategies that work regardless of teaching style or method.

Effective teaching strategies include devoting a large percentage of time to content, spending minimal time on management tasks, providing students with optimal practice time, ensuring high rates of on-task behavior, matching task demands to student abilities, setting high expectations for achievement, making lessons smooth, and holding students accountable for achievement.

Models for teaching include direct instruction, task/station teaching, reciprocal/group teaching, contracting, PSI/mastery learning, and contingency management. Some of these models can be combined with one another, and each is more or less useful depending on the activity, the school, and the interests of the teacher.

Important teaching tips reflect the characteristics of effective instruction. Make instructions clear and appropriate. Be sure that demonstrations are well prepared, efficient, and informative. Actively supervise student practice. Deliver behavioral and skill feedback accurately and often. Ask appropriate questions. Make sure that accountability systems are consistent and absolutely clear to students.

Suggested activities

1. Prepare a brief report on the best teacher you ever had. Describe what the teacher *did* to win your favorable judgment. Compare his or her strategies to those described in this chapter.

2. Divide into groups. Each group is to examine one model for teaching physical education with special attention to what demands the model places on the teacher and report the group's findings to the class.

3. In class, discuss the teaching tips provided in the chapter. Then add to the list with suggestions from your own experiences.

4. Debate the following issue: Teaching effectiveness should be judged primarily on the basis of student achievement. Have three students argue the affirmative and three the negative.

5. List the major effective teaching strategies presented in the chapter and then indicate the degree to which you believe you have mastered each strategy. Use the results as a basis for class discussion of how and when the strategies may be acquired and refined.

21

Current Issues in Teaching

The purpose of this chapter is to examine current issues in professional physical education that exert an impact on day-to-day teaching in middle schools and junior and senior high schools. The chapter defines the issues, places them in perspective, and where appropriate, offers potential solutions to problems associated with them. The major topics covered in the chapter are as follows:

Terms and concepts related to legal liability in teaching

Guidelines for teachers to protect against negligence

Accountability concerns surrounding assessment and grading in physical education

Rules for and challenges deriving from coeducational teaching

Suggestions for coeducational competition

Relative merits of arguments for an emphasis on lifetime sports versus team sports in school programs

Factors that make competition either good or bad

A physical education teacher in a midwestern state is sued by a student and his parents for failure to teach sufficient progressions in a gymnastics unit in which the student suffers a spinal cord injury. Coeducational instruction in school physical education becomes the law of the land with the passage of Title IX. Girls are guaranteed equal access to facilities and support both in physical education and interscholastic sport. Problems continue to occur in youth sport and interscholastic sport. As a result, a movement in physical education begins to stress fun and noncompetitive activities. Students in physical education classes are held accountable for attendance, proper dress, and minimal participation; that is, if they show up, dress up, and stand up, they earn not only a passing grade but often the top grade. Physical educators seem to believe that success in teaching is related to students' being "busy, happy, and good" (Placek 1983). Seldom are students held accountable for improvement in skills, fitness, or ability to play games well. Competitive team sports are thought by many to be inappropriate for high school curricula; instead, there is a call for greater emphasis on lifetime sports.

No profession is without its current issues. The issues reflected in the preceding paragraph happen to be of current importance in physical education. Most of these issues are reflections of general concerns in society. For example, legal liability is an issue in teaching physical education because we live in an era when more and more people turn to the courts to redress their grievances against others. Equity in sport and physical education for girls and women reflects a 30-year emphasis in our society toward equal opportunity, an emphasis also reflected in the civil rights movement and in education for the handicapped. Questions about competition have always been present in society and seem never to get resolved. Accountability for performance is an issue in industry and government as well as in schools. There is a great deal of discussion about teachers being held more accountable. Therefore, it seems natural that concern should develop over accountability for students too.

The purposes of this chapter are to address these issues, to provide some factual information about them, and to present views toward them. Thus you will be better able to form a point of view and develop an *informed* attitude toward these issues.

Safety and liability considerations

A student in a physical education class is under the care of the teacher. That responsibility cannot be assigned to someone else. It cannot be avoided. As the common phrase goes, "it comes with the territory."

Safety is important in physical education. It is important first of all because nobody wants a student to be injured. It is also important because students should *feel* safe and be willing to take physical risks that are within their skill capabilities. Thus, both physical and psychological safety are major ingredients in well-planned and well-implemented physical education programs.

We live in an era in which people are more willing than ever to use the judicial system. Doctors get sued. Manufacturers get sued. Teachers get sued. Teachers sue school boards. Legal liability has become a dominant issue in virtually every professional endeavor.

Teachers are not liable for injuries that occur to those under their care if they have acted as reasonable, prudent people would have acted under similar circumstances. The basis for liability suits against teachers is almost always a claim of negligence. *Negligence* is defined as failure to act as a reasonable, prudent person would have acted. The crux of the matter, then, is what constitutes reasonable, prudent behavior for the practicing physical educator. This section attempts to answer that question.

Important terms and concepts

Teachers need to understand a number of terms and concepts in order to deal adequately with the entire issue of legal liability in teaching (Drowatzky 1978).

- *Liability* is the breach of a duty, most often through a negligent act.
- *Negligence* is conduct that falls below an established standard of care to protect others against unreasonable risk of physical or mental harm. Negligence can occur through acts of commission or acts of omission.
- The *"but for"* test refers to establishing negligence as a causal factor in injury; that is, the injury would not have occurred *but for* the negligent act.
- *Duty* refers to the responsibility to protect others from unreasonable physical or mental harm and to avoid acts of omission that could produce such harmful situations.
- Being a *professional* means that one who undertakes to provide services in the practice of a profession (such as being a certified teacher) is required to exercise the knowledge and skill typically demonstrated by members of that profession who are in good standing in similar communities.
- *Risk* is typically assigned on the basis of the facts and circumstances involved in the individual situation, and in school cases risk is based on the following priorities:
  1. The student (the person exposed to the risk) is given the highest value.
  2. The reason for taking the risk; that is, did the student undertake the activity voluntarily with knowledge of all of the potential consequences, or did the student do it because the teacher said to do it?
  3. The magnitude of the risk, which typically relates to the potential for physical harm.
  4. The utility of the risk.
  5. The necessity of the risk; that is, was there some other activity that might have produced the same instructional outcome with less risk?

The notion of a duty owed students by their physical education teachers does not present a completely clear picture from which we can draw guidelines to help teachers perform in reasonable and prudent ways. However, a sufficient number of court cases have been decided to allow for a series of recommendations that have some basis in court precedents. Teachers who follow these recommendations will have done the best they can to behave as reasonable, prudent professional teachers.

Guidelines for teachers

The first guideline is that teachers should have *procedures* related to class management and specifically to activities in which safety is a specific concern. These procedures need to be stated with great clarity, and teachers need to communicate them to students early and often. Special equipment or special activities that might involve risk require special procedures.

A second guideline deals with supervision of students. We have made a strong case for active supervision as an important teaching skill. Adequate supervision is almost always an issue in teacher liability cases. Several points are important here. A teacher cannot supervise unless he or she is at the site. Teachers should never leave classes unsupervised or unattended. Teachers should utilize the strategies for active supervision suggested earlier.

A third guideline pertains to planning. If a lesson plan is well done and is related to a curriculum syllabus that is on file at the school, then it is clear that the activity in which students are engaged is part of the approved curriculum of the district. Lack of evidence of planning invites questions about the legitimacy of the activity and the degree to which it was an "approved" activity.

A fourth guideline involves the design of instruction within the activity unit. We have made it clear that we believe it important that teachers match the demands of an activity to the abilities of students. This is what is typically meant by the term *teaching progressions*. To ask a student to do an activity for which he or she does not have adequate prerequisite skills is not only ineffective teaching but can be dangerous.

A fifth guideline deals with the teacher's skills relative to the activity he or she is teaching. Teachers should generally lead only those activities for which they have adequate preparation themselves. This is one very good reason for teachers to upgrade their own preparation continually. They need to be able to teach a variety of activities in a competent manner.

A sixth guideline deals with equipment. Teachers need to make sure that equipment is in good repair and is appropriate for the activity they are teaching. Equipment should not be left out in a space that is unsupervised between classes or during periods in which no classes meet. Facilities should not be used in ways for which they were not designed or in ways that represent safety hazards. Lines on floors were put there for specific purposes. They should not be used for other purposes unless the safety implications have been thoroughly resolved.

A seventh guideline deals with violations of class procedures and particularly of class safety rules. Teachers must deal with violations quickly and completely. They must stop unsafe behavior immediately.

A final guideline deals with student help in the instructional process. If students are to act in assisting roles (for example, as spotters in gymnastics), teachers must train them to do so and use them in a consistent manner.

A note of caution: Exercise judgment

How does one acquire good judgment? How does a teacher get in the habit of thinking about the safety implications of what he or she plans and implements? All of the suggestions we have made in this section are important, but they do not entirely take the place of good judgment. We cannot list all situations in which students may experience harm or provide all relevant guidelines. Teachers must *pay attention* to safety issues and be sensitive in terms of what they ask students to do.

Teachers should not put students in risk situations to "build character." Running on uneven surfaces should be done only under clear and well-supervised conditions. When running is used in any activity, students should have ample space to slow down before reaching a barrier or a wall. Students should not be mismatched in activities that involve physical contact. Students should not be asked to do activities for which they have not acquired the prerequisite skills. These situations, and many others, require good judgment on the part of the teacher.

It is important for every teacher to have liability insurance. This type of insurance is widely available and reasonably inexpensive. It is often available to members of professional teacher organizations. It can also often be added to renter's or homeowner's insurance. No teacher should be without it.

Liability is often a frightening prospect to the new teacher. However, a thoughtful teacher who develops clear procedures and enforces rules is unlikely to be judged by a court to be negligent. The courts are not out to get teachers. Although safety issues and potential liability situations should cause all teachers to think carefully about what they do, liability concerns should not prevent teachers from moving forward with the design and implementation of educationally sound activities that happen to involve some physical risk.

Accountability, assessment, and grading

During the early part of the twentieth century, professional physical educators struggled long and hard to have their subject accepted as a regular school subject. A major form of acceptance was the provision in state law that physical education was a required subject. Most states did eventually pass laws requiring participation in physical education either on the basis of a certain number of minutes or periods per week or on the basis of a certain number of credits toward graduation.

As physical education became more accepted as part of the regular school curriculum, it began to be treated in the same ways that other regular parts of the curriculum were treated. Teachers had to hold students accountable for achieving goals. Teachers had to assess performance to see if students had achieved the goals. Quite often teachers had to give reports to parents, and in many cases, teachers had to assign grades. Thus, accountability, assessment, and grading became relevant areas for physical educators. The issues of how best to assess performance in physical education, what to assess, how to report it, and what kind of grading scheme is most useful arose and continue to be relevant in physical education today.

Assessment is important in physical education for many reasons. It is necessary in fitness programs to provide information on fitness entry levels, progress, and attainment of goals. Assessment of some kind is often necessary to group students for instruction and/or competition. Skill assessment is often necessary as a diagnostic tool to detect skill deficiencies that can then be remediated. Teachers have traditionally used assessment as a means for assigning grades.

Physical educators have developed a large number of assessment tools to deal with specific sport skills, cardiovascular fitness, strength, flexibility, agility, posture, and knowledge. These assessment instruments are useful in many ways other than for grading, and occasionally they have been used as a basis for grading. It is not our purpose here to discuss assessment generally or to discuss individual assessment instruments but rather to discuss the role that assessment plays in accountability and how it is related to grading.

From time to time, physical educators have been surveyed to determine the basis on which they grade students (Fox 1959; Mathews 1968; Morrow 1978). Teachers are asked, either through an interview or questionnaire, to identify the factors they use when computing grades. The problem with this

---

WHAT SHOULD GRADES REFLECT?

In its now famous report, *A Nation at Risk*, the National Commission on Excellence in Education spoke strongly about the need for schools to have high expectations for students. The commission suggested that high expectations include notions about hard work, investments of time, appropriate behavior, self-discipline, and motivation. It also suggested many ways in which high expectations are expressed to students, including rigorous examinations, graduation requirements, and the general difficulty of the subject matter students are asked to confront in their daily and weekly assignments. The commission also made it clear that high expectations are expressed to students through grades. And it was *very* clear about what a grade should reflect.

Such expectations are expressed to students in several different ways:

- by grades, which reflect the degree to which students demonstrate their *mastery of subject matter*. (p. 19)

Should grades in physical education reflect the degree to which students have mastered the subject matter?

SOURCE: *A Nation at Risk: The Imperative for Educational Reform.* A report to the Nation and the Secretary of Education by the National Commission on Excellence in Education, David Pierpont Gardner, Chairman, April 1983.

kind of research is that it is based on what teachers *say they do* rather than on direct evidence of *what they do*. Still, it is the only historical evidence available, and it is both interesting and instructive.

The factors that seem to stand out across time as consistent contributors to grading in physical education are (1) attendance, (2) dress, (3) conduct and/ or attitude, and (4) effort or participation. Research indicates that at one time measures of fitness and skill were also used in the computing of grades, but those factors appear to be less prevalent in current grading practices. Measurement of skill seems sometimes to be embedded in "effort" and is typically made on a subjective basis by the teacher. Improvement is also mentioned occasionally, but it too appears to be based on impressions rather than on direct assessment of students.

Recent research on teaching physical education has provided some interesting data. For example, Tousignant and Siedentop (1983) observed three levels of accountability among teachers. At one level, a student can earn a top grade in physical education by being a "member in good standing" of the class. This is achieved by regular attendance, no tardiness, appropriate dress, no disruptive behavior, and minimal participation in the activities. The researchers found a slightly more rigorous type of accountability in classes where teachers require the preceding behaviors and also some student *effort*. At this level, students who "try hard" can be sure of earning a top grade. At the third level of accountability, teachers add some assessment of skill performance to the formula. Students are expected to be members in good standing, but they are also graded on how well they perform the skills identified in a unit. From this research it seems clear that students in today's physical education classes commonly earn top grades without having to demonstrate skill or fitness or any improvement in those areas.

How can such lack of attention to performance in grading in physical education be explained? One study (Placek 1983) sought to discover how physical education teachers determine whether they have been successful in their teaching, that is, what factors in the gymnasium they believe provide evidence that they have been successful. Neither student learning, student performance, nor even improvement appear to be a significant factor in their accounting for successful or unsuccessful teaching. What does seem to matter to these teachers is that students be active, enjoy the class, and not misbehave. In other words, a successful teacher is one whose students are busy, happy, and good. These findings are strikingly similar to those reported by Tousignant and Siedentop (1984). They show that teachers do indeed *intend* that level of accountability and most often seem to achieve it.

It is also interesting to compare what teachers perceive to be *successful* teaching with what research shows is *effective* teaching (see Chapter 20). And it is interesting to speculate on how physical education has developed to a point at which teachers do not include learning and performance in their definitions of successful teaching.

If physical educators focus their accountability systems on factors such as attendance, dress, and minimal participation, that is what they will achieve.

Within that kind of accountability system nobody should expect students to become more fit, more skilled, or more knowledgeable about physical education. Some students who happen to be vitally interested in physical education will no doubt learn anyway. But many more students will do what the system demands of them and very little else.

The "busy, happy, and good" approach appears to be very close to a supervised recreation period. If this is what we are achieving, then we should not be surprised when people question the worth of our programs or the laws that require them. Professional teachers are not needed to supervise and administer recreation programs. That can be done by paraprofessionals at a great savings to school districts.

We suggested in Chapter 2 that in order to be successful physical education programs must accomplish something tangible in terms of improvement in student performance. This requires some form of accountability that is directed toward performance. To accomplish specific goals, teachers need to develop and maintain adequate accountability systems. Grading is one such system—but, it is not the only one. Teachers can establish accountability for improvement and performance through tournaments, league play, the keeping of statistical records, the use of games with scoring instead of drills, the charting of objectives or tasks completed, and through contingency management systems in which performance leads to rewards such as extra activity time. Teachers can also use badges, ribbons, charts, public recognition, and other forms of reward to motivate students to continue to strive for improvement.

Obviously, we want students to enjoy physical education, but a fair and rigorous accountability system does not destroy the "fun" of the experience. Students will enjoy improving and getting better at the activities. They will enjoy having their improvement recognized in some meaningful way. Eventually, they will enjoy doing the activities because skilled performance produces its own rewards. This kind of motivation has enduring qualities and may lead eventually to a lifetime commitment to regular participation.

Coeducational teaching

The education amendments of 1972 include a section commonly referred to as Title IX. Title IX is a federal antidiscrimination law that aims to provide equal opportunity for girls and women; it is directly relevant to sport and physical education. The key sentence in Title IX reads as follows:

> No person in the United States shall, on the basis of sex, be excluded from participation in, be denied the benefits of, or be subjected to discrimination under any educational program or activity receiving federal financial assistance.

Many of the provisions of Title IX apply to interscholastic sport, and educators seem to be fairly knowledgeable about them. However, the legislation also applies to instructional physical education classes, and educators are much less familiar with this.

Title IX initiated an era in which coeducational instruction in physical education has become the rule rather than the exception. Historically, boys and girls were separated for instruction in physical education with boys taught by male teachers and girls by female teachers. The curriculum was often developed around "boys' activities" and "girls' activities."

Title IX makes it illegal to discriminate on the basis of sex in such areas as class scheduling, teaching assignments, budgeting, and use of facilities. Policies regarding such matters as attendance, dress, showering, dressing time, and grading must apply equally to both sexes. Rules that denote standards of conduct and appearance and disciplinary actions that might result from violations must be the same for both sexes. As one physical educator put it, coeducational gym is "a whole new ballgame" (Mikkelson 1979).

The intent of Title IX implies the following stipulations for instruction in physical education:

- Classes are to be sex integrated. Designating certain sections of multi-section classes for single-sex instruction is unacceptable.
- Counseling students about what classes to take cannot be based on the sex of the student or any other means of exclusion (intended or unintended).
- Students are to be grouped for participation without regard to sex except in contact sports (boxing, wrestling, football, basketball, and rugby).
- Students can be grouped by ability if their skills are assessed by objective standards of individual performance that were developed and then applied without regard to sex.
- Requiring one activity (for example, slimnastics) for girls and a different activity (for example, weight training) for boys is unacceptable.
- Teaching assignments are to be made without regard to the sex of the instructor.
- In assessment, students can be compared to a single norm only when its application does not adversely affect members of one sex.
- Students cannot be denied access to instruction in an activity on the basis of sex.
- Facilities are to be shared equally.

You probably realize that although these provisions are clearly implied in the law, not all schools are in compliance with them. Laws such as Title IX are only as strong as their enforcement mechanisms. The legal system will eventually define and specify the various interpretations of the law, but it cannot do so until suits are brought concerning the many provisions. Many suits have been filed over the application of Title IX to interscholastic sport. Fewer suits have been brought concerning its application to physical education.

Thus, many schools no doubt continue to program and teach physical education in the same way they did prior to Title IX.

Implementation of Title IX has caused many professional physical educators to examine their philosophies and commitments. Regardless of how vigorously the government enforces Title IX or how the courts eventually interpret it, the physical education profession cannot return to the days when girls were systematically denied access to instruction in many physical education activities. In fact, it is the physical educator's responsibility not only to carry out the specific provisions of Title IX but also to emphasize the *intent* of the law in school physical education programs.

In some respects it is more difficult to teach coeducational classes than one-sex classes. Often a coed class presents a wider range of skill levels than a sex-segregated class. As a result, teachers face some different managerial challenges and more complex instructional challenges. Different behavioral problems may develop simply because boys and girls not only behave differently together than apart but also misbehave differently. Nonetheless, coeducational classes offer many opportunities for skill and social development that are not present in traditional sex-segregated classes. In order to take advantage of these opportunities, teachers must plan their strategies to meet the challenges.

One of the most important features of coed teaching is how students are grouped for participation. Clearly, boys and girls can be grouped together for drills and can receive instruction together. It is at the moment of *participation* in game activities that coed teaching succeeds or fails. In activities such as archery, canoeing, gymnastics, and bowling, there is little problem with coed participation or competition. However, in basketball, soccer, volleyball, and softball coed participation/competition often fails. We believe that it fails because it tends to violate one of the basic features of play—that in order for an activity to be playful, the competition must be fairly even (see page 189). Un-

Co-ed participation will continue to be an issue in the future.

even competition is not much fun for anybody, and it certainly does not present a situation in which students are likely to learn and improve. The question, then, is how a teacher can overcome the problem of uneven competition in coed classes.

The simplest way to overcome the unequal competition problem is to provide a boys' competition and a girls' competition and then to allow girls who are sufficiently skilled to participate in the boys' competition and boys who are sufficiently skilled to participate in the girls' competition. Many interscholastic sports programs respond to Title IX in this manner, and it appears to be a successful strategy for fulfilling the intent of the legislation, that is, to provide equal opportunity regardless of sex. This strategy allows physical educators to provide *coed instruction* while competition remains primarily sex segregated. We should emphasize, however, that coed instruction is something quite different from *coed competition*. There are goals to be achieved in coed competition that are entirely lost within this strategy.

Another approach to grouping for competition is by skill level. Here teachers assign students to competition on the basis of the results of demonstrated skill performance. In activities such as archery, bowling, or skiing, where many learners are new to the activity, we feel this is the preferred strategy because skill is the most relevant factor to good, equal competition. In activities such as soccer and softball, however, girls have not typically been given the opportunity to learn and compete to the same extent as boys have. Therefore, grouping by skill in these activities often results in better teams being dominated by boys and less-skilled teams being dominated by girls. Obviously, the reverse is true of activities in which girls have more experience. To be sure, some girls will be among the better skilled and some boys among the less skilled. For adolescent students that creates some problems. It is one thing to be on a team composed mostly of girls (or boys) when you want to be, but it is another to be assigned to that team because of your skill level.

Grouping by skill needs to be handled carefully and sensitively so that the positive outcomes are maximized and the negative potential is minimized. It is a valuable lesson for all students to learn that some girls are better than some or most boys in an activity that is traditionally considered a "male" activity and that good competition is based on equal skill levels rather than on the sex of the participants. But these things do often matter to adolescent students, and teachers should not ignore their concerns.

Another approach to grouping for competition is to create coeducational activities in which coed grouping is part of the definition of the activity. In this approach both instruction and competition are coeducational because the activity is *designed* as a coeducational activity. By means of this approach many of the social outcomes of coeducational participation and competition can be more fully realized. Johnson (1977) has suggested that rules be adapted so that competition is equalized and so that full participation is emphasized among all players regardless of sex. Some examples of this approach follow.

1. *Coed basketball.* Teams consist of three girls and two boys. Girls' field goals count three points, boys' two. All free throws are one point. Boys may not score more than six consecutive points except by free throws. Boys may dribble a maximum of five times before passing or shooting. Defense is boy–boy and girl–girl. Only one boy is allowed in the lane on offense at any one time.

2. *Coed soccer.* Teams consist of four boys and four girls. A girl's score equals two points and a boy's one. More than two consecutive passes among boys on the same team constitute a foul, and the opponents get a free kick at the site of the third touch.

3. *Coed softball.* Teams have equal numbers of boys and girls. Boys and girls alternate in the batting order. The offensive team supplies the pitcher, and each batter gets a maximum of three pitches. On defense, two infielders must be girls.

4. *Coed volleyball.* Each team consists of three boys and three girls (or four and four for greater participation). Boys and girls alternate serving order and defensive positions. When more than one player per side hits the ball, one of the hits must be made by a girl. The net should be set to girls' rules height (or lower) and the ball slightly underinflated.

5. *Coed floor hockey.* Teams consist of three boys and three girls each. Games are played in three 12-minute periods, and the floor is divided into offensive and defensive halves. Two players are on offense (one a girl), three are on defense (at least one girl), and one player is allowed to move in both areas. A girl must play the roamer position for at least one of the periods. Goals by girls count two points. Players must change positions (offensive to defensive and vice versa) at least once per game.

In each of these examples the rules for scoring and participation have been changed to encourage full participation among all the players. Students who play these modified games quickly develop strategies that involve the girls fully simply because the rules of the game tend to reward such strategies.

Lifetime sports versus team sports

One of the major changes in school physical education programs since World War II has been the addition of lifetime sports to what had been for many years a curriculum dominated by team games. A lifetime sport is an activity that is generally available in communities and can be pursued throughout life. Thus sports such as golf, bowling, and tennis have become part of the physical education curriculum.

Ever since lifetime sports became accepted components of the school program, some people have argued that they should *replace* team sports in the curriculum, especially at the high school level. For example:

> Physical education as a profession must get away from competitive team games and get into lifetime activities that give students a desire for lifelong fitness. Secondary level physical education programs need to be more individualized, and less emphasis should be placed on athletics. (Johnson 1983, 9)

We would like to present our perspective on this issue in the hope that it will help you to clarify your own point of view.

In Chapter 2 we suggested that the activities of physical education are of equal value *when viewed from the perspective of the participant* (see page 25). We also acknowledged that when viewed from the perspective of the physical educator, one activity may have more value than another relative to a specific educational goal. For example, soccer and field hockey are better activities in terms of cardiovascular fitness than are golf and archery.

We recognize and support the right and the obligation of the professional educator to choose activities and to counsel students into activities because of their benefits relative to specific educational outcomes. But we cannot support the lifetime sports argument in its entirety.

Golf, bowling, tennis, and other so-called lifetime sports are fine activities, and they belong in physical education programs. Many adolescent students obviously enjoy learning and performing these activities. They do not need to be justified by reference to lifetime participation. They are worthwhile activities in their own right, and students learn and enjoy them because of their *immediate* benefits.

Team sports are also fine activities, and adolescent students should have the opportunity to learn and participate in them during their physical education classes. We do not believe that team sports are limited only to youth. Adult participation in softball, volleyball, soccer, and basketball is increasing steadily. Society is changing its views on the *appropriateness* of adult participation in team sports. The running and fitness movements show that adults can participate in strenuous activities for most of their lives. There is no longer any reason to confine team sports to the young. The point is that team sports can be lifetime sports too!

Thus, although we support the inclusion of lifetime sports in school programs, we urge caution in the ways in which these activities are explained and defended. We urge caution so that we do not become guilty of what one physical educator described as promoting *pedigeriatrics*—teaching the young to be old before their time

Good and bad forms of competition

Another recurring issue in physical education revolves around the matter of competition. There are many bad practices in sport at every level: problems in youth sport in community programs, problems in interscholastic sport, problems at the collegiate level and the professional level. Some of these problems develop because too many people are willing to be irresponsible with athletes and rules in order to gain some imagined competitive advantage. Physical educators need to do everything possible to protect sport from these bad practices, to make sport better at all levels, and to speak out against abuses. However, we cannot remedy bad competition by doing away with all competition. Instead, we must develop and protect good competition.

Rather than characterize this issue as the overemphasis of competition, we would do well to approach it as an issue of good and bad forms of competition. What does competition mean? What constitutes good competition? These are questions we need to understand and answer. Playful competition in the form of games and sports is a major sustaining force in human experience, both for individuals and for the societies in which they live. Good competition has four major attributes.

1. Good competition is first and foremost a *festival*. Competitions have traditions, rituals, and celebrations. These features provide the context within which competitors share significant experiences (Siedentop 1981). This is the most fundamental and important meaning of good competition and the one that is the least understood. This characteristic is often neglected or seriously violated in physical education.

2. Good competition creates a *forum* within which people can demonstrate competence. The forum (a game, a league, a tournament, etc.) is created by rules, standards for judging performance, records, and generally accepted criteria for excellence. Within the context of these forums, athletes set goals, strive to achieve them, and then set new goals. The terms *compete* and *competence* both derive from the Latin *competere*. The pursuit of excellence sustains good competition.

3. Good competition involves *rivalry*. Competition thrives on adversarial roles in which one person or group wins. What is important to understand is that this characteristic of competition rarely is of a zero-sum type. Zero-sum competition means that your victories are necessarily my defeats. Zero-sum competition is rare in sport. Some coaches or fans would have us believe otherwise, but the evidence suggests that they are wrong. There are many ways to "win" in competitive endeavors. One wins when one plays well. One wins when one has participated in a particularly good contest. One wins when one improves. Sometimes these forms of winning occur when the contest itself has been lost.

4. Good competition means *striving* hard within the rules and traditions of the forum. It means little to win a game or a contest when the victory is gained because one has bent the rules or taken unfair advantage of an opponent. However, to win in a fairly fought contest against a worthy opponent provides great meaning. But its meaning exists only within the context of the forum. Once the contest is over, the winning and losing should mean very little. This is what makes the contest playful. Clearly, one of the major features of bad competition is that the results too often have meaning that carries over into other spheres of life. An athlete should always strive to win; to do less dishonors the opponent and the competition. But to paraphrase a famous sportsperson, once it's over, it's over!

With these characteristics in mind, it is easier to judge what constitutes bad competition. All students should have the opportunity to experience good competition, and school physical education should provide that opportunity and show young people what good competition is all about.

Summary

It is important for physical educators to develop an informed attitude toward issues that affect not only their own teaching but the profession as a whole. Safety and liability are one such issue. Teachers must practice physical education safely and develop procedures that minimize the risk of injury to students. Procedures, planning, and supervision are important for minimizing risk.

Accountability for outcomes is another issue in physical education, one that is related to assessment and grading procedures. Teachers should hold students accountable not only for appropriate behavior and basic cooperation but also for performance in skill and fitness activities. Teachers need to be aware of the tendency to trade accountability for student cooperation, a trade that often results in a happy and cooperative class but one in which little learning takes place.

Title IX mandates that male and female students share equally in facilities, equipment, and the opportunity to learn. Often this results in coeducational teaching in physical education. Coed instruction differs from coed competition. Although boys and girls can receive instruction and practice together, coed competition often works best when the teacher adapts an activity to meet the needs of the coed participants.

Physical educators often promote lifetime sports in physical education because of their carry-over value in later life. However, adolescent students also enjoy team sports. As society changes its views on the appropriateness of adult participation in team sports, physical educators can begin to teach and promote team activities for their lifetime benefits as well as their immediate benefits. Physical educators should always remember that the primary value of an activity is decided by the individual and that the distinctions a teacher may make are not always similar to distinctions students may make.

The term *competition* refers to the festival nature of activities, to the creation of forums within which skills can be tested against well-defined standards, and to rivalry. It is not appropriate to think about *less* or *more* competition but rather about *good* and *bad* competition. Physical educators need to design competitions that meet the festival, competence, and rivalry meanings of the term—and to do so within the rules, traditions, and strategies that define a particular activity.

Suggested activities

1. Invite a local legal expert to discuss liability cases with the class. Prepare questions for the expert in advance.

2. Debate the following issue: Grading in physical education should be based primarily on student achievement. Have three students argue the affirmative and three the negative.

3. Debate the following issue: High school physical education should emphasize lifetime sports rather than team sports. Have three students argue the affirmative and three the negative.

4. Using your own experiences as a guideline, develop a list of major teaching challenges that result from coeducational classes. Try to determine whether each problem is primarily instructional or primarily social.

5. Divide into small groups. The instructor will assign each group an activity unit such as gymnastics, track and field, etc. As a group, identify the major safety issues in the unit and the options for dealing with those safety issues. Discuss your conclusions in class.

22

Gaining Support for the Program

The program of physical education that we have described in this text suggests a wide range of activity interests, some of which extend beyond the school and into the broader community. The development of such a program requires physical educators to generate support from other people both inside and outside the school and to develop resources to match program needs. In brief, physical educators want people to know about the program, to believe in it, and to support it. This requires careful planning and hard work.

The major topics in this chapter are as follows:

Sources of support for the program, including students, parents, members of the community, and school personnel

Ways of gaining support for the program

Important support groups

Physical educators must gain the support of at least three groups if their program is to succeed: students, parents and other members of the community, and other school personnel. Let's look at each of these groups in turn.

Students

The demonstration of competence is a vital part of the developmental process of adolescence. Adolescents have questions about their bodies, how strong they are, how much they weigh, how they measure up to others, whether they are improving, and whether their efforts are producing results. Physical educators must help students answer these questions to their satisfaction if students are to value physical education. To do this physical educators need to provide feedback on student performance and behavior.

Feedback itself is reinforcing. However, teachers should also provide periodic rewards for achievement that promote even greater levels of student enthusiasm. There are several ways of doing this: (1) provide individual awards for students based upon national standards such those of the Red Cross and AAHPERD; (2) provide T-shirts indicating major achievements such as membership in a 5000-mile bicycle club or a 1000-mile jogging club; (3) display photographs of successful endeavors on school bulletin boards and get them published in local papers; (4) establish a roster of all-star performers in physical education classes comparable to that in athletics; (5) create a physical education hall of fame; (6) institute award assemblies for public approval; (7) see to it that physical education is part of academic award festivals as are music and art.

Parents and other community members

Parents do want to know about their children's progress or lack of progress in school. They are immediately concerned about academic subjects, but their interest extends to every aspect of their children's lives, certainly their health, safety, and happiness. Parents take great pride in the accomplishments of their daughters and sons, be it in music, art, sports, or any other aspect of school performance. Yet for the most part, teachers and schools do little to inform parents and other members of the community of the success of their students. The report card, an occasional end of season celebration or award banquet, and a chance remark from a teacher on a school visitation day are the usual forms of exchange with parents and the community—that is unless something goes wrong and then contact is swift, decisive, and unfortunately negative.

The report card, at least in physical education, is not very informative. It usually includes a check mark, an S or a U, or perhaps a letter grade. This really does not mean much to a parent. "Can my son swim? Has my daughter learned new skills? Give me something I can understand when I discuss their report cards with them." Specific suggestions for keeping parents informed appear later in this chapter.

Award ceremonies usually honor the best students: the best student in history, the American Legion essay winner, the outstanding athlete. Why do we not publicize the many successes of other students? Perhaps they need a pat on the back more than the highest achievers. Certainly their parents want them to be recognized, and teachers can usually find ways to do this.

Remember that adult members of the community who have no school-aged children or who send their children to private school also support public education through their taxes. Keeping these citizens informed of school and physical education matters will assist in the development of community pride and a positive attitude of cooperation and support. Specific strategies for achieving this goal are outlined in the last section of this chapter.

Other school personnel

The school is a collection of program areas, each seeking resources from the same modest resources base. The administrative officials adjudicate this process but also must bear the brunt of parental or other criticism.

Physical education represents a risk area to administrators. The risk comes from the immense parental pressure generated by athletics, from the injury incidence of motor activities, and from the great expense involved in high-ceilinged, large activity areas. It may also come from locker-room theft, liability suits, and sex discrimination charges. To many other teachers physical education is a field without the usual academic problems they experience with students. Many students will get out of bed two hours earlier than usual on a Saturday morning to play ball, but they will not spend 30 minutes at night to complete a homework assignment. Physical education deliberately creates a stressful program to challenge students' potential. It is important, it has great merit, but it is sufficiently unique to cause others in the system discomfort.

Physical educators must recognize these issues and respond to them. Here are some suggestions for doing so.

- Attend other school functions and the special events of other teachers.
- Do not infringe on the time of other school programs with practice, game, or tournament schedules.
- Share parental support with other teachers and programs.
- Do not raise money in a manner that challenges the integrity of school policy or creates a different life-style for your activities.
- Specifically invite teachers and administrators to physical education program events.
- Share students with others; do not be exclusive.

Techniques to gain support

Physical educators can gain the support of the groups we have been surveying in several ways. They can provide feedback to students, information to parents, community members, and administrators, and support to other teachers. In this section, we examine techniques for accomplishing those ends.

Maintaining student records

It is ironic that physical education represents an area of sports and games that sustains itself on statistics related to performance yet school files rarely contain any records related to physical education scores. One can find attendance records, reading and mathematics scores, and ACT and SAT scores but no physical education scores. Math and reading scores frequently depict a student's progress from the early grades through high school. Such a record can provide important feedback on the student's progress or lack of progress.

Why are there no physical education records? How can physical educators afford not to maintain systematic records and provide appropriate feedback based upon such information?

It is easy to keep track of sit-ups per minute, number of chin-ups, and other fitness measures. Teachers can easily chart students' participation patterns in sports, their progress in skill achievements, even their responses to sportsmanship episodes during their career in physical education. Currently, about the only record maintained in school files pertains to any limiting medical conditions to activity. Adding to the irony is the fact that physical education is one of the very few subjects in the formal school curriculum mandated by law for most of the 12 years of elementary and secondary schooling.

An overview of student achievement in physical education should be maintained in the physical education office and also in the central office of the school. It should be a cumulative record that provides a history of the individual's development. Physical educators could use information from such a record to provide feedback to students and also to report to parents about their children's progress.

Obviously, a series of letter grades or satisfactory-unsatisfactory notations are not very meaningful. However, there are records that do have meaning to students, their parents, and school officials. Figures 22.1 and 22.2 (p. 418) show records that are useful.

Figure 22.1 provides for the cumulative notation of fitness, activity, and teacher observations of the student. Physical educators can periodically make copies of the chart for student and parental review. This kind of record has the additional advantage of showing student and parent that physical educators care enough to monitor and evaluate the student.

The inventory profile shown in Figure 22.2 is used to record a student's sports and leisure interests at periodic intervals, in this case grades 6, 8, 10, and 12. Students answer a series of questions keyed to seven major headings (combatives, outdoor pursuits, etc.), and then the teacher records the student's degree of interest on a five-part Likert scale (low interest to high interest). The resulting "score" card gives a schematic profile of the student's activity interests.

Modeling

SCENE   *A father and daughter are driving home from volleyball practice.*

DAUGHTER   Thanks for picking me up. Its almost 9:00 and I still have to study for a French test.

FATHER   Why were you so late?

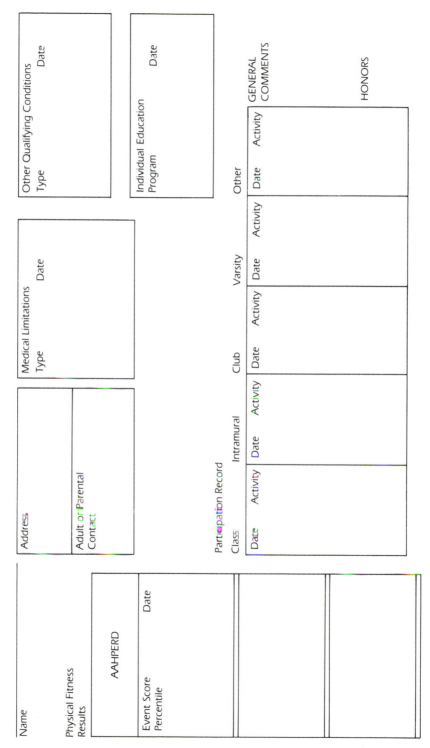

Figure 22.1 A physical education record card.

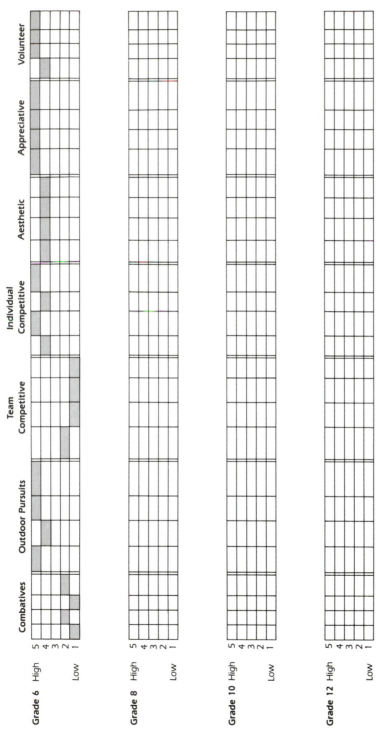

Figure 22.2 A sports and leisure interest inventory profile.

DAUGHTER   There was some problem about using the gym. I didn't mind that but practice was useless.

FATHER   Why useless?

DAUGHTER   The coach, Mrs. Sullivan, is just terrible.

FATHER   Well, I know she's the guidance counselor and really more of an adviser than a coach. She's just helping out—at least that's what you told me. How much can you expect?

DAUGHTER   Yes, she's just helping out, but we really try hard. Maybe it's unfair, but if she criticizes me or expects a lot of me, then I think she should try just as much. Tonight she sat on a chair by the court eating potato chips the entire practice!

FATHER   Just eating potato chips?

DAUGHTER   Yes, just eating, stuffing herself. Between bites she had a few smart remarks that were really irrelevant. She volunteered to coach; nobody twisted her arm. She makes the volleyball court an extension of the lunchroom. I can't respect her.

Perhaps the most significant way for a physical education teacher to create support among students and players is to be an appropriate model. Is the teacher a player enthused about physical activities, interested in the world of sport, reasonable about healthy habits, prudent about fitness? If not, he or she should find another profession. Students deserve something better, and they can readily detect lack of commitment.

Using a computer

By means of a personal computer, standard software, and a simple printer, a physical educator can quickly and easily produce a variety of analyses, statistics, and student and class records.

For example, the Physical Educational Management System developed by Luke Kelly* is a software program for Apple computers that allows a teacher to manage performance data for 250–500 students on a wide range of fitness, skill, and knowledge objectives. Teachers can input their own specific objectives into the program and provide data on an individual or class basis. The program offers a variety of ways to analyze and present these data. Figures 22.3 through 22.6 on the following pages show sample printouts from this software package.

Keeping parents informed

As we suggested earlier parents are concerned with the performance and well-being of their children. Nevertheless, physical educators must sharpen this general level of interest with tactics designed to focus attention upon physical education.

The first priority is to report student progress to parents. See Figures 22.7 and 22.8 for examples of productive interactions between teachers and parents.

* © Copyright 1985 by Luke Kelly, Ph.D.

PHYSICAL EDUCATION MANAGEMENT SYSTEM

OBJECTIVE WORKSHEET

DIRECTIONS: LIST THE OBJECTIVE NAME OR PHRASE (25 CHARACTERS MAX.) DESCRIBING
EACH OBJECTIVE, THE MASTERY LEVEL THAT CAN BE OBTAINED, AND THE
SCALE DIRECTION (1 = POSITIVE OR 2 = NEGATIVE).

TOTAL NUMBER OF OBJECTIVES TO BE ENTERED = _4_

	OBJECTIVE NAME	MASTERY LEVEL	SCALE DIRECTION
1.	*Abdominal Strength*	*35*	*1*
2.	*Leg Strength*	*6.5*	*2*
3.	*Soccer Rules Test*	*90*	*1*
4.	*Kicking*	*10*	*1*
5.			
6.			
7.			
8.			
9.			
10.			
11.			
12.			
13.			
14.			
15.			

Figure 22.3 Teachers can enter their own objectives on the computer software program.

P H Y S I C A L   E D U C A T I O N   M A N A G E M E N T   S Y S T E M

D A T A B A S E   S T A T U S

THIS DATABASE IS CURRENTLY MANAGING 6 STUDENTS ON 4 OBJECTIVES.

OBJECTIVE: ABDOMINAL STRENGTH

	STUDENT NAME	ENTRY	TARGET	EXIT
(1)	DAN GARDNER	000020	000023	000025
(2)	MARY RYAN	000017	000021	000023
(3)	FRANK KINNER	000023	000028	000026
(4)	SALLY ELSPAR	000021	000024	000026
(5)	HARRY SMITH	000007	000011	000012
(6)	DENISE LEWIS	000016	000021	000019

Figure 22.4 Printout example showing entry, target, and exit performances for one objective.

PHYSICAL EDUCATION MANAGEMENT SYSTEM

STUDENT PROGRESS REPORT

BIG VALLEY SCHOOL DISTRICT
SMITH MIDDLE SCHOOL

STUDENT NAME: DENISE LEWIS   REPORT DATE: 3/15/85

GRADE LEVEL: SIXTH   TEACHER: MR. JOE JOHNSON

NUMBER OF STUDENTS IN THE CLASS = 6

	ENTRY LEVEL	ACTUAL EXIT	NET CHANGE	MASTERY	% MASTERY TO DATE	CLASS AVERAGE (EXIT)	DIFF. FROM CLASS
ABDOMINAL STRENGTH	16.00	19.00	3.00	35.00	54.00	20.83	-1.83
LEG STRENGTH	7.10	6.80	.29	6.50	95.00	7.88	1.08
SOCCER RULES TEST	71.00	97.00	26.00	90.00	107.00	90.83	6.16
KICKING TEST	7.00	10.00	3.00	10.00	100.00	9.33	.67

Figure 22.5 Printout example for one student, showing data for four objectives.

PHYSICAL EDUCATION MANAGEMENT SYSTEM
CLASS REPORT

BIG VALLEY SCHOOL DISTRICT
SMITH MIDDLE SCHOOL

REPORT DATE: 3/15/85   TEACHER: MR. JOE JOHNSON
GRADE LEVEL: SIXTH   CLASS: MRS. SMITH'S CLASS
NUMBER OF STUDENTS IN THE CLASS = 6

OBJECTIVES	CLASS MEAN ENTERY	CLASS MEAN EXIT	CLASS MEAN NET CHANGE	MASTERY	CLASS MEAN % MASTERY	% OF CLASS ACHIEVING MASTERY
ABDOMINAL STRENGTH	17.33	20.83	3.50	35.00	59.52	******
LEG STRENGTH	8.55	7.88	.66	6.50	82.45	16.66
SOCCER RULES TEST	68.33	90.83	22.50	90.00	100.92	66.66
KICKING TEST	5.33	9.33	4.00	10.00	93.33	66.66

Figure 22.6 Printout example for one class, showing data for four objectives.

Obviously other reporting schemes can also be helpful. For example, see Figure 22.9.

Increasing school and community awareness

The American Alliance for Health, Physical Education and Recreation* provides a rich panoply of materials to publicize a program. See Figure 22.10 (pp. 428–29) for examples. These materials are self-explanatory and can be used on bulletin boards in school and the community, on local radio and television stations, and in local newspapers.

Teachers can also publicize a physical education program in the following ways:

- Include parents and community members in selected physical education activities. For example, schedule hours when adults in the school district can use the weight room. Arrange and schedule parent-child activities.

- Showcase physical education activities. Physical education nights, demonstration events, and sport festivals are a means of capturing some of the enthusiasm ordinarily reserved for varsity sports.

---

* Materials can be ordered from Publications Orders, American Alliance for Health, Physical Education and Recreation, 1900 Association Drive, Reston, Virginia 22090.

Mr. and Mrs. John Smith
2 Supportive Way
Encourage, Ohio 44444

Dear Parents:

It is a pleasure to have Jim in my seventh grade
physical education class. We meet three times per week
for approximately 45 minutes. Our goals include
improving sports skills and levels of physical fitness,
learning the rules and etiquette of games, and generally
enjoying using the body successfully. Jim seems to like
sports, and he is an enthusiastic, responsible and well-
behaved young man. You should be proud of him.

I do note, however, that Jim is having more than
normal difficulty with fundamental motor skills such as
throwing and catching. This interferes with his ability
to play the typical team games of his age group. Also,
his fitness scores, particularly for shoulder girth
strength, are below standard for his age. In part this
is undoubtedly due to his very rapid growth in the past
year. I believe extra instruction and activity time
will help correct these deficiencies.

Each Monday, Wednesday, and Friday at 7:30 A.M. I
conduct a class for approximately 10 youngsters such as
Jim to provide additional instruction and opportunity
for skill and fitness development. This is 50 minutes
before classes start and 35 minutes before the buses
arrive. If you can bring Jim to school on those days or
arrange transportation with the parents of other
children in the group (a list of parents and their phone
numbers is attached), I believe it will be helpful for
him.

The first session of the class is on January 6,
1986.

Sincerely yours,

Ruth Jones
Ruth Jones
Everett Middle School Physical Education Teacher
(889-2929)

Figure 22.7   A letter from a teacher to parents.

Ms. Ruth Jones
Physical Education Department
Everett Middle School
Encourage, Ohio 44444

Dear Ms. Jones,

Thank you for the letter inviting Jim to your
extra class in physical education. He will be there
and looks forward to the opportunity. Is there
anything we can do at home to help him with his
physical skills? Any suggestions will be helpful.

Let me add how nice it is to know that some
teacher cares enough not only to teach an extra class
but also to pay attention to individuals. This is
really reassuring.

Sincerely,

Beverly Smith

Beverly Smith

Figure 22.8   A letter from a parent to a teacher.

```
      To:   The Parents of John Smith

    From:   James Jones, Physical Education Teacher,
            Hiawatha High School

 Subject:   Strength training results for your son during
            the period August-December 1985


Individual Result

     John Smith - 16 years, 7 months

     Upper-body strength  Bench press    = 185 lb
                          % difference   = 22.1%
                          August to December

     Lower-body strength  Knee extension   = 115 lb
                          % difference     = +18%
                          August to December


Group Results

     76 participants

     Upper-body strength  85% of participants increased
                          strength an average of 17%.

     Lower-body strength  90% of participants increased
                          strength an average of 8%.



For further information call instructor James Jones
at 889-3942 during school hours.
```

Figure 22.9   Strength training results for one student and how his results compare with the group's results.

Figure 22.10 Examples of publicity advertisements for physical education.

- Arrange a personnel and resource exchange with a local industry or business. Some industries and other business enterprises attempt to assist schools by exchanging personnel and resources. This occurs most often in technical and computer program areas. In many cases these same organizations sponsor fitness and other activity programs for their employees. This represents an exchange opportunity between an organization and a school physical education program that can benefit both.

- Establish a booster club for the entire physical education program, not just a specific athletic team. Permit only members in good standing to vote on issues; have parents earn their participation rights as their daughter or son earns a grade (Olson 1982, 18).

Finally, Dougherty and Bonanno (1979, 200) list 15 ways to win support for a program. Use this list as a start for your own list.

1. Be sure that students see the educational purpose behind their school experience.

2. See that students do a good job of communicating these objectives to their parents.

3. Keep fellow educators and administrators informed of innovations in the field.

4. Note newsworthy events in your program and call them to the attention of local media through appropriate channels.

5. Encourage laypeople to speak for the field and do so yourself.

6. Keep alert to enthusiasts in the community who could be enlisted as advisers or supporters of the school program.

7. Formulate in your own mind why you are in physical education, and relay this to your students.

8. Use points of contact with the public, especially in the school environment, to get across at least one fact about the benefits of health, physical education, and recreation programs.

9. Participate actively in state, district, and national association projects.

10. Keep up-to-date on new ideas and opinions relating to the profession. Express your ideas and experiences in a way that can be shared by others.

11. Use all of the resources available to you.

12. Relate to other professionals in the field in terms of common goals within the community.

13. Promote the lifetime aspects and benefits of health, physical education, and recreation learning experiences.

14. Express pride and appreciation to students, parents, and administrators for their participation in and support of your work.

15. Write to local and national media thanking them when they do a good job of reporting events related to the profession or when they provide public service time.

Summary

To gain support for the physical education program, physical educators must engage the support of students, parents, members of the community, school administrators, and other teachers. Students want to believe that they have achieved and improved their performance in sports and levels of fitness. Parents expect teachers to recognize their child's progress and promote wholesome activities. Members of the community want to be informed of school programs and to know that their tax dollars are being spent wisely. Administrators want a balanced program that does not create conflict in the school or community. Other teachers expect some positive reinforcement for their efforts with students.

The techniques to respond to these concerns include providing adequate feedback to students, parents, and community members; sharing space and time with other teachers; and informing administrators of program developments.

National associations and their publications can assist the teacher in discovering new techniques to generate support for physical education. However, the principal strategy for program acceptance and recognition is to be found in the achievement of students, which is a direct product of good teaching and a good program.

Suggested activities

1. Visit a local school district and find out how it publicizes physical education to parents and other adults in the community. Discuss your findings with the class and draw up a joint list of effective publicity techniques.

2. Describe the feedback techniques that a teacher can use for students engaged in a physical fitness program.

3. Design a brochure to communicate to parents and other adults in the community the experiences a physical education program provides for students during an entire school year.

4. List and discuss in class five ways in which a physical education teacher can support other teachers and programs in the school.

5. Design a record form and record system for students in physical education. Emphasize the use of your system to offer feedback to each student as well as a continuous record of performance throughout his or her school career.

Appendix

Resources for Recreation and Competitive Sports for Students with Special Needs

Publications

Cathey, M., and P. Jansma. "Mainstreaming Orthopedically Disabled Individuals in Various Physical Activities." Parts 1–4. *The Directive Teacher*, Fall 1979, Winter, Spring, Summer/Fall 1980.

Fluegelman, F. *The New Games*. San Francisco: The New Games Foundation, 1976.

Gross, S. J. "Mainstreaming the Physically Handicapped Student for Team Sports." *Practical Pointers* 1, no. 8 (1978):1–8.

Kearney, S., and R. Copeland. "Goal Ball." *Journal of Health, Physical Education and Recreation* 50, no. 7 (1979):24–26.

Klesisus, S. E. "Wide Width of Acceptability Games." *Journal of Health, Physical Education and Recreation* 50, no. 4 (1979):66–67.

Marlowe, M. "Motor Experiences Through Games Analysis." *Journal of Health, Physical Education and Recreation* 52, no. 1 (1981):78–80.

———. "Games Analysis Intervention: A Procedure to Increase Peer Acceptance of Socially Isolated Children." *Research Quarterly for Exercise and Sport* 51, no. 2 (1980):422–26.

———. "Games Analysis: Designing Games for Handicapped Children." *Teaching Exceptional Children* 12 (1980):48–51.

Morris, D. G. S. *Elementary Physical Education: Toward Inclusion*. Salt Lake City: Brighton, 1980.

———. *How to Change the Games Children Play*. 2nd ed. Minneapolis: Burgess, 1980.

Winnick, J. P. "Techniques for Integration." *Journal of Health, Physical Education and Recreation* 49, no. 6 (1978):2.

Winnick, J. P., and J. Hurwitz, eds. *The Preparation of Regular Physical Educators for Mainstreaming*. Brockport, N.Y.: State Univ. College Press, 1979.

Organizations

AIKIDO
Paul Linden
Larkins Hall
The Ohio State University
Columbus, Ohio 43210

AIR TRAVEL
Marilyn Wullschleger, R.N.
Nursing Education 118E
Veteran's Administration Medical
  Center
Long Beach, Calif. 90822

Aircraft Hand Controls
Ed Stadleman
PO Box 207
Sturgis, Ky. 42459

Portable Aircraft Hand Controls
Union Aviation, Inc.
Sturgis Airport-G
Sturgis, Ky. 42459

Wheelchair Pilots Assn.
John Green
3953 West Evans Drive
Phoenix, Ariz. 85023

ALL TERRAIN VEHICLES
Wheelchair Motorcycle Assn.
Dr. Eli Factor
101 Torrey Street
Brockton, Mass. 02401

ARCHERY
National Wheelchair Athletic Assn.
Ben Lipton, Chairman
Nassau Community College
Garden City, N.Y. 11530

National Archery Assn.
Ronks, Pa. 17572

BASEBALL/SOFTBALL
National Beep Baseball Assn.
3212 Tomahawk
Lawrence, Kans. 66044

National Wheelchair Softball Assn.
Dave Van Buskirk, Commissioner
PO Box 737
Sioux Falls, S.Dak. 57101

BASKETBALL
National Wheelchair Basketball Assn.
Stan Labanowich, Commissioner
110 Seaton Building
University of Kentucky
Lexington, Ky. 40506

New Life, Inc.
#514
2300 Good Hope Road, SE
Washington, D.C. 20020

BOATING
Handicapped Boaters Assn.
PO Box 1134
Ansonia Station, N.Y. 10023

BOWLING
American Wheelchair Bowling Assn.
Robert Moran, Executive Secretary
6718 Pinehurst Drive
Evansville, Ind. 47711

Women's Wheelchair Bowling Comp.
W. Bennett Avenue
Milwaukee, Wisc.

American Blind Bowling Assn.
James Murrel
105 N. Bellaire Avenue
Louisville, Ky. 40206

CAMPING
Committee for the Promotion of
  Camping for the Handicapped
2056 South Bluff Road
Traverse City, Mich. 49684

Handicapped Unbound, Inc.
PO Box 1044
Prescott, Ariz. 86302

Outdoor Wilderness Program
Crotched Mountain Center
Greenfield, N.H. 03047

Colorado Outdoor Education Center
  for the Handicapped
PO Box 697
Breckenridge, Colo. 80424

Courage Camping Programs
Courage Center, Camping Dept.
3915 Golden Valley Road
Golden Valley, Minn. 55422

Greater Kansas City Epilepsy League
4049 Pennsylvania
Kansas City, Mo. 64111

CANOEING
Mississippi Project Aquatics
Box 172 Southern Station
University of Southern Mississippi
Hattiesburg, Miss. 39401

Art Javes Designs
ROWCAT
4914 17th Avenue
Gulfport, Fla. 33707

FLYING CLUBS
American Wheelchair Pilots Assn.
Dave Graham
PO Box 1181
Mesa, Ariz. 85201

Southern California Wheelchair
   Aviators
3800 Dixie Canyon Drive
Sherman Oaks, Calif. 91423

Wheelchair Pilots Assn.
11018 102nd Avenue N
Largo, Fla. 33540

FOOTBALL
Rehabilitation Education Center
University of Illinois
Oak Street at Stadium Drive
Champaign, Ill. 61820

GOLF
Dennis Walters
250 Jacaranda Drive
Plantation, Fla. 33324
or
63 East Overlook Bay
Englishtown, N.J. 07726

National Amputee Golf Assn.
24 Lakeview Terrace
Watchung, N.J. 07060

DeDe Owens
USPGA Professional
US Blind Golfers Assn.
225 Baronne Street
28th Floor
New Orleans, La. 70112

National Amputee Golf Foundation
George C. Beckman, Trustee
St. Joseph's Mercy Hospital
11705 Mercy Blvd.
Savannah, Ga. 31606

HAM RADIO
Courage Handi-Ham System
3915 Golden Valley Road
Golden Valley, Minn. 55422

HORSEBACK RIDING
Don Drewry
College of HPER
Texas Woman's University
Denton, Tex. 76201

Linda McCowan, Executive Director
Cheff Center for the Handicapped
RR 1, Box 171
August, Mich. 49012

Diane Schechter
Berkeley Outreach Recreation
   Program
2539 Telegraph Avenue
Berkeley, Calif. 94704

North American Riding for the
   Handicapped
Leonard Warner, Executive Director
Box 100
Ashburn, Va. 22011

KAYAKING
Rick Ciccotto
Route 2, Box 589
Monck's Corner, S.C. 29461

Handicapped Boaters Assn.
PO Box 1134
Ansonia Station
New York, N.Y. 10023

MARATHON RACING
National Wheelchair Marathon
380 Diamond Hill Road
Warwick, R.I. 02886

New England Spinal Cord Injury
   Foundation
369 Elliot Street
Newton Upper Falls, Mass. 02164

SKATING
International Council on Therapeutic
  Skating
Ice Skating
PO Box 13
State College, Pa. 16801

SKIING
Chris Kolb, Executive Director
Ski for All Foundation
521 Wall Street, Suite 326-A
Seattle, Wash. 98121

Adapted Sports Assn.
Allen Hayes
PO Box 299
Miller Place, N.Y. 11764

National Handicapped Sports and
  Recreation Assn.
c/o Jack Benedick, President
PO Box 19664
Denver, Colo. 80218

Blind Outdoor Leisure Development
c/o Jack Helst, Director, Aspen BOLD
533 East Main Street
Aspen, Colo. 81611

United States Deaf Skiers Assn.
c/o David O. Riker,
Secretary-Treasurer
9915 Good Luck Road, Apt. 103
Seabrook, Md. 20801

Hal O'Leary, Director
Handicapped Ski Program
Winter Park Recreation Assn.
Box 36
Winter Park, Colo. 80482

William E. Steiler
6832 Marlette Road
Marlette, Mich. 48453

ARROYA (ski sleds)
PO Box 5249
Stanford, Calif. 94305

Amputee and Blind "Learn to Ski"
  Program
The 52 Association, Inc.
441 Lexington Avenue
New York, N.Y. 10017

US Ski Assn.
Central Division
Amputee Skiers Committee
PO Box 66014
Chicago, Ill. 60666

Disabled Skiers Assn. of British
  Columbia
Box 3433
Main Post Office
Vancouver, British Columbia
Canada V6B 3Y4

Canadian Assn. for Disabled Skiing
Box 2077
Banff, Alberta, Canada TOL OCO

British Amputee Ski Assn.
Box 1373
Banff, Alberta, Canada TOL OCO

References

American Alliance for Health, Physical Education, Recreation and Dance. 1976. *Ideas for secondary school physical education.* Reston, Va.: AAHPERD.

———. 1980. *Lifetime health-related physical fitness test manual.* Reston, Va.: AAHPERD.

Atwell, L. A. 1983. Outdoor adventure education course. Unpublished manuscript, Lake Forest, Illinois, High School Physical Education Department.

Bain, L. September 1980. Socialization into the role of participant. *Journal of Physical Education, Recreation and Dance.*

———. 1983. Teacher/coach role conflict: Factors influencing role performance. In *Teaching in physical education,* edited by T. Templin and J. Olson, 94–101. Champaign, Ill.: Human Kinetics.

Bain, L., and J. Wendt. 1983. *Transition to teaching: A guide for the beginning teacher.* Reston, Va.: AAHPERD.

Bronfenbrenner, U. 1973. *Two worlds of childhood: U.S. and U.S.S.R.* New York: Pocket Books.

Bruner, J. 1971. *The relevance of education.* New York: Norton.

Caillois, R. 1961. *Man, play, and games.* New York: The Free Press.

Charles, C. M. 1981. *Building classroom discipline: From models to practice.* New York: Longman.

Chu, D. 1981. Functional myths of educational organizations: College as career training and the relationship of formal title to actual duties upon secondary school employment. In *1980 National Association of Physical Education in Higher Education proceedings,* edited by V. Crafts. Champaign, Ill.: Human Kinetics.

Coleman, J. S., E. Q. Campbell, C. J. Hobson, J. McPartland, A. M. Mood, F. D. Winfield, and R. L. York. 1966. *Equality of educational opportunity.* Washington, D.C.: U.S. Department of Health, Education and Welfare.

Conrad, D., and D. Hedin. 1983. *Experiential education—Executive summary of the final report, Center for Youth Development and Research.* St. Paul: Univ. of Minnesota.

Craig, C. J. 1976. *Human development.* 2nd ed. Englewood Cliffs, N.J.: Prentice-Hall.

Crass, D. B. March 1976. Fun that's contagious. *Journal of Health, Physical Education and Recreation.*

Dick, W., and L. Carey. 1985. *The systematic design of instruction.* 2nd ed. Glenview, Ill.: Scott, Foresman and Company.

Dougherty, N. J., and D. Bonanno. 1979. *Contemporary approaches to the teaching of physical education.* Minneapolis: Burgess Publishing Co.

Doyle, W. 1979. Classroom tasks and students' abilities. In *Research on teaching: Concepts, findings, and applications,* edited by P. Peterson and H. Walberg. Berkeley: McCutchan.

Drowatzky, J. May 1978. Liability: You could be sued! *Journal of Physical Education, Recreation and Dance* 49:17–18.

Duke, D. January 1977. A systematic management plan for school disciplines. *National Association of Secondary School Principals Bulletin* 61:1–10.

Earls, N. 1979. Distinctive physical education teachers: Personal qualities, perceptions of teacher education and the realities of teaching. Ph.D. diss., University of North Carolina, Greensboro. University of Michigan microfilm no. 8011201.

———. Fall 1981. Distinctive teachers' personal qualities, perceptions of teacher education and the realities of teaching. *Journal of Teaching in Physical Education* 1:59–70.

Erikson, E. H. 1963. *Childhood and society*. 2nd ed. New York: Norton.

Fast, B. September 1971. Contingency contracting. *Journal of Health, Physical Education and Recreation*, 31–32.

Feldhusen, J. 1979. Problems in student behavior in secondary schools. In *78th Yearbook of National Society for the Study of Education*. Chicago: Univ. of Chicago Press.

Fox, J. 1959. Practices and trends in physical education programs for boys in selected Oregon schools. Ed.D. thesis, University of Oregon.

French, R., and P. Jansma. 1982. *Special physical education*. Columbus, Ohio: Charles Merrill.

Hall, G. S. 1904. *Adolescence: Its psychology and its relations to physiology, anthropology, sociology, sex, crime, religion, and education*. Englewood Cliffs, N.J.: Prentice-Hall.

Headlee, Barbara. May 1978. Expanding a physical education program through community facilities. *The National Association of Secondary School Principals Bulletin* 62:32–34.

Hellison, D. 1978. *Beyond balls and bats: Alienated youth in the gym*. Washington, D.C.: AAHPERD.

———. July 1983. Teaching self-responsibility (and more). *Journal of Physical Education, Recreation and Dance*.

———. 1984. *Goals and strategies for teaching physical education*. Champaign, Ill.: Human Kinetics.

Horrocks, R. September 1978. Resolving conflict in the gymnasium. *Journal of Health, Physical Education and Recreation*.

Hunsicker, P., and G. C. Reiff. 1976. *AAHPERD youth fitness test manual*. Washington, D.C.: AAHPERD.

Jansma, P., and D. Wyatt. 1977. Ideas to combine regular and special pupils in physical education. Presentation given at the State University of New York, Brockport.

Jensen, J. R. Winter 1975. Cooperative relations between secondary teachers and students: Some behavioral strategies. *Adolescence* 10:469–82.

Johnson, L. January 1977. Coed sports in high school. *Journal of Health, Physical Education and Recreation* 48:23–25.

———. July 1983. Issues and insights. *Journal of Physical Education, Recreation and Dance*.

Johnson, P., W. Updyke, D. Stolberg, and M. Schaeffer. 1966. *Physical education: A problem-solving approach to health and fitness*. New York: Holt, Rinehart & Winston.

Keniston, K. 1975. *Youth: The seventy-fourth yearbook of the national society for the study of education*, Part I, edited by R. J. Havighurst and P. H. Dreyer. Chicago: Univ. of Chicago Press.

Kneer, M., and F. Grebner. 1983. Teamed for excellence. *Journal of Physical Education, Recreation and Dance* 54:20.

Kounin, J. 1977. *Discipline and group management in classrooms*. Huntington, New York: Krieger.

Kraus, N., and R. P. Hirschland. 1954. Minimum muscular fitness tests in school children. *Research Quarterly* 25:178.

Lawrence, G., and J. Branch. June 1978. Peer support system as the heart of in-service education. *Theory into Practice*, 245–47.

Lawson, H., and J. Placek. 1981. *Physical education in the secondary schools: Curricular alternatives*. Boston: Allyn and Bacon.

Lezotte, L. 1981. Climate characteristics in instructionally effective schools. *Impact* 16:26–31.

Locke, L., and J. Massengale. 1978. Role conflict in teacher/coaches. *Research Quarterly* 49:162–74.

Lovins, M. Spring 1978. Physical education—Making changes to fit the times. *NASSP Bulletin*.

Loy, J. May 1968. The nature of sport: A definitional effort. *Quest* 10:1–15.

Mackenzie, D. E. 1983. Research for school improvement: An appraisal of some recent trends. *Educational Researcher* 12:5–17.

Mancini, V. H., D. A. Wuest, E. K. Clark, and N. Ridosh. 1983. A comparison of interaction patterns and academic learning time of low and high burnout of secondary physical educators. In *Teaching in physical education*, edited by T. Templin and J. Olson, 197–207. Champaign, Ill.: Human Kinetics.

Mancuso, J. July 1983. Issues and insights. *Journal of Physical Education, Recreation and Dance*.

Mann, D., and J. Lawrence. 1981. Introduction. *Impact* 16:5–10.

Marsh, D. February 1983. Issues and insights. *Journal of Physical Education, Recreation and Dance*.

Maslow, A. 1970. *Motivation and personality*. 2nd ed. New York: Harper & Row.

Massengale, J. 1981. Role conflict and the occupational milieu of the teacher/coach: Some real working world perspectives. In *1980 National Association of Physical Education in Higher Education proceedings*, edited by V. Crafts. Champaign, Ill.: Human Kinetics.

Mathews, D. 1968. *Measurement in physical education*. 3d ed. Philadelphia: W. B. Saunders.

McCase, R., and P. Hardin. June 1981. Intramurals at six. *Journal of Physical Education, Recreation and Dance*.

McEwin, C. K. Spring 1983. Schools for early adolescents. *Theory into Practice*.

McLeish, J. 1985. An overall view. In *Teaching effectiveness research*, edited by B. Howe and J. Jackson. Victoria, B.C.: Univ. of Victoria, Physical Education Series #6.

McNergney, R. Autumn 1980. Responding to teachers' individual needs. *Theory into Practice*, 234–39.

Meyer, D. Autumn 1979. The management of risk. *The Journal of Experiential Education*, 10–14.

Mikkelson, M. October 1979. Coed gym—It's a whole new ballgame. *Journal of Physical Education, Recreation and Dance*.

Morrow, J. December 1978. Measurement techniques—Who uses them? *Journal of Health, Physical Education and Recreation*, 66–67.

Mosston, M. 1981. *Teaching physical education*. Columbus: Charles Merrill.

Mueller, P., and J. W. Reznik. 1979. *Intramural recreational sports: Programming and administration*. 5th ed. New York: John Wiley & Sons.

National Commission on Excellence in Education (D. P. Gardner, Chairman). April 1983. *A nation at risk: The imperative for educational reform*. A report to the nation and the secretary of education. Washington, D.C.: U.S. Department of Education.

Novak, M. 1976. *The joy of sports*. New York: Basic Books.

Olson, H. E. October 1982. Establishing a booster club. *Athletic purchasing and facilities*. Madison, Wisc.: Athletic Business Publications.

Oregon State Department of Education. 1962. *Motor fitness tests for Oregon schools*. Salem, Ore.: State Department of Education.

Placek, J. 1983. Conceptions of success in teaching: Busy, happy and good? In *Teaching in physical education*, edited by T. Templin and J. Olson. Champaign, Ill.: Human Kinetics.

1979. Renewing urban schools. *Theory into Practice* 27, no. 2.

Rhudy, E. January 1979. An alternative to Outward Bound programs. *Journal of Health, Physical Education and Recreation* 50:26–27.

Rosenshine, B. V. 1979. Content, time, and direct instruction. In *Research on teaching*, edited by P. L. Peterson and H. J. Walberg, 28–56. Berkeley: McCutchan.

Rowan, B., S. T. Bossert, and D. C. Dwyer. 1983. Research on effective schools: A cautionary note. *Educational Researcher* 12:24–31.

Seagrave, J. 1981. Role preferences among prospective physical education teacher/coaches. In *1980 National Association of Physical Education in Higher Education proceedings*, edited by V. Crafts. Champaign, Ill.: Human Kinetics.

Seavey, D. 13 December 1983. *U.S.A. Today*.

Sherrill, C. 1976. *Adapted physical education and recreation*. Dubuque, Iowa: Wm. C. Brown.

Siedentop, D. 1973. How to use personalized systems of instruction in college teaching. *NCPEAM proceedings*, 77th Annual Meeting, Kansas City, 116–25.

———. 1980. *Physical education: Introductory analysis*. 3rd ed. Dubuque, Iowa: Wm. C. Brown.

———. August 1981. Must competition be a zero-sum game? *The School Administrator*.

———. 1983. *Developing teaching skills in physical education*. 2nd ed. Palo Alto: Mayfield.

Steinman, G. October 1979. The Newton plan—An intramural program for the middle school. *Journal of Health, Physical Education and Recreation*.

Stewart, M. July 1983. Implementing the concepts approach. *Journal of Physical Education, Recreation and Dance*.

1981–1982. *Statistical Abstract of the United States*. 103d ed. Washington, D.C.: U.S. Department of Commerce.

Tanner, J. M. 1981. *A history of the study of human growth*. Cambridge, Mass.: Harvard Univ. Press.

Taylor, J. September 1980. Styles of secondary school physical education curricula. *Journal of Physical Education, Recreation and Dance*.

Tenoschok, M. September 1981. Intramurals, above and beyond . . ." *Journal of Physical Education, Recreation and Dance*.

Thompson, M. M. 1951. *An outline of the history of education*. 3rd ed. New York: Barnes & Noble.

Tomlinson, T. M. April–May 1981. Effective schools: Mirrors or mirage? *Today's Education*, 48–50.

Tousignant, M. 1982. Analysis of task structures in secondary physical education classes. Ph.D. diss., The Ohio State University.

———. July 1983. PSI in PE—It works! *Journal of Physical Education, Recreation and Dance*, 33.

Tousignant, M., and D. Siedentop. June 1983. A qualitative analysis of task structures in required secondary physical education classes. *Journal of Teaching in Physical Education*, 45–57.

Tucker, R. A. January 1974. A touch of nostalgia. *Journal of Health, Physical Education and Recreation*.

Wilson, G. April 1975. Legal concerns in special education. *Theory into Practice*.

Yankelovitch, Shelly & White, Inc. 1978–1979. *Family health in an era of stress*. Minneapolis: The General Mills American Family Report.

Index